FLORIDA SOUL

UNIVERSITY PRESS OF FLORIDA

Florida A&M University, Tallahassee
Florida Atlantic University, Boca Raton
Florida Gulf Coast University, Ft. Myers
Florida International University, Miami
Florida State University, Tallahassee
New College of Florida, Sarasota
University of Central Florida, Orlando
University of Florida, Gainesville
University of North Florida, Jacksonville
University of South Florida, Tampa
University of West Florida, Pensacola

FLORIDA SOUL

From Ray Charles to
KC and the Sunshine Band

John Capouya

University Press of Florida
Gainesville · Tallahassee · Tampa · Boca Raton
Pensacola · Orlando · Miami · Jacksonville · Ft. Myers · Sarasota

This book may be available in an electronic edition.

22 21 20 19 18 17   6 5 4 3 2 1

Library of Congress Control Number: 201793559
ISBN 978-0-8130-5452-0

The University Press of Florida is the scholarly publishing agency for the State University
System of Florida, comprising Florida A&M University, Florida Atlantic University, Florida
Gulf Coast University, Florida International University, Florida State University, New
College of Florida, University of Central Florida, University of Florida, University of North
Florida, University of South Florida, and University of West Florida.

University Press of Florida
15 Northwest 15th Street
Gainesville, FL 32611-2079
http://upress.ufl.edu

To the late Doris Shapiro, who first played James Brown, Johnnie Taylor, and Archie Bell & the Drells for me and took me to hear B. B. King

And for Felix Hernandez, host of the Rhythm Revue on WBGO-FM in Newark, New Jersey, keeping the faith—and replenishing mine—for thirty years and counting

Contents

Introduction: *The Soul State of Florida*   1

1. Ray Charles: *Greenville/Jacksonville/Orlando/Tampa*   21
2. Ernie Calhoun: *Tampa*   55
3. Noble "Thin Man" Watts: *Deland*   68
4. The Twist Came from Tampa: *Tampa/Miami*   76
5. Linda Lyndell: *Gainesville*   95
6. Lavell Kamma and the 100 Hour Counts: *Jacksonville/Pahokee*   111
7. Sam Moore, Soul Survivor: *Overtown*   123
8. James Purify: *Pensacola*   149
9. Bobby Purify: *Pensacola*   162
10. Papa Don Schroeder: *Pensacola*   170
11. Wayne Cochran: *Miami*   178
12. Willie Clarke and Deep City Records: *Miami*   192
13. Helene Smith: *Miami*   211
14. Henry Stone: *Miami*   221
15. The Miami Sound: *Little Beaver, Chocolate Perry, and the T.K. Family*   241
16. Frankie Gearing: *St. Petersburg*   257
17. Timmy Thomas: *Miami*   270
18. Latimore: *Riverview/Miami*   287
19. Jackie Moore: *Jacksonville*   302
20. KC and the Sunshine Band: *Miami*   320
    Epilogue: *The State of Florida Soul*   334
    Acknowledgments   349
    Notes   353
    Bibliography   371
    Index   373

FLORIDA SOUL

Introduction

The Soul State of Florida

IT'S A WINTER NIGHT IN AMERICA, and "Monday Night Football" is about to air on ESPN. First, though, comes the lead-in show, "Monday Night Countdown." The inherent challenge here, it seems to an outsider, is to make more than two hours of older men sitting down, talking, and *not* playing football remotely compelling to watch. To keep the energy level high, the network uses brash-talking commentators, action-packed game highlights, fancy graphics, and, very selectively, music.

As the show goes to its last commercial, the camera pulls back from the broadcasters and an up-tempo song blares briefly. It's "Hold On, I'm A Comin'," powerfully declaimed by Sam and Dave, the classic soul duo formed in Miami's Overtown neighborhood. That anticipatory song was a #1 hit on *Billboard* magazine's Hot Rhythm & Blues Singles sales chart in 1966—and just about a half-century later, ESPN's producers chose it to introduce their football game.

Now it's May, and thirteen-year-old New Yorker Elena Messinger is celebrating her bat mitzvah in a 6th Avenue hotel. The entertainment includes much food and a man cutting uncannily accurate silhouettes of guests out of folded paper, followed by music and dancing. A saxophonist plays over recorded music, while the DJ exhorts the throng to "come on!" via their wireless mikes. Smiles of recognition break out across the crowded, high-ceilinged hall at the very beginnings of "Get Down Tonight" and "That's the Way (I Like It)," 1970s hits by KC and the Sunshine Band. Multigenerational dance gyrations ensue.

As the weather reference in its name infers, that band is from Florida, too. Originally, they were called the Sunshine Junkanoo Band, a nod to the Bahamian music Harry Wayne Casey, aka KC, heard in Miami and incorporated into their sound. Improbably, Casey still leads a current iteration of the Sunshine Band, touring and performing in his mid-sixties.

Now it's autumn. Walking toward East 6th Street, Austin, Texas', main drag for bars and entertainment, passersby can't help but notice an outpost of the Coyote Ugly Saloon chain. For one thing, the smell of spilled beer is rank. For another, the music coming from the bar's outdoor speakers is resoundingly loud. The college students in this contingent immediately recognize "Hotline Bling," a 2015 hit by the Canadian rapper Drake. But it's their "old school" professor (that's their term; I think they mean it affectionately) who identifies the haunting organ track underneath Drake's singing. It's "Why Can't We Live Together," a plea for peace and tolerance by Florida soul singer Timmy Thomas, released in 1972. (The "Bling" lyrics are concerned with very different matters.)

Thomas' song, born of the Vietnam War and the African American civil rights struggle, has since been covered by Sade, Joan Osborne, and Carlos Santana, among others. The song's greatest impact, however, was felt halfway across the world from Florida. "Why Can't We Live Together," which contains the line, *No matter what color, you are still my brother,"* became an anthem of the black liberation movement in apartheid-era South Africa. Thomas performed the song in Johannesburg while Nelson Mandela was in prison and returned to sing it again in 1994 when Mandela was elected that country's president.

These Florida songs and artists all surfaced during my writing of this book, so, naturally, I noticed. My antennae for passionate vocals and funky sounds with Florida origins were up. Here's the other thing I noticed: None of these artists' Florida origins were discussed or even alluded to; it never came up. Perhaps the loudest silence came when the Seattle Symphony performed its "Tribute to Ray Charles." Press coverage declared that Charles "spent a significant part of his career in Seattle." There was no mention of the fact that Charles was a Florida soul artist, perhaps the greatest of them all. The late singer, piano player, composer, arranger, and bandleader—known during his Florida decades by his given name, Ray Charles Robinson—was raised here, went blind here, became a musician here, and made his first recordings here. At one point he even played in a Tampa country and western band, the Florida Playboys, and in 1951 recorded a composition of his called "St. Pete Florida Blues."

Ray Charles circa 1949, just after he left his home state of Florida. Courtesy Joel Dufour.

In the years immediately following World War II, the talent level was so high and the pool around him so deep that, talented as he was, "RC" struggled to make it as a working professional—and at times, to eat. Later in his career he attributed his success in part to this cutthroat environment, saying, "Florida toughened me up."

Much of the music that he and the other Florida performers above produced endures today—still enjoyed, still part of our collective culture and our collective commerce—forty to fifty years after it was first issued into a very different country. These artists and the classic songs of the Florida soul canon continue to demand attention, renewed or continued.

Somehow, though, Florida soul in the aggregate remains largely unrecognized, both in and outside of this state. Although the term "southern soul" is widely used and accepted, the South it conjures up seems to end before it reaches Florida's borders. In the otherwise excellent 2004 soul documentary, *Only the Strong Survive*, the narrator says: "When soul spread north from Memphis to Philly, Chicago and Detroit, where it became Motown, pop music was changed forever." Again, Florida gets no play.

When most listeners, even knowledgeable devotees of this genre, think of soul hotbeds, their minds will likely move to Memphis, with its illustrious Stax and Hi record labels; to Muscle Shoals, Alabama, home to the FAME recording studio; or to Detroit and the Motown sound. (That is, if they consider Motown soul; many don't, calling it pop.) New Orleans may deservedly come up, as can Macon, Georgia, from which Little Richard and James Brown emerged in the 1950s, and Philadelphia, where Kenny Gamble and Leon Huff created TSOP, the Sound of Philadelphia, in the 1960s and 1970s.

And that's not right—or that's not entirely right. Soul soared in those places, but Florida's contributions—to soul, rhythm and blues, funk, and 1970s dance-soul or disco—are equally rich, and deep. In the thirty-five-year swath between 1945 and 1980, Florida produced some of the most electric, emotive soul music this country's ever heard. Great singers, musicians, and songwriters plied their crafts here in the service of a fine, funky art. DJs on local AM radio stations like WTMP in Tampa, WBAS in Tallahassee, WJAX in Jacksonville, and WFEC and WMBM in Miami spun little vinyl 45-rpm discs with Florida labels on them—labels with names such as Jayville, Tener, Marlin, Leo, Alston, D & B, Glades, and Bound Sound. Performed live, this music rang out—and found responsive audiences—in nightclubs, dance halls, ballrooms, "casinos," and juke joints all over the state, from Miami and Tampa Bay to Gainesville, Jacksonville, and Pensacola, and in between.

Then as now, this music's reach extended far beyond the Sunshine State, stirring limbs and loins all over the United States and beyond, especially in the United Kingdom and Japan, where American soul music has long had strong followings. Especially in soul's golden age, the 1960s and 1970s, Florida soul shone. Yet that remains a hidden history, an underappreciated cultural heritage.

This book aims to document and celebrate that legacy. Its most ambitious goals are to expand the history and cosmology of soul and to prove that Florida and its cities deserve their own prominent places therein—to redraw that misshapen musical map. Until that happens, though, millions will continue to listen, dance and sing to this music—to love it—without understanding just how many of their beloved touchstones have Florida in their geological makeup.

I didn't. Growing up in New York and New Jersey I was drawn to the soul music of the 1960s and 1970s. When Betty Wright came on the radio singing her hit "Clean Up Woman" or when one by Sam and Dave or Timmy Thomas came on the radio, I turned those songs *up*. I especially remember banging on dashboards to the driving rhythm and blasting horns of "Funky Nassau" by the strangely named group, the Beginning of the End. But the DJs on WABC and WNJR (in Newark) didn't say—had no reason to say—"You know, Betty Wright is from Florida" or "'Funky Nassau' is on the Alston label, based in Miami."

I was too young to get caught up in the global outbreak of Chubby Checker's song "The Twist" in the early 1960s. But millions who did, from San Francisco to Scandinavia, had no idea this little hip-shimmy of a dance and the song celebrating it almost certainly originated in the black enclave around Central Avenue in Tampa. As chapter 4 relates, R&B singer Hank Ballard wrote that tune, and first recorded it, in Florida.

Until I began teaching at the University of Tampa I had never heard of the late Henry Stone—the Berry Gordy or leading impresario of Florida soul. As I discovered, he recorded virtually all the important soul artists who came from or passed through Miami at his T.K. Productions, from Ray Charles, James Brown, and Sam and Dave to Betty Wright and including KC and the Sunshine Band. (Both Casey and Rick Finch were working for him when they cofounded that group.) This state's soul yield was not as concentrated as in Memphis, where two labels, Stax and Hi, essentially held sway. Yet, especially in the 1970s, Miami still dominated, through its size and stature, and through Stone. (See chapter 14.) In 1976 an Associated Press story on T.K. went out across the country with the headline "'Miami Sound' Dominates Floors," meaning dance floors.

Artists and groups with Florida roots have certainly earned respect and renown. But that glory is specific, individualized; it doesn't acknowledge any shared context or the ways and reasons they became so accomplished where they did. One likely underlying reason is that some important artists, including Ray Charles and Sam and Dave, lay the foundations of their success in Florida but gained their greatest fame after they'd left the state. Sam and Dave, for example, broke through nationally after they teamed up with songwriters/producers Isaac Hayes and David Porter at Stax.

An even more important reason why this state's contributions go unrecognized, I believe, is that there is no one distinct Florida soul sound, nothing as identifiable as, say, the Memphis soul stew. Instead, there's a unique amalgam of styles, trends, and regional approaches that other states and soul enclaves are hard-pressed to match. That lack of one metanarrative—or the profusion of sonic narratives—may actually be the essential Florida soul story.

No doubt the state's enormous size contributed to this musical diversity. Due to geography and their Alabaman influences and collaborators, the music of James and Bobby Purify, created in the Panhandle, has been called Flora-Bama soul. Although they did hard-driving soul tunes as well, some of their work with Muscle Shoals songwriters Dan Penn and Spooner Oldham has pop and country flavorings. The deliberate, forlorn song the Purifys are most famous for, "I'm Your Puppet," sounds nothing like the driving funk their contemporary Lavell Kamma, of Jacksonville, put out nightly on Florida's chitlin' circuit. And in neither of those cities would you be likely to hear soul music with Caribbean inflections, as you would in Miami.

It's not just due to geography; this variety of styles in Florida soul is also based in the differing sensibilities of individual producers. Papa Don Schroeder, for example, who produced "Puppet," had a way of combining deep soul and pop sweetness that simply clicked, musically and commercially. Willie Clarke of Deep City Records in Miami wanted to hear lots of horns and plenty of percussion, sounds he helped produce when he was one of the Marching 100, the famed band of Florida Agricultural and Mechanical University (FAMU). Helene Smith, the Deep City singer profiled in chapter 13, says their Miami soul label emulated "that full, kick-butt sound, like the FAMU marching band with all the horns."

The Miami sound that came out of Stone's T.K. Productions in the 1970s is the most distinct and dominant musical aesthetic, a product of the stellar house band or regular studio musicians there. That group included Timmy Thomas on organ and Willie Hale, aka Little Beaver, who remains a cult figure among guitarists. (See chapter 15 for more on the T.K. musical family.) "Funky Nassau" and the junkanoo music that KC and the Sunshine Band drew on show how island culture enriched the Miami sound, and of

Sam Moore (*right*) and Dave Prater in an early performance; they met and formed their great soul duo in Overtown. Photo by Michael Ochs Archives/Getty Images.

course in that location there were Latin influences as well. Little Beaver, who's from Arkansas, said "the Latin flavor was something I picked up on in Miami." He already had the African part of the Afro-Cuban musical blend inside him, the guitarist noted.

Willie Clarke of Deep City (who later worked with Stone at T.K.) went even broader, including northward, in describing the acoustic admixture he contributed to: "The Miami sound is stirred up with the ingredients from the Bahamas, Jamaica, Alabama, Georgia—all mixed together." Steve Alaimo, a Miami-based blue-eyed soul performer and T.K. producer, even detects an element of rock and roll in this South Florida fusion. He calls it "white-boy bass," referring to Ron Bogdon, who played on many T.K. hits. (Chocolate Perry, the other T.K. bass stalwart, is African American, though his nickname derives from his sweet tooth, not from his skin color.)

WHAT IS MEANT HERE BY "SOUL?" Succinctly and therefore a bit roughly put, this is an African American musical form that combines gospel-derived vocal styles with blues- and jazz-based instrumental underpinnings. In her early (1969) and important book, *The Sound of Soul: The Story of Black Music*, Phyl Garland describes soul as "a fusion of blues, jazz and gospel."

Soul vocalists certainly employ blues singing techniques, especially flatted or "blue" notes, but most would agree that gospel—especially gospel singing—is the heart of soul. When producer Brad Shapiro worked for Atlantic Records, producing music by Wilson Pickett and Jacksonville's Jackie Moore, among others, he was often teamed up with Floridian musician, songwriter, and producer Dave Crawford. Praising Crawford's piano work in a *Florida Soul* interview, Shapiro said: "His playing was straight out of the church; he played that church groove, which was where soul came from. After all, 'soul' is a church term, right?"

In chapter 7 Sam Moore of Sam and Dave explains how he and his partner brought the passionate exhortations and call-and-response of the black church to their dynamic soul performances. (Singers in both genres also use melisma: extending single lyrical syllables into multinote runs.) Quite a few soul classics, including Ray Charles songs, were direct transpositions of gospel songs, with more earthly sentiments expressed (see chapter 1).

Many experts see rhythm and blues, or R&B, as distinct from soul, usually pegging the former as an earlier style, most prominent in the 1940s and 1950s. Soul emerged later than classic R&B, in the 1960s and 1970s, and in a very different cultural context. Rhythm and blues was performed and patronized almost exclusively by African Americans, and the term "race records," used during times of legal segregation, emphasized that distinction. Soul crossed over, gaining a significant white audience and integrating Top 40 radio and sales charts even as it helped drive and define the African American civil rights movement.

Up-tempo rhythm and blues, sometimes called jump-blues, was primarily meant for dancing. Like the jazz-oriented big bands or swing bands that preceded them, R&B bands placed great emphasis on the instrumentalists' ensemble and solo work. The chapters here on Floridian tenor saxophone players Ernie Calhoun and Noble "Thin Man" Watts reflect that priority. Soul, on the other hand, is seen as primarily a sung genre, a vocal, emotional art—think Aretha Franklin and Solomon Burke. Of course, it's hard to imagine soul without the contributions of instrumentalists such as guitarists Steve Cropper and (Miami's) Little Beaver, or saxophonists Junior Walker and King Curtis, just as the singing of Amos Milburn, Ruth Brown, and Big Joe Turner, to name a few standouts, was always crucial to rhythm and blues.

This book carries the *Florida Soul* title but chronicles the development of both R&B and soul in this state—and insists little on their differences. (Some would also question whether the dance-oriented music that came out of Henry Stone's Hialeah studio in the 1970s, including those by KC and the Sunshine Band, truly qualifies as soul, calling it—and, often, dismissing it—as disco. For more on that loaded discussion, see chapters 14 and 20.) The main, consistent emphasis here will be on specific artists and the music they created, rather than distinctions between genres.

It may be simplistic but still useful to consider that rhythm and blues evolved and divided into two main musical forms. One was rock and roll, which took its cues from artists like Louis Jordan, Ike Turner, and Big Mama Thornton. The other R&B stream mingled with gospel and evolved into soul. (Soul also followed 1950s doo-wop, another genre at least partially derived from gospel vocals.)

In his book, *Sweet Soul Music: Rhythm and Blues and the Southern Dream of Freedom*, Peter Guralnick, probably the genre's preeminent chronicler, emphasizes one essential point of demarcation in his definition of soul. He calls it a "gospel-based, emotion-baring kind of music that grew up in the wake of the success of Ray Charles." So in this learned version, the catalyst of the entire soul explosion came from Greenville, Florida.

Impassioned delivery—the emotion and sincerity—is ultimately what sets soul apart. Author Guralnick puts it this way: "Soul music is a message from the heart." Yet musically, in its underlying architecture, soul does show some more quantifiable traits, including differences from and commonalities with its predecessors. As the name suggests, rhythm and blues relied heavily on the musical basis of traditional blues, a repeated three-chord progression. These songs use the I, IV, and V chords, meaning chords based on the first, fourth, and fifth notes in whichever key or scale is being used. (In C major, those chords would be C, F, and G.) A great many 1940s and 1950s R&B hits used this musical format, often combined with faster tempos and more humorous or upbeat lyrics than a typical blues lament would contain. These songs also adhered to the blues' AAB lyrical structure: an opening line; that line repeated; and then a third line concluding each verse. A prime example with Florida roots is Hank Ballard's "The Twist," released in 1959, which then became a huge crossover hit for Chubby Checker in 1960 (see chapter 4). As readers of a certain age may remember, the first line, *"Come on baby, let's do the Twist"* (sung over the I chord) is repeated (over the IV chord) and then the singer finishes the proposition with: *"Take me by my little hand, and go like this"* (V, IV, I).

Both 1950s R&B and 1960s soul tended to use more than three chords and more varied structures. Eventually, the three-chord blues progression phased out almost completely. In his book *The New Blue Music*, Richard J. Ripani calculates that 60 percent of the top-selling R&B songs of the 1950s used the I–IV–V. In the 1960s that number went down to 12 percent. (Ripani also says the biggest 1960s hits were, on average, 10 beats per minute faster than those of the previous R&B decade.) By the 1970s, when, as Ripani puts it in his chapter title, we saw "Funk and Disco Reign," not one of the twenty-five top-selling songs used the blues basis.

Especially in the earlier years—what Miami singer/songwriter Timmy Thomas calls "the Jackie Wilson time, the Sam Cooke time"—the music underlying soul singing tended to resemble gospel. "We had almost exactly the same chord structures in our secular songs," Thomas says. "I got a lot of my early stuff from [gospel's] Dixie Hummingbirds." (The two great singers he mentions both came to soul from gospel careers.) A key difference, though, is that soul musicians tended to be freer and looser in their approach and adherence to these musical templates. According to Scott Swan, a veteran soul guitarist who teaches music history and appreciation at the University of North Florida, "There was greater variability in the way they applied these progressions in soul music than in gospel, where you find fewer solos and less harmonic improvisation." Overall, Swan contends, southern soul was "more experimental and improvisational than the northern soul of Berry Gordy and Motown." That's one reason it sounded "more 'raw,' expressive and emotionally charged," he says, "especially in live performances."

One frequently used progression, seen in soul songs as disparate as Aretha Franklin's "Baby Baby Baby" and Marvin Gaye's "Mercy Mercy Me," is the I–VI–II–V. (Often the middle two chords used are minor rather than major; those minor chords are denoted with lower case letters, as I–vi–ii–V.) "Another very common R&B progression is the I–VI–IV–V [or I–vi–IV–V]," according to Longineu Parsons, trumpeter and professor of music at FAMU. This series is sometimes called the doo-wop progression; well-known examples include the Ben E. King hit "Stand By Me" and Otis Redding's "These Arms of Mine." "It's basically the same circular motion you might see in gospel," Parsons says.

Parsons is classically trained and an esteemed performer in the jazz world—where the charts can get considerably more complex—but he got his start playing in R&B bands on the southern chitlin' circuit. Parsons notes that the interplay of gospel and soul "was not just a one-way thing. R&B ended up influencing church music as well as the other way around."

Typically soul songs, both ballads and up-tempo numbers, start out with several lyrical verses. Here the words vary but the melody is essentially unchanged. Then, as in most popular song forms, there's a bridge, in which the music changes to different underlying chords and the singers work over them in these new tonal ranges. An instrumental solo can also cover this passage; think of King Curtis' tenor sax work in Aretha Franklin's "Respect." Very often these bridges are based in or begin on the IV chord, says Thomas, including many he played as part of T.K. Productions' house band in the 1970s. Other soul songs rely more on the V or VI chords than on the IV. (The bridge in Florida duo James and Bobby Purify's "I'm Your Puppet" goes first to the V chord; in "Pain in My Heart," sung by Otis Redding, it starts on the VI.) To hear this in one well-known example, listen for the IV-chord bridge in Sam and Dave's "Hold On, I'm A Comin'," which arrives when they sing: *Reach out to me for satisfaction / Call my name for quick reaction.*

In the 1970s, roughly the second half of the soul era and the heyday of Miami's T.K., "we started writing a little differently, using some different chords," says Timmy Thomas. "For one thing, we very often used dominant seventh chords." These are formed by adding the seventh note from the root of a given chord, and that note is lowered or flatted a half-step as it is in minor and blues scales. So to a C major chord or triad, consisting of C, F, and G, the player adds B flat (instead of B). This sounds richer and creates tension, musicians say, and lends a bluesy coloration. Dominant seventh chords are very common in jazz, Thomas says, and less so in gospel.

During this latter-soul era the number of different chords songs typically contained increased significantly. Natalie Cole's hit "I've Got Love on My Mind" contained nine chords, Ripani writes, and jazzier ensembles such as Earth Wind & Fire also used more complex arrangements ("Serpentine Fire" used seven chords). Some of Al Green's hits, many of which he wrote or cowrote, contained unusual progressions. Even as more sophisticated patterns emerged, though, so did a contrary trend. Some 1970s funk relied on even fewer chords than did I–IV–V blues; "Flash Light" by George Clinton's Parliament, for example, is essentially a relentless two-chord outing. Of course that stripped-down, doing-it-to-death approach goes back—and owes much—to the earlier grooves of soul and funk Godfather James Brown. Guitarist Robert Berry remembers that when he was covering Brown's hits in Florida bands in the 1960s and 1970s, "sometimes you'd just be riding the I," by which he means staying on the single chord based on the keynote or tonic. Around the same time, when T.K. was "focusing on dance music, or you might call it disco," Thomas says, "we also stayed on the same chord[s] longer."

FLORIDA SOUL IS NOT MEANT to be an exhaustive—nor, I hope, exhausting—encyclopedic compendium, covering everyone who ever plucked an E-string in this state, every juke joint open late, or every Florida singer who gave it up and turned it loose. This aggregation is necessarily selective and subjective. I don't tell the story, for example, of Benny Spellman, best known for "Lipstick Traces (on a Cigarette)," who was born and died in Pensacola, because in my view he was truly a creature of New Orleans. Still, I believe that this book—to my knowledge, the first of its kind—will be comprehensive if not definitive and that a satisfying soul survey will emerge.

I've tried to tell not only the most important stories but also the most intriguing and engaging ones, and that naturally favors soul folks who are alive to tell their tales. (Through historical research and interviews with survivors, however, Florida Soul does chronicle the work of some artists who are deceased, including Ray Charles and Noble Watts.) This book is based primarily in my original reporting; that is, in-person interviews with surviving musicians, singers, promoters, producers, arrangers, and DJs, plus other writers and experts. Some are familiar, big-name soul acts, but others

Rick Finch, Henry Stone, and Harry Wayne Casey with their gold record for the album *KC and the Sunshine Band*, 1975. Photo © Larry Warmoth.

profiled here are less well known, such as Ernie Calhoun, St. Petersburg singer Frankie Gearing, and Miami bass man Chocolate Perry.

Throughout, their stories are rendered here as they told them to me, firsthand. Whenever possible I have verified the facts and specifics in their accounts—through published accounts, public records, and interviews with their peers—but some parts of some stories have proved unverifiable. Of course, that doesn't mean they're not true.

The chronology of these narratives begins with Ray Charles Robinson of Greenville, in north Florida, who became a professional piano player at fifteen, working with Henry Washington's big band and Tiny York's combo in Jacksonville, circa 1945. The last *Florida Soul* story ends in 1980, when KC and the Sunshine Band left Henry Stone's T.K. Productions, ending that company's run of hits. (Stretching as far as possible, the story could be said to end in 1984, when Columbia Records reissued Jackie Moore's hit single "This Time Baby.")

At times my own journey of discovery becomes part of the *Florida Soul* story. Listening to singer Linda Lyndell describe the thrill of recording her 1968 classic "What A Man"; sitting next to Timmy Thomas as he ran through the chord progression of "Why Can't We Live Together" on his home keyboard—those were immensely satisfying times for this soul fan and chronicler. I hope readers feel the same way about the time they spend vicariously on the Florida soul trail.

Soul is fundamentally an African American art form, born in the era of segregation and come to maturity during the civil rights movement. Thus its story is inextricable from the ongoing, complex story of race in this country. That is neither the subject of this book nor my area of expertise, but it is undeniably the context. In Florida, as in black music everywhere, some white producers and label owners are accused of profiting excessively or unfairly at the expense of their African American artists. Lyndell, who's from the Gainesville area, ran headlong into a different kind of racial resistance that derailed her career. Stories of conflict, discrimination, and injustice are proffered here via those who lived (and live) them, in their words and from their varied perspectives.

At the same time, there's another true thing at work here, a parallel narrative. As at Stax Records, the American Sound studio in Memphis, and the FAME recording studio in Muscle Shoals, Florida soul featured interracial groups, among them, T.K.'s house band, KC's Sunshine Band, Lavell Kamma's Counts, and Weston Prim and Blacklash. Within those units we see abiding friendships, inspired collaborations, and mutual respect. More than one chapter deals with "blue-eyed soul": credible, popular black music performed by white folks, memorably seen in the person of high-octane, bleached-blond-bouffant-wearing Wayne Cochran, the "white James Brown" who held forth with his C.C. Riders at the Barn in Miami in the 1960s.

The audience for soul music was and is integrated; that's another possibly useful distinction between it and earlier rhythm and blues, which was created almost exclusively by African Americans for black audiences. Soul crossed over and continues to straddle the biracial fault line. This was intentional: The Motown slogan, "the sound of young America," was deliberately inclusive, and that label targeted whites as much if not more than African Americans. In Florida, Willie Clarke and Johnny Pearsall, who founded Deep City Records in the mid-1960s, tried to follow their crossover example, as did Pensacola native Papa Don Schroeder with the groups he produced.

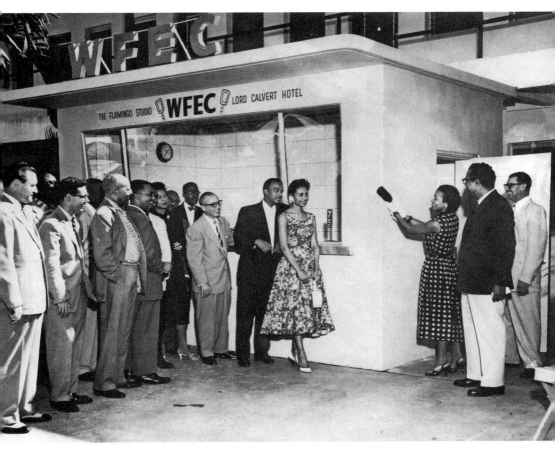

Radio station WFEC opens its studio in the Lord Calvert Hotel in Overtown, 1950s. Courtesy State Archives of Florida.

In both individual narratives and the overall soul saga, Florida's segregated black communities are themselves important characters. These enclaves, especially the cities' black business and entertainment districts—LaVilla in Jacksonville, The Deuces in St. Petersburg (centered on 22nd Street South), Central Avenue in Tampa, and Overtown in Miami, to name a few—incubated R&B and soul. Little Harlems, as they were often referred to, held the clubs and restaurants African Americans could patronize, the hotels they could stay in, and resonated with the music they made.

Florida had an exceptionally long tail of cities, and not just due to the state's length. As historian Gary R. Mormino notes, after World War II Florida became "the most urbanized state in the south. In 1950, almost two-thirds of Floridians lived in cities. . . . By 1960, three of every four

Floridians were city dwellers." All these urban centers, within reasonable driving distances of each other, created a five-hundred-mile string of paying gigs. (That's just the north-south trajectory; of course there were many more cities to stop in and bandstands to mount going east and west.)

This state, along with Texas, presented the densest and richest segment of the chitlin' circuit, the southern network of clubs, halls, and juke joints that flourished during segregation. Between 1957 and 1959, for example, circuit veteran and legendary touring bluesman B. B. King, a Mississippian, played 126 Florida gigs, more than in any other state. He made repeated stops at the Palms of Hallandale, just north of Miami, and Jacksonville's Two-Spot, two of the bigger, classier clubs in that long musical loop. Local musicians and fledging performers found inspiration and opportunity in many of those same urban venues—usually on weeknights, rather than weekends—along with exacting training and cutthroat competition.

Those cities thrummed with dance and concert halls, swanky nightclubs, and ghetto dives, but musical work was plentiful in between the population centers as well. Florida's stoop-laboring agrarian workforce, much of it black, was sizable and, though poorly paid, eager to make its weekends count at local venues. In their interviews for this book, singers Sam Moore and Lavell Kamma both spoke of playing to sugarcane workers in "the muck," as they called the Everglades region. These gigs didn't usually pay all that well. But as the late musician and bandleader Sax Kari told Preston Lauterbach, author of *The Chitlin' Circuit and the Road to Rock 'n' Roll*, "the circuit was never about making big money—it was about making constant money."

When integration came it was of course welcome and overdue. But it also eroded many of the urban soul centers even as it opened other social and financial avenues. Then, too, quite a few black entertainment districts, including Overtown and Tampa's Central Avenue neighborhood, were literally laid waste to by the placement of huge highways in and through black communities. As an elderly man named Joseph Grant of Jacksonville told the *Florida Times-Union* about the lost LaVilla district: "We [have] the equal rights now but we just don't have these places to go anymore."

While R&B held sway and then gave way to soul, Florida was expanding—exploding, really. Transformative growth took no breaks between sets, in full swing twenty-four hours a day. Between 1950 and 1970 in-migration, including by white and black World War II veterans, multiplied the state's total population by 2.5 times and the African American population by 1.7 times, to more than one million. Some of those folks pouring in

The FAMU Marching 100 band in 1963, shortly after Deep City Records producer Willie Clarke marched and drummed in Tallahassee. Dave Woodward (David Luther), courtesy State Archives of Florida.

were musicians, and others were entrepreneurs and record men, like New Yorker and erstwhile trumpeter Henry Stone. And of course many more of the 3.5 million new Floridians became record-buyers and cover-charge payers.

As in almost every other realm, Florida sunshine played a role in soul. The sensational singer and Detroit native Little Willie John understandably made Miami an informal second home, including during wintertime, as did Hank Ballard, another soul notable based for a time in Detroit. "My dear fellow," says soul DJ, vinyl record dealer, and producer Jan Lisewski. (He's a Brit who moved here in 1992.) "Do you know how many people toured in Florida because of the weather conditions in the old days? Florida was not some sort of happy accident in soul music. This was the nurturing ground where so many acts came to play on the circuit and enjoy their merry sunshine."

Florida Agricultural and Mechanical University (FAMU) in Tallahassee, a historically black community of a different kind, was also a musical driver.

The superlative jazz and marching bands there trained many a working musician, including Deland tenor man Noble Watts (see chapter 3), who studied there in the 1940s along with jazz alto sax star Julian "Cannonball" Adderley and his brother, cornetist Nat Adderley. Deep City founders Willie Clarke and Johnny Pearsall were also alumni, along with their horn arranger, Arnold "Hoss" Albury, to name just a few more.

Florida was also home to the traveling variety show "Harlem in Havana," which performed at state fairs all over the United States from the mid-1930s to the mid-1960s. This Tampa-based all-black revue featured acrobats, comedians (Redd Foxx was one), and scantily clad "brown showgirls" as well as musicians. Singers whose careers were launched or sustained in this "Harlem" include Floridian Little Jake Mitchell; Rufus Thomas ("Walking the Dog"); Fontella Bass ("Rescue Me"); and Chuck Berry. In an ironic twist—bitter is probably a better descriptor—the revue's performances were usually off-limits to blacks except for one time each engagement, on "Negro Day."

MORE THAN RACE, more than demographics, and more than commerce, though, this book is about craft. As happens with bluesmen and women, R&B and soul performers are sometimes romanticized (and patronized) as soulful black folk whose art simply pours out of them, unbidden, unrefined, and unrehearsed. In this view the atmospherics of soul music—the heat and sweat and guts, especially in live performance—outweigh and obscure the artists' ideas, techniques, and countless hours of practice that made their art possible, and made it superb. Soul is soulful, yes, but it's also a carefully wrought expression of emotion. While acknowledging the spontaneity and heartfelt inspiration in these performers' work, I want to emphasize the purposeful rigor and precision—the intention—that channeled and amplified their passion. In his book *The Real Rhythm and Blues*, Hugh Gregory cites two well-known, albeit extreme, examples, writing that Ray Charles, "with his Orchestra . . . and [James] Brown, with the Famous Flames, applied a musical discipline that appeared almost draconian."

In these chapters, songwriters, singers, musicians, and producers discuss their training and their creative decisions, explaining how they became learned in the language that is music. (And this is equally true of those who couldn't read musical notation.) Tenor sax man Ernie Calhoun talks about the solitary afternoon practice sessions in Tampa's Ybor City that led to his hiring by a touring R&B band, sessions that his mother was forbidden to interrupt. Singer Ben Moore, who took the stage name Bobby Purify, says

Miami's Betty Wright, circa 1970. Her "Clean Up Woman" became a huge hit on Alston Records the following year—when she was 17. Photo by Michael Ochs Archives/Getty Images.

he and James Purify "rehearsed our harmonies so tight, our voices blending so close," that when they performed in Florida clubs, "we had people *crying*, man."

The stories of this music being made are organized by artist and told in chronological order. That sequence is approximate, however, as some soul folks were fortunate enough to have their careers extend across decades. As in life, the personal narratives in this book tend to overlap—lives intertwine and characters recur. Betty Wright recorded for Deep City Records in the 1960s and for Henry Stone's T.K. Productions in the 1970s (see chapters 12 and 14). Sax man Charlie Blade (the stage name of one Charles Steadham) of Gainesville played behind Linda Lyndell (chapter 5) some fifty years back; today, he is one of three horns riffing and soloing behind Little Jake Mitchell, whose story is told here in the epilogue.

While this is largely an oral history, it's also an aural history. Through vinyl, CDs, and MP3s, Florida's soul music tells its own stories. My appreciation and interpretations of this music are parts of what I want to convey here, in the hope that readers will be drawn to explore this legacy for themselves.

Why chronicle soul music at all, in Florida or elsewhere? Because it's glorious. Like the good news that is gospel and the bad news of blues, the best soul music is thrilling, cathartic. Like God and good fortune, this uniquely American art form works in mysterious ways, but it most certainly works on the human organism. Its power to move bodies and stir hearts derives from an elusive but immediately, viscerally recognizable combination of rhythm, blue notes, and emotion, as conveyed by the wondrous human voice.

In the documentary *Only the Strong Survive*, Sam Moore gave filmmaker D. A. Pennebaker a deliberately reductive definition of soul. "Soul is a feeling," he said. "You put a little extra emphasis on what you're singing, and that's soul." Listen to him sing, though—or to any of the greats—and "little extra emphasis" will seem a completely inadequate description. "Feeling," on the other hand—both in the deliverer and in the recipient—will be abundantly, wonderfully evident.

Call and response between a preacher and their congregation is crucial to church gospel and, as noted, to the twofold vocals of Sam and Dave. Similarly, soul issues an invitation of its own, to respond to—and with—heartfelt feeling. To let this music, so artfully constructed and conveyed, move you is to tap into some emotional commonality, shared bandwidth within the human experience. Back in soul's heyday and even today, DJs sometimes chide listeners, telling them that if they can't feel the groove of a particular piece being played, "You've got a hole in your soul." But this can be construed in reverse and in a more inclusive way as well: When we listen and respond to this music, those holes begin to be filled.

Like anything rich, the Florida soul story is complex. I'm sure I missed some important tales and sounds along the way and have made mistakes in fact and in judgment. For those errors and omissions I apologize in advance.

Thank you for listening.

1

Ray Charles

Greenville/Jacksonville/Orlando/Tampa

"Well, he walked like a parrot."

"I'm sorry, what?"

"You know how a parrot walks, don't you?"

"Um . . . no, actually."

"He walked with his toes pointed inward; we used to call that parrot-toed. Same thing as pigeon-toed."

That's the first thing tenor saxophone player Ernie Calhoun remembers about Ray Charles. In 1947 and early 1948, he and Charles worked together in the Tampa-based Manzy Harris Orchestra. Calhoun was twenty and the other musician just seventeen—and blind. The sax man would come across Charles walking down Central Avenue—the main artery of Tampa's black business and entertainment district—by himself, on his way to rehearsal with their jazz/blues combo. Charles' gait stayed in his mind, Calhoun explains, because "Ray would take his foot and put it in the groove in the center of the sidewalk. He'd follow those grooves to get where he was going. When he got to a corner, he'd listen both ways, then cross and when he got close to the other side he'd stick one of those parrot feet out to find the curb. He never did use a cane."

The younger man dressed older, always in the same somewhat formal get-up: black pants, white shirt, black shoes and socks. This was his nighttime performance outfit, minus the black tie and black suit jacket. At that time this "undertaker" outfit, as Charles would later call it, was pretty much all he had.

The way Calhoun remembers it, Charles had another technique that helped him navigate the Tampa streets: "He'd make a buzz sound as he was walking. *Bzzz, bzzz*, like that. So when he got close to an object or a person, he'd get a kick-back; the sound would come back to him like sonar, and he wouldn't run into it." When they met on Central, with Charles en route to rehearsal at Watts Sanderson's Blue Room, or to a gig on the patio of the Cuban Club, or to the room he rented on Short Emery Street, the young piano player wouldn't stop to chat, much less ask for help. "He'd be telling me, 'Out of the way, man. I got to go. You're holding me up.'"

Charles doesn't seem to have mentioned the sonar technique Calhoun ascribes to him. However, the tenor man remembered Charles' speed and impatience accurately. While working some of his first professional gigs in Jacksonville, Charles wrote in his memoir *Brother Ray*, "I got to know the city quickly and had no trouble racing around on my own." Of Orlando, Tampa, and other Florida cities he lived in, the musician said: "I don't want to sound like I'm bragging, but when I walked around those towns, my pace wasn't halting or even cautious. Man, I moved."

He was much skinnier then, not as solid in body as the iconic entertainer he'd become. He wasn't yet Ray Charles, either; audiences in his home state knew him by his birth name, Ray Charles Robinson, while friends and colleagues called him RC. Musically he'd be close to unrecognizable today as well. Manzy Harris, the leader of that six- or seven-piece Tampa group, hired Robinson as a piano player, a sideman, but he sometimes let him contribute vocals. The young man sang well, but his voice was still quite light. More significantly, "he didn't have his own style yet," says bandmate Calhoun. Instead, this singular, distinctive artist was intentionally, slavishly mimicking two older, better-known musicians of the day.

Young RC was also focused as much on his alto saxophone playing as he was on piano. That's the instrument he'd play when he and alto man Harold Young came over to Calhoun's house, on Central near Cass Street, to work on tunes and study theory. This was a careerist move; the success of Louis Jordan and Illinois Jacquet had made sax the glamor instrument and Robinson was intently—even desperately—focused on making his living in music, the only career he thought he could have and the only one he wanted. He had mastered the clarinet, which made the saxophone much easier.

He was already displaying one quality that would help that career become a reality: a rare, full-spectrum musicality. In his biography, *Ray Charles: Man and Music*, author Michael Lydon says his subject had perfect pitch. Calhoun, a trained musician (see chapter 2) who's certainly familiar with that term, expresses it another way. "Ray had a gift of hearing," he says. "He could hear all the intonations. He got here and right away he's telling us who's playing the right notes, who's playing the wrong notes. He'd tell us: 'You don't want to be playing B-flat there; you want B-natural.'"

Even the more experienced players they worked with weren't offended, Calhoun remembers. "Those criticisms were right, for one thing," the tenor player says. "I mean, the man was a genius."

There may be no good definition of, or explanation for, genius. But this fact seems to confirm that Charles was indeed what Calhoun calls him: No one in RC Robinson's family sang well or played a musical instrument. The man himself could only conclude, "I was born with music inside me."

Less appreciated than either his genius or his musical legacy is that both those things were born and took form in Florida. True, this iconic American entertainer was born in Albany, Georgia, in 1930. Yes, he famously—unforgettably—sang "Georgia on My Mind." But Ray Charles Robinson, who died in 2004, was truly a Floridian. His mother, Aretha Robinson, brought him with her to Greenville, Florida (about 45 miles due east of Tallahassee and 125 miles west of Jacksonville) when he was less than six months old. RC remained in the Sunshine State for roughly the next two decades; Florida is where he became a musician and a man. And as the lyrics of his "St. Pete Florida Blues" testify, his first great love was a Florida love.

Post–World War II Florida was flooded with first-class musicians, Charles later explained, and, beginning when he was fifteen, he was immersed in this competitive crucible. He struggled as he worked his first paying gigs in Jacksonville, Orlando, and Tampa, and those hard times are reflected in the titles of successive chapters in his autobiography: "Suffering"; "Scuffling in Jacksonville"; "Hungry in Orlando"; and "Floppin' Round Tampa." His early tribulations forced him to work harder, improve at his craft, and reconsider the possible.

If mastery takes ten thousand hours of practice, as is popularly believed these days, this is where RC paid those dues, even as he made actual, financial payments to Florida musicians' unions. The young man also came to realize the limitations of the musical and vocal imitations he engaged in for much of his early career, which would allow him to create his unique musical identity.

If Ray Charles did not invent soul music, he certainly pioneered it and raised it to its highest exponent. While it's important that Florida lay claim to this phenomenal—and phenomenally successful—musician, his importance in the history and evolution of soul music extends well beyond any state borders.

As noted in the introduction, author Peter Guralnick invokes this Florida artist in his definition of soul. On the second page of his seminal 1986 book, *Sweet Soul Music,* he also gives that musical form an origin story, one in which Calhoun's former colleague is both protagonist and catalyst. Soul music, Guralnick writes, "grew up in the wake of the success of Ray Charles."

One way to explain his vital role (and one factor in his decades-long appeal) is to consider that Charles first excelled at the thing that came *before* soul music: dance-band rhythm and blues. Charles, or Robinson at this stage, made his name as an accompanist, soloist, arranger, and singer, in the seven- to twelve-piece blues-based dance bands of the 1940s and 1950s. These midsize combos, smaller versions of the bigger pre–World War II bands, took their cues and often their charts from Charles Brown, Louis Jordan, and Lucky Millinder, among others. (As a bandleader Charles would later expand the Ray Charles Orchestra back to the prosperous size of the Basie and Ellington Orchestras, featuring backup singers, sophisticated arrangements, strings, and full horn sections stocked with star players such as David "Fathead" Newman.)

Next, and just as vital, Charles was without peer at the thing that *defined* soul music: searing, soaring vocals. The second strand of Charles' unique musical DNA was his utterly compelling voice, instantly recognizable and often imitated. The beautiful power of his vocals, the emphasis his recordings put on singing, and his gospel-derived vocal style were crucial to the creation of the soul template.

Charles was never very religious, but he was well churched as a young man, made to attend at least every Sunday. If the dogma he heard there didn't make a big impression, the music did—especially the singing and the call and response between the preachers and the congregation. After he left his musical and biographical home, Charles would directly transpose gospel into pop, substituting a female love interest for the Lord in his lyrics in songs such as "I Got A Woman" and "Hallelujah, I Just Love Her So." His great achievement, Guralnick writes, was the "transformation of dignified gospel standards into cries of secular ecstasy." Those cries contained strong elements of the blues—his rasp or strain, the use of flatted notes—to which Charles was able to add falsetto range. To those qualities he also added the capacity to render a ballad sweetly and soulfully.

These two streams—the jazz-fluent musicianship and gospel- and blues-inspired vocals—suffused the humid air and percolated up from the Florida soil he walked on as a barefoot boy. Combined they produced in him an inimitable triumph: instantly recognizable, soulful music that virtually anyone could appreciate but that no one could quite reproduce.

Aretha Williams was the ward or adopted daughter of a Greenville couple, Mary Jane and Bailey Robinson. After Aretha became pregnant at sixteen, it emerged that Bailey was the father. The Robinsons sent her to their former home, Albany, Georgia, where she gave birth to Ray Charles Robinson in 1930. Soon after Aretha and child returned to Greenville, Bailey left Mary Jane and moved away; he'd have little to do with his son.

Greenville, which locals pronounced "Greensville," was a little country town—Charles called it "the real backwoods"—founded around a stop on the Florida Central and Western Railroad. Originally called Station Five, it was renamed by a resident who came from Greenville, South Carolina. The town produced cotton, cattle, lumber, and pine slats used for Florida orange crates. And of course this 1930s Florida enclave was "segregated to the teeth."

Even compared to the other African Americans in Greenville, 'Retha, her firstborn, RC, and her second son, George, born a year later, were poor. There were two black enclaves in Greenville and the Robinsons lived in the rougher, more transient one farther from the town center, a collection of shacks known as Jellyroll. (The more established "colored" section of town was called Blackbottom.) In the Great Depression, dinner at the Robinsons might consist of homegrown greens and/or raw sweet potatoes. 'Retha couldn't always make the rent, so they moved often. She was small, frail, and couldn't do the heavy work other black residents, including the women, put their backs to. While Mary Jane worked in one of the sawmills, dragging soaking wet boards to the blades, RC's mom took in the extra washing and ironing for white folks that the other black laundresses couldn't handle.

Despite the family circumstances, Mary Jane, 'Retha and, RC remained close; Charles said often that he had two mothers. His birth mother was the strict, demanding one when it came to chores like chopping kindling and fetching water, while Mary Jane was indulgent. Charles would later describe his life then as "a simple time and a simple place. We were back in the woods, and the feeling of life and the spirit among the people was good."

Ray Charles' boyhood home in Greenville, Florida, which locals pronounced "Greensville." Courtesy of the author.

The Robinson family went to the Shiloh Baptist Church. In his earliest years the sole accompaniment to the singing there was the sound of tambourines; only later in his childhood did the church get a piano. So young RC found his instrument and his calling elsewhere: in Wiley Pitman's Red Wing Café. Jellyroll's general store, it also served as a gathering place and weekend juke joint. A few tables sat in the middle of the store's biggest room and, along one wall, the adult Ray Charles remembered, were two entrancing things: a piano and a jukebox.

The jukebox played blues by Tampa Red (who, despite his origins and moniker, had most of his success in Chicago) and boogie-woogie piano by Meade Lux Lewis, as well as the big bands of the 1930s. The only radio signals reaching Greenville played white music—pop crooners and country, or hillbilly as it was called—and RC and his mom listened to the "Grand Ole Opry" program out of Nashville every Saturday night.

The kid heard and liked them all, but he wanted to make music, too. Mr. Pit, as RC called him, was a very accomplished boogie-woogie piano man. Starting when RC was three, Mr. Pit let him climb up on his stool with him and bang away on the keys. "That's it, sonny! That's it!" Mr. Pitt would tell him and by the time he was six, Charles claimed, he could play a little blues of his own. When not at the piano, doing his chores, or in school, RC was crouched in front of the jukebox speaker.

As much as he wanted to create sounds like those he heard, the boy wanted to understand them, to know how music came together and how it worked. He and George were both mechanically minded; they'd watch older men work on car engines, and they built toys, repaired bicycles, and tinkered with any machines they got their hands on. As he wrote in *Brother Ray*: "There's a mechanical side to music which has always fascinated me."

When he began to compose and write arrangements he would tap this structural knowledge and mechanical approach, layering components and combining musical forces like an architect. After he went blind, having seen and felt the layout of the piano keyboard—all the octaves, sharps, and flats—no doubt enhanced his musical vision.

Before that catastrophe, though, there came another. When RC was five and George four, he saw his little brother and close companion drown in a backyard washtub. In one later telling the adult Charles said the two had been horsing around; it seems possible that RC actually pushed his brother into the water. If so, the guilt must have been nearly unendurable.

Not long afterward, RC began waking up with a "crust" or mucus coating his eyes. Gradually his field of vision telescoped inward and light and colors dimmed. His mother took him to both local doctors and got a diagnosis of "congenital juvenile glaucoma," for which they had no remedy. "By the time I was seven," Charles said, "I was completely blind."

He wasn't devastated, or so he always maintained. Perhaps because his loss was gradual, over two years, it didn't feel that traumatic. 'Retha kept RC at all his chores and trained him to live as independently as possible. But she knew he couldn't go to Greenville Training, the local school for colored children. A white couple who employed friends of Aretha's called the Florida School for the Deaf and Blind in St. Augustine. The school year had already started, but they said he could attend right away, in October 1937. RC had lost his brother and his sight; he still slept with his mother. In Greenville, he also had Mary Jane, Mr. Pit, and other adults who knew and looked out for him. He was inconsolable at the idea of leaving; his twenty-three-year-old mother, implacable. RC went.

When Robinson arrived, writes Michael Lydon, the school a mile north of St. Augustine's Spanish fort was "modest: a dozen low wooden dormitories and classroom buildings connected by cinder paths winding between mossy oaks and tall palms." It was also, if possible, more deeply segregated than the world outside its acreage. South Campus was for the roughly one hundred black students—who could not be taught by white teachers or study with the three hundred or so white students—and their African American teachers, plus live-in staff. The curriculum on the black side was geared more to "industrial arts like broom-making than to higher education," according to this biographer, and made do with hand-me-down equipment. (The deaf students were kept somewhat separate from the blind ones, and of course, the girls were housed separately from the boys.) The racial apartheid didn't really bother Charles at this point—that was all he'd known—but later he saw the irony. "Imagine the nonsense of segregating blind kids," he later wrote. "I mean, they can't even see!"

Seven-year-old RC was terribly homesick his entire first year—and ridiculed for it by the older students. In his first year at that school he had to have his right eye removed as well. Fortunately, there was music at FSDB as well as loneliness. In his second year, Charles got his first formal piano lessons, which were based in—and only in—classical works. He played Chopin études and Strauss waltzes and listened to Beethoven; RC thought that last composer had a lot of feeling in his music, which he admired.

No boogie-woogie was allowed, and no blues. He'd play them anyway, get reprimanded, and go back to the classical work. But to him it was always "a means to an end. . . . I wanted to learn how to arrange and I wanted to know how to write music, and in order to do that I had to study classical music. But I wanted to play jazz, and I wanted to play blues—that was my heart."

Fortunately for the blues-minded, the school had three pianos and only so many hours of supervision. After classes the student musicians would get together in the practice rooms and jam. The big dog on piano was an older boy named Joe Lee Lawrence, but RC eventually took over that first chair. He'd play "Honky-Tonk Train" or "Beat Me Daddy" and get the other kids dancing.

The young musician was still listening to the big bands—Glenn Miller, Tommy Dorsey, Benny Goodman—and other current jazz releases on WFOY, a St. Augustine station. He "flipped" when he heard clarinetist Artie Shaw, taking up that instrument when he was ten or so. Big-band arrangements continued to fascinate and his perfect pitch or gift of hearing, as Ernie Calhoun calls it, allowed RC to make his arranging "debut" when he was twelve years old. "We had a small orchestra [at FSDB], maybe nine or 12 people," Charles wrote in *My Early Years*, an autobiographical booklet published by the Ray Charles Foundation in Los Angeles. "The first time I wrote an arrangement and heard it played back to me, you can't imagine how excited I was. I mean, you hear your ideas, your thoughts—that was the most exciting thing to me, and I've never forgotten."

As he had been at home, he was an indifferent academic student—a quick study, impatient, and quickly bored. RC did well in math, probably because of its similarities to music and things mechanical. He was mischievous, playing practical jokes that could become disruptive, and stubborn. By his own admission he was also vindictive; if he'd been slighted he was sure to take revenge, but sneakily, never in face-to-face confrontations. As RC got older he was also determined to make his forbidden way to the girls' dormitory.

The young man, like the older man he would become, could not abide any affront against his self, the strong personhood that he somehow already possessed and felt he had to keep inviolate. Years before psycho-jargon like "inner-directed" and "self-actualizing" was invented, Ray Charles embodied those things to an astonishing degree. Later he would insist that he could handle heroin, and for most of the sixteen years he used the drug he seems to have done so. The adult Charles was also determined to control the business side of his career, a rarity in his day, by, among other things, starting his own record company, Tangerine, in 1962. (James Brown, another soulful southerner who lost his mother at an early age and also an inveterate womanizer, likewise took control of the business his talent created.)

RC spent parts of his summer vacations in Tallahassee, staying with Henry and Alice Johnson, who formerly ran a café like Mr. Pit's in Greenville. Mr. Johnson founded a Tallahassee social club and persuaded the other members to buy the young musician a clarinet. During one of those summers RC met the young saxophone player Cannonball Adderley, who was still going by Julian, and sat in with his Florida A&M jazz band. A guitarist named Lawyer Smith led one of Tallahassee's busiest jazz bands and he liked what he heard from the visiting piano player, hiring him occasionally for something like two dollars a night. RC already banged away forcefully at the keys, the same way he struck the Underwood typewriters at FSDB, and he'd play that way always. As he put it, "I'm no soft touch." At times Smith would also let RC sing.

RC had previously been "hired" to play proper popular tunes for groups of middle-class black ladies in St. Augustine, but they paid him mostly in candy or fruit (tangerines were his favorite) and loose change. So these Tallahassee gigs were RC's first true professional jobs, playing jazz and blues. He was thirteen years old and skinny, still an immature kid in many ways, but his musicianship approached that of an older man. Charles said he also had his first sexual encounter during one of those Tallahassee summers, in a gas station bathroom.

Back at FSDB the blind boy took to walking into town, exploring St. Augustine by himself. He'd done that in Greenville and claimed to have ridden a bicycle around his hometown after he went blind. Charles also maintained that he drove a motorcycle around Tallahassee and, famously, that he was given to driving friends' cars, without any disastrous results. Those anecdotes may have been exaggerated, but Aretha had certainly raised him to be capable, independent, and not to rely on anyone else, a message that clearly sunk in and only intensified after he lost his vision.

For that reason he would continue to reject three things associated with blind people—helpless blind people, that is. Ray Charles never used a cane, wouldn't consider a guide dog, and, gifted as he was on multiple instruments, never picked up a guitar. Those first two were signs of weakness and the third, a stereotype: "Seems like every blind blues singer I'd heard about was playing the guitar," he explained in *Brother Ray*. He would not become Blind Lemon Robinson or Blind Boy Charles.

His methods for getting around independently, which he described in *Brother Ray*, would serve him for the rest of his life:

> If I was in a part of town for the first time and needed to find my way somewhere, I'd have someone take me. I'd pay attention to the path we took—remembering a building here, a step down there, listening to the changing sounds and memorizing as much of the trip as I could. I'd never count steps; that'd be too complicated. On the return trip I'd have another chance to see where I was going. And before long I'd be able to do it myself.

Ernie Calhoun, the tenor saxophonist who worked with RC in Tampa, says he once saw him flying down Central Avenue with alto player Harold Young on the handlebars. Suddenly, Young bailed out, dropping off the handlebars and turning around to grasp them and stop the bike.

"Man, didn't you see that car?" he yelled.

"What, you think I'm gonna kill myself?" RC bellowed back. "Yeah, I saw that car!"

Meaning, one supposes, that he heard it.

Getting around *musically* required more strategizing and adaptation, for RC as with all blind musicians. An unsighted pianist can't use the most basic technique: playing as they read the score in front of them—even a score written in Braille. To learn a piece, Charles would read five bars or so with his hands, play and memorize them, and repeat that process until he had the entire thing down. When it came to arranging he would devise the parts for each instrument in his head and dictate each one to someone who would transcribe them in standard musical notation for the other musicians. Then he'd listen to his ideas played in ensemble and make more verbal adjustments. He used this method his entire career, from the rendition of "Jingle Bell Boogie" he orchestrated for "The Shop Boys" at a FSDB Christmas party to the lush, complex arrangements the Ray Charles Orchestra played for five decades.

Soon after he left Florida at the end of the 1940s, RC's voicings and combinations would impress an even younger musical prodigy in Seattle. The fifteen-year-old trumpeter and would-be arranger couldn't figure out how to write different musical parts for each member of an eight-man horn section. His new colleague, still going by RC Robinson, delivered an oral chart that used the most sophisticated jazz techniques of the day. "He added a B-flat-seventh chord in root position and C-seventh above that, and there it was: the eight-note chord with the Dizzy Gillespie sound," the younger man remembered. A lifelong friend of Charles', his name was Quincy Jones.

IN MAY 1945, 'RETHA DIED. She was thirty-one at most; RC was not quite fifteen. (His mother's health was chronically poor, but the reasons for her death were never fully explained.) He left school and went home to Greenville and Mary Jane, but neither she nor anything else could console him. As he would later recount: "For a while I went a little crazy. . . . My mind couldn't handle the fact that there was no possibility of seeing or hearing Mama again." RC didn't eat, didn't sleep, didn't cry—and he didn't pray.

He'd lost his brother, his vision, and now his mother. These were the scarring, defining crises in his personal life during his Florida years—and, perhaps, a painful source of the soulful musicality that emerged there. "From these experiences as much as any," writes biographer Lydon, "springs the empathy that vibrates in Ray Charles' music. [His mother's death] engraved itself on the young man's heart, to be worked out in song for the rest of his life."

Ray Charles the performer certainly conveyed emotion deeply and convincingly, as much when singing "America the Beautiful" as in his rendition of, say, "Lonely Avenue." Charles had another take, however, on the impact of this latest loss. "Silence and suffering also made me harder," he acknowledged in *Brother Ray*, "and that hardness has stayed with me the rest of my life."

That fall he returned to St. Augustine, but he had lost interest in school. An FSDB document obtained by biographer Lydon shows he was sent home—expelled, it seems clear—as an "unsatisfactory pupil." In Charles' telling, however, leaving was his decision: "I was already curious about what the rest of the state looked like—even the rest of the world." So he didn't return home to Greenville or even to Tallahassee. Instead, he went to the big city.

Jacksonville was a shrewd choice and, whether or not RC was conscious of it, an intrepid one. The biggest city in Florida was home to some seventy-five thousand Negroes, as they had begun to be called, and going back to the 1920s, that community had one of the most highly developed black entertainment districts in the state and perhaps the country. Jacksonville's African American musical heritage was long and deep, going back to James Weldon Johnson, who wrote the black national anthem "Lift Every Voice and Sing" in 1900, and the 1920s/1930s blues singer Blind Blake. Stanton High School, on Ashley Street between Broad and Clay, also featured a well-regarded jazz band directed by James P. Small, who also led a local professional outfit, the Blue Devils.

The city's economy had gotten a wartime boost when its port was put to shipbuilding. Nightclubs, theaters, and other black-owned businesses lined Ashley Street and others surrounding it in the LaVilla neighborhood, east of downtown. National touring acts such as Cab Calloway, Duke Ellington, and Erskine Hawkins played the fifth-floor Knights of Pythias ballroom and other halls; tickets were available at the Hollywood Music Store near Ashley and Broad. Manuel's Tap Room and the Two Spot, which was a few minutes north of LaVilla by car, were the most prominent nightclubs. In 1942, not that long before RC arrived, *Crisis*, the magazine of the NAACP, called the Two Spot "the finest dance palace in the country owned by a Negro." The story, on owner James Craddock, added that "the hardwood floor has a capacity of 2,000 dancers. A thousand persons may be seated on the main floor and mezzanine."

Many African American enclaves in the South looked to New York City's legendary quarter, with locals calling their neighborhoods the "Harlem of the South" or "Little Harlem." Jacksonville went even further, calling the Ashley Street area the Great Black Way, after the Great White Way, Broadway, in New York City.

The dance floor at the Two Spot nightclub in Jacksonville, which reportedly held two thousand customers, 1947. Spottswood Studio, courtesy of State Archives of Florida.

Like RC, trumpeter Teddy Washington was born in 1930, and he grew up on Clay Street, near Ashley. "Ashley and Davis Streets was where the action was for black people," he said. "This was our turf." Washington and his musician friends competed in talent shows at the Roosevelt Theater and knew all the restaurants and cafés on Ashley the professionals would frequent, including Ms. Daisy Ford's Boston Chop House. As for night-clubs, "El Chico on Ashley Street would jam all night long." Washington lived across the street from Charlie "Hoss" Singleton, a performer and lyricist who cowrote the Sinatra hit "Strangers in the Night" and the pop standard "Spanish Eyes," as well as writing songs performed by Nat King Cole. According to Washington, he and RC both worked in an annual show

Singleton ran at Myrtle Avenue Park called the April Follies (it may have been called the April Frolic).

RC's luck at finding kind adults held. Mary Jane had a connection to Fred Thompson, a Jacksonville carpenter; he and his wife, Lena Mae, had an extra room and took the young man in. The couple lived on Church Street, just one block over from the Ashley main drag. That put RC just a block or so from the Egmont Hotel, one place prominent black entertainers stayed—were allowed to stay—along with the Richmond and the Wynn hotels (the Egmont also housed the Lenape Bar, a local hotspot). More importantly he was a very short walk from the Clara White mission building and, therein, Jacksonville Local 632 (colored) of the national musicians' union. After Fred Thompson walked him there a couple of times, RC knew the way and began haunting the place.

The union office was on the third floor of the white building, but the ground floor held an upright piano. RC would hang around, listen intently, and wait his turn at the keyboard. The older musicians were struck by his ability to copy their licks after hearing them once—and not always in an admiring way. Soon, RC wrote in *Brother Ray*, "When those guys saw me coming, they stopped playing. They were right. Once I heard what they'd be putting down, I started running with it. Like a thief in the night."

Luckily, not everyone in a position to hire was a piano player and thus a competitor. RC got occasional jobs with drummer Henry Washington's big band, including their regular gig at the Two Spot, for four dollars a night. Tiny York's smaller combo played around the state as well as locally, and they sometimes needed a fill-in piano man, too. York just fronted this band, though he did play sax on other jobs, doing a high-energy imitation of or homage to Louis Jordan, immensely popular at the time with his Tympany Five. To get these gigs young RC would even offer to play on spec, or on a contingency basis: If the bandleader didn't like his work, he didn't have to pay. RC always got paid.

Many favorable forces were aligned: The demand for music was high, and there were scores of seasoned jazzmen from whom RC could learn and who appreciated what he could do. In Jacksonville, unlike in many other Florida locales, black bands worked in the white community as well as in their own, playing at private parties, country clubs, and big social events that called for dance music. Tiny York played New Year's Eves for a white doctor and his wife twenty years running.

Robinson's main difficulty, though, lay with that same cadre of experienced, highly skilled players. The best naturally gravitated to the big cities.

During Ray Charles' 1940s sojourn in Jacksonville, he frequented the Clara White Mission on Ashley Street, as the building housed the local ("colored") musicians union; see also the Hollywood Music Store to the right. Eartha M. M. White Collection, University of North Florida, Thomas G. Carpenter Library, Special Collections and Archives.

Many were returning from the war, in which they'd gotten even more proficient playing in the top-notch military bands. (Henry Stone, who would record some of RC Robinson's earliest singles in Miami, played trumpet in a crack Army band. The other trumpeters were so much better than him, he said, that he knew he had to make his living on music's business side.) Jacksonville had a glut of "first-quality musicians—I mean real motherfuckers—you never heard of," Charles said. "Cats could play their instruments, and I mean from top to bottom."

This was certainly a boon for the Jacksonville music fan with a few dollars in his or her pocket; less so for the up-and-comer. RC was extravagantly talented, and he wanted badly to be a great musician—he'd wanted that since the days he still lived barefoot. But, not surprising for someone fifteen or sixteen years old, he had not yet reached his full potential. Sure, he was a quick study, but why hire a promising learner when there were so many learned musicians available? Plus, this piano player was blind (though he got to gigs by himself, walking or taking cabs) and underage. Enforcement was loose, but why take a chance using him in venues where alcohol was served and minors were not allowed?

Here and later in his Florida career, jam sessions were late-night proving grounds, with the potential to get RC hired. But they also weeded out the weak. With a rhythm section and a few horns or other lead instruments in place, the leader would call out songs with tricky chord changes and/or unusual tempos and see who could cut it. A common test, Charles remembered, was Coleman Hawkins' rendition of "Body and Soul," which modulated a half-step from D flat to D natural in mid-song. He also encountered the musical stress test that alto saxophone great Charlie Parker encountered during his 1930s Kansas City apprenticeship: The group would launch into and speed through a tune chromatically, playing it in all twelve keys in sequence. "It was merciless back then," he remembered. "Cold blooded. If you'd be fumbling around, you'd get laughed out of the place. You either cut the mustard or had the mustard smeared all over your sorry face." Often young RC could hold his own, but at times he'd get lost, discouraged, or even humiliated. "It became part of my education," he wrote, looking back. "We called it developing chops. Sure it was cruel and hard-nosed, but, baby, you did learn how to play."

It wasn't just this one musician, five to ten years younger than most of his prospective bandmates, who had to hustle and scrape to get by. No one was getting rich playing music, even in this thriving scene, and not that many were even making a decent living. Tiny York kept a second job as a landscaper for much of his career.

Perversely, the fact that Jacksonville was big, hip, and prosperous enough to draw national touring acts hurt the local musicians. When Count Basie, Billy Eckstine, or Nat "King" Cole came to town, locals couldn't work that club during the occupation. Those stars would also draw patrons away from locals' gigs on those nights.

Sometimes, too, the big names might not have their next engagement nailed down, or it would fall through, and they'd end up, as the professionals put it, "stranded." They'd immediately try to find more work where they were stuck, further reducing the Jacksonville musicians' chances of a well-paid gig. RC, hardly a fixture or mainstay among those working pros, had even less of a shot.

Fortunately he still had the cushion the Thompsons provided. Gigs could be scarce, and they were, but those two—not kin—still fed him, clothed him, and kept a roof over his head. The young man, who at this point had grown to his full height of five feet eight and weighed about 160 pounds, knew, though, that he would not live with surrogate parents forever. He didn't want to. He had to be able to make a living as a musician in order to eat, and to live the way his instincts told him he needed to. What other kind of work could he, a blind teenager, do to earn money? Whatever that might be, he didn't want that, either.

Struggling didn't make RC a humble supplicant or any less irascible and independent. (Just before leaving for Jacksonville he turned down an offer of a Seeing Eye dog, which a Greenville couple offered to pay for.) Teddy Washington remembers one night in particular when the blind piano player literally went his own way. Those two and some other young Jacksonville musicians were playing an engagement in Fitzgerald, Georgia. The bandleader, a Mr. Burgess, was driving the group back home, Washington wrote in his memoir, while sipping some Four Roses whiskey:

> We traveled down the highway through a cold damp fog. Suddenly there was a loud grinding sound and a sudden snap as the [limo's] axle broke. We pulled off to the side of Highway 90 . . . It was pitch dark and freezing cold with no help in sight. We didn't know what time it was and the only one we could find out from was RC. He had been given a Braille watch; it was about 2:30 a.m.
>
> We got out of the limo and built a fire. As we were sitting around the fire trying to keep warm, we called out to RC to see what time it was again. We also wanted to make sure he wouldn't get lost. He was nowhere to be found. Mind you, this was the blind guy! Lo and behold, RC had hitched a ride back to Jacksonville and left all of us "seeing" guys out on the highway.

At one point in 1946 Tiny York asked him to go on a road swing, and RC eagerly agreed. But when they got to Orlando their gig fell through—they were stranded. RC wasn't upset or daunted; based on that inauspicious beginning the sixteen-year-old, who had no foreseeable income, decided to stay there and try living completely on his own for the first time. RC found a room to rent for three or four dollars a week, which he promptly began to default on.

A quarter century before Disney, Orlando was a smallish city of less than one hundred thousand, of which one quarter to one third were African

Americans. Here there were two high-end nightclubs: the Sunshine Club and the South Street Casino. It would be a while before RC could gain admittance to that echelon.

As in Jacksonville, "musicians were coming out of the woodwork . . . the competition was ferocious. Work was tough to come by." A can of sardines, soda crackers, and a glass of water qualified as dinner; beans with a little fatback boiled in them was a fancy dinner. His poverty here was even more onerous than the Robinson family's in Greenville—these were his hardest days.

Eventually he got some lower-level jobs at fish fries, juke joints, and dance halls, mostly in cities like Deland and smaller towns surrounding Orlando. In these joints—typically with only one entrance that was also the only exit—the piano man and sometime singer made sure he knew where the windows were. Should all the liquor and beer being served lead to trouble at 1, 2, or 3 a.m., that would be his way out. RC tried to avoid another kind of blind-musician trouble—getting ripped off—by insisting he be paid in singles, keeping track as each bill was counted out into his palm.

Tenor man Joe Anderson led the fifteen-piece band that held court at the Sunshine Club on West Church Street. He started giving the blind cat a few nights' work, and then got more invested when he found out RC could arrange, too. Instead of buying other bands' published charts off the rack Anderson got original arrangements from the kid who could hear every part in his head and would call them all out, note for note. Plus, the young orchestrator was so excited at this new responsibility that he didn't charge the bandleader a cent. Unfair as that might have been, it helped RC develop his arranging chops, which in turn increased his marketability—and chances of survival.

Making himself even more versatile, the pianist/singer/arranger began playing alto saxophone. The jazz- and jump-blues-based big bands of the 1930s and prewar 1940s were giving way to smaller R&B combos. Public taste began to favor them, it seemed, and, not insignificantly, they were cheaper to book and to maintain. RC hooked up with a couple of them in Orlando, including with trumpeter Sammy Glover's. A.C. Price, who ran the South Street Casino, also threw some much-needed crumbs his way.

In another Florida first, he wrote a song instead of interpreting them, composing "Confession Blues." This was a twelve-bar blues that began: "*I want to tell you a story of a boy who was once in love.*" After that line repeated, the verse ended with "*and how the girl that I loved robbed me of the happiness*

I dreamed of." It's not known whether any particular girl inspired this particular boy to tell this particular story.

Although it cost him some meals, Charles was feeling confident enough to buy a phonograph and all the records in the classic "Jazz at the Philharmonic" series he could get his hands on. (These 78-rpm discs were made of shellac, which had been virtually unavailable during the World War II industrial effort.) This was a series of all-star jam sessions organized by impresario Norman Granz and recorded in New York's Carnegie Hall and other prestigious venues around the country. They showcased jazz as an African American art form and in Orlando the young piano player listened raptly and repeatedly. "Way down in Florida, those records were the only way we knew what the heaviest cats were up to," he wrote.

He learned not just from the pianists but also from horn players like Charlie Parker, Lester Young, and Benny Carter. Guitarist Charlie Christian taught him about "phrasing and ad-libbing" and the drummers "taught me the importance of keeping time. And as far as I'm concerned, there's no greater lesson." As Ray Charles he would go on to play with virtually all the greats on those discs; Benny Carter later arranged for him. At the time, though, RC and others were able to use the "JATP" records like today's massively open online courses, or MOOCs: They allowed musicians anywhere to learn from the best players and singers. And once enrolled, students had access to this instruction anytime, day or night, as many times as they wanted.

All his musical training and influences were coming together, arraying themselves at his command. RC was all of sixteen, yet he had formidable jazz chops on more than one instrument. His voice, which was completely untrained, was also getting him more attention in the more intimate context of the smaller ensembles. Then as now, this was an extremely rare combination, one that would, in its maturity, sustain Ray Charles and set him apart for his entire career.

When an East Coast tour brought Lucky Millinder and his sixteen-piece outfit to RC's new hometown in 1946 (possibly 1947), that gentleman had been running his own bands for the better part of a decade. Born Lucius Venable, he was a pure front man, a bandleader who didn't play an instrument and rarely sang. Seemingly perpetually smiling, he had a broad, open face with a high forehead and straight (or straightened) dark hair parted on the side. His big hits included "Who Threw the Whiskey in the Well?"; "That's All"; and "Shorty's Got to Go." Top players, including trumpeter

Dizzy Gillespie, sax man Bull Moose Jackson, drummer Panama Francis, and singers such as Wynonie Harris and Ruth Brown, worked for him. At the time of this Orlando swing, Sister Rosetta Tharpe, who RC admired, was singing for Millinder. Originally a gospel singer who "crossed over" to pop, melding elements of both, she may have set a precedent that Ray Charles would follow.

Word went around that Millinder was looking for a piano player, and RC wrangled an audition on a Saturday afternoon at the Sunshine Club. The place was empty; Millinder, always well dressed, sat and listened. Charles tells it this way in his memoir:

> I sing a couple of songs, I play a couple of tunes. I give it all I got. And when I'm through, I just sit there, waiting for the verdict.
>
> "Ain't good enough, kid."
>
> "W-w-w-what?" I stammer.
>
> "You heard me. You don't got what it takes."
>
> Those are the man's words . . . and brother, that hit me between the eyes like a bolt of lightning! No one—I mean nobody at no time—had ever said that to me before. And for a self-assured little motherfucker like me, that was a very heavy blow. I just wasn't prepared for out-and-out cold rejection.
>
> Lucky wasn't mean, just matter-of-fact. And that almost made it worse. I went back to my room and cried my eyes out for days.

Years later Lucky told him he'd thought RC had potential; he just wasn't there yet. And in Florida in the 1940s, Charles concludes at the end of that anecdote in *Brother Ray*, "potential wasn't enough. There were so many cats who could play good, no one needed to wait around while *you* developed."

Whether or not it disqualified him with Millinder, RC Robinson did have one musical weakness, one that had more to do with style than with skill. At this point in his evolution, and for much of his Florida years, RC Robinson sang and played like other people altogether. Just like them.

ONE EVENING ABOUT FIVE YEARS LATER Bronx-born Henry Stone found himself in the Mary Elizabeth Hotel in the black neighborhood of Miami called Overtown. Stone was a record distributor and would-be producer trying to get his Chart and Rockin' labels off the ground.

Stone was at the hotel, he remembered in a *Florida Soul* interview, to see the great singer Sam Cooke, whose gospel records he was distributing. As they talked Cooke introduced Stone to another guy at the bar, RC

Robinson. (It's unknown who else was in that tavern at that time, but those two alone brought the talent level up to stupendous. Soul lovers can only imagine what might have been produced if, somehow, Cooke and Charles had begun a collaboration that night.)

"I understand you're a record man," Robinson said, according to Stone. "Well, I need to make some bread."

As it happened, Stone had spent some time in Jacksonville the previous year, and he'd heard about this singer who'd attended the school for the blind in St. Augustine. "I have a little studio, do you want to come in and cut some sides?" he replied.

At this time, 1950 or 1951, RC Robinson was almost certainly under contract to Jack Lauderdale of Down Beat Records in Los Angeles, but that doesn't seem to have bothered either party. Generally speaking, both men were interested in making bread, and over the years both would produce great music.

Using a four-track Ampex recorder and his "nice piano," Stone put down four Robinson tracks: "Why Did You Go?"; "Walkin' and Talkin' To Myself"; "I'm Wonderin' and Wonderin'"; and "I Found My Baby There" (aka "St. Pete Florida Blues" or "St. Pete Blues"). Heard today, that last performance is immediately recognizable as an imitation—a strikingly adept imitation—of Charles Brown, the postwar California singer and piano player best known for "Driftin' Blues." ("*I'm driftin' and driftin', like a ship out on the sea.*") Although in some ways Brown's work with his group, the Three Blazers, was typical of that day's West Coast sound, his singing was very distinctive: He wasn't desperate and declamatory (or boastful) like so many other blues singers; instead, he was mournful, rueful, in a quieter vein. His words and enunciation were quite clear despite his less forceful delivery; it was almost as if he were singing with baited breath.

So sang RC Robinson. "I Found My Baby There" is a very slow blues ballad, just two-and-a-half minutes long, with only two vocal choruses. The first one went: "*Down in St. Pete . . . Florida . . . I found my baby there / St. Pete, St. Pete, Florida . . . I found my baby there / No one's ever loved me like my baby, any place, anywhere.*"

The third and last stanza consists of RC scatting while simultaneously playing the same riffs on the piano. These duplicated musical and vocal lines are another signature of the West Coast sound, often associated with guitarist T-Bone Walker. The entire piece is rendered in Brown's deliberate, intimate style: a small combo, using light to nonexistent bass, fills of jazzy guitar chording, and tinkling right-hand piano under light, smooth vocals.

Even though RC's lyrics are actually upbeat—he's found his baby, not lost her—his tone is quite melancholy. That's also typical of Brown; his "Black Night" is one of the (greatest) bleakest songs in the blues repertoire.

During his Florida years and even after, RC Robinson was consciously, conspicuously imitating Charles Brown and, even more so, his main idol, Nat King Cole. The smooth Cole, eleven years older than RC, was riding high with his versions of "Laura," plus Cole Porter and Gershwin tunes. He was a jazz pianist, too, and a very good one; the younger man especially admired the way he accompanied himself with inventive fills. RC loved Cole's singing, too, which to the still thin-voiced RC sounded deep and romantic. Cole "changed my life," Charles said later. "I followed him for nearly a decade. Musically I walked in his footsteps until I found a stride of my own." Biographer Lydon, who got to interview Charles, says, "RC had been imitating him since Greenville. The teenager struggled to fit his piano fills around his voice as the King did. . . . Doing a slow Charles Brown blues was, in contrast, like rolling off a log."

RC wanted to be where the money was—where some money was, at least. Charles Brown and Nat Cole were nationally known, wildly success-ful, and their sounds were within his reach. They were also popular with white people, appearing frequently on mainstream radio, including "Kraft Music Hall."

It's hard to believe of this artist whose later work was so singular and distinctive, yet he made an early decision to *not* be himself. "I didn't really think about my own style yet, didn't even dawn on me that I needed one," he wrote in *Brother Ray*. "Hell, I was so happy to be able to duplicate things I was hearing around me, I didn't see any problems. And besides, I did my imitations with real feeling."

Cole and Brown fans in Florida were delighted to hear their favorites impersonated so well in their local clubs and jukes. Whatever rewards RC got in these early years came to some extent from impersonating others, so why would he change, and for what musical personality would he forsake them? Yet until he became and fully inhabited Ray Charles—the performer he alone could realize—RC Robinson could only be so good.

Later, he'd be great—and help make soul great—following his own pro-prietary path, a musical way that was soulful like Brown, commercial like Cole, and authentically his. Blues and ballads would truly belong to him after he stopped acting them out in assumed personae. But when Robinson sat down at Henry Stone's piano in 1950, the producer recalled, "He started to sing like Nat King Cole. I said 'No, no, no, I want some blues. I know you can do the blues.' He said, 'Yeah, man I can do it.' So that's when we came up with 'St. Pete Florida Blues' and the other three cuts." That switch satisfied the producer, but those songs, though skillfully done, show that the young musician was no more emancipated: Instead of Nat Cole, Stone got Charles Brown.

WELL BEFORE THOSE QUASI-ILLICIT RECORDINGS, RC lived through a year of sardines and soda crackers in Orlando. Then, to try to better his lot—and perhaps to escape the memory of Millinder's rejection—RC took a friend's suggestion and relocated to Tampa in late 1946 or 1947. Here his luck was better, and came sooner. He quickly met the guitarist he remembered as Gosady McGee, who biographer Lydon more reliably identifies as Gossie McKee. RC stayed briefly in one of the hotels on Central Avenue, then McKee found Robinson a place to stay with his girlfriend, Frederica, and her sister, Lydia, on Short Emery Street in an adjacent neighborhood known as the Scrub. (Charles later remembered the sisters' last name as Spencer, but Lydon and local musician Ernie Calhoun say their name was Simmons.) The family had a piano in their living room, a first for RC Robinson.

Nelson Griffith was about seven when RC came to Tampa. He became a musician, too, a trumpeter who later switched to sax, and he managed the 1970s Tampa soul and funk bands the Montereys, the Childs of Friendship, and the Mighty Good and Strong. He recalls the young piano man dating his aunt, who lived with Griffith and his mother on North Boulevard. Griffith remembers RC as "easy to get along with, and soft-spoken, never a harsh word." RC called Griffith's mother, Essie, "Miss Lady." However, the frequent visitor would tell the occasional off-color joke, which Nelson only later understood.

RC quickly found work with Tampa's most successful outfit: Charlie Brantley and His Original Honeydippers. Accidentally, or more likely, intentionally, that name evoked Joe Liggins and the Honeydrippers, whose song "The Honeydripper" was a huge hit in 1945. An alto player, the bandleader was "into Louis Jordan with both hands and both feet," according to Charles. Honeydipper trumpeter and Tampa native Frank Shellman remembers that "the guy who was driving for Charley knew RC from Jacksonville. So when we needed a piano player at some point, we picked him up."

Brantley was usually leading a seven-piece band then, and all eight men rode in one station wagon, with a trailer in back carrying the equipment. Shellman says he got to know RC well, sitting next to him en route to

Honeydippers gigs "from Key West to Pensacola." Shellman was twenty, and RC about three years younger. The blind man had a pair of dark sunglasses back then, Shellman says, but he didn't like to wear them. Sometimes, though, the trumpeter would tell him that his eyes were leaking pus, and that he should wipe them out, or put the glasses on. (McKee later claimed that he was the first to get RC those trademark dark glasses, as did L.A. producer Jack Lauderdale.)

The seatmates passed some of the time playing "Dirty Hearts" with a pack of Braille cards. "I had to deal, otherwise, he would know what cards I had by feeling them," Shellman says. The loser had to drink salty water or undergo some other minor humiliation; that was the "dirty" part. When they were home in Tampa, Shellman would have RC over to dinner at his mother's house on East Columbus Drive. "He usually didn't have 25 cents to his name," Shellman says. "And that boy could eat!"

Shellman calls him a boy because Charles was still a skinny teenager. "But he acted like a grown man. He always knew about current events from listening to the radio, and you never had to do anything for him. He'd come to rehearsal at the Cuban Club, or anywhere, by himself, just walk or catch the bus." Shellman refutes his former bandmate Ernie Calhoun's recollection that RC was pigeon- or parrot-toed and that he used the lines in sidewalks to help him navigate. "No, that was the amazing thing: He would just walk right up to my house and up the steps, same as you did."

Charles didn't need or seek any help as a musician, either. There were no Braille charts for him to use while the other Honeydippers read their arrangements, done by Tampa's Michael Rodriguez and others. "Our piano players mostly played chords back then," rather than leads or solos, Shellman says, "and RC had a good head. He would just listen and pick up right away what we were doing." Clarence Jolly was the lead vocalist; Brantley did a little singing; and RC would occasionally get to sing, too. "Charley was doing Louis Jordan and RC was our Nat Cole," Shellman says.

The trumpeter, eighty-seven when interviewed for this book, claims he saw RC's genius back in the 1940s, and told him so. "We were standing there on 22nd Street one day when he was waiting on the bus, and I said, 'One day you are going to be big.' He just said, 'Oh, I don't know.'" Years later Ray Charles the established star sought him out on his return to Tampa. "His driver parked his Cadillac right across the street, and he came in this house," Shellman remembers. "He told me he was thinking of buying his own plane [which Charles did] and that he was gonna do a country album. And he was confident about it, said it would be big." That prediction came true as well.

After Brantley RC got his next steady gig with the Manzy Harris Orchestra, which included Ernie Calhoun. Harris also played piano and guitar, but as a bandleader he featured his drumming; a vintage advertisement for a gig at Sanderson's Blue Room touts: "Manzy Harris: His Drum and His Orchestra." Using RC in a trio, a quartet—which also featured Gossie McKee on guitar—and other configurations, Harris put the spotlight squarely on the young pianist's singing for the first time. RC sang his Cole and Brown homages, plus some blues songs he'd written. To compensate for the lightness of his voice, he picked up techniques other singers used when working amplified. Using the amp's tone controls he'd add both bass and more treble, which deepened his sound without sacrificing clarity. As he got older, Charles said, his voice "developed more resonance of its own." It remained hard to categorize: "You can't call it a tenor 'cause it ain't high enough: you can't call it a baritone 'cause it ain't low enough. If there's such a thing as a true lead singer, that's me."

Harris, who had been working Tampa's Central Avenue black business and entertainment district, got a lucrative new gig at a white club, the Skyhaven, located at a former military airfield. McKee sang a little along with his guitar work, but RC was the big draw. With tips, each man took in more than thirty dollars on good nights.

All told, his first few months in Tampa were his best yet. Adding to the sweetness was his new girlfriend, sixteen- or seventeen-year-old Louise Mitchell. He met and impressed her while playing the piano at a friend's house; soon the unsighted singer came to understand that she had "quite an enticing figure. Might say fabulous." The young lovers wanted to move in together, but her parents were not in favor. RC and Louise ran away to Miami for a few weeks and then returned to Tampa and rented a room together in West Tampa. "I Found My Baby" or the "St. Pete Florida Blues" is said, by Stone and others, to be about Mitchell. She lived in Tampa, though, not across Tampa Bay in St. Petersburg. One plausible explanation for the song's title was offered by the late Kurt Curtis, a Tampa DJ and author of an encyclopedia of popular music recorded in Florida. RC's song was originally written with Tampa in the lyrics, Curtis maintains, but because St. Pete, already something of a tourist destination, was much better known nationally at the time, RC and producer Stone agreed to change the musical venue.

THE WAY HE TOLD IT IN RETROSPECT, RC did not let the obvious, onerous facts of segregation dismay or deter him during his Florida years. "Ever since I was a little kid, I'd understood that white folks could go wherever the hell they pleased, but that we were restricted to our own place. . . . I could comprehend the system, and I knew it was rotten. But I was just too busy trying to stay alive to let it drive me crazy."

In that context it's quite surprising that, around the time he turned eighteen, in 1948, RC met a white musician at the Arthur Smith music store who was looking for a piano player. Somehow this piano player's most obvious attributes—black and blind—didn't diminish the white man's interest. Soon RC was installed in the Florida Playboys, an otherwise all-white country band featuring guitar, pedal steel, two fiddles, upright bass, drums, and piano. "We played all the country hits of the day—'Kentucky Waltz' and 'Anytime,'" Charles wrote. "Every once in a while I'd get to sing. I also learned how to yodel."

After all those nights listening to the "Grand Ole Opry," RC knew hillbilly music, felt it, and certainly could perform it. If true, it's amazing that, as Charles always maintained, he encountered no racial problems working with the Playboys, no patrons "making fun of the blind nigger trying to play white music. I was accepted and applauded along with everyone else." After the Playboys gigs he and the other members went their separate ways, "but that was no different from when I played with black bands. I was a loner."

One reason there was no racial drama, Charles surmised, was that his blindness made him less of a threat when it came to the white female patrons. In the minds of the white men present, "there was no way I could be checking over their little ladies. So they thought I was cool."

In April 1962, Charles' producers at ABC Records were extremely uncool about his latest project and vociferous in their doubts. Many soul fans were also taken aback when Charles released the first of his two country albums, *Modern Sounds in Country and Western Music*. Confounding expectations, Charles' version of "I Can't Stop Loving You" was a #1 pop single. (His other songs that made it to #1 on the pop chart were "Georgia on My Mind," in 1960, and "Hit the Road Jack," in 1961.) *Modern Sounds* topped the album sales chart for fourteen weeks, supplanting the soundtrack from *West Side Story*.

Those same producers and executives then became just as adamant that a second volume of *Modern Sounds* be released, which it was in October of the same year. It included "Your Cheating Heart" and a remarkably soulful version of "You Are My Sunshine," which made it to #1 R&B and #7 pop.

The idea for these albums—a black artist working in this genre—was surprising and unprecedented; the results, astonishing. Yet, looking backward to Charles' Florida years and his work with the Playboys, the quality of these country works, if not their acceptance, begins to make more sense.

WHILE HE WAS IN TAMPA, playing "hot hillbilly piano," Ray Charles Robinson made his first recordings. These weren't studio recordings and no physical discs were produced, but they were recordings nonetheless. Earning more than he'd ever made, RC saved up for a wire recorder. This was one of the first magnetic recording devices that captured sound using a spool of steel wire as the recording medium. He may have paid as much as $150 for the machine, a fortune at the time. He and some other working musicians—in later life he couldn't remember who—worked their way through his tune "I Found My Baby There" (aka "St. Pete Florida Blues") and a couple more. For the first time, the musician heard himself play and sing while he wasn't actually doing those things. Whatever else he thought and felt, he was not impressed by the wire recorder's fidelity: "It sounded like we were all locked away in a closet."

Charles would often claim that versions of these songs that circulated (on vinyl and audiotape) after he became successful must have been the wire recordings, which had somehow fallen into the hands of unscrupulous music producers. More likely, this explanation was cover for the fact that he made unauthorized recordings while under contract to others. It's clear that at least one of those same songs, "I Found My Baby There"/"St. Pete Florida Blues," was released on Henry Stone's Rockin' label in 1951 and it may be that all of them were. (They may also have been leased to a New York label called Sittin' In With.) None of these tunes appear on the official discography on raycharles.com—and none of the discoverable versions of these early songs sound as if they were produced in a closet.

Work was steady, more attention and respect were being paid, and money was coming in. Life with Louise was likewise good. So, naturally, RC wanted to leave. "It suddenly dawned on me that I had never been more than three or four hundred miles from Greensville," he wrote. "By this time I knew Florida as well as anyone needed to. I had been through the state—east, west, north, south, the big cities and the little towns wedged in between. Now it hit me that I have to get away."

He was determined to become great at what he did; to that end he was a close observer of all the national touring acts passing through. RC noticed that "the cats in those bands always seem to come from far away places" like Chicago or New York. "Everyone was from somewhere except Florida." He had done as well there as he could, and now it was time to move on. He didn't want to leave Louise, he said, but he "had to."

The older Ray Charles recounted what happened next this way: He tells Gossie McKee to bring him a map of the United States, to find Tampa on the map, and then locate the big city as far away as possible, without leaving the country. Gossie reports that he has pinpointed Seattle.

"Well, brother, count me as good as gone," RC replies. "Cause that's where I'm going. And I be leaving soon."

He undercuts the serendipity of it a bit in his memoir when he says he considered New York or Chicago, "but I didn't think I was ready. Besides, I was afraid of those big-sounding cities."

In the Lydon biography, however, McKee comes up with and sells RC on the idea. One enticement is that black men could date white women in the Northwest without reprisal. After RC agrees and his *Jazz at the Philharmonic* records are packed, though, he loses his resolve and Gossie goes to Seattle first by himself.

In all scenarios, RC eventually takes a five-day, five-night bus trip to Seattle, in March 1948. He carries something like five hundred dollars that he's saved. The next day he talks his way into a local nightclub called the Rocking Chair, even though he is not yet eighteen years old. It's talent night. RC gives them some of his best Charles Brown and immediately a man offers him work, asking him to put a trio together. Done, or soon done. He also soon discovers that "in one respect [Seattle] was just like Tampa: there were lots of musicians roaming the streets would blow your ass off the stand if you gave them half the chance. But I wasn't about to get blown off the stand." The reason he could hold his own, he concludes in his memoir: "Florida toughened me up."

A short time later he formed a second trio with his pal Gossie on guitar and Milt Garred on bass. They called themselves the McSon trio, combining the Mc in McKee and the son in Robinson, and played all over Washington State. Radio and TV work followed.

He sent for Louise and she came out from Tampa. But tensions were high, no doubt exacerbated by Charles' womanizing, a lifelong predilection. At eighteen he also began drinking a little, smoking pot, and, like some of the older musicians he worked with, shooting five-dollar bags of heroin. Louise's family sent her a return ticket home and she used it. As it turned out, she was pregnant and gave birth to their daughter, Evelyn, in 1950. (She still lives in Tampa.)

Jack Lauderdale, the African American owner of Down Beat Records, based in Los Angeles, knew the Rocking Chair and heard the McSon Trio there. He had singer Jimmy Witherspoon and pianist Lloyd Glenn on his label and decided to record McSon, too, first in Seattle, and then again in L.A. These were RC's first real, released recordings. "Confession Blues," his composition, became something of a hit, reaching #2 on *Billboard*'s "Most-Played Juke Box Race Records" chart, which became the Rhythm and Blues chart. The label identified the players as the Maxin Trio (at other times they were called Maxim), and back in Seattle the band renamed itself accordingly.

But the trio wouldn't last. Lauderdale asked Robinson to come back to Los Angeles to record without the other members, which he did. Soon thereafter the band broke up. One of the singles from that second session, "Baby Let Me Hold Your Hand," also became a race-chart hit in 1951, reaching #5. Down Beat had changed its name to Swing Time at that point, and for the first time the label on Swing Time 250A read: The Ray Charles Trio. The writing credit also went to him, under this new name. Lauderdale or RC, or both, had decided that RC Robinson wasn't mellifluous enough, and Ray Charles Robinson sounded too much like the boxer Sugar Ray Robinson. So Ray Charles it was and would be.

He put in a year on piano with bluesman Lowell Fulson; worked with drummer Joe Morris; and did some freelance work as well, including playing on and arranging Guitar Slim's "The Things That I Used to Do," a huge hit in 1953. Charles cut at least forty more sides for Lauderdale. Then Atlantic Records founder Ahmet Ertegun bought his recording contract for $2,500 in 1952. Two early cuts on his new label, "Mess Around" and "It Should've Been Me," made some noise, but his seventh Atlantic single is a soul touchstone. In what is perhaps a sign, though, that Charles and/or his producers still had doubts about their new creation, this landmark single was backed with "Come Back Baby," a traditional eight-bar blues.

"I Got A Woman," performed by Ray Charles and his Band, writing credited to Ray Charles, was released on Atlantic in December 1954. Charles based it on a current gospel song he had been listening to, "It Must Be Jesus" by the Southern Tones. But instead of the gospel accompaniment he grew up with in Greenville—tambourines and perhaps piano—Charles added complex backing by skilled, jazz-steeped musicians, the accrual of

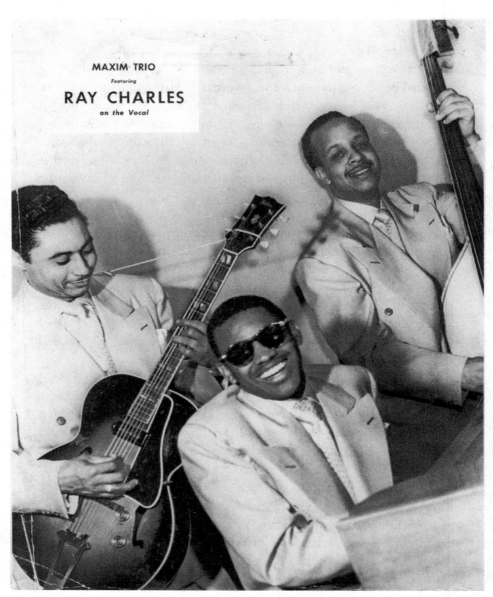

The Seattle trio: Charles, Gossie McKee on guitar, and Milt Garred on bass.
Courtesy Joel Dufour.

his Florida training in jazz, rhythm and blues, and arranging. Stop-time intervals after a saxophone solo added propulsive energy in the fourth chorus, as did a fade-out vamp—another rhythm and blues trope—under the repeated vocal line: "*Don't you know she's alright.*"

Then—or, perhaps foremost—Charles layered on his impassioned, blues- and gospel-based vocals. (The lyrics unfold in an A-A-B-C-A pattern rather than the standard blues A-A-B structure.) British critic and author Hugh Gregory says Charles' singing of this song was "fired by a gospel-laden fervor." Crucially, he also notes that by this time "all echoes of Charles Brown and Nat 'King' Cole had been eradicated from his vocal style."

Charles came into his own and, some maintain, soul was born. Innovative as they were and distinctive as they remain, however, both Charles' work and soul music are clearly amalgams as well as departures. Listened to anew, Charles' fervent vocals evoke gospel but do not seem incompatible with the work of the "shouters," male and female, who fronted the earlier, bigger R&B bands of the 1930s and 1940s. Like blues singers before and during the big-band era, Charles leans heavily on and makes frequent use of blue notes; there's a familiar strain to his voice, especially when he reaches high for the last syllable of "*mon-ey*" in the line "*She gives me money, yes, indeed,*" and all the way into falsetto as he elongates the word "*she-eeee*" in the second chorus.

And while soul is often characterized as primarily a vocal genre or one that "privileges" singing, without the sophisticated musical underpinnings Charles and his cohorts brought to their work, its impact and transcendent quality would both be diminished. This was the formula—if such a potent, alchemical brew can be described as formulaic—that led to Charles' great success and drove the explosion of soul music that followed.

Whatever the exact admixture of elements and influences, craft and inspiration, "I Got A Woman" became Charles' first #1 R&B hit. (A later version charted again in 1965.) Guralnick, admittedly a soul partisan, declares that Atlantic 45-1050 "had as profound an impact on American pop culture as any single record before or since."

"This Little Girl Of Mine," released in 1955, also blatantly transposed "This Little Light Of Mine" from gospel song to secular. In both cases the tempos were accelerated to fast, quick-shuffle speeds, and the beats given heavy emphasis. It's worth noting, too, that in almost every case the gospel songs Charles worked with were not covered by copyright, so he could use them at no expense, and he did so as avidly as he had previously used the vocal stylings of others.

To many church-going and God-fearing African Americans, he went too far. As happened after Sam Cooke's first pop forays, a substantial part of the gospel audience felt Charles' new bag went beyond secular to sexual and, thus, profane. Jerry Wexler, his producer at Atlantic and a mightily important soul figure himself, said: "When Ray Charles did this radical, unheard-of thing of taking gospel songs and putting the devil's words to them, a lot of ministers and a lot of churches found this blasphemous."

Ernie Calhoun, RC's Tampa bandmate, remembers that reaction well. Charles' music "sounded kinda sanctified but it wasn't holy rolling, and the church got on him," he says. But, as Calhoun also notes: "Too many people were dancing to it" for the record to get suppressed. "Hallelujah I Love Her So" and "Lonely Avenue," both based on spirituals as well, came out in 1956, and by 1959, when Atlantic released "What'd I Say," with its completely churchy call-and-response, the record-buying public was convinced and converted.

So was Ray Charles. He had found his musical identity, and commercial success that far exceeded what he'd achieved as a gifted follower. "These are the years . . . when I became myself," he wrote. "The minute I started being me, that was all I knew, I couldn't be nothing else but that."

To ACCOMPLISH ALL THAT he was capable of, RC Robinson felt he had to leave Florida. Yet it was his early decades in that state that allowed him to become—that made him into—Ray Charles. To understand and acknowledge that, the performer would have to live and age a bit more, and then go back home.

In 1954 Mary Jane, Charles' second mother, died and he returned to Greenville for the funeral. He'd been gone about six years at that point, and during this trip, he seems to have come to a realization. For decades afterward, whenever he described his evolution as an artist and his role in the creation of soul, he would invoke the music he was reared on in his Florida home. "I'd been singing spirituals since I was three, and I'd been hearing the blues for just as long," he wrote in Brother Ray. "So what could be more natural than to combine them?"

His imitating others, especially Nat Cole, "required a certain calculation on my part," he admitted. "It certainly wasn't effortless. This new combination of blues and gospel was. It required nothing of me but being true to my very first music."

By the mid-1950s his hewing to that truth, and the public response to it, allowed him to take control of his music in ways few artists could. He wrote his own songs, handpicked the best musicians, and wrote his own arrangements. In effect, he made producers extraneous. Charles was "the first self-produced artist I'd ever known," wrote Wexler, "and the model for people like Marvin Gaye and Stevie Wonder [in the] early seventies." Unusual as it was for him to be a spectator, the producer said, "it was a privilege to watch him work, to see how he—and American music, for that matter—evolved through his own unique instincts."

One inspired choice Charles made around the time of his return to Florida was hiring and featuring David "Fathead" Newman on baritone and tenor in his newly formed seven-piece combo. (That group also included two trumpets; a second tenor sax; drums; bass; and notably, no guitar.) Hank Crawford, another jazz master with a funk/soul tone, would soon become a ten-year stalwart on alto. From that smaller group the maestro would later build out a full orchestra, adding strings and the backup singers closely identified with him, the Raelettes. But that smaller group was the first that was truly his own. His goal and guiding vision when forming it, Charles said, was to "rebuild my own little musical world that I first heard in Greenville."

On the earlier return trip, in 1950 or 1951, when he recorded those songs in Henry Stone's Miami studio, Charles had essentially left for good. Yet in that recording session he laid down not only "St. Pete Florida Blues" but also a second composition of his in which he paid tribute to his home state, and to the late 'Retha Robinson.

"Walkin' and Talkin' to Myself" opens with a rippling, jazz-tinged twelve bars of blues, played at quite a slow tempo. The piano sounds like a tinny instrument, but the playing is sure. Then Charles comes in with the first vocal lines: "*Well, I'm walkin' and talkin' to myself / I'm walkin' and talkin' to myself / My baby's gone, and I can't find nobody else.*"

His singing, while not overly strong or full-throated is less muted than in the more overt Charles Brown homages in that session. To this point the lyrics are standard blues fare, and as the second chorus begins he falls back on another familiar theme, the "I'm gonna leave this town" or "hit that lonesome highway" sentiment. In what is probably an improvisation, he varies the first, or A, line the second time around: "*Well, I'm going where the sun shines every day / I'm gonna change my climate; going where the sun shines every day.*" He then concludes this three-line section with: "*Going back to my home town, way down in the state of F-L-A.*"

In the third and last chorus, he breaks form, employing only two lyrical lines instead of three and moving early to the chord change that resolves the blues progression. The song's final words have much greater resonance if one knows of the young man's great loss five years before and the impossibility of what he narrates: *"I'm going to write my mother a letter / Mother, please, ma'am, look for me / Well, I'm coming home, Mother / Yes, this is your son, RC."*

2

Ernie Calhoun

Tampa

ERNIE CALHOUN PICKED HIS ALTO SAXOPHONE UP off the bed and began to play. As usual, the nineteen-year-old was practicing during his midafternoon break from managing Joe Pullara and Sons grocery store, just a block or so away on Tampa's Central Avenue. He'd started as a bicycle delivery boy there when he was eleven.

On this day in 1946 or possibly 1947, Calhoun still had the first chart he'd ripped from the Carl Fischer Saxophone Method book pinned to the back of the bedroom door. When he'd picked up the horn he sounded awful, and the neighbors complained; "They were raisin' hell," he says. But he'd progressed, holding the first alto chair in the Middleton High School band until he graduated, and was now practicing two hours a day. His mother knew not to interrupt, yet on this particular day, she knocked.

"Ernie," she called out, "there's someone here to see you. A Mr. Mayfield."

"Who?"

"Percy Mayfield, he says."

"Oh. Well, send him on in here, Mom."

Young Ernie knew the name. Percy Mayfield, who's been called "the poet of the blues," is best known today as the writer of the much-covered "Please Send Me Someone to Love," a #1 R&B hit for him in 1954. He also wrote "Hit the Road, Jack," made famous by Ray Charles, who signed Mayfield to his Tangerine label in the 1960s. An underappreciated artist, he had a knack for crafting poignant, idiosyncratic takes on the eternal themes of love and, most often, heartbreak. The slim Mayfield was also a moving singer, rendering bluesy ballads (ones that generally didn't rely on the blues' traditional twelve-bar chord structure) in his smooth, resonant baritone. When he dropped in on Calhoun in Tampa he was leading a fourteen-piece band and may have been touring behind his first successful single, "Two Years of Torture" (this one was a straight blues).

The young Tampa alto player was still a rank amateur; his L.A. visitor, a significant personage in postwar R&B, part of the West Coast sound that included one of Ray Charles' idols, Charles Brown.

"You sound all right with that horn, boy," Mayfield said, entering Calhoun's bedroom.

"Yes, sir."

Seeing Calhoun's book open on the bed, the bandleader asked: "Can you read?"

"Yes, sir."

"Play that," the bandleader said, gesturing to an open page.

Satisfied by what he heard, Mayfield told Calhoun, "I just left one of my alto players behind." His musicians, like many others at that time, had a fifteen-minute grace period after the appointed departure time to show up at the band bus. If you were late, Calhoun says, you were done.

"You think you can cut my book?" Mayfield demanded, meaning: Can you sight-read my charts?

"I don't know, sir. I'll try."

"Well, we're having a rehearsal this afternoon. You come up there to the Apollo and if you can cut it, I want you to play with us tonight."

CALHOUN WAS BORN IN 1927 and his father died when he was four. He remembers being on relief in Jacksonville during the Depression, which he calls the Hoover days: "We used to go down to Forsyth St. and pick up the peas, beans, bags of flour, sugar, and fatback, the fat part of the hog. They had clothes for you, too, so you could go to school."

When Ernie was nine (his brother, Alexander, was a year and a half older) his mother married a seaman, Richard E. Banks, and they moved with him from Jacksonville to another deepwater port, Tampa. The family settled in a tiny street called May Alley and Ernie went to the local segregated public schools, including Middleton, named after African American business leader George S. Middleton. "My mother had only been to third grade," he said. "But she read very well, she wrote, and she could multiply and divide. Her thing was that I was going to be better than what she was,

The marching band at Middleton Senior High School, Tampa, 1951, shortly after Ernie Calhoun held the first alto chair. Courtesy Tampa-Hillsborough County Public Library System.

so when I wanted to leave school and help take care of her, she said, 'No way.'"

In the time he came up in, Calhoun says, "things were bad for the black community, but we did have people you wanted to emulate. We had our own black businesses, black dentists, doctors, and finally we got our lawyers and our bookkeepers and all. So I made up my mind to excel."

His mother, Martha, did day labor, including on farms, for fifty cents a day plus carfare. But she did much better, her son said, shooting dice and playing blackjack in clubs that catered to blacks and Cubans. "Tampa was wide open. We were the Las Vegas of this area," he says. Besides bolita, the wildly popular daily numbers game, Tampa "had gambling houses all over" offering poker, blackjack, and dice games. "There was Tito's, Serafino's, the Yellow Shack, and Big Joe Porty's. . . . My mother used to take me to them and sit me in the corner while she played." His stepfather was lost at sea during World War II; after that, Calhoun says, gambling was how Martha supported herself and her sons.

All along, Ernie saw the rhythm and blues bands coming in to play this lucrative stop on the black nightclub or chitlin' circuit, one that offered additional earning possibilities at its Cuban nightclubs. "Jimmy Lunceford, Louis Jordan, Cab Calloway, Lucky Millinder—Tampa was a Mecca for music," he says. "My grocery store was right across the street from the Apollo Ballroom and on the weekends everybody would get dressed out, to go to the dances." As in many other black enclaves in Florida and the South, local hotspots were often named after those in New York's Harlem: Tampa had a Savoy as well as the Apollo, and across Tampa Bay in St. Petersburg the top black venue was the Manhattan Casino (see chapter 16, on singer Frankie Gearing).

The constant stream of working musicians in the thriving Central Avenue district gave Calhoun his first ideas about becoming one of them. He'd been serious about the saxophone ever since joining some friends in the Middleton band. "I was new boy on the block but I was very aggressive," he says. "I told them I was gonna play in the number one chair, and in about five or six months, I had it." He also took private lessons from band director Professor Michael Rodriguez, who mentored many Tampa jazz and R&B musicians over a long career. "I used to ride the trolley all the way out to where he lived around North 48th or 49th St," Calhoun remembers. "There were no streetlights then and I had to walk in the dark to his house. A lot of times he'd be playing with his [professional] band so he wouldn't get back there until 10:30 or 11 p.m. I'd be sitting up in his house waiting on him so I could get my lesson."

Craftily, he used his day job to get additional instruction. Calhoun would monitor which musicians checked into the Central Hotel. Then, using his employee discount at the grocery, "I'd get me some baloney and salami, some luncheon ham and mayonnaise, cut me some bread, grab some milk and juice, and I would go up to their rooms and knock on the door. We had Early Times whiskey back then, and I'd bring that, too.

"'Here you go, fellows,' I'd say. 'You all have a good time.' I'd bring my book, and gladly they would help me learn. I was just a beginner, and I was feeding some top-flight musicians—one of them was Bill Harvey, heck of an alto player, who used to be the bandleader for B. B. King. He taught me more theory and composition."

He'd already learned his "bite," how to best position and hold the mouthpiece. Some horn men hold theirs on one side of their mouth or the other; some clamp it right in the middle. Calhoun learned to move his mouthpiece around, a technique he developed due to his occasional part-time job as a boxing sparring partner. If he got hit in the lip, he'd need to hold the horn differently for a few days afterward.

Ernie was a big kid on his way to being a big man; full grown he stood six feet one and weighed 225 pounds. Like jazz great Julian "Cannonball" Adderley—also from Tampa, along with his cornet-playing brother, Nat—he got a big sound out of his alto. (Later Calhoun would switch to tenor.) That biting, forceful tone carried his thirty-second-note and sixty-fourth-note practice runs out onto Central Avenue where Percy Mayfield noticed them, just as the neighbors had. But Mayfield reacted differently than they did: He liked what he heard.

ERNIE SHOWED UP AT THE PYRAMID HOTEL (also known as the Rogers Hotel) that afternoon and climbed the stairs to the Apollo Ballroom, one of Tampa's most prestigious venues. "I'm gung-ho," he remembers, "bright-eyed and bushy tailed. A little nervous." Mayfield's band was rehearsing, and the youngster was struck by how relaxed they were, "wearing do-rags on their heads, slides [slippers] on their feet, they had their shirts open."

The singer carried a full reed section: two altos, two tenors, and a bari-tone sax. When Calhoun took out his horn and stepped up on the bandstand, the first alto player saw he was a little nervous and coached him. "Son, you just listen to me," he said, "and phrase as I phrase." Calhoun's part was harmony to the older man's lead. The nineteen-year-old had a good ear, and Professor Rodriguez had developed his pitch sense by playing notes on the piano and asking his pupil to identify them: "That's D . . . that's B-flat." He'd also play triads—three notes that form a chord—and quiz Calhoun on those.

Before the first song kicked off, one of Mayfield's players asked, "How are we going to spell it?" Calhoun didn't know that referred to tempo: How fast will we play it? They started spelling it slowly and Ernie followed along as best he could, reading a bar or two ahead, and if he couldn't decipher what was coming fast enough, he'd sit out briefly rather than play the wrong thing.

"After a few numbers they asked me, 'Alright, you got all the notes?' and I'm thinking, 'Yeah, I got it.' But then they say, 'It's show time,' and the tempo doubled. Before we were doing it like this," Calhoun says, tapping his knee slowly. "Now, it's like this!" He taps much faster.

The verdict came in. "Son, you did alright," they told him. The next thing he knew, not only was he playing that night's Apollo gig but Mayfield asked him to go on the road with him. "I said, 'No, I can't just go, Mr. Mayfield. I have to ask my mom.' I was a good Christian boy. I didn't curse, I didn't smoke and I didn't drink."

Back at the house, Mayfield told Martha he'd be responsible for her son. She agreed but added a warning. "I know how you musicians are," she told him. "If anything happens to him, you will belong to me," meaning there would be consequences. As Calhoun puts it: "My mother didn't play."

The ensuing road swing covered seven southern states, and every night was a rich lesson in ensemble rhythm and blues. Calhoun was grateful and also amazed at the sound Mayfield got out of *his* instrument. "He was a little fellow, but he sure had a big old voice."

When the tour brought the band back to Winter Haven, Ernie gave in to homesickness and came off the road. He quickly hooked up with the Manzy Harris Orchestra, featuring the blind piano player RC Robinson. "Manzy played mostly drums. Sometimes, we had three horns, sometimes two, and a four-part rhythm section: guitar, bass, drums, and piano. This was a blues band, but we really played everything," Calhoun says, including jazz and some Latin dance numbers.

Then, at the end of 1949 or beginning of 1950, "they called me to go to Korea. I didn't want to go, because of the conditions that my people were under here, in this country. I didn't feel that I should go and fight and didn't know who I was fighting. Didn't know where Korea was! But it was either accept being drafted or go to jail, so I went."

He stayed in for two years, got well-versed in big guns, including the .40-, .90- and 120-millimeter varieties, and moved up the ranks to sergeant. "We were segregated when I first went in, and then we became integrated. We had hell with that because some boys from Alabama and Mississippi said, 'No nigger is gonna tell me what to do.' And they wanted to fight. We said, 'Okay, we'll go outside and fight you, but after that, we need to start fighting the enemy.'"

In 1952 Calhoun came home from the service; the last leg was Jacksonville to Tampa by train. He showed up to catch the Seaboard Line's Silver Star "spit-polished, shoes shined; I'm well-dressed and well-groomed. I've got that [sergeant's] chevron on my sleeve, and I represent the uniform well." But the clerk at the ticket window insisted on serving every white customer first, and then called Calhoun "boy." The way he tells it, the Shore Patrol and MPs had to pry him off the clerk and put him on the train.

Melvin Webb, drummer in a 1950s version of the Manzy Harris Orchestra. In the previous decade band members included Ernie Calhoun and Ray Charles. Cal Adams/*Tampa Bay Times*.

Then, arriving home, "I get the same damn thing," he says, his voice rising. "The train station was right where it is now, on Nebraska Avenue, and I was living up on Cass and Central. I had this big old duffel bag so I decided to take the bus.

"When I got on, it was full, everybody's hanging on those handles. I look in front, and right behind the driver, there's a seat. So I moved on up and sat down. I noticed the white lady next to me started cringing. Then the bus driver looked up in the mirror and saw us. After a while, he pulled over along the side of the road. He addressed me properly as 'Soldier,' but told me I couldn't sit there."

Calhoun knew that even if the bus was full, "colored" folks were expected to stay at or behind the back door. But he was fed up. "I've been over there getting shot at," he says, "and this is my reward, my reception."

Two white cops boarded the bus and another confrontation began. "Everybody on the bus starts to panic; they think I'm shell-shocked, crazy, including my people in the back. So finally I said, 'Just give me my fare back, the 15 cents I paid, and I'll get off your bus.' I threw my duffel bag over my shoulder and I walked home.

"When I got there my mother ran out and hugged me, but she could tell something was wrong. She said, 'Son, what is the matter?'

"And I told her, 'I can't live here. I have to find a place where things are different because if I don't, I'll kill somebody.'

"She said, 'Son, you can't leave, you have to stay and do something about it, make things better.'"

He'd become a civil rights lawyer, Calhoun decided. He stayed in Tampa and began taking courses in business administration, law, and shorthand at a local technical college, intending to transfer to Morehouse, the historically black college in Atlanta, using his GI Bill benefits. He got there briefly, years later, but returned home when his mother fell ill.

Music still beckoned. Calhoun rejoined Manzy Harris, playing all the local clubs, including the Cuban Patio, part of the *Centro Cubano*, or Cuban Center, built by dues-paying cigar rollers in the Ybor City neighborhood. Harris and the Orchestra played their jump-blues on the patio while, upstairs, a Cuban band played for Latin dancers. By day they'd rehearse at Watts Sanderson's Blue Room on Central, where the lunch crowd got a free show with their beer, crab chowder, or chicken with yellow rice. In that wide-open part of town Monday night was the night off for pimps and working girls, Calhoun remembers. "All the pimps would dress up and go out to the bars, bring the girls in their silk skirts, play the jukebox and party down. They called that Blue Monday."

Soon, though, he got a call that a band gigging in West Palm Beach needed a sax man, so down he went, and soon afterward he went to Miami. "I played there for a while; you had the Fontainebleau, the Eden Roc, the Cadillac Hotel, the Americano. . . . Miami was another Mecca of music with the big beaches." Those beach gigs were for white crowds. "You didn't have many black customers because for us to cross going to the beach, we had to get an ID card. The police would stop you and ask, 'Boy, what are you doing over here, boy?' Yeah."

He settled in for a while at the Rockin' MB Lounge at 21st Street and Collins Avenue, where, as a 1956 Miami-Miami Beach nightlife guide described it: "Two bands take turns blowing away for the edification of the younger set (but still over 21, because this is still basically a saloon). Never a cover or minimum. Open from 9 p.m. to 5 a.m." There Calhoun hooked up with the D.C. drummer and showman TNT Tribble. In his trademark move, Tribble would leave the bandstand and walk into the crowd with a big tom-tom strapped in front of his torso, singing and banging out rhythms on patrons' tables and chairs as well as his drum.

Calhoun went with Tribble on an East Coast swing and north to Montreal, playing mostly white venues and some chitlin' circuit clubs. In Canada, including at Montreal's Esquire Show Bar, "they treated a black musician like royalty, as long as you maintained that stature, by doing the right things."

Through most of the 1950s, he "was bouncing around band to band." One of his longer jobs included backing up singer Lloyd Price, who had gutsy R&B hits including "Lawdy Miss Clawdy" and "Stagger Lee," and then had bigger mainstream success with the teenybopper-friendly "Personality" in 1959.

Life as a sideman suited him; Calhoun enjoyed it at the time and in retrospect it's a source of satisfaction. "I played with renowned people and got to see the world," he says, "and it didn't cost me anything. I went to San Francisco, Portland, Seattle, Montreal, Vancouver, Toronto, lots of places. I was a young man learning and everything was brand-new to me. At times, it was insane—girls in those clubs hollering and screaming and grabbing at you."

Edifying as it may have been, this wasn't a life of comfort. The money wasn't great; "we were riding the bus all that time, yeah." Sidemen often had to wear uniforms or matching outfits bought and maintained at their expense, though the more successful bands like Price's had valets who took care of the cleaning and mending. On that long road, Calhoun learned how to save on living expenses. "When we hit town, I got off the bus and told one of the guys to keep my horn for me. They're going to the hotel, but I'm going to find me a mom-and-pop house, regular people who had a room for rent in their house. See, that only cost like $2 a night or maybe $5 with breakfast, lunch, and supper. Hotel prices then were pretty high: $10, $15, like that."

For a short time Calhoun toured with the great Lionel Hampton, the vibraphone player and bandleader best known for his 1942 hit, "Flying Home." That song originally featured renowned tenor man Illinois Jacquet and later, in other iterations of the Hampton band, Arnett Cobb and Dexter

Gordon. By the time he took their place Calhoun was a converted tenor man, and something of a showman as well. He'd "walk the floor," going from table to nightclub table as he soloed, walking outside into the street and even climbing up on top of parked cars, with clapping patrons following along. "I was like the Pied Piper, you might say. I enjoyed it but at the same time, I saw how the public is easily fooled. They tend to appreciate the floor showing you're doing more than the way you're playing those chord changes."

During an earlier sojourn in the New York area, respected tenor sax player Don Byas heard Calhoun play. "Man, you're overpowering that alto, you're over-blowing it," the alumnus of the Count Basie and Duke Ellington bands told him. "You need to switch to tenor." Subsequent work with Ralph Duty, a former trombone player who'd already made the switch, also helped in his transition.

Calhoun says there was also a vogue at that time for tenors combined with Hammond B-3 organs, after Bill Doggett's "Honky Tonk," featuring Clifford Scott (at one time a Ray Charles sideman) on tenor, was such a huge R&B hit in 1956. In the jazz realm, Jimmy Smith and other B-3 organists were establishing a "soul jazz" genre with the likes of Stanley Turrentine, Sonny Stitt, and Eddie "Lockjaw" Davis on tenor. Calhoun's sound got fuller and deeper, and he quickly came to feel that tenor was his best avenue for expression—his musical home.

It fits him. Sitting in his physical home, his living room in Ybor City, he passes the tenor from hand to hand. It's more than three feet long with the mouthpiece and weighs almost eight pounds—seeming in proportion to this still-big man. His close-cropped hair is gray, as are his eyebrows and the moustache that extends to the ends of his mouth. "I had a unique sound," he says, the closest he will come to self-aggrandizement over a series of interviews. "It was still strong, naturally; the closest comparison is probably those Texas tenors, like David 'Fathead' Newman. [Others in that Texas cadre included Jacquet, Cobb, Herschel Evans, Buddy Tate, and Buster Smith.] But I listened to 'em all: Lester Young, Lucky Thompson, Chu Berry."

At times he worked with another Florida tenor man, Noble "Thin Man" Watts, of Deland, who had instrumental hits in the late 1950s and early 1960s with "Hard Times (The Slop)" and "Jookin'." (See the next chapter.) "He had the same kind of sound," Calhoun says. "And Noble could play."

His new instrument gave him greater power, but like jazz masters John Coltrane and Coleman Hawkins, Calhoun also had a melodic, nuanced way with ballads on tenor. (In Hawkins' obituary *New York Times* critic John Wilson described the way he combined "grace and strength in a jazz ballad.") Calhoun's approach was centered in his temperament: patient, thoughtful, careful in the ways he expresses himself.

Yet his work is not just an intellectual exercise. "You got to have soul," he says. "There are technicians who play 9,000 notes, and they're all up and down the horn, but they don't have soul. Then another guy comes by and plays 10 notes and you'll say, 'This guy really sounds good, my man is down here *playing*.'" You play your instrument, Calhoun believes, but in many ways you are the instrument and play yourself—you make your deeply personal offering to the audience and to the gods of music. "That's the way I've always played, from the heart."

In 1958 or so he came off the road for good. Back in Tampa he fronted his own (integrated) band, Ernie Cal and the Soul Brothers, and gigged locally for quite a few years. Although he never became a civil rights lawyer, Calhoun is proud of his work placing low-income workers and students in training and jobs through the Comprehensive Employment and Training Act (CETA), passed in 1973. "Over the years I helped a lot of folks, white, black, and Latin," he says.

He can't play that big horn anymore. At the last interview for this book, he was eighty-seven; bypass surgery and congestive heart failure had left him without the requisite power. So, to make a point about tenor playing he plays a CD put out by the Tampa Bay Jazz Association, which Calhoun cofounded in 1981 with pianist and St. Petersburg native Al Downing. "My Foolish Heart," the 1949 popular tune that has become a jazz standard, comes on the boom box and fills Calhoun's front room facing 17th Street.

He's partial to the 1950 hit version sung by Billy Eckstine and still remembers most of Ned Washington's sentimental lyrics evoking the *"line between love and fascination"* that ends with the singer's hopeful insistence: *"It's love this time, it's love, my foolish heart."* The Jazz Association rendition is instrumental, and when the song moves into Calhoun's tenor solo, he has a complicated reaction. Listening to himself ply his craft, he seems first empowered, then burdened.

"That's a beautiful song," his visitor tells him.

"Yes, it is," he replies, with evident satisfaction. "You know, jazz is our African American heritage, just like classical is for the Europeans. It's a means of expression for us, like the blues was. But while blues came from servitude and has just one musical profile—three chords—jazz has

Ernie Calhoun at his home in Ybor City, Tampa. Photo © Suzanne Williamson.

a multitude of chord changes. So the trick, especially when you're play-ing rhythm and blues or soul music, is to present your improvisation over those changes to a general audience and try to get them to understand what you're doing, what you're feeling."

Then, as the song continues, another association kicks in and a dif-ferent mood takes hold. "I told you I was in Korea, right?" Calhoun asks. "Well, at night when we were in those foxholes—it's freezing, mind you, 20 below at times—the North Koreans and Chinese would play stuff at us over loudspeakers. It was propaganda, like Tokyo Rose did in World War II; you can look that up.

"First they'd play some jazz tunes to get our attention and I remember 'My Foolish Heart' was one of them. Then a voice would come on, saying: *'Hey, black GI, why you fight us? You ride back of the bus; you can't use white man's bathroom. You could be home with your girl right now—what you doing here?'*

"Or they'd say something like: *'White GI don't care about you. You need to fight him next to you, not fight us!'*"

"Yeah," Calhoun says, nodding his head as he remembers those nights. "We all heard that. Then you'd be looking at the white soldiers around you, and they'd be looking at you. . . . That was something."

He sighs, shakes his head and leans back into his chair, placing those big hands on the tops of his thighs. "But yes, you're right," he says. "It's a beautiful song."

3

Noble "Thin Man" Watts

Deland

NOBLE WATTS WAS SIX FEET THREE AND A HALF, and he barely weighed 140 pounds. That gave him a striking appearance, as well as his nickname, the Thin Man, bestowed on him by a fellow band member at FAMU, in Tallahassee. The entertainer, born in 1926, was also "extremely well dressed" and fastidious about clothes, according to his widow, singer June Bateman. "He had some 'swag,' as they say today." When he played, the tenor sax man's deep-set eyes remained intense and focused. All told, he had quite a presence. "When you'd walk into a room you'd recognize him," Bateman says. "You'd look around and say, 'Oh, there's the Thin Man.'"

When Bateman, a New Yorker, met Watts, who hailed from Deland, Florida, she found him intimidating, mean as well as lean. In 1961, she was nineteen and had recorded a couple of R&B singles for Enjoy Records, with King Curtis on saxophone and, she recounts, a striking array of talent singing background: Dionne Warwick, her sister Dee Dee, and Cissy Houston (Whitney's mother). Watts was leading the house band at Sugar Ray's, boxer Sugar Ray Robinson's Harlem nightclub, when a relative of Bateman's suggested he give her a listen.

When Bateman showed up there during a daytime rehearsal, she saw this tall, intense man berating his drummer. "I can't remember the poor man's name; he was off beat somehow and Noble was letting him have it. I thought, 'Oh, no, this guy's a nut.' He was always very hard on drummers; you had to be good to play with Noble."

Watts was rough on himself as well. Fellow tenor man Ernie Calhoun became friendly with Watts at Tampa jam sessions in the late 1940s, when

Calhoun was working with Manzy Harris and Watts played with Charlie Brantley's Honeydippers. "Noble was a good guy, and he could really play. Noble could play," he repeats and emphasizes. "But he was a perfectionist, and in music you can't be perfect, you can just play well. If Noble played a solo and missed a chord change, he'd get angry, and he might take that saxophone and throw it up against the wall."

After one such evening Watts came to Calhoun's house on Central Avenue and said, "Hey, I had a problem with my horn last night, can I use one of your tenors? You sound just as strong on the alto, and I don't want to miss this gig." But Calhoun understood just what kind of horn problem had arisen, and told him: "No, I can't, because if you tear up your tenor, mine wouldn't stand a chance."

One night in the 1980s, after Watts and Bateman moved back to Deland, she got a call from her husband. "The notes just weren't coming out the way he wanted," she says, "and he told me, 'I just threw my horn in the [St. Johns] river.'"

THE STICKLER, who was thirty-four or thirty-five when he met Bateman at Sugar Ray's, liked what he heard and hired her. She was singing more blues and R&B and admired LaVern Baker and Ruth Brown, but he steered her toward jazzier material, plus crowd-pleasing standards like "All of Me." It was difficult for her at first: "Thin Man's patience wasn't the greatest." But she learned what he wanted and to like singing that new material, and the nightclub audiences took to their combined act. Soon they were a couple offstage, though they didn't get married until eight years later, in Orlando.

In the early 1960s the two recorded some singles together, with Bateman singing on "I Don't Wanta" and the raucous (and oddly countrified) up-tempo blues "Possum Belly Overalls," as well as at least one duet, "What Ya Gonna Do." When not holding down the Harlem gig at Sugar Ray's, they went out on the road in revues with Brook Benton, Jackie Wilson, and Frankie Lymon and the Teenagers. They traveled with a twelve-piece band, Bateman remembers, and many of the arrangements they used were by the Thin Man's friend and mentor, Paul Williams.

That bandleader and baritone sax player had the #1 R&B hit of 1949 with the instrumental "Hucklebuck," leading to the band's renaming as Paul Williams and His Hucklebuck Boys. Watts played tenor with him from 1952 to 1956, including at the Apollo in Harlem when Williams led the house band there and appearing with him on the early TV show, "Showtime at the Apollo," on which the two sax men backed up Dinah Washington

Noble Watts, "The Thin Man," recorded his biggest instrumental hits in the 1950s for Baton Records. Photo by Gilles Petard/Redferns/Getty Images.

and other illustrious guests. He was also featured on Williams recordings, including "Give It Up," "Pass the Buck," and "South Shore Drive," all on Vee Jay records. (During that time he also recorded two sides under his own name for the Deluxe label.)

"Noble was a star with Paul Williams," said jazz cornet and trumpet player Nat Adderley. Along with his brother, renowned alto sax man Julian "Cannonball" Adderley, Nat played and studied with Watts at Florida Agricultural and Mechanical University (FAMU) in the late 1940s. Adderley said Watts was an exciting musician but a dignified performer as well. "He was never crass or crude—he didn't have to lie on his back or crawl around on the stage [while playing his sax] like a lot of players," Adderley said. "He could get the audience on his side without honking."

In the 1940s and into the 1950s, many performers, sax men included, channeled Cab Calloway and Louis Jordan, antic showmen who'd become huge record sellers and live draws. Jordan played mostly alto, and Tampa's Charlie Brantley was a Jordan follower. Another entertaining cadre of tenor men put out bigger, rougher sounds as they performed the crowd-pleasing stunts and athletic gyrations Adderley described. They became known as "honkers." (Producer, music executive, and author Arnold Shaw called his history of rhythm and blues *Honkers and Shouters*.)

Despite Adderley's protestations, Watts is celebrated and most widely remembered as a proponent of that tenor saxophone style—as a honker. Other influential tenor men included Big Jay McNeely, Sam 'The Man' Taylor (heard on Big Joe Turner's "Shake, Rattle, and Roll"), Plas Johnson, Joe Houston, and fellow Floridian Willis "Gator Tail" Jackson (Ruth Brown's bandleader and soloist). From roughly 1946 to 1960, these sax players were often front men or featured instrumentalists in rhythm and blues bands, a role they maintained as R&B, or some strains of it, evolved into early rock and roll. Another group of tenor sax specialists, most notably King Curtis and Junior Walker, would enhance R&B's other outgrowth, soul music, though, those two aside, these horn players were more often sidemen than stars.

In a 1987 review of one of Watts' later albums, *Return of the Thin Man*, British critic Richard Williams characterized Watts and his instrumental ilk this way:

Noble "Thin Man" Watts is a member of that group of tenor saxophonists who, trained in jazz and steeped in the blues, enlivened the pioneer years of rock and roll. . . . These men punctuated many of the classic early hits with raucous, wailing solos. In the evolutionary chain, they belong somewhere between Illinois Jacquet and King Curtis.

Watts would certainly have been comfortable placed between those two tenor men. But, though he hired on as a sideman to 1950s rock and roll acts such as Chuck Berry, Fats Domino, and Jerry Lee Lewis, he considered himself a jazz artist and bluesman. As he made clear to a *St. Petersburg Times* reporter in the late 1980s, when his second career or comeback was in full swing, he did not admit or aspire to the kind of pioneering Williams credited him with. Wagging "a long, bony finger" emphatically at the interviewer, he told him, "I wasn't nowhere near rock."

GROWING UP IN DELAND, Watts first studied violin and piano, paying for lessons from a Stetson University music professor by doing yard work. He later took up the trumpet; one story holds that Watts' mother gladly bought him any instrument he wanted to keep him from pursuing his other interest: boxing. The young trumpeter specialized in high notes, like instrumentalist/bandleader Maynard Ferguson. "They used to say I was gonna come out of the bell of my horn 'cause I liked to play so high," he once said.

In 1947 his talent took him to FAMU, in Tallahassee. As a music major in that famed program, Watts studied harmony, composition, and chord progressions alongside the Adderley brothers—but blew out his lip going for those high notes. He switched to tenor sax and left school after just one or two semesters to work with Brantley's Honeydippers and then the Griffin Brothers. Watts made his first recordings with that Virginia-based R&B band in 1949. He also toured in jazz great Lionel Hampton's reed section, with Tiny Bradshaw's jazz/R&B band, and then with Paul Williams.

In 1957 he left Williams' Hucklebucks to front his own band and signed with Baton Records in New York. Baton put out eight singles of his in the next three years, including "The Slide," "The Creep," "Flap Jack," and "Hot Tamales." Those cuts drew respectful attention from *Billboard*, including in a 1957 review of "Easy Going Parts 1 & 2." The magazine called it a "powerful instrumental with strong deejay and juke appeal. Strong musicianship . . . the very danceable sides should go over big with audiences."

Another of those Baton singles, also an instrumental, went over the biggest. In *Honkers and Shouters*, Arnold Shaw quotes Baton owner Sol Rabinowitz on that 1957 release:

> Noble "Thin Man" Watts, a fine tenor saxophonist, recorded an instrumental for us, which we named "The Slop," after the new dance that

was just getting started at the time. . . . WHK, a major pop station in Cleveland, persuaded us that the title should be changed because they could not play a record entitled "The Slop." We did a new run of labels . . . with the new title, "Hard Times." This was the first Baton record which reached the Top Forty on the national pop charts, quite a feat at that time. Only our inability to get this record on the *Dick Clark Show* kept [it] from reaching the Top Ten.

Perhaps. In December 1957 Watts' tune sat at its highest point, #44, in *Billboard*'s "Best Sellers in Stores" ranking for pop songs. ("April Love" by Perry Como was #1; "At the Hop" by Danny and the Juniors, #2; and Elvis Presley's "Jailhouse Rock," #3.) Oddly, this blues-based number never cracked the R&B chart.

Compared to some other tenor men, Watts' tone and playing range was higher, including in the solo opening lines of this mid-tempo, loping blues. Less full or deep than other tenor men—including Watts' friend Ernie Calhoun; Gene Ammons, who Watts admired; and jazz players such as Dexter Gordon—his playing does incorporate the burr or raspy slur that is a signature of the honking style, as well as some accentuated, repeated, and staccato sixteenth and thirty-second notes. While some honkers' playing feels frantic, insistent, almost desperate for attention, Watts seems assured and unrushed. As Nat Adderley once said, "Musically, he's hard to categorize. He has always liked the blues rhythm and feeling, but he has a great degree of musicality . . . and sensitivity. He lends [blues and rock] bands some jazz sophistication."

Conversely, his widow says, though Noble had the chops and theoretical knowledge to improvise in "way out" ways, like his bebop-playing contemporaries, he intentionally kept his playing accessible to the lay listener. "You could relate because Noble would stick to the melody. He was so soulful with it, too, you could get a beat and pat your feet to it."

On "Hard Times"/"The Slop," as on his next biggest hit, the 1962 Enjoy single, "Jookin'," Watts featured his guitar player, Jimmy Spruill, the relative of Bateman's who introduced her to Watts back at Sugar Ray's. Spruill was also heard on the Wilbert Harrison version of "Kansas City," Buster Brown's "Fannie Mae," and quite a few other R&B/soul hits. He died in 1966 on the way back to New York from Florida, where he was visiting Noble and June Watts.

IN THE LATE 1970S AND EARLY 1980S, the work that had sustained Watts for more than thirty years, and Bateman for twenty, began to slow down. Disco was the thing, she remembers, and they emphatically did not play that. Instrumentals like Bill Doggett's "Honky Tonk," Williams' "Huckle-buck," and Noble's "Hard Times" weren't in vogue anymore either. June remembers: "A lot of musicians, like [singer] Big Maybelle, all got day gigs because the music just wasn't there anymore." Her husband was worn out, she says, "and he didn't know where to turn."

In New York and on the road other musicians had made fun of Deland, telling Noble that it wasn't really a town, just a couple of stoplights. But he remained loyal. "He always loved Florida dearly," says June. "Deland was his home, and he never tried to be anything but a plain ol' Florida boy." Watts wrote and recorded two songs that paid homage to Florida: "Florida Shake" and "F.L.A.," on the Jell and Brunswick labels, respectively. As it turned out, Florida would reciprocate that loyalty.

The couple settled in on West Howry Avenue in Deland, just a half mile from where Noble grew up on East Howry. June went to work for the state government and Watts, sixty or so, still went to New York for occasional gigs and played lounge music in spots around Deland. Then by chance, bassist Bob Greenlee heard him playing at a picnic in New Smyrna Beach. Greenlee, who had played with Duane and Gregg Allman growing up in Daytona Beach, led a local blues band called the Midnight Creepers and owned King Snake Records. He immediately brought Watts into the band and began recording him again. (King Snake, based in a converted garage at Greenlee's Sanford home, released more than one hundred blues albums over twenty years, including LPs by Lazy Lester, Rufus Thomas, Lucky Pe-terson, Kenny Neal, and Root Boy Slim.) Greenlee, who died of pancreatic cancer at fifty-nine, a few months before Watts passed in 2004, was "one of the greatest friends I ever had," Watts said. "I was in bad shape and he revived my career."

In 1987 King Snake put out two Watts albums, *Daytona Blues* and *Return of the Thin Man*, and in 1990 Ichiban, a Japanese label, released *King of the Boogie Sax*. That year, Greenlee also released an album of Watts playing with Nat Adderley, his friend since FAMU, called *Noble & Nat*.

Alligator Records rereleased *Return of the Thin Man* in 1990, and it was favorably reviewed in *People* magazine's Picks and Pans section. That "pick" mentioned: "Bluesman Taj Mahal plays guitar on the jumping 'Blow Your Horn,' and contributes a written appreciation of the tenor man's 'big sax sound.'" (Though *People* did call his vocals "sorrowful and satisfying" the review truthfully pointed out, "His singing isn't on a par with his playing.") Soon Watts began to get invited to Europe, with and without the Midnight Creepers. As Bateman put it, "His career just zoomed."

During the last decade or so of his life, Watts' embrace of and by Deland also deepened. In 2004 an amphitheater was named after him on Clara Avenue, across from the African American Museum of the Arts. The inaugural Thin Man Watts Jazz Fest was held that year as well; it's now an annual event.

The most moving and unexpected tribute came about four years earlier. Noble and June were on their sunporch one afternoon when a vice president at Stetson University's Deland campus came by to tell them that, instead of having a speaker for their 117th commencement in May, they would like to have a commencement performer: the Thin Man. And they would give him an honorary degree, a doctorate in music.

Watts, with music professor Harold Blanchard on piano, plus bass and drums, improvised on themes from "The Grand Canyon Suite" by Grofé and, for unknown reasons, the out-of-state "Georgia," by Hoagy Carmichael. "That was a beautiful, beautiful thing," his widow says. "One of the highlights of his life, right here in his hometown. We had family and friends with us, including some who came down from New York."

She remembers seeing him in his cap and gown and thinking he looked "so calm, though I knew he must have been excited and proud." Ever the snappy dresser, the seventy-four-year-old wore a white suit and looked elegant. "He just played so beautifully, everyone really enjoyed it, and he did, too. I hadn't really seen my husband cry—he was such a hard-nose—but that night I saw the tears come from his eyes." So special was this occasion that on this gig, Watts even left the drummer alone. There were no rhythm criticisms from the Thin Man.

4

The Twist Came from Tampa

Tampa/Miami

SAM COOKE WAS THE HEADLINER, and the heartthrob. Dead-handsome and glamorous, wearing a short, tight-fitting bolero jacket, Cooke sang his romantic hits of that year, 1961: "Cupid" ("*Draw back your bow, and let your arrow go . . .*") and "Wonderful World" ("*Don't know much about history . . .*"). Rhythm and blues shows were usually segregated back then, says Ronny Elliott, a Tampa singer/songwriter who was thirteen or fourteen when he attended this one at Tampa's Fort Homer Hesterly Armory. But he distinctly remembers Cooke causing this biracial reaction: "All these young African American women, and Caucasian girls, were screaming at the point of fainting."

It was a soul summit, a star-stacked bill. Little Willie John ("Fever") performed a short set that evening on North Howard Avenue, too, as did LaVern Baker ("Jim Dandy") and Marv Johnson ("You Got What It Takes"). But Elliott was knocked out by Hank Ballard and the Midnighters.

While Cooke was a romantic, Ballard had made his name with raunch. His songs such as "Get It," "Sexy Ways," "Work With Me Annie," and the follow-up, "Annie Had a Baby," were known for their suggestive lyrics and had been banned from the radio in some parts of the country. They also provoked risqué answer songs, such as "Roll With Me, Henry" by Etta James. The Midnighters then riposted with "Henry's Got Flat Feet (Can't Dance No More)."

A slender man in his mid-thirties, about six feet tall with narrow shoulders, Ballard was belting out up-tempo dance numbers, pouring it on under the hot lights hanging from the high Armory ceiling. Sweat droplets formed on his broad forehead, and his distinctive tenor voice rang out, cutting through the overheated space to the five hundred or so people swaying in their ranks of metal folding chairs. Although his singing was intense, Ballard stood surprisingly still, even stiff, in performance; the Midnighters, his four backup singers, performed all the synchronized dance moves typical of that era. They ran through their recent hits "Finger Poppin' Time" and "Let's Go, Let's Go, Let's Go," and then kicked into another up-tempo tune Ballard had written. He called it "The Twist."

"I see lascivious grins," Elliott remembers as he casts his mind back to that show. "I see grown men having more fun than I knew you could have, and they are *in the music*, it is just phenomenal. I see these men dancing like nothing I've ever seen and at the same time doing this wonderful singing. That seemed impossible to me. That *still* seems impossible to me. In my entire life that may be the best rock and roll performance I've ever seen." This from a man who's been a professional musician since 1964 and shared bills with Jimi Hendrix, the Allman Brothers, Chuck Berry, Bo Diddley, and Van Morrison.

At the time of this Armory show, Ballard's song "The Twist" had already become a monster hit—for another man. Ballard's original version, on Cincinnati-based King Records, debuted in 1959 and did well, getting to #16 on *Billboard*'s R&B chart. Six months or so later Chubby Checker, an eighteen-year-old from Philadelphia, recorded it for hometown label Cameo Parkway. This second "Twist"—a note-for-note, word-for-word cover—went galactic.

That simple, catchy two-and-a-half-minute song hit #1 on *Billboard*'s pop music chart, the Hot 100, in September 1960, bumping Elvis Presley's "It's Now or Never" off that spot. Checker's Ballard cover also made it to #2 on the R&B ranking. A year and change later, gaining momentum from Checker's appearance on Dick Clark's TV show *American Bandstand*, Checker's version charted again and took the top spot for the second time, in January 1962.

Slews of other twist songs—including Sam Cooke's "Twistin' the Night Away," Joey Dee and the Starlighters' "Peppermint Twist," and the Isley Brothers' "Twist and Shout"—followed and became hits as well. That Isley Brothers number was later covered by four young Englishmen who went by the strange name of the Beatles. (They were Hank Ballard fans, and when they visited the United States, those four came to hear him and get his autograph at Miami's Peppermint Lounge.) Ballard's "Twist" was rereleased in 1960, in the wake of Checker's success, and went up to #6 R&B and #28 on the Hot 100 or mainstream pop chart.

If you remember the song, you must remember the dance. That's what transformed "The Twist" from a hit record into a social phenomenon, in this country and abroad. In the early 1960s, seemingly everyone was doing a little hippy shimmy-shake that, Checker told the audience of the *Dick Clark Show*, went like this: "Just pretend you're wiping your bottom with a towel as you get out of the shower and putting out a cigarette with both feet." The East Room of the White House reportedly "reverberated to the sound of 'The Twist,'" though Press Secretary Pierre Salinger denied that First Lady Jacqueline Kennedy was doing the deed. The *St. Petersburg Times* confirmed that "from Alaska to Florida the dance has swept the country." This was almost certainly the biggest song and dance craze of the Baby Boomer era or the latter half of the twentieth century. In 2008 *Billboard* ratified that by declaring Checker's "Twist" the most popular song of the previous fifty years. Not surprisingly, then, it is indelibly associated with those two sons of Philadelphia, Checker and Clark.

Yet, it's really Hank Ballard's "Twist." That song is his creation, his legacy. Outside of the African American community, where Ballard had his greatest success, few have any knowledge of this achievement. Fewer still, white or black, are aware that the original "Twist"—the one the Midnighters rocked Tampa's armory with in 1961—is a Florida product. As it turns out, Hank Ballard was almost certainly inspired to create that song in Tampa and it was recorded for the first time in Miami. That first rendition, committed to reel-to-reel tape in 1957, was never heard by the public. The true, Florida genesis of this massive music phenomenon is convoluted, and in parts controversial—call it the Twistory.

ON ANOTHER FLORIDA NIGHT, during another rendition of "The Twist," a ten-year-old girl stood off to the side of the stage, near a dressing room, at the Knight Beat. This was in 1966 and that club, in the Sir John Hotel in Miami's Overtown district, was one of the premier black nightspots. As Hank Ballard sang, the young girl, Lynn Williams, thought: "'I have a good-looking father.' I felt so good because he saw me—he was just smiling. He was really handsome, and I felt so proud. And that was the first time I saw my father."

Lynn Williams, born in Jacksonville, became a singer herself, recording for Marlin, Suncut, T.K., and other Miami labels in the 1970s and backing up Overtown neighbor Betty Wright on vocals. Her mother was Vernetta

Hank Ballard. After an unauthorized Miami version that was never released, his song "The Twist" came out on King Records in 1959. Courtesy of the author.

"Vanilla" Williams, a "shake dancer" (akin to a go-go dancer) at the Knight Beat and other clubs and later a popular DJ on WMBM in Miami.

Hank Ballard, who died in 2003 at age seventy-four, had five children by four different women that she knows of, Williams says. And Billy Davis, who played guitar with him from 1958 to 1965, remembers him as an intent, focused ladies' man. As a result the singer was "kind of a laid-back boss," Davis says. "He'd come to sound check, but he really wasn't around all that much. He had all these women . . ."

While pretty-faced Sam Cooke projected a wholesome earnestness, Ballard was a dangerous male; women loved watching him sing, and, to quote a Midnighters song title, he had sexy ways. That persona, his way with a catchy lyric, and above all his smooth, powerful singing made him a compelling performer and the Midnighters a rhythm and blues force.

Ballard, born John Kendricks, grew up in Alabama listening to and singing gospel. Another early influence, he said in later years, was the singing cowboy Gene Autry. He had moved to Detroit when he met fellow singer Sonny Woods of the Royals. Both men were working at a Ford plant, but Ballard wanted to make his living singing, as his cousin, Florence Ballard, would do with the Supremes.

Woods brought him into his group as a backup singer, and producer Johnny Otis got them a deal with Federal Records, a subsidiary of King Records in Cincinnati. Another act on that label was the Famous Flames, featuring James Brown, who was a lifelong Hank Ballard fan and later featured him in his long-running revue. To distinguish itself from another group, The "5" Royales, the Royals changed their name to the Midnighters, and they had some minor successes, including Otis' "Every Beat of My Heart" in 1952.

The Royals were singing doo-wop, essentially, as were a slew of other groups. They were able to distinguish themselves when Ballard began writing harder R&B tunes for them, beginning with "Get It" and then the even-more-suggestive "Annie" songs, including "Annie's Aunt Fanny." This new style called for Ballard to do more than just croon in a round, pleasing tone and to exploit the force of his voice and his ability to drive a song forward with intensity—to rock with soul. He became the clear front man of the group, despite his semirigidity onstage. "He wasn't really a dancer; he didn't have it," concedes guitarist Davis. "Hank depended on the Midnighters to do that. But I just loved his voice, his singing," Davis continues. "He had a very unusual sound, [his] natural sound. That's what first attracted the fans—they were with him right away because he didn't sound like anybody else."

The smooth force of Ballard's instrument far exceeded its size. When Davis first auditioned for the Midnighters in 1958 at Detroit's East Side Show Club, the nineteen-year-old guitarist kept waiting for Hank Ballard to show up but never saw him. Then Davis recognized the elaborate "process" or straightened hairdo on the skinny guy, about thirty or so, looking through some arrangements on the side. "I had an image of him in my mind of this big black guy, goes about 200 pounds, because of that voice," Davis remembers. Instead "he was about 6 feet tall, maybe a little less, but he was so thin, maybe weighed about 135, and he never gained more than five or six pounds. And he stayed young-looking as long as I knew him."

After their initial harder-edged transformation Ballard and the Midnighters lost some momentum and didn't have another substantial hit for three years. During that late-1950s fallow period, the Midnighters continued to tour nationally, including regular trips to Florida. And it was on one of those southern swings, the story goes, that "The Twist" was born. Tampa's Ronny Elliott makes that case in one of his songs: *"Hank Ballard came through Tampa on a chitlin' circuit show / pushed his way up through the crowd to the very first row / A little girl in a red dress recognized the vocalist / he asked her, 'What's that they're doing?' / She said, 'that's the Twist.'"*

This scene might have played out at the Cotton Club, the Apollo, the Little Savoy, or any of the clubs and theaters on Central Avenue, the center of the black business and entertainment district. As the names of those clubs suggest, this was the Harlem of Tampa. In other versions of this urban legend Ballard saw those twisting kids—it's usually girls—out on the Avenue, when he stepped out of his hotel. It may well have been the Pyramid Hotel (later named the Rogers Hotel), or it could have been the Jackson House, the boarding house on Zack Street where Cab Calloway, Ella Fitzgerald, and many other black musicians stayed when white hotels were off-limits. This genesis story is echoed in the liner notes to a rock and roll compilation album entitled *1960: Still Rockin'*. Ballard wrote the song, writer Joe Sasfy says, "after seeing kids do the pelvis-swiveling maneuver in Tampa, Florida."

In some Tampa enclaves, this is a fervently held belief. "I've been in the music business a long time and I've lived in Tampa since 1968," says the Soulman, aka Bob Scheir, a producer, DJ, and artist manager who for many years hosted *Blues with a Groove* on Tampa's public radio station, WMNF.

"And Little Milton, Bobby Bland, and I can't tell you how many other artists, have all told me that the kids on Central Avenue started the Twist, that's where Hank Ballard saw it. That's what I *know*."

"I was there," confirms Artis Clayton, in a *Florida Soul* interview. He was a member of the Star Lighters, a late 1950s Tampa vocal group who opened for the Midnighters in Tampa and St. Petersburg. "It was 1958 in the Apollo on Central Avenue," Clayton continues. "The fans were twisting, then the Midnighters started doing it." (Other facts make it more likely that this would have been in 1957.)

Ballard himself seemed to endorse versions of this story at times, and not at others. In the 1993 documentary *Twist*, Ballard says his Midnighters were the inspiration for the song. "I was watching my group, they were twisting their bodies," he says. "I don't know where they got it from, I really don't." But he's sure of this: "I gave the world the biggest dance craze ever." He doesn't mention Tampa.

He does, though, in a 2002 radio series, *A History of the Blues in the Tampa Bay Area*, that aired on local public radio station WMNF. In his introduction to Ballard's sound bites, narrator and producer P. W. Fenton says Ballard noticed high schoolers in Tampa "doing some kind of new dance." He also puts the year at 1958. "We were playing a gig there somewhere," Ballard is heard saying. "And they were twisting their bodies, and the lyrics just came to me."

In this quote Ballard doesn't specify who "they" are. (Fenton declined to discuss his interview with Ballard further.) His words could mean that teenagers twisted at a Midnighters dance, as the narrator has it, or that the Midnighters were twisting their bodies while playing a Tampa gig. In both of these scenarios, though, Hank Ballard says he first saw the dance performed in Tampa, and that's what inspired him to write the song.

Just how the lyrics came to him can be interpreted in more than one way as well—and probably should be. Author Jim Dawson interviewed Cal Green, the late Midnighters' guitarist, for his book, *The Twist: The Story of the Song and Dance that Changed the World*. Green remembered someone in the gospel group the Sensational Nightingales approaching Ballard with "something scribbled on a piece of paper. He said, 'We can't record this, we're a spiritual group, you can have the song.' So Hank says, 'Get your guitar, Cal, let's see what we can do with it.'" According to Green this lyrical handoff took place in 1957 "in Tampa, Florida. The Nightingales were staying at the same hotel [as the Midnighters]."

That's his understanding as well, says Billy Davis, who replaced Green in the Midnighters. "The [lyrics] were written by a guy singing with The Sensational Nightingales. I know the guy, I just can't think of his name."

Jo Jo Wallace?

"That's him."

Strange. This very secular song, first a soul hit and then a rock and roll smash, had some fairly salacious undertones. Could a sacred singer have created one of the biggest touchstones in American pop?

"I surely did, and that's the God-knows truth," said Brother Joseph "Jo Jo" Wallace, from his home in Durham, North Carolina. At the time of this *Florida Soul* interview, Wallace, then eighty-four, still sang tenor, played the guitar, and toured with the Nightingales. "In our younger days," he explained, "the late Bill Woodruff—a member of our group—and I would sing secular music, blues, sometimes. One time we were in these ladies' house, in the parlor, in Camden, New Jersey, just balling. I was playing the guitar and singing blues, and I came out with, 'My baby can twist . . . Who taught you how to twist like that?' Well, those girls were shaking their tails like mad, shakin' 'em so hard the candles shook."

Use of "the twist"—as an exhortation to dancers and a euphemism for sex—goes back at least as far as that time (Wallace was born in 1926, so this would have been the 1940s). As author Dawson points out, a 1912 composition called "Messin' Around" urged dancers to "stand in one spot nice and tight, and twist around, twist around with all your might." Duke Ellington recorded "Harlem Twist" in 1928, one of at least three songs with this theme released that year, followed by Jelly Roll Morton's "Turtle Twist" in 1929. "The sexual implications of the word 'twist' became more overt in a song called 'Winin' Boy Blues,' recorded at least five times by Morton," Dawson writes. "The lyric—'Mama, mama, look at sis, she's out on the levee doing the double twist'—referred to a whore working the [New Orleans] docks."

Whether or not Wallace's "Twist" lyrics were entirely his invention, he maintains he was indeed the conduit to Hank Ballard. In a handwritten note to this author, Wallace said he told another Nightingale, David Edrington, about the song "and how much empack [sic] it had on the girls in Camden. I sang it to him and he really were empress [sic]." Edrington then passed it along to a cousin of his in the Royals, Wallace says (though by this time they would have changed their name to the Midnighters). His thinking was: "If it do well for them, maybe they would remember me with a little money (smile)." There's no indication that kind of remembrance ensued. Wallace's recollection of where he sang his song to Edrington echoes Cal Green's: "In a hotel room in Tampa, Fla. David's cousin's group was staying at the same hotel."

Ballard didn't mention Wallace or the lyrics being handed to him in any of his accounts. Musically, Ballard and Green both acknowledged they based "The Twist" on a tune they'd already released called "Is Your Love For Real?," which had a twelve-bar-blues chord progression and a boogie-woogie bass line: "*Ba-by, won't you tell me how you feel / I want to know if your love, is your love for real.*" That song was in turn a variation on Clyde McPhatter and the Drifters' "Whatcha Gonna Do?": "*Whatcha gonna do about half past eight? / It would knock me out if we had a date.*"

In that 2002 radio interview Ballard said that, soon after inspiration struck, "we left Tampa and went to Miami, and I got in touch with a guy named Henry Stone. He had a record company down there. We went into a high school with some portable recording equipment. That was the first version [of 'The Twist']."

Henry Stone produced blues, R&B, and soul on a dozen or so labels in Miami for something like sixty years, beginning in 1948 (see chapter 14). Ray Charles and Sam Moore both recorded early work for him. In 1957, though, when he recalls this visit from Hank Ballard, he was just distributing records for other labels. But he still managed to record the original "Twist."

"Ballard came into my Tone Distributing office," Stone says, "and told me his contract with King Records was over and that he was shopping for a new label. We discussed Chicago's Chess and Vee Jay Records labels and he decided on Vee Jay. I called Ewart Abner, the president of Vee Jay, and he told me to go ahead and record him and the Midnighters in Miami. At the time they were very big."

What was in it for Stone? "A lot of the business was done in records back then," he explains. "As payment I might get, say, 1,000 of them. I'd sell them for 50 cents apiece, make $500. So Abner said he'd pay me 10,000 free records for my recording session work with Ballard."

Stone remembers the venue as an armory, not a high school: "So I take Ballard and some portable sound equipment into the North Miami Armory to produce some songs. And Hank came up with one song after another, good blues songs, good dance songs." Then Ballard got to his latest composition, and typically, perhaps even truthfully, Stone says that he made all the difference. "Hank came up with 'The Twist' but it was in sort of a slower blues tempo: '*Come on, baby / let's do the Twist . . .* '

"Cal Green was on guitar and he started tuning up, and he does it *bing bang, bing bang*—faster than Hank was going, in a much more danceable tempo. It sounded good, so I said, 'Hey, why don't we try a dance number on this?' which we did. And I sent all the tapes to Abner at Vee Jay in Chicago."

But then, Stone continues, Abner got a phone call from King Records head Syd Nathan, telling him: "'Yeah, Ballard's contract is up, but he owes me $300. And I know that that Henry Stone son of a bitch is recording him. If Ballard don't pay me the $300 I'm going to sue you and Stone and the whole world.' So Abner just sent the tapes to King and Nathan. Syd then released [a rerecorded version of] 'The Twist' as the B-side to 'Teardrops on Your Letter,' which was a pretty good hit."

Stone confirms that Ballard and his group came to him, with that song, directly from Tampa. But when he thinks back to that Ballard session Florida's historical claim to "The Twist" is not his biggest concern. "The sad side of the whole story," Stone says, "is I had also made a deal with Abner to get half the publishing [rights and fees] to all those songs we recorded with Ballard. And I can't tell you how big that record was for 30 years."

As STONE RELATES, on November 11, 1958, Ballard and the Midnighters rerecorded his composition in the King Records studio on Brewster Avenue in Cincinnati. They were backed up by pianist Sonny Thompson's session men. Guitarist Cal Green was there, too, as he was at the Miami session. To accomplished session man Edwyn Conley, who played upright bass on the King side, it was "nothing special. Just a 12-bar blues. We didn't need a lot of takes." What did he get paid for his part in this historic tune? "Something like fifty bucks."

This second "Twist" sounds much more polished overall, and the prominent twangy guitar and bass lines in the Miami version are much more subdued. In both takes, Ballard goes in and out of adhering to the traditional A-A-B lyrical structure. Both versions also employ stop-time intervals at the ends of choruses.

On this second version, the one the public got to hear, Ballard made a crucial change in the lyrics. The Miami song was narrated in the third-person: "*Everybody is doin' the Twist / it's a crazy thing, goes like this.*" Now it became a second-person exhortation, beginning in the first line: "*Come*

on, baby / let's do the Twist." And Ballard added another verse that resonated with teenagers across the country: *"My daddy's sleeping, and mama
ain't around / My daddy's sleeping, and mama ain't around / We gonna twist it,
twist it, twist it, till we tear the house down."*

King impresario Syd Nathan didn't think much of it. (Ballard later
pointed out that Nathan didn't like James Brown's "Please Please Please"
either, until it became a huge success.) Thus the song was relegated to the
B-side of the 45-rpm "Teardrops" single. That soulful but traditional ballad,
written by producer Henry Glover, was a sort of throwback to the Midnighters' doo-wop days. It became the group's biggest hit in several years, reaching #4 on the R&B charts in April 1959. Then, DJs and listeners recognized
what Nathan couldn't and the danceable "Twist" cracked the charts as well,
and stayed there for ten weeks.

While Ballard's *Twist* was still charting, Dick Clark suggested covering
it to producers at the Cameo Parkway label in Philadelphia. They brought
in Ernest Evans, who'd recorded an audio Christmas card for Clark and
his wife, and had one decent hit the year before with the novelty song,
"The Class," on which he'd sung his impressions of popular artists. Mrs.
Clark reportedly gave him the stage name Chubby Checker, a riff on Fats
Domino. Their "Twist" would be a duplicative effort in every conceivable
aspect.

Dave Appell, who produced Checker's "Twist" session, acknowledged
he set out to make a musical copy, using the same key (E major), the same
number of choruses, and the same saxophone break between the fourth
and the fifth. Checker's impression of Ballard is as close as possible, and
Ray Felder, the Cincinnati tenor man on the original Ballard recording, says
of the solo on the Cameo Parkway version, "To me, that guy is trying to copy
mine."

Why didn't Clark simply promote the original? Explanations are muddy
and varied. One holds that Ballard was touring and unavailable to appear
on *American Bandstand*; Ballard said as much on occasion. Others suggest
that Clark, who supplied some remarks on "The Twist" through a publicist,
but declined to be interviewed on specifics, wanted more control of what
he sensed could be a monster hit. Or that Clark had a financial interest in
Cameo Parkway. Clark may also have felt that teenage, extroverted Checker
would have more appeal than the older Ballard. Ballard was also quite dark-
skinned, whereas Checker was light; some feel that figured into Ballard
being replaced. Clark certainly knew the Midnighters' bawdy lyrics and

reputation as well; they were even known to have enlivened performances by dropping their trousers.

Checker put it across very well; his voice has a nice sonority to it. He's sensitive about "imitation." In an e-mail interview he points out that the cover is a music industry staple. "Look, I sang his song," he wrote. "Elvis sang Big Mama Thornton's song, 'Hound Dog.' Jerry Lee Lewis sang Big Maybelle's song, 'Whole Lotta Shakin' Goin' On.' It's not a big deal." Later he adds: "If Hank Ballard wasn't born, I wouldn't be here, and I always give him credit. But I was the one who took it to glory."

He's right, and for that reason, the glory that ensued—and, at times, the approbation of "The Twist"—went to Philly, not to Florida.

WHEN CHECKER'S "TWIST" made the Hot 100 for the first time in August 1960, at #49, Ballard's version was still in residence, at #53. After a Saturday night Chubby appearance on *American Bandstand*, the cover version became, as Checker put it, "the biggest song on the planet." "Let's Twist Again" was Checker's inevitable follow-up; it stayed on the pop chart for twenty-three weeks in 1961 and went gold. In October of that year, after Checker appeared on the *Ed Sullivan Show*, Cameo Parkway rereleased his "Twist" with a different B-side, and in January 1962 it hit #1 on pop for the second time. This effort made #4 on the R&B chart; all told it spent a combined seventy-seven weeks on both *Billboard* charts.

As we might say today "The Twist" went viral. And, with no Internet yet in existence, it became a global phenomenon as well. In the fall of 1961 celebrities—including Marilyn Monroe and Noel Coward—had begun to descend on a dingy biker dive on West 45th Street in Manhattan called the Peppermint Lounge. Joey Dee, born Joseph DiNicola, a twenty-three-year-old from across the river in Passaic, New Jersey, led the house band there. "I was doing the Hank Ballard version of 'The Twist,'" he says from his home in Clearwater, Florida, where he's lived since 1989. "I first heard it in a little club in Newark called Ben's Cotton Club, and saw the reaction, and it became the mainstay of my show."

One Sunday in October Dee sat down with Henry Glover—formerly a Midnighters producer, then A&R man at Roulette Records in New York—at the piano and knocked out "The Peppermint Twist" in about an hour and a half. In February 1962 that song one went to #1—knocking off Checker's reissued "Twist."

Time magazine and *Newsweek* weighed in, and then *LIFE* magazine told the whole country. A seven-page text-and-photo spread in November 1961 declared: "A Pulsating, Gyrating, Hip-Swinging Mania Sweeps the U.S. and Europe." Among other photographs, the story showed extras gyrating on the set of Elizabeth Taylor's new movie, *Cleopatra*. Chubby Checker was credited with "starting it all," though the story added: "Both the Twist song and dance were dreamed up by another Negro singer, Hank Ballard."

Sam Cooke's subsequent "Twistin' the Night Away" was inspired by the madhouse at the Pep (*"Let me tell you about a place / somewhere up New York way"*) and became part of a bigger wave of Twist tunes pouring forth. At its unlikely edges were found "The Alvin Twist" by the Chipmunks; "Mr. Oliver Twist" by Rod McKuen; and even Frank Sinatra's "Everybody's Twisting." ("That's my favorite other Twist song," says Checker. "It's very tasteful. Hats off to Mr. Sinatra.") At least four low-ambition Twist movies were rushed out, too, starring Checker, Dee, and Louis Prima. Bob Hope made twist jokes. Sean Connery twisted in the first Bond film, *Dr. No*.

Florida was at least as susceptible to the virus. Peppermint Lounges sprang up in Miami and elsewhere around the song's home state. Jacksonville was twisting, appropriate given it's the hometown of Gary U.S. Bonds, who had a hit with his "Dear Lady Twist." In February 1962 that tune was one of three Twist songs, along with Checker's and Dee's, in the top 10 simultaneously. The *St. Petersburg Times* sent their women's editor to the Pep. She was grateful to be admitted, Gloria Biggs reported; it seemed former U.S. vice-president Richard Nixon had just been turned away. The dance floor was tiny, she told her South Florida readers: "24 crowd it. Thirty turn it into what looks like a madhouse." On it she saw "gyrating bodies twisting in violent rhythm to the music."

In December 1961 *Times* writer Bill Dunn wrote of his Twist attempts at Ronnie's Peppermint Lounge on Madeira Beach. He ended with a very sixties, *Mad Men* take on the dance sensation: "I think I'll take my twist on a lemon peel in a nice dry martini." Over the following New Year's weekend twenty-four Tampa Bay couples tried to set a Twist endurance record while sailing to Longboat Key and back on two cabin cruisers. They claimed they Twisted for eleven hours each way.

Teenagers made "The Twist" a hit and kept doing the dance that Ballard first saw in Tampa. But the second, bigger surge was driven by their parents, as they decided, en masse, to get down with it. "All of a sudden," Dick Clark said through his publicist, "an older generation was able to

Florida State students doing the hip-swiveling dance in 1962 or 1963; whether they danced to Ballard's or Chubby Checker's version is not known. Courtesy State Archives of Florida.

admit they really liked rock & roll." A product that draws from multiple demographics is a marketer's dream, and this one checked each box in a rare pop-culture quadrant: black teens; white teens; black adults; and white adults. Not at the same dances, of course.

Ronny Elliott was twisting at South Tampa's Woodrow Wilson Junior High, and at the equivalent black school, Booker T. Washington on Estelle Street, Fred Hearns was doing the same. "Everybody I knew was doing the

Twist," says Hearns, who was for many years the city's director of community affairs. "We saw the kids on *American Bandstand* doing it, but to us that was our little dance."

IT WAS SO EASY: Just swivel those hips—joints that some pop culture savants believe were preloosened by Elvis Presley and the hula hoop craze—from side to side, and rotate your arms in the opposite direction. To the beat, if possible. Arthur Murray, the nation's dance teacher through his chain of instructional studios, offered Twist lessons, even though, he said, "There are no steps, just swivels." Chubby Checker agrees the thing succeeded "because it was simple. Anybody could do it. It's a natural form of human behavior, and we just happened to stumble upon it."

One Tampa Bay area psychologist took the Twistian analysis further. For young people, he said, the dance was "an expression of a basic need for individuality, a need to show the climate is different today than it was 5 or 10 years ago." And their Twisted parents? "They're trying to prove they're getting younger, instead of older."

Beyond the racial and the generational, the Twist straddled another crucial divide. The movements—pelvic, but not outright pumping—were nicely balanced between the sexual and the innocent, the carnal and the cute. On one level, what Sis was doin' was the nasty; that's what the old songs meant by twist, and in Ballard's rendition it was yet another euphemism for doing the dirty. Suggestive? Try explicit, says music historian and author Dave Marsh in a *Florida Soul* interview. "If you can look at people doing the Twist and not see people screwing, you oughta get a medal," he says. "The Pope couldn't miss it."

And yet, take another look at Sis. She's Twisting by herself, really, not grinding against anyone, not touching her partner at all the way you did in the Charleston, the Jitterbug, or the Lindy Hop. That lack of contact gave Twisters the perfect out: sexuality with deniability.

Chubby Checker maintains that this, not selling all those records and setting off the craze, is his greatest legacy: changing the way Americans dance. Although others would disagree, he says that before the Twist, "we didn't dance apart, to the beat. We began with the Twist, then came the Pony, the Fly, the Shake, and the Hucklebuck—all danced that way. Before Chubby Checker, the boogie wasn't there."

Checker also insists that this nonstick swiveling and accompanying arm jive did *not* originate with Hank Ballard—or in Tampa, for that matter. "The Twist was a dance the black kids made up to the lyrics of Hank

Ballard's song, not the other way around," he wrote. "I saw Hank Ballard and his band perform that song at the Uptown Theater on Broad Street in Philadelphia when I was a kid. The Midnighters were dancing around him, in a circle. No one was twisting." He says the moves he took onto *Bandstand* and that then spread out across the globe were those he'd seen in his Philly neighborhood, plus a few little fillips of his own.

As Checker's words make clear, "The Twist" still provokes strong feelings more than fifty years after its inception, including bitter ones. To detractors, Clark and Checker's cover is not just inferior musically but a blatant rip-off, a cruel soul-jacking of Hank Ballard's original work. Ronny Elliott's song "The Twist Came From Tampa" sums up that line of thought: "*Hank got a lot of miles out of the song and the dance but a young Dick Clark wasn't about to take a chance / Found himself a hack, called him Chubby Checker, pulled his finger out of the pie with a number one hit record / A social phenomenon . . . an inferior version of Hank Ballard's perfect record.*"

Guitarist Billy Davis remembers the first time he, Ballard, and the Midnighters heard the other version of their song. "We were in the car, less than 40 miles from Miami. We played there for three or four weeks sometimes. We were sleeping and suddenly we hear, '*Come on, baby*' on the radio. I sense something different. . . . Everybody's sitting there; we all got quiet. They say, 'It's gotta be us but it ain't us.' Afterward, they said 'Chubby Checker' and everybody's just, 'Who the hell is Chubby Checker?'"

Over the years Ballard was often quite gracious about this saga, even thanking Checker at times for making him money via his songwriting royalties. Legally—meaning, theoretically—Ballard got compensated every time Checker's "Twist" was played, as well as his own. At other times, though, Ballard accused King's Nathan of making a complicated deal with Dick Clark that sold out his "Twist" in favor of Checker's.

Not everyone took to the new fad. There were haters, including in Florida. The book *The Twist* lays out all the silly backlash—undertaken with high seriousness—against this scourge of a dance: The Society of New Jersey Chiropractors came out against the Twist, citing hip and knee injuries. Dwight Eisenhower, who had just left the presidency, said the Twist dance "does represent some kind of change in our standards. What has happened to our concepts of beauty and decency and morality?" In the Soviet Union, an apparatchik went further, explaining: "American dances allow people to forget themselves, which is required by people who are leading joyless lives." Of course, after officialdom denounced it, Soviet youth twisted even harder.

Stunningly, Tampa turned on its own. Like many parents, the city grew alarmed at its progeny's behavior and brought the disciplinary hammer down. The Twist was grounded in January 1962, when the city Recreation Department prohibited the dance at all its community centers. "We discourage all weird or off-beat dancing," said Recreation Director David Barksdale. "We don't feel the Twist has any part in our program."

City Councilman Bill Myers tried valiantly to have the ban overturned, dancing "with a pretty City Hall secretary," as the *St. Petersburg Times* called her, in front of his fellow councilmen to show the Twist's essential decency. "You lose weight doing it," he also argued, "and it helps keep your skeleton straightened out." But the ban held. St. Petersburg was considerably more relaxed. "We won't ever ban fad dances from our recreation centers," said that city's recreation director, Jack Puryear. "If I could do the Twist, I would."

BALLARD AND THE MIDNIGHTERS continued to have success, propelled in some ways by Twist-mania. In all, they had twenty-two singles that made the R&B chart. The group continued to perform "The Twist" in their live shows; they closed their sets with it, Billy Davis remembers. Ballard, who later began performing solo, remained quite popular in England and recorded a double album there. *Hank Ballard Live at the Palais* is considered his finest work after the Midnighters' early 1960s heyday. (Despite the French name, the Palais was a London venue.)

In 1990 Ballard was inducted into the Rock and Roll Hall of Fame, and he was recognized for his contributions to rhythm and blues—and to the rock and roll that followed, built on an R&B foundation. Irwin Stambler cited the Midnighters' influence in his *Encyclopedia of Pop, Rock & Soul*, writing: "The Allman Brothers . . . recall that their early bands often played Hank Ballard songs in Florida clubs in the early and mid-1960s. Quite a few other groups that were to spawn the most successful rock bands of the late 1960s similarly used Ballard material as an important part of their repertoires."

Later in his life Ballard moved to Miami, where he reconnected with his daughter, Lynn Williams. During their frequent visits he didn't talk about or express any bitterness toward Chubby Checker or Dick Clark, she says. During that time Williams got to perform with her father, singing backup for him at the Newport Hotel on Miami Beach (along with Jeanette Wright, sister of Betty Wright). A lifelong smoker, Ballard died of throat cancer in 2003.

Central Avenue, heart of Tampa's "Harlem," in the 1960s. See sign for Joyner's Cotton Club, named after the one in New York City. *Tampa Tribune*.

The Central Avenue nightlife district where Ballard was inspired to create his classic song disintegrated in the 1970s and is no more. That thriving center of African American life in Tampa was a casualty of "urban renewal" and of racial integration. Still, nostalgia for Twisting times remains strong in Tampa Bay. In the early 1960s Marvin Flemmings spent his summer afternoons at one of those St. Petersburg recreation centers—the ones where the Twist wasn't banned. He was eleven or so, and around 3 or 4 p.m. the kids and counselors at Jordan Park Elementary School would go inside, push all the tables and chairs to the cafeteria walls, put their 45s on the record player, and dance. He was already steeped in "The Twist" from the AM radio at home; DJ Chuck C. was playing Hank Ballard's song all the time on WTMP.

"Those were good times," says Flemmings, who's retired from the United States Army and from teaching in the Pinellas County school system. Segregated times, too. "Yeah, but we had a real community there," he says. "Everyone knew each other. We grew up together. I wish that togetherness could happen today." Flemmings can't Twist anymore, though: "It's too much gyration on my knees."

It was silly, and it was sexy. It was funky, and it was innocent. It was a fine expression of Hank Ballard's R&B art, and it became a huge, crass commodity. When it comes to Ballard, the originator, perhaps the way the Twist story unfolded was a shame, but it was also a joy—one he created. Twisting is a happy act, says Fred Hearns, the amateur African American historian in Tampa who did his dancing at Booker T. Washington Junior High. As he notes: "It's hard to Twist and not have a smile on your face."

He thinks there should be some tangible commemoration of the song, the dance, and, especially, their Florida origins in downtown Tampa. Hearns sees a statue of Hank Ballard, with his hair in that high process, holding a microphone, belting out his historic work. In the meantime, he's done some consulting for a new mixed-income housing development just north of downtown, called Encore! Its musical theme extends to buildings named Tempo and Trio and to a senior residence called Ella, after Ella Fitzgerald, who is said to have written one of her signature tunes, "A-Tisket, A-Tasket," while staying at the nearby Jackson House. Hearns' influence is seen in the name of one of this community's new roads: Hank Ballard Street. So far, though, no statue.

5

Linda Lyndell

Gainesville

IF, IN THE LATE 1940S AND EARLY 1950S, you took Archer Road south-west out of Gainesville about eight miles or so and then followed a dirt road further out into the country for another seven, you'd reach the Rowland farm. "We had milk cows and a garden we ate out of and we sold some, too," says Linda Rowland, born in 1946. "We also gave away a lot. It was not a good time; people who lived back in those woods did not have a lot."

From their farm it was just a three-quarter-mile walk to the Bethel AME (African Methodist Episcopal) church. Starting when she was very young—four or five, she thinks—Rowland would make that walk every Sunday. Her parents weren't religious, and work on their farm, in what was then rural Florida, occupied them "pretty much 24-7-365," the daughter says. So they let the little girl go by herself. Linda didn't have too many clear ideas about religion, either. She went to Bethel "because I wanted to sing."

Like most soul singers of her generation, Rowland got her training and inspiration singing gospel in the black church. She'd run down the long central aisle to join the choir behind the preacher and the pulpit and, in her youngest Sundays, they'd lift her up to stand on top of the piano, facing the congregation. "I did some solos," she says. "Even then, I had a voice. We didn't have microphones; you just had to belt it out, so I learned to sing loud and strong."

Her powerful instrument and passionate, full-on delivery gave her a career in music as Linda Lyndell, a stage name she created using her middle name, Wynell. In 1968 she made it to southern soul's promised land: Stax Records in Memphis, home to Otis Redding, Sam and Dave, and other

Linda Lyndell in a promotional photo, 1965 or 1966. Photo by Sam Johnston, Courtesy of Charles Steadham / Blade Agency.

top-tier national acts. There Lyndell recorded her best-known song, "What a Man." The compulsively catchy refrain—"*What a man, what a man, what a man, what a mighty good man*"—boosted the song onto *Billboard* magazine's R&B sales chart, and today it's considered a classic. Salt-N-Pepa and En Vogue had a combined hit with their cover version in 1994.

As a little girl Linda already had dreams of being a famous singer, a star. She also craved the attention and approval she got at those Sunday church services, things that weren't in long supply at home. "Daddy was drinking a lot back then," the adult Lyndell says. The middle-aged and older women who so warmed to her at Bethel, she considered her "aunties." Their children, with whom she played, were like her cousins. Linda had no sense of being different or an outsider: "I didn't really understand that I was Caucasian, or that I was the only white person there."

Lyndell believes—wants to believe—that the church folks didn't consider her an outsider, either. "They just figured I would be there come Sunday, and I was. It was like a color-blind place, and it was beautiful, it really was."

If so, it was the last such place she would inhabit. The story of soul music is inextricable from race and racism, but Lyndell—a white woman singing black music—traced her own convoluted and anomalous arc. In her years performing across the segregated South, she was both marketed for her whiteness and reviled for it. For a time, Lyndell wore an Afro wig and tried to pass for black.

Her talent and sincerity were indisputable, yet at a crucial point in her musical life—and a particularly raw period in American race relations—her skin became her sin. And as so many African Americans have experienced, this involuntary, ineluctable quality would not go unpunished.

Lyndell, turning seventy at this writing, lives with her third husband twenty miles outside Tallahassee. They run a plant nursery together. She's out of public life and reticent; Lyndell declined to be interviewed until a good friend and former musical colleague interceded. She wouldn't be photographed. "It's sad what happened," Lyndell says, "but I'm over it now." Then, in the next sentence, she adds: "I'll really never get over it, because there was so much more for me to do."

As SHE GOT OLDER LINDA was forced to confront segregation, at school, for instance. But perhaps in part because both her parents had some Native American lineage, Lyndell was taught to treat everyone equally. "Momma called black folks 'colored people,' which was the respectful term at that time, while the more redneck types around us used the N-word," she says. During the summers she and her older brother worked the nearby tobacco, cantaloupe, and watermelon fields for "a whole dollar a day. We were shoulder to shoulder [with the black workers] there," she says, "and when you work with somebody like that, you just get to be friends." She's not sure why, but at their midday break she and her brother would eat their bagged lunches under some trees with the black workers, while the other whites ate separately.

She'd started playing her aunt's piano by ear, with one finger, when she was three, and later her parents bought one. After immersing herself in gospel every Sunday she'd come home to find her father playing his bluegrass records—Bill Monroe, the Wilburn Brothers—and she loved their harmonies, especially *a cappella* harmony. After the family moved to Gainesville (first to a neighborhood called Blacktown, then to a mostly white one), she became an ardent admirer of Stax artists Carla Thomas, Sam and Dave, and Otis Redding, as well as Little Richard and Elvis. To her black music wasn't an alluring taboo; it felt natural, and she considered it her birthright.

The piano player for a rock and roll band called the Mark IVs lived in the neighborhood, and one day he heard her singing in her living room. She became their vocalist while still in high school and dated the guitarist, Al Towles. Some of the other Marks were attending the University of Florida, including saxophone player Charles Steadham. Steadham, who remains Lyndell's close friend, says the Mark IVs were "the least soulful band of all time." But soon she and Steadham were regulars at the jam sessions at Sarah's Place on NW 5th Avenue and at the Checkerboard (the outside was painted in black and white panels), south of town on U.S. Highway 441, both clubs that featured black music.

After a two-year apprenticeship at those jams and gospel sings, Steadham and Lyndell were asked to join Gordon Henderson and the Blues Rockers, the house band at Club Bali in Ocala, roughly forty minutes south. "This was an uptown place, with a balcony overlooking the stage, owned by a prominent black physician," says Steadham, who took the stage name Charlie Blade. Club Bali was an established chitlin' circuit stop that hosted major touring acts, including James Brown, Bobby "Blue" Bland, and Sam and Dave.

Listeners' first reaction was usually astonishment at the power of Lyndell's singing. "'That little thing, and she's putting out all that voice?' I got that all the time," she says. Her next employer, the late singer and bandleader Lavell Kamma, remembered that Lyndell didn't have or didn't use great vocal range. "But back then singing wasn't about having range of this or that many octaves," he said. "It was about delivery." Hers was unabashedly emotional, a quality likely instilled in those Sunday morning church sessions. Her stage persona was dynamic and extroverted as well; she even makes the audacious claim that her performances had "just as much movement as James Brown did—I worked that hard. I jumped like a Pentecostal person and I danced. You couldn't just stand up there and sing."

"She had the show-time personality," agrees Weston Prim, who worked and recorded with her (and Blade) in the 1970s in a band called Blacklash. "It was amazing the way she got out there and worked that crowd, worked the room. She was good, and she knew it."

From Club Bali Lyndell and Blade jumped—as a two-person package, which would become their pattern—to join Kamma's revue. At that point his band, the Counts, was called the 100 Hour Counts, a name earned in a publicity stunt at the Club El Morocco in Fort Lauderdale, when they played for more than 100 consecutive hours. (For more on Kamma's career, see the next chapter). The Counts' two new members drove to and from Florida gigs in Blade's blue 1965 Plymouth Fury. Much of the band's work was in the southern part of the state, and many of those gigs were for sugarcane workers.

In 1966, when Kamma booked a southern tour into Louisiana, Texas, and Arkansas, as well as Georgia and Alabama, Lyndell and Blade went with him. He dropped out of the University of Florida to go. Lyndell's mother was apprehensive, especially with Linda's older brother serving in Vietnam, but "she knew how I loved to sing and dance; I used to sing to her all the time. So she didn't try to stop me."

"Tour" is perhaps too glamorous a word for life on the chitlin' circuit. "It was absolutely hand-to-mouth," says Blade, who remembers eating lots of potted-meat sandwiches and that peanut butter and jelly "was a delicacy." Kamma's entire revue, roughly ten pieces then, would play to as many as five to six hundred people sharing a single Electro Voice 664 microphone and one Bogen amplifier with two twelve-inch speakers. After their advance man for that tour took five hundred dollars of their earnings up front from each venue and absconded with it, that sound system got hocked for $80 somewhere on the road, never to be reclaimed. In Houston, their motel rooms were robbed.

In a much more glamorous publicity photo from that time, the young white soul singer stands alone, wearing a form-fitting, floor-length gown.

She's fairly tall—five feet seven and a half—and slender, her torso narrowing to a tiny waist. High heels accentuate that length, and her body is attenuated by the gown's sharp narrowing, as it dives inward from her hips to hug her thighs and knees. Her hair is brown, her eyes a darker brown, and her teeth shine whitely. Like other female artists in the mid-1960s, such as the Supremes and Martha Reeves and the Vandellas, who were sent to Motown's "finishing school" for elegant young ladies, Lyndell wears elbow-length white evening gloves. She's nineteen, possibly twenty.

"You are talking about a beautiful young lady," Kamma said in an interview shortly before his death in 2015. "What's more," he added, "she could sing her ass off." Like many other R&B and soul bands, Kamma had his promotional posters or placards made by Globe Poster in Baltimore. On them Lyndell's name appeared under Kamma's—he was the headliner, billed as "Mr. Knockout"—but sometimes, he said, "I'd make her picture bigger than mine, to highlight Linda. You have to understand, at that time, a white girl fronting a black band was *unheard of*. People couldn't believe it and their curiosity made her a great draw. And after they heard her sing, the response was unbelievable." Lyndell was hailed on the placards as the "New Queen of Soul" or the "Vivacious New Queen of Rock 'n' Roll."

When she and Blade were performing with the Counts, in 1966 and 1967, singer Robert Castleberry would come on first and do some blues. Then two male backup singers, the Dynamites, did a short set. Lyndell still remembers their MC introducing one of them, Cy Hightower, braying, "*Ladies and gentlemen, Mr. Cy Hi-Tow-Ah!*"

Lyndell took the next set, the penultimate one, before Mr. Knockout. "That was something else," says Counts guitarist Robert Berry. "We were the only black group with a white guy on sax and a white girl singing back then, I can tell you that." He remembers Lyndell "used to do Aretha's 'Chain of Fools,' and she tore the house down with that. Linda was a strong singer, man," he continues. Then, as becomes inevitable in the reporting of this story, he adds: "She sounded black."

As she was pictured on those posters, "I wore long gowns with spanglies and sequins onstage," Lyndell says. They'd need to be cleaned at least once a week: "It was *hot* in those clubs, and we were working hard. And of course there was no AC." They usually did two shows a night, and all the Counts would change their sweat-soaked outfits after the first set.

Then it was star time, when Kamma—who idolized Frankie Lymon and Sammy Davis, Jr. growing up and did a spot-on James Brown homage—sang

LAVELL KAMMA SHOW

IN PERSON

PARADISE CLUB

SATURDAY — Nite — MAY 21 — 1966

Belle Glade, Fla. — 9 P. M. Til ? — Admission $1.75 — Table Free

☆ LIVE ON STAGE ☆

LAVELL
"mr. knockout"

KAMMA

AND THE DYNAMITES

Cy HIGHTOWER ★ Jerry O'BRYANT

— plus —

VIVACIOUS
Queen of Rock 'n' Roll

LYNDA LINDELL

— AND THE —

100-HOUR

COUNTS

ORCHESTRA

The "vivacious" singer, whose name is misspelled, featured on a Lavell Kamma placard. Kamma said the white female soul singer was a "great draw" on the black chitlin' circuit. Courtesy Lavell and Johnnie Mae Kamma.

and danced the crowd into a frenzy. "I have to say, all of us together, we put on a super show," Lyndell says. "Nobody left disappointed."

The places they played ranged from classy ballrooms in the bigger cities' black neighborhoods to country jukes, where, Kamma remembered, you could see the dirt beneath the buildings through gaps in the wooden floorboards. Within that broad social range, though, the hues of the audiences didn't vary; they played to black audiences only. "It was very, very rare to see a white person there," Lyndell says. "If that ever happened, they were probably musicians."

The circuit could get rough. Blade remembers diving behind a pool table in one chitlin' circuit joint to avoid bullets. From the stage he'd clearly seen a raised arm—with a handgun at the end of it—pointing up toward the ceiling, with two other hands grabbing for the weapon. But the two white band members say no hostility, much less violence, was directed at them; Lyndell and Blade insist they had no racial problems with their African American audiences. "We were accepted and made welcome," Blade says. "They *loved* Linda, and we both felt privileged to be there."

They may be romanticizing a bit, but it's plausible: These two particular white people—willingly led by a black man—posed no threat and had made the effort to learn a foreign language, in a sense, and spoke it sincerely and well. "We were fine when we stuck with our own kind," says Lyndell. She means black people.

STILL, TROUBLE FOUND THEM. An all-black group was something everyone could accept, if not respect, but whites consorting with blacks was another inflammatory thing altogether. "Back then," says Berry, "you must know that some people didn't want to see a pretty white girl with us." At times the sight of her on their posters would attract the attention of local (white) law enforcement. Kamma remembered sheriffs' deputies lingering near club doors and eyeing the integrated Counts, but when they saw there was no outright miscegenation in progress onstage, they usually stood down.

One night in the spring of 1967 they were playing the Pearl Harbor Club in Leesville, Louisiana. It was a pay weekend in this military town where, Blade remembers, prostitution, gambling, and other vices were rampant, including in the flophouse rooms surrounding the club. Those transgressions were tolerated, Blade says, but the mayor, with two big deputies at his side, raided the club three times that night, to hassle him and Linda for, essentially, race-mixing. Finally, Blade promised the mayor that if he would let them go peacefully to the parish line, they would never set foot in Leesville again. "I kept my word," he says. "Even today, I would drive 400 miles out of my way to avoid it."

They were booked into one white club on that tour, in Lufkin, Texas. When the band began playing their first set in the back room that night, not one customer paid the cover charge to enter. Bored, one of the male backup singers said, "Come on, Linda," and led her out onto the dance floor. Not for a slow, close grind but just a friendly twirl. "That was really the wrong thing to do," she says. In the adjacent front room, she heard "some guy slam his beer down on the bar and say, 'We don't do that kind of thing around here.' And then he called me an N-word lover."

The manager told them the Ku Klux Klan had been called and was on the way, with guns and sheets. The Counts all helped the drummer, Sticky, break down his kit as quickly as possible and threw their equipment into their pink Chrysler Imperial and Blade's Fury. Then, Lyndell says, they drove away as fast as they could. She lay down on the seat so her white skin wasn't visible amid the blackness.

Hours later, after they checked into a black motel one county to the north, Kamma and the band's manager Bill Jones asked Blade to go back and get their clothes; they'd abandoned them in the makeshift dressing room behind the bar. He drove back alone, strapped with a knife and a small-caliber pistol in his waistband. "As I was backing out with a double armload of clothes," he says, "the manager glared at me and snarled, 'We killed Kennedy just a few miles from here, and we'll goddamn sure kill people like you and that girl!'"

LYNDELL AND BLADE had always tried to fit in musically and socially. Kamma didn't allow drug use or anything more than social drinking, which was easy for them to adhere to. (Lyndell even claims that the other Counts didn't avail themselves when women, later known as groupies, made themselves available, though that's harder to give credence to.) Somewhere along the way, the two white band members began trying to fit in even more—to pass for black. This was for safety's sake, Blade says. "If people thought we were light-skinned black people [amid other blacks] that would be a lot less troublesome than if we were white."

Blade went first. "Do you know what a process is?" Lyndell asks, referring to the straightening technique for black men's hair, or the conk. "I gave him a process, and he wore a do-rag on his head." So, in this twisted racial tangle, in order to appear black, the white man Blade wore his hair in a way that Malcolm X and others derided as trying to look white.

Linda Lyndell in her Afro wig, circa 1970, when she was performing with Weston Prim and Blacklash. Photo by Charles Steadham, Courtesy of Charles Steadham / Blade Agency.

In the late 1960s and into the 1970s, when the process became unfashionable, they both wore Afro wigs (Blade says he still has his). Did they really pass? "I felt black, I sounded black, and now I looked more black," Lyndell says. "And there were some very light-skinned guys in the band. So I think maybe I did."

After she and Charlie Blade left Kamma's group, they went to New Orleans together, where they got work with local stalwart Tommy Ridgley and his band, the Untouchables. With them the two Floridians once opened for one of their idols, James Brown, at the Municipal Auditorium, which held upward of seven thousand. Demand for Lyndell grew to the point where, she and Blade say, a bagman for a local Mafia boss came to their motel one night and told them that she now worked for them and would perform in venues the boss owned. They'd put Blade in another local house band. Frightened and unwilling to be indentured servants, they borrowed twenty dollars in gas money from Frank Painia, owner of the Dew Drop Inn on Lasalle, and fled town.

They returned to Florida and worked with the Georgia Soul Twisters, led by Clarence Griffin and based in Eustis. (That band's biggest hit, released in 1967, was "You Shot Me Through the Grease"). "We featured Linda as a star," Griffin says. "Two or three people would precede her, including our drummer, Johnny Lee, who sang, and then she would come on." Florida singer Gene Middleton ("When a Boy Becomes a Man") hired her and Blade as well.

Lyndell made her first recordings in Tampa, for Gainesville-based D&B Records, which were not released; some of them recently came to light on the British reissue label Ace. Atlanta lawyer Joe Williamson signed her to a management contract and, after an ill-conceived country music session in Nashville, Lyndell cut three soul singles in Jackson, Mississippi, on the Grits and Soul label. Under Williamson's auspices, Lyndell went to an Atlanta film studio, as did Griffin, to perform in a movie called *Soul Has No Color*. But Williamson died and the film was never released.

In these early sessions Lyndell recorded songs by David Crawford, a Jacksonville, Florida, writer, producer, and disc jockey. She knew he had played piano with the prominent gospel group Albertina Walker and the Caravans and suggested to Williamson that Crawford be involved in her career. (Crawford also wrote and produced for Wilson Pickett and Jackie Moore at Atlantic Records; see chapter 19 for more on him and Moore.) Lyndell recorded one of his tunes, "Here Am I," in Jacksonville, and Crawford, who had strong connections, sold the cut to Stax. The company released the single on its Volt subsidiary, with one of her Grits and Soul songs, "Bring Your Love Back To Me," on the flip side, in early 1968. At that point Al Bell was running the company for owners Jim Stewart and his older sister, Estelle Axton (the name Stax derives from their combined last names). In the spring of 1968 Crawford persuaded Bell to book a Lyndell recording date in Memphis.

"Soulsville, USA" was home to artists she admired, like Carla Thomas, and one she worshipped: Otis Redding, who she met through Crawford and befriended, along with his family. Lyndell told Rob Bowman, author of a 2001 feature on her in the *Oxford American*, that on entering Studio A, "you felt like you were walking on hallowed ground. . . . Walk over there by that microphone where Otis had sung. Wow! It was an anointed place."

Crawford had a gift for distinctive lyrics; this time, though, he just had an upbeat refrain, which he sang to Lyndell in her motel room the night before their session. "What do you think, Buck Jones?" he asked her. (Crawford came up with various nicknames for Lyndell, most of them mocking racial references, including Buck Jones, Cornbread, and Cracker.) "Those couple of lines were all we had when I went into the studio the next day," she remembers. "At first David was trying to record these three girls from the University of Memphis he was working with, called the Vans. Then we went to my song and they sang backup. And, I mean, it just sort of fell together."

Most of the stellar Stax house musicians were in place, she remembers, including Steve Cropper on guitar and Al Jackson on drums. Booker T, the leader of the MGs was absent, but others filled in on both piano and electric keyboard. As usual there were no written charts; instead the group huddled at the middle of the room and worked out a head arrangement. The lyrics, atypically for Crawford, are pretty inconsequential, mostly improvised by Lyndell and the Vans, she says. "Somebody would give a line and I would do that, plus an ad-lib."

> "*Let me put it on your mind*
> *He thrills me, kills me*
> *He's a lovin' kind*
> *Another ounce of his love*
> *And I think I'm a gonna slip*
> *Lose my grip*
> *And do back-over flips*"

But Crawford had come up with that killer hook, and the energy—in the room and later on vinyl—was sky-high and tight, seeming to ratchet up with each repetition of: "*What a man, what a man, what a man / what a mighty good man . . .*"

Referencing current dances—the Camel Walk; the Funky Broadway; the Tighten Up—came easy, Lyndell says, "'cause those were the dances that everyone was doing at the time." One such nod went out to the Godfather of Soul: "*[He] makes me do the James Brown / Every time I get on my feet.*"

The session horn players were waiting outside the studio, toward the front of the former movie theater and could hear Lyndell's funky southern

wail through the walls. When the time came to add their parts, "Andrew Love played baritone sax," Lyndell says, "and he was so good. It was great—the whole thing just came together."

"What a Man" had only taken three takes or so, but they stayed to cut a B-side, cowritten by Crawford, "I Don't Know." It's more of a lament, with a minor, bluesier tonality: *"If you ask me when he's coming home / I have to tell you, I don't know."* Lyndell sings a bit higher and belts less stridently on this cut, suggesting the more polished singer she could have become. The Vans again contributed strong support. (Although it's been completely overshadowed by "What a Man," this is a sinuous and distinctive song, listenable to on YouTube.)

When they got done at 9:30 or 10:00 p.m. enthusiasm was high, Lyndell says: "We knew we had a hit." In his Lyndell profile, Bowman describes Bell listening to a playback of "What A Man" and modifying a snatch of the lyrics to express his reaction: "Lose my grip, and do motherfucking back-over flips." Meaning, the author says: "He damn well knew his company had just cut one unbelievably monstrous hit."

IT WASN'T, THOUGH; NOT REALLY. "What A Man" (released on Volt) broke onto the *Billboard* R&B chart in August 1968, but it remained there for just two weeks, never getting higher than #50. It didn't help that the distribution deal Stax had with Atlantic Records, the conduit for all their hits, had just ended. Al Bell later said the company should have done more to promote the record; given his enthusiasm and his power there, why he and Stax didn't get behind it fully is hard to fathom.

In-house producer Isaac Hayes wanted her to come back and do another session, Lyndell says, and there was talk of recording at another soul epicenter, Muscle Shoals, Alabama. But neither of those things materialized. Instead, Crawford found her a dumpy apartment in Atlanta and got her a job singing in one of the city's black clubs. That's when, she remembers, "I started getting these terrible calls. At first I brushed them off, but it kept happening."

HER SONG, THOUGH NOT A HUGE HIT, got just enough attention to make her a target. All the phone calls were anonymous, and venomous. Some were from white supremacists. "They wouldn't say, 'We are the KKK,'" Lyndell remembers. "They'd say 'I'm calling for the white people,' or something like that." Using the N-word, they warned her to stop consorting with that kind—or else.

Just as many of these hateful calls, she says, came from African Americans. "They told me they didn't need any white chicks at Stax. Then they said they knew where my family lived and that they'd kill us all if I didn't get out of the business."

Her record came out just a couple of months after Dr. Martin Luther King, Jr., was killed, in Memphis, in April 1968. (During her short stay there, Lyndell stayed at the Lorraine Motel, where Dr. King was shot.) "The South was going to pieces," Lyndell says. "People were mad, and it became dangerous for me to be around people who'd been friends of mine all my life. Nobody wanted to see black and white together."

Some of the threatening callers tried to disguise their voices, raising an awful question: Did she know them? She took the threats from both sides seriously; "I did what they said to do."

She ran. Charlie Blade had gone to San Francisco and now Lyndell followed him. He had a regular gig at the Stardust Lounge in the Fillmore district, and Blade assumed she would join him and perform. But for a good while after she arrived, Lyndell stayed home nights, in the apartment she was sharing with Blade. For the first time since he'd known her, Linda didn't want to sing.

After two or three months, Lyndell moved "just as far away from sing-ing rhythm and blues as you could be." Her older brother was working in rodeo and she joined him on a very different circuit, running barrels or competing in barrel racing. Lyndell married a rodeo man, and that lasted about two and a half years.

She came back to Gainesville and worked in banks. Soon, though, she ached to perform again. "When you're really a singer it's always inside you. Like we say down South: 'That don't wash out.' I craved it, and that brought me back to Charlie." He'd returned to Florida in 1969 and soon they were a team again. In 1972 or 1973, she joined Blade and the powerful vocalist and sometime trumpet player Weston Prim in his funk/soul band, Blacklash. Blade booked the band and promoted Prim as "265 Pounds of Pure Soul." Prim, now retired and living in Alachua, was impressed by Lyndell's vocals as well as her showmanship. "Linda could [sing] a lot of stuff that black girls I knew couldn't sing," he says.

Those kinds of comments—usually admiring and well meant, as Prim's is—were a constant in her career. Lyndell is both amused and frustrated by them. "Thinking white people can't sing soul is like that movie, *White Men Can't Jump*," she says. "Well, some of us can, especially when you are born and raised to it like I was."

Lyndell recorded a few more songs in Nashville in the mid-1970s, and in Jackson, Mississippi, in the 1980s. None of them ever saw the light of day. She moved back to California and worked for the USDA for quite a few years, singing a little on the side. She married again, divorced again, and moved back to Gainesville again in the early 1990s. While working for the University of Florida Alumni Foundation, Lyndell heard from Al Towles, the guitarist she'd dated when they were both in her first band, the Mark IVs. "He had lost his wife of 25 years," she says, "and I was not married, with no children. We reconnected in September of 1997 and were married the next January."

Around that time Rob Bowman, who'd written a book, *Soulsville, U.S.A.: The Story of Stax Records*, worked to get her sampling fees owed from the Salt-N-Pepa/En Vogue cover of "What A Man." That money helped the couple build their log house on four hundred acres south of Tallahassee and launch their plant nursery, where they sell bromeliads and orchids as well as more ordinary varieties. Even though they work and live together, they don't fight, Lyndell says. "We read the Bible every day. We're both Jesus people."

In 2003 Lyndell returned to Stax and Memphis, performing at the "Soul Comes Home" concert. In the company of soul royalty—Isaac Hayes, Mavis Staples, Booker T. & The MGs, Al Green, Solomon Burke—she felt she belonged. "It was like I was *back*," she says, "and that was a super feeling." The next year she returned to perform a one-woman tribute to Otis Redding. "I did 'These Arms of Mine,' 'Hard to Handle,' 'Dock of the Bay'—I think it was the best show I've ever done because I loved him so much."

Occasionally there's some renewed attention to Lyndell and her music, as in 2014 when Ace Records released some vintage material of hers on one of their compilations. In 2016 Chase Bank licensed her version of "What A Man" for a TV commercial, and that seemed likely to provide a significant windfall. But these glimmers tend to be brief and bittersweet. Linda Rowland certainly had times she cherishes and accomplishments to be proud of. But she still thinks about intervening years, all the time she *didn't* spend performing and recording hit songs, and the ways and reasons her career veered off track. Lyndell thought—believed deeply—that cutting "What A Man" at Stax would be a beginning and not the end. "But I guess God has more for me to do in other places," she says.

Charlie Blade, a friend for fifty years now, knows she still has regrets. "Being a soul singer was all she ever wanted in her whole life; she was so passionate about it. And she didn't really get to where she wanted to be."

A while back she and Al started attending a black church near their home so Linda could sing there, as she'd done with her aunties in childhood. But going there became uncomfortable. Remarks about white people were made, not in the church, but outside, in the street. So now they go to a different church, called River of Life. There are some black families there, she says, but it's mostly filled with white people—who either are or are not her kind.

6

Lavell Kamma and
the 100 Hour Counts

Jacksonville/Pahokee

WHEN YOU WALKED INTO CLUB EL MOROCCO in north Fort Lauderdale, the stage was straight ahead, the tables facing it, and to your right was a long mahogany bar. It was a pretty classy place, say musicians who played there, and in the mid-1960s, "you couldn't even get into a club like this if you weren't dressed well," according to one circuit veteran. No food was served at El Morocco; it was strictly a place for listening, drinking, and dancing in the black part of the city.

At 4 a.m. on this weeknight in 1964, however, there were very few patrons doing any of those things. Only a handful remained scattered around the place that could hold a hundred, and half of them were asleep, heads down on the tabletops. Yet, up on the bandstand, a seven-piece soul outfit wailed away, seemingly oblivious to the hour—and the obliviousness of their audience.

A smallish trim vocalist launched into a James Brown number, his voice pitched higher than JB's but with the requisite rasp, three horns blaring behind him, along with guitar, bass, and drums. That was followed by Lloyd Price's "Lawdy Miss Clawdy"; Willie John's "Fever"; the dance number "Hully Gully," a pop hit for the Olympics in 1959; and ninety-six other popular songs of that time and the previous decade. Then, when the Counts, for that was the name of this Florida soul band, got through that one-hundred-song set list, they played it again. And again. Twenty-four hours a day, for just over four days.

The Counts, who came together in Jacksonville, had come to Fort Lauderdale six or eight months before. Their manager, who was also their MC onstage, had relatives there, so the band moved in with them. They quickly got hired at the Downbeat, another club in the same area, north of Sunrise Boulevard, on a weekly salary. (Other black Fort Lauderdale clubs of note included the Embassy and the Windsor.) "We were bringing the latest sound and we were just a step ahead of the local boys," said Counts leader and lead singer Lavell Kamma in one of several *Florida Soul* interviews. (Kamma died in April 2015.)

As a result, he said, they were recruited by El Morocco's owner, who had a proposition. "You guys want to make a name for yourselves that will last forever?" he asked. The Counts were intrigued. "I want you guys to play for 100 hours straight," the owner continued. "I will set up publicity and I will have a doctor on hand to make sure you're okay." Some band in California had recently played eighty hours straight, Kamma remembered, and that's where the owner got the notion.

"We were young back then and stayed up all night anyway," Kamma explained, "so we agreed. Sure enough, we played 100 hours—45 minutes on and 15 minutes off every hour. I'm pretty sure we started on a Wednesday night. We didn't want to start in the day; we felt like if we could make it through that first night we stood a chance."

The only vocalist, Kamma had to perform every song that wasn't an instrumental from the list of one hundred that guitar player and arranger Robert Berry put together. "It was hard for me to keep my overall stamina up," Kamma said. "After a while you really start to wear down." His voice held up pretty well under the strain, though. One reason for that, he surmised, was that "back in the day, if you had a decent voice the band would play down so you could be heard. They had respect."

The Counts played long, extended versions of each song, Berry says. "We still went through the set list several times but there were always new customers who hadn't heard it all before." He was seventeen or eighteen at the time, several years younger than Kamma, and full of energy. Still, Berry reports, "we had so many pots of coffee up onstage."

Supportive locals would stop in on their way to work to check on the band's progress and then come by again that night. "It felt like the whole city of Fort Lauderdale was behind us," Kamma said. They weren't really paid much extra for the stunt, just a little supplement to their monthly salary of $120 per person. (Kamma said he made the same as the others.) In a

For just $1.50 patrons were entertained by Mr. Knockout, the Dynamites, the 100 Hour Counts, and the entire traveling revue, from 10 p.m. until . . . Courtesy of Lavell and Johnnie Mae Kamma.

normal week the Counts would have just played 10 p.m. to 2 a.m. on three nights. But no one, it seems, was counting. "Hey, man," Kamma said, "to us, this was a fun deal and a way to make our name. We weren't looking for money, we were looking for fame."

THEY GOT SOMETHING LIKE FAME: a very specific kind of renown. Lavell Kamma and the 100 Hour Counts Orchestra—renamed after their successful Fort Lauderdale stunt—was one of Florida's longest-running, tightest, and most musically adept soul groups. Although they recorded a handful of singles, the Counts were not primarily recording artists; they were a show band and, according to one-time Count, saxophonist Charlie Blade, "everything you'd want a show band to be."

The success they had, and the pride Kamma evinced in later years, was based on their electric live showmanship and in making a sustained living—including in a later incarnation as the Afro Soul Revue—on the southern chitlin' circuit. "I am a true circuit performer," said Kamma. "My bands and I played Florida, Georgia, South Carolina, Alabama, Mississippi, Louisiana, Texas, Oklahoma, and Tennessee. That's where I spent something like 15 to 18 years, and for much of that time, we did not have a home." Instead, he explained, "We'd go to an area, rent a house, and then work 50 or 100 miles around there in our tour buses, then we'd go to the next area and do the same thing."

On a poster advertising a 1966 appearance at the Paradise Club in Belle Glade, Florida, Kamma is pictured with his male backup singers, the Dynamites, on either side. The rest of the orchestra—guitarist Berry, four horn players, and the drummer, Enoch "Sticky" Henderson—appear on the bottom right, all in matching white jackets and black pants. Admission, says the placard, is $1.75. The biggest photo is given over to Linda Lyndell, the "Vivacious Queen of Rock 'n' Roll." Kamma was both open-minded enough to hire the white singer at a time when that was extremely rare and shrewd enough to exploit that novelty.

On another poster, this one in lurid color, promoting a Savannah, Georgia, gig, the revue is declared "Florida's Finest Attraction." Kamma is pictured front and center. He's wearing tight pants, a vest, and a bowtie and holding his jacket over one shoulder, à la Frank Sinatra. Like backup singers Cy Hightower and Eddie Hudson, his hair is sculpted into a pompadour-height process. As on the other poster, Kamma is billed as "Mr. Knockout."

"After we changed our name," Kamma said, "people used to come to see us just because they couldn't figure the name out. 'What in the world is a 100 Hour Count?'"

Another crucial career boost preceded their Fort Lauderdale marathon, and Lyndell's hiring. They were playing the Windsor Club, in the same city, when singer Wilson Pickett came to town. As was customary for all but the most successful acts, he came without a band, and the Counts both opened for him and backed him up. "We made a big impression," Berry says, and that led to a run of road gigs, including some in New York City. "We did shows with Ben E. King, Laura Lee, Etta James, Garnett Mims and the Enchanters, Earl Gaines, and others I can't remember," Kamma said. "And in between, we'd practice, practice, practice."

They did have trouble working with one headliner, a colossus: James Brown. Kamma was short, as was Brown, and both were athletic dancers and showmen. It seems Kamma took his admiration for that soul man quite a ways into imitation. At times, Lyndell remembers, "he basically did the James Brown show." Kamma sang JB's songs, fell down and slid across the floor on his knees while singing, and even had the MC ask the audience, as Brown's crowd's were asked before he came on, "Are you ready for star time?" Guitarist Berry, a lifelong friend of Kamma's, agrees: "He was really geared up on James Brown."

They were on a package tour, Berry remembers, "working with Ted Taylor, Johnnie Taylor and James Brown. I think we did the Cleveland Arena and Cincinnati Gardens, among other places." JB, known to be difficult, understandably did not think his opening act should be his own. He decreed that on those nights Kamma would not sing. "Lavell was kinda upset" at the ban, Berry says. But at that time Berry, who was self-taught and couldn't read music, had started teaching Kamma the guitar, so the front man still managed to get onstage and perform.

In five or more consecutive holiday seasons, the Counts also played at an annual Memphis festival sponsored by the important black radio station WDIA, called the Goodwill Revue. Kamma recalled working there with Stax Records artists Rufus Thomas and his daughter, Carla.

More commonly their reputation as a hard-working, energizing band that knew how to defer to stars brought them Florida gigs. "I remember getting a call," Kamma said, "saying, 'Little Johnnie Taylor, who has the hit, 'Part Time Love,' is coming to Florida, and he needs a band.' Same thing happened with Eddie Floyd, who did 'Knock On Wood,' and Sam and Dave used to call us and say, 'Hey, we are at the Sunset Lounge in West Palm Beach,' or 'We're at the Mary Elizabeth Hotel in Overtown, can you come down here?'"

As it seems from that reminiscence, many of their gigs in the mid-1960s were in the southern part of the state, including many much less glamorous ones for sugarcane workers in and around the Everglades. At that time, Kamma says, Florida was markedly more tolerant racially south of Orlando than it was to the north, including in his hometown of Jacksonville. "That was our Mason-Dixon line, or reverse Mason-Dixon line," he said, "because above it things were much worse than they were below." Although many black Miamians would certainly disagree, to Kamma, that southernmost city took racial permissiveness to unheard-of extremes. "I remember one time we were playing the Palms of Hallandale [roughly twenty miles north of Miami], backing up Sam Cooke, and Willie John walked in, with a white girl on his right arm and another white girl on his left arm. We almost passed out—we had never seen that!"

For much of their time on the road, though, and in many of their most memorable times, the Counts were the main attraction, the headliners on those posters and at their circuit stops. And the circuit never seemed to stop. "In one stretch, I remember we did 91 one-nighters," Berry says. Their schedule evolved into two long tours a year, and when they returned to cities and towns they'd played six months earlier, Kamma said, "we'd have a brand-new show for them." A show would always consist of at least two sets, sometimes more.

Money was bad before it was good. "As we started to get known, a good night's pay would be $75 dollars" for the whole band, Kamma said, "and not everybody got that, just the bands that could draw. A bad night's pay would be a chicken sandwich and somewhere to lay down and get some sleep before the next job." (Blade's recollections are in the same range; he says he averaged ten dollars a night and that on the band's best night, he got twenty dollars.)

Berry was in charge of the band's outfits and uniforms, which he had made by a Chicago seamstress. "I had pink and black ones made, pink and purple." Once in the 1970s, he remembers, they were doing a gig in Enterprise, Louisiana, and Berry was about to debut a special outfit he'd had made for himself, a lavender and pink suit, with big bells on the pants, worn in those days with stacked heels. When Berry went to change into it, however, he saw Kamma coming out of the dressing room wearing it. "We were roughly the same size," Berry says. "Lavell told me, 'It's so fine, I had to wear it!'"

KAMMA'S FULL NAME WAS FAROUK LAVELL KAMMA. He claimed not to know the derivation of it, saying only that his family "has no tie to what the name may suggest," meaning, presumably, that it wasn't Muslim in origin. Growing up in Jacksonville Kamma idolized Frankie Lymon; they were within a year of each other in age, and both had high male voices. But he also modeled himself on an older entertainer: dance man Sammy Davis, Jr. Scott Swan, who played guitar in the Gainesville-based Lavell Kamma Band in the mid-to-late 1990s, wrote his master's thesis on the bandleader while studying at Florida State. In it he notes his subject's unusual musical influences—or more precisely, the ones that Kamma did *not* share with other artists in his genre. "Musically, he had no background in gospel or blues," Swan writes. "Instead, he started in a doo-wop group and later became a soul performer."

When Kamma sang with the local doo-wop outfit the Joylocks, John Price, several years older, sang most of the leads. "He had a Jackie Wilson voice, he could really sing," Kamma said. Kamma sang first tenor behind Price, along with a second tenor, a baritone, and a bass singer who went by Blue. But he got to sing lead on a local recording of a song he'd written, "Betty Is My Love."

In 1957, Kamma thinks, they won a talent contest at the Palms of Jacksonville club, which was not in the LaVilla neighborhood, like many of the other black music rooms, but in the Edgewood area on the northwestern side of town. First prize was a huge one, especially for a high school kid: A two-week engagement opening for Sam Cooke, with the B. B. King orchestra behind them. Kamma explained that King, though he toured prodigiously, would take time off in February, and during those times his band hired out independently. The Joylocks did one week at the Palms of Hallandale—"we had to get waivers signed by our parents to go," he says—and the second week at home at the Jacksonville Palms. (These clubs and the Palms in Bradenton Beach were a mini-chain.) The Joylocks also recorded a single in New York City during a summer-long visit, though the label, understandably, changed their name to the Floridians.

Robert Berry, several years younger than Kamma, grew up listening to his father play guitar and to the jukebox in his dad's no-name bar in that Eastport section of Jacksonville. After teaching himself that instrument and competing in local talent shows, Berry dropped out of high school in 1961 to go on the road with the original version of the Counts. At the time they consisted of Kamma on vocals; Berry on guitar; Tim Wilder on bass; Sticky Henderson on drums; and "Jabo," real name David Darty, on C-melody sax, and later tenor.

After a year and a half or so of apprenticeship in Georgia and Lake City, Florida, the band rented a house in Gainesville and held the stage in one of local impresario Sarah McKnight's clubs. "We were red hot, that's the only way to put it," Kamma said. "We would get up as a unit and practice, practice, take a break, get something to eat, go chase the girls for a while, and if we weren't working that night, we came back to the house and practiced some more. We did everything together, and we perfected our skills." From there the Counts made their way to Fort Lauderdale and their 100 Hour date at El Morocco.

Kamma may have skipped over gospel and the blues, but the mix of influences he did carry—Frankie Lymon, Sammy Davis, Jr., and James Brown—helped make him a standout stage performer. Charlie Blade, his one-time sax player, says Kamma's revue became Florida's preeminent show band "due to his showmanship. He was an entertainer, with a crystal-clear soulful voice, and he danced every bit as good as James Brown."

In 1967 Kamma recorded one of his compositions, "Try to Keep Yourself Uptight," for the Houston-based Sure Shot label. (This was one of the labels owned by songwriter, producer, and music mogul Don Robey. His better-known labels included Duke and Peacock.) On that tune you can hear the urgency of Kamma's singing: "*You're always telling me 'bout the things that I do / but don't forget you do the same things too.*" The bridge is then given over to a horn break, arranged by Berry.

"*Now, lookee here,*" Kamma semishouts, before launching into the next verse, which concludes: "*Before you tell me I ain't right, keep yourself uptight.*" He riffs and improvises over the fade-out in a way James Brown would certainly recognize if not approve of: "*Try! Try it baby. You gotta be uptight, and outta sight . . .*"

That early single, with "Begging" on the B-side, also shows off the high-energy, tightly synchronized backing of Kamma's band. Much of that, Kamma and Blade both say, is due to Robert Berry. When he first started playing Berry thought Chuck Berry (no relation) was the guitarist he wanted to emulate, but by the time he went on the road, he'd progressed to jazz great Wes Montgomery. Berry also learned a lot from Wayne Bennett, the jazzy guitarist with Bobby Blue Bland. "He never played straight blues or rock and roll with us," Kamma said. "He played jazz guitar with our soul band, which made us sound fantastic. It actually made us sound better than we were."

Kamma remembered one night in particular when Berry's playing took the locals by surprise. "So here we are playing in the little town called Eunice, Louisiana. When you pull up to the club—it might have been an Elks Club—you can smell chicken cooking, and when you get inside you can see through the wooden boards of the dance floor to the very ground. That way, when they mop the floor, the water runs through. This was the kind of place where guys throw beer bottles at each other.

"Anyway, those people were still listening to John Lee Hooker and all this funky blues and soul. So here comes this kid with the smooth guitar sound—he's killing this Wes Montgomery. I mean, they never heard anything like it. So they had to stop and really listen, and you know what? After a while they really liked it. It was different, but they knew it was good."

Charlie Blade recognizes Berry's jazz chops but also remembers him as "an incredibly talented, flashy, crowd-pleasing guitarist, alternately playing portions of his guitar solos with his teeth, with the guitar slung behind his back, or holding it high over his head. He'd pick it with his teeth, too—he was really quite a showman." Lyndell adds that Berry would also be a part of the Counts' synchronized dance moves when backing her, the Dynamites, or Kamma.

Berry used Montgomery's signature "octaves" technique—playing notes simultaneously with those an octave above, accomplished by brushing the flat of the thumb over the strings and modifying the fretwork. He would also solo using only chords, as opposed to single-note melodic lines. "When I did the octaves with the horns surrounding me, man, that was some strong stuff," Berry says. Once when he was leading the numbers that preceded Kamma's "star time," he remembers, "I had that band going so strong, that Lavell told me, 'Hey, you need to do that *after* I come on, not before.'"

Berry, who says he has perfect pitch, also did the horn arrangements. Late in the Afro Soul years, he recalls, they carried a combined five saxes and trumpets. "On the bandstand," he says, "If a guy forgot his part, I would play his part on the guitar and then he'd pick it back up." Berry studied Bobby Bland's orchestra here as well. "I patterned some of the more sophisticated things we did after what Joe Scott, their arranger, had them doing," he says.

As much as he admired his friend's work, Kamma believed there was such a thing as *too* sophisticated. At times he'd complain to their man-ager, Bill Jones—with the guitarist present—that "Berry's trying to make us sound like a jazz band!"

To which Berry retorted: "That's good!"

They reached a compromise, one that likely contributed a good deal to the Counts' and the Afro Soul Review's sounds and success. Berry says he told Kamma: "We'll keep the funk on the bottom end, but I'll make my horns and my guitar lines on top of that a little different." Today he elabo-rates, saying, "I had the horns playing violin lines I'd heard; I'd drop in 9th chords—so it was funk on the bottom and jazz lines over that."

Kamma's former band members praise his leadership as well as his talent and musical acumen, saying the rapport he created stayed in place offstage, after the performances ended. "Nobody did drugs, nobody got re-ally high or drunk," Lyndell says. "Sticky would drink a little wine, but that was it. Anything more was not allowed. This was our job, our paycheck, and we loved what we were doing."

Kamma's embrace of the two white members was also extended by the rest of the band, Lyndell and Blade say. As the race-mixing whites, they were often the primary targets of any backlash. "We protected them, man," says guitarist Berry. "In those days it wasn't cool to have a pretty white girl sing-ing with a black band. But we all looked out for each other, and we didn't have *too* much trouble, even when we were working in Georgia, Texas, and Alabama."

To Blade, the most striking thing about Kamma's leadership was his equanimity. Poise and resilience were definitely called for on the circuit, where payment could be arbitrary and life unpredictable. "When a major setback would befall the band," Blade says, "Lavell would pause for a second or two as if in deep thought, frown, turn his head just a bit to the right and left, and say, 'Yes sir, that's a hell of a thing!' Then, in the next moment, he refocused and locked in on what needed to be done to get the next show onstage or get the band to the next engagement."

And when something unexpectedly positive happened? "Lavell would pause for a second or two as if in deep thought, smile, turn his head just a bit to the right and left . . ."

THE COUNTS' MANAGER BILL JONES, an athletic as well as musical pro-moter, made his home in in Pahokee, Florida, on the edge of Lake Okeecho-bee. For a good part of their run, the Counts were based there, too, though the road was just as much of a home. Their show expanded to a dozen performers or more, including female dancers as well as the MC, musicians, and singers who opened for Kamma. (Lyndell and Blade had left the group.) In the early 1970s, they took on a new name: The Afro Soul Review. "We all had big Afros at the time," Berry remembers.

They traveled, according to Kamma and his chronicler Scott Swan, in "a luxuriously appointed Scenicruiser, a top-of-the-line touring bus with a Cummins V-8 diesel engine. Made originally for Greyhound, the Scenicruisers were the largest commercial buses on the road at the time."

During all that bus time, Kamma learned to play practically every instrument the band used, including alto and tenor sax, guitar, bass, drums, and keyboards, so he could replace anyone who got sick or had to miss a gig for any reason. "I wasn't trying to be cute," he said. "I had to make a living and this was the only living I knew." He also learned to read music from an alto player he hired, who had been in Ray Charles' band. "When he found out most of us couldn't read, he said, 'I am opening class here on the bus. Anybody who wants to learn how to read, write, play better, you better catch me while I am here.' I was the first one in line," Kamma said.

In 1972 Kamma's best-known recording—which means not very well known at all, except to deep-diving soul fanatics—appeared on the Mississippi label Tupelo Sound. Early in "Soft Soul" (backed on the 45-rpm single with "I Know Where It's At") Kamma interjects a *"Good God! Ain't it funky now!"* that is once again very reminiscent of James Brown. Overall, though, the song is much smoother, mellower, and slicker (in a positive sense) than either Brown's work or Kamma's earlier releases. The background vocals are restrained as he leads with: *"It's a feeling that'll make you move / it's a thrill that'll make you groove."*

The soul may be soft but it is certainly not weak. The unusual title Kamma came up with is never explained lyrically, but this slower, insistent groove seems to embody it. The horns take the bridge more or less by themselves, and in one of Berry's jazzy touches, they modulate (changing key) and veer almost into dissonance before bringing it back to the original chords and Kamma's vocals: *"If you really wanna know how it feels / to have a love that you know is real."* ("Soft Soul" is included on the twenty-two-cut compilation *Florida Funk: 1968–1975,* issued by Jazzman Records in 2006. Other musicians treated or quoted in this book appear as well, including Weston Prim and Blacklash; Little Beaver; Clarence Reid in his rapper persona Blowfly; and the Montereys, a Tampa band managed by trumpeter Nelson Griffith. This album also features worthy Florida artists not treated here, including Miami's James Knight and the Butlers and the Mighty

Dogcatchers; the Universouls from Daytona Beach; and Bobby Williams & His Mar-Kings, out of Orlando.)

Robert Berry spent his whole career with Kamma, yet in the mid-1970s, he was the first to leave the band. "I met a little lady and she was complaining about me being on the road," Berry says. Kamma, usually quite gentle, remonstrated with him, telling Berry: "You don't *ever* let a female get you to quit a band!" The bandleader added a warning: "You're a *musician* now, people want to see you. If you leave, then you're just a regular guy." But Berry left anyway and, he says, with a laugh tinged with regret, "I got a hard-labor job."

After that the band dispersed. Despite his admonishment of Berry, Kamma became a civilian as well, going to Gainesville in 1977 or 1978 and becoming a surgical technician, assisting in operating rooms. He worked at that for twenty-some years, taking occasional gigs singing with others' bands and maintaining his own four-piece Lavell Kamma Band so as to not entirely forsake his musician status. After he retired from his day job Kamma worked around Gainesville in a trio and later as a one-man band, before he died of cancer in 2015, at age seventy-three. (Kamma was married twice and left grown children.)

It was uncharacteristic for Kamma to end as a solo act, and though he took pleasure in it, perhaps a bit sad. In his thesis Scott Swan writes of the immense satisfaction Kamma—and, as a result, his band members—got from "creating a musical family, a brotherhood and sisterhood, on the highways of the chitlin' circuit at a time when ignorance and prejudice sought to destroy it all."

The ethos of the ensemble was vital to Kamma. Swan told the writer of Kamma's *Gainesville Sun* obituary, "It was never about showing off. It wasn't about him. It was about the band." To inculcate that close connection, and to demonstrate it to the chitlin' circuit audiences, Swan said, Kamma had his musicians and singers stand and work close together—which meant close to him—on the bandstands. He didn't want them to seem, or to be, apart.

[7]

Sam Moore, Soul Survivor

Overtown

"I was brought up on a side street
Learned how to love before I could eat
Was educated, from good stock
When I start lovin' I can't stop.
I'm a soul man . . ."

—"Soul Man," by Isaac Hayes and David Porter,
performed by Sam and Dave

PRAYER MEETING WAS ON WEDNESDAY NIGHT. Thursday nights meant usher boy meetings. On Friday night, choir rehearsal. When Sunday came, after a Saturday night barbecue, "you'd sing all day, all night. That's what we all did."

That was life in the church, the way young Sammy Robinson lived it in Overtown, an African American enclave in Miami, during the 1940s and 1950s. The adult Sam characterizes his childhood home more bluntly, calling it "the black ghetto." At the time, though, he adds, "I didn't understand that."

The boy was raised by his mother, Louise Robinson, a devout four-foot-eleven woman everyone called Baby, and her mother, Virginia. Sam went by "Bubba," a nickname he thinks came from his early inability to say the word "bottle." The family lived at NW Third Avenue near 15th Street, across the street from a barbershop and Charlie's, a juke joint in the literal sense: a bar with a jukebox but no live music. Their house didn't have electricity or a gas line, so Sam learned to light the wood stove with kerosene and fry eggs with lard. (Most Overtown houses in the 1940s lacked electricity and indoor plumbing, according to historian Marvin Dunn.) Baby taught school and worked long hours; Virginia looked after him, took in laundry, and did day work in other folks' homes. Much of their off-hours and Sam's after-school time was spent at the Israel Bethel Primitive Baptist Church.

His biological father, John Richard Hicks, wasn't around much; Sam was five or six when he saw his dad for the last time. It wasn't until much later—seven decades later—Moore says, that he realized he'd woven an elaborate fantasy about his absent father, one that had a profound impact on his childhood, and thus his entire life.

Mr. Hicks wasn't a preacher, Moore has since come to understand, but with the church such an early locus—and the Reverend Brantley exhorting the gathered into a frenzy—Sam imagined his father was one of those charismatic older men. Starting when he was five or so, the boy would make a pulpit out of wooden soda crates out in his front yard, and then open his *Archie Comics* on top; that was his Bible. He'd imitate everything he'd seen preachers do, and envisioned his father doing, on Sundays: singing, getting down on his knees to deliver a prayer, and working himself up into a righteous lather, using a handkerchief as another prop. Sam loved singing, but faith played little part in his fervor. Brother Bubba, as he called himself, "didn't know the Bible," he said. "The point of preaching was the lather."

Sam's true devotion was to attention, especially female attention, to getting even more of it than he got at home, and boosting his precocious male vanity. One vivid impression he did have of his father—seemingly a more accurate one—was that he was a womanizer. Baby had shed herself of Mr. Hicks after he took his young son with him on visits to various "aunties." (When Baby later married Charles "Charlie" Moore, Sam was legally adopted by him and took a new last name.) Sam set out to become the person he imagined his father was, and succeeded, becoming a ladies' man who would tell a lie faster than the truth; a poolroom hustler; and, briefly and very unsuccessfully, he says, a pimp. For nearly fifteen of his adult years, he was a heroin addict.

Then, in a narrative worthy of a sermon, he was redeemed. In his precocious boyhood, while his attention was focused on the girls in the pews, he was also getting church-trained in gospel, and God saw fit to give him one of the great voices in American popular music. In a chance meeting at the King O' Hearts nightclub in Miami's Liberty City neighborhood, Moore would team up with Dave Prater to form the duo Sam and Dave, raising soul to its highest exponent in one of the genre's most successful. From 1965 to 1968 they delivered a string of soul classics—including "You Don't Know Like I Know," "Hold On, I'm A Comin'," "Soul Man," and "I Thank

You"—that are still heard, performed, and beloved. Music critic and author Dave Marsh called their work "the most sophisticated expression that Southern soul achieved." Marsh astutely points out that they were the rare compelling live act—he calls their shows "thrilling"—that also made great records.

Others, including Ray Charles and Aretha Franklin (whose father was renowned preacher C. L. Franklin), had successfully used gospel chord progressions and modified sacred songs and lyrics to create pop hits. Sam and Dave brought gospel's call-and-response to their live performances, alternating and improvising impassioned vocal lines as they preached, shouted, and sweated in front of fervent audiences, in this country and abroad. They were billed as "Double Dynamite" and "The Sultans of Sweat," and their passionate delivery (with Moore singing most of the leads) came through in the duo's recorded work as well. When Moore sat down for an extended *Florida Soul* interview in his Scottsdale, Arizona, home, he called their style "Holy Ghost preaching."

Sam and Dave had their great success on Stax Records in Memphis, and, in their heyday, the duo was probably most responsible for that essential soul label's success. (Moore's close friend Otis Redding also sustained Stax artistically and financially, much of that occurring after that great singer's untimely death.) Beyond Stax, this duo formed in Florida helped soul music cross over into the white mainstream and stay there. In the 1960s, a vital time for the African American civil rights movement, Sam and Dave songs, along with those by other black artists, were integrating the *Billboard* Hot 100 or pop chart. "Soul Man," #1 on that magazine's R&B charts, made it to #2 on the mainstream Hot 100 as well and won a 1967 Grammy award.

The duo disbanded for the last time in 1981, and Prater, from Ocilla, Georgia, died in 1988. Since that time their work has become and remains a part of American popular culture, due in part to the Blues Brothers, the ersatz soul duo created by comedians John Belushi and Dan Ackroyd that appropriated—but paid homage to—Sam and Dave on "Saturday Night Live" in the late 1970s and in two big-studio movies. The real duo was inducted into the Rock and Roll Hall of Fame in 1992.

Since then, Moore has been in demand for decades, a soul eminence. A broad spectrum of musicians has recognized him as an artist, and, importantly, not as an artifact of times gone by. In the living legend stage of Moore's life—which has lasted far longer than Sam and Dave's run—he has sung and recorded with Bruce Springsteen, the late Amy Winehouse, Sting, Bon Jovi, Usher, and country music's Conway Twitty, with whom he

An early Roulette album, before their breakout success on Stax Records. Courtesy of the author.

covered the Brook Benton hit "A Rainy Night in Georgia." Moore's collaboration on "You Are So Beautiful" with his best friend, the late Billy Preston; Eric Clapton; Robert Randolph; and the Italian singer/songwriter Zucchero earned them a 2006 Grammy nomination. (Moore was already a Grammy winner with Prater for "Soul Man" in 1967.)

In 2014 Moore performed at a Kennedy Center event in Washington, D.C., honoring Al Green, with then-President and First Lady Obama in attendance. More than a half century after he first took an Overtown stage, Moore closed the show with Mavis Staples, singing a rousing "Take Me to the River." It's not hard to envision the tribute to Sam Moore that might follow.

The saga of soul's most successful duo is implausible to begin with, surpassed in improbability by this survivor's second act. All of this was unthinkable to Miami's Sam Moore, who initially had no ambition to be a star. "Dave was much more serious about [singing] as a professional pursuit," he wrote in his 1998 book, *Sam and Dave: An Oral History*, a collaboration with Dave Marsh. "I thought I always had my hustle to fall back on."

Still performing in his early eighties, Moore can no longer do all the stage gymnastics Sam and Dave were famous for, including some moves he copied back in Miami from his idol, Jackie Wilson. Along the way, however, the powerful gospel shouter has also honed his craft and become a true, thoughtful singer. "I always had a voice," he says. "But there's more to it. All these years later, now I really know how."

Like Ray Charles, Sam and Dave were formed in Florida, had their earliest success there, and then surpassed it elsewhere. As Moore tells his story, it becomes clear how much this singer, too, was inspired, nurtured, and forged by his early years and musical upbringing in his home state—specifically, Overtown of the 1950s and 1960s, when doo-wop and R&B ruled and then gave way to soul.

Moore also embodies soul music's origins in and reliance on the gospel tradition. He was born in 1935, five years after Ray Charles, who, like many in that slightly older generation of rhythm and blues singers, was steeped in blues and, like many of his contemporary R&B instrumentalists, trained in jazz. But Moore, though he can deliver a mean rendition of "Part-Time Love," was never a blues singer. In fact, in two days of talking about his career, he didn't utter the word "blues" once. "My background is in gospel," says the ultimate soul man. "That's who I am."

SECULAR MUSIC WASN'T ALLOWED in the Moore house, only gospel. But to find popular, sinful sounds, all the teenage Sam had to do was "leave out the house, go to the corner, find your friends and sing a little doo-wop." He idolized The "5" Royales, the name the Winston-Salem, North Carolina, gospel group the Royal Sons used for their secular efforts. (Sam and Dave later recorded their "I'm With You.")

Overtown, formerly known as Darkey Town, then Colored Town or the Central Negro District, sat literally across the railroad tracks from white Miami. In Moore's day it was home to roughly forty thousand inhabitants. Northwest Second Avenue, one avenue over from the Moores,' was the main artery of a vital black business and entertainment district, much like Ashley Street in in Jacksonville or 22nd Street South in St. Petersburg, aka The Deuces.

In this racially segregated era, Miami was an important stop on the chitlin' circuit; actually, two stops, which made it that much more attractive to national touring acts. "Folks like Nat King Cole, Dinah Washington and Billy Eckstine could play at the Miami Beach hotels and clubs," Moore explains, "but they were not allowed to stay there." (Several musicians interviewed for this book recalled that black people could not enter the beach area after dark unless they had a "night pass" signed by an employer.) So, after their beach gigs, they would come back across the causeway to Overtown, stay at the Mary Elizabeth Hotel, or the Sir John—and, more than likely, hit the black clubs to work a second gig, sit in, or just enjoy. As *Miami Herald* reporter Jordan Levin detailed in her 2009 article, "The Sweet Sound of Overtown," "national stars and their bands jammed with local musicians, trading riffs and ideas, lovers and companionship, day and night." Many of those visiting stars would hire locals to back them up and/ or work as their opening acts.

Prominent clubs included the Harlem Square (which became the Island Club), the 535 Club, the Fiesta in the Mary Elizabeth, the Rockland Palace, the Mr. James, and the Knight Beat. (The last was located in the Sir John Hotel, owned by the Sir John whiskey company. Earlier it was the Lord Calvert Hotel, property of that distiller.) Black Miami's astonishingly deep talent pool, plus the constant influx of touring national acts, created a musical milieu as rich and competitive as the Florida jazz scenes that produced Ray Charles. Almost casually Moore rattles off a series of illustrious names, great singers he easily came into contact with and learned from as they came through Overtown: the Soul Stirrers, Sam Cooke, Jackie Wilson, Johnnie Taylor. Hank Ballard and Little Willie John, who Moore says "may have been the best of all of us," were semilocals; they made their second homes there and were recognized figures in the community. And those were just the male singers, and ones who became well known.

One small skein of musical relations and relationships in Overtown may help evoke the broader web. Moore was a close neighbor to the Wright Spiritual Singers, a family gospel group. Betty, the youngest, was probably the most gifted. She looked up to Moore, roughly eighteen years her senior, calling him Uncle Bubba. "She'd say, 'I want to sing like Bubba!'" he remembered. And she did: "Clean Up Woman" was the first of her many national hits in 1971, when she was just seventeen. Lynn Williams grew up across the street from the Wrights, and she was a gifted singer, too; she later sang backup for Betty. Her father was Ballard, the singer who wrote and first recorded "The Twist," in Miami, for Henry Stone, who also recorded Betty Wright, as well as some of Sam and Dave's early work.

Throughout the 1950s and early 1960s, some adventurous white fans would follow the entertainers from the beaches to the Overtown clubs. As reporter Levin puts it, "the action also brought in white musicians and music fans, creating a racial mix unique for the time in a segregated South." Steve Alaimo, a pop and blue-eyed soul singer who would become a key producer for Stone's Miami labels, was a premed student at the University of Miami. "I would only go to Overtown," he says in a *Florida Soul* interview. "It was the only place. There was the [Mr.] James Club, that was on 7th Avenue; the Harlem Square, the Knight Beat, and then later on there was a place called Birdland." (That last club, and the Birdland in New York City, were owned by Morris Levy, also the proprietor of Roulette Records, one of Sam and Dave's pre-Stax labels.) There was no problem, no "white boy" resistance to his presence, he said, either in the audience or on the bandstand. "I drove a white Cadillac convertible. I used to drive that car at 11:00 at night in front of the Knight Beat, flip my keys to whoever was on the corner, go in the club and sit in with the bands until 5:00 in the morning. When I'd come outside sometimes my car was washed. They'd give me the car and I'd drive home."

Joyce Greenberg, who would later become Joyce Moore, Sam's wife, was part of a younger white contingent at the University of Miami that listened to black radio stations WEDR in Miami and WRBD in Fort Lauderdale and then came to the Overtown clubs. "We would go to the Sir John in a group, dance, and never think twice about it. This is in '62, '63, before the Civil Rights Act," she says. Then, as racial tensions escalated in the mid- to-late 1960s, that atmosphere changed. "When my first husband and I went to see Jackie Wilson in December of '66, after the law's passage, we were the only white people in the club. It was much more like, 'What are *they* doing here?'"

As happened elsewhere, integration released African American customers from this enclave, allowing them to spend their time and money elsewhere. Then, as also happened in other Florida cities, a deliberate decision taken in the early 1960s to run Interstate 95 right through Overtown proved the community's "death knell," according to Marvin Dunn. An alternate route that "would not have decimated black Miami was considered," he writes, "but rejected." When Sam Moore was coming up, though, all that aggregated talent—still confined and concentrated by segregation—made the soulful music heard every night in Overtown and, later, in Liberty City clubs, the equal of that in any other U.S. city.

Moore graduated from Booker T. Washington High School a year late, the delay coming after he was shot by an angry husband. He already had a daughter, conceived in Fort Lauderdale, where his fed-up mother and grandmother had sent him to live with his aunt and uncle, Estelle and Charley Pinkett. Sam joined the band at Dillard High School because he thought girls would be impressed, and he liked the look and sound of the alto saxophone. Aunt Estelle purchased a brand-new shiny sax for him, and Sam had the great Julian "Cannonball" Adderley as his teacher and bandleader. But Moore couldn't spare the time to practice or learn to read music, so when Adderley, after hearing the boy's bragging, asked him to play a solo, he confiscated the instrument and showed Sam the door.

Sam returned to Miami, where Baby was raising his daughter, Deborah, for his junior year of high school. A football-playing classmate at Booker T. Washington High School, John MacArthur, had an a capella gospel group called the Nightingales, later renamed the Gales. Moore joined around 1953, forming a quartet that sang in local churches for the next two years or so. True to tradition, the young men practiced on street corners and in bathrooms, "looking for an echo," as Moore put it, that would reverberate off the tiled walls. Then MacArthur, who fancied himself the next Frankie Lymon, and Moore came up with an idea for a "rock" group, which they called the Majestics. His partner somehow wrangled a recording session with local distribution kingpin Henry Stone. With some locals backing them up, they cut their attempt at a pop novelty tune called "Caveman Rock," featuring Sam's Tarzan-esque yells, backed on the Marlin Records single with a slow number called "Nightie Night." Their single, for which Moore says he was paid nothing, did some business in Miami and Fort Lauderdale, he remembers, and got them gigs at local school dances.

"Then John MacArthur and all the rest of the guys went to college at Florida A&M," Moore says, "and I made a decision to go on the road with a gospel group, the Mellonaires. This was about 1958." They performed in churches, delivering multiple shows each Sunday, and would walk through the congregations afterward to collect their pay. With the Mellonaires Sam also returned to Overtown street corners, singing lead with a hat or cigar box on the sidewalk in front of the group for donations from passers-by. And in those days, when gospel shared preeminence with rhythm and blues in Florida's black communities, people would give.

"Don't you ever
be sad
Lean on me
When times get bad . . .
Hold on, I'm coming
Hold on, I'm coming"

—"Hold On, I'm A Comin'," by Hayes and Porter,
performed by Sam and Dave

EARLIER IN THE 1950S THE SOUL STIRRERS, the renowned gospel group, had come to town to perform. In those days gospel singers often stayed in active church members' homes. Sam was related to a few of the greats, including the Davis Sisters and Albertina Walker of the Gospel Caravans. Baby and her husband, Charlie Moore, one of the first black architects in Miami, had moved the family to a much bigger home in Liberty City at NW 60th Street and NW 12th Avenue at this point, so it was natural that they would host the Soul Stirrers' charismatic lead singer, Sam Cooke. Cooke heard Moore sing on that visit, as the Mellonaires opened for the Soul Stirrers, and though Cooke was four years older, the two became friendly.

On subsequent visits, after the Stirrers performed at a Miami assembly hall or a VFW, Cooke would often hang out with a friend named Willy, who worked as a tailor and dressmaker downtown. Replacing R. H. Harris in the country's most successful and beloved gospel group had made Cooke a nationwide celebrity in upright, Christian black communities. But, Moore remembers, "Sam was comfortable around the ghetto, he loved hanging out, getting drunk or whatever, and talking to the 'common man.' And I would go with him."

When the Stirrers came to town in 1958 or so, though, Cooke had left the group to pursue his pop music career. "He left a message with Willy, 'cause he knew he could find me at the pool room or Nat's barbershop," Moore says. "He told me the Stirrers were looking for a new lead singer, and that Sam wanted me to try out." Moore went to their hotel and auditioned, he remembers, "and they liked my voice and my singing style. I was told I had the job; I had made it."

Sam was to meet the Stirrers the next day and join them on their tour, heading first to Chicago. Despite his raw talent, this was a colossal break for the local, part-time singer and full-time ne'er-do-well. His mother and grandmother could only praise God, begin packing the boy-king's clothes, and make him a packet of sandwiches for the road. Once again, though, the pull of the secular—the profane, really—was much stronger on Moore than were any right-thinking inclinations. That night, Jackie Wilson was performing at the Knight Beat. (That club was managed by impresario Clyde Killens, who did the same for many Overtown venues in the 1950s and 1960s, including the Harlem Square and the Fiesta Club in the Mary Elizabeth hotel.)

Sam loved Wilson's work with Billy Ward & His Dominoes and his secular, solo efforts—"Reet Petite" and "To Be Loved" in 1957; "Lonely Teardrops" in 1958—so he made sure to catch Wilson's last set that night. This was the first time he saw Wilson live, and the singer did not disappoint, showcasing his soaring range and melismatic style. But young Sam came away amazed by something else entirely:

"The *wo-men!*" he exclaims, his voice going up an octave as he recalls that night. "I remember so well, when they said, 'Now ladies and gentlemen, Mr. Excitement, Jackie Wilson!' And here this guy steps onstage and right before he gets to the mike he does a spin that takes him right in front of the mike—*bang!* The minute he does it the women are screaming, and kicking their legs up, and I was kicking my legs up. . . . Then I see the women in the front grabbing and kissing him, they're sticking their tongues in his ears. . . . I'm sitting there, wide-eyed, and I think: 'I want some of that for myself.'"

"I knew I could never sing like no Jackie Wilson," Moore adds quickly. "I never believed I was that great vocally. But I saw the response he got and how he got it." Moore later took what he saw Wilson do onstage—"the spinning and twisting and splits and knee drops"—and incorporated those moves into the dynamic Sam and Dave live act. "Early on, believe it or not, I was leaving most of the singing to Dave," he says. "I would do all that [athletic] stuff and then when I stopped, I would sing. That's how I got bad knees today," says the man, now in his early eighties, "trying to do all that stuff Jackie did."

After the Knight Beat show Moore went to the dressing room, uninvited, and saw Wilsons' charisma working on the "nice shapely women all over him, at his beck and call." And he knew that would not be nearly as forthcoming with the more decorous Soul Stirrers.

Waking up the next morning Sam was "too chicken" to tell his mother and grandmother he had changed his mind. He took their sandwiches and well wishes and slunk off to a girlfriend's house, then to another's, finally returning three days later to admit what he'd done. "Them being

Christian-hearted ladies, it was kind of a betrayal, you know." Johnnie Taylor, who would later become a successful secular singer ("Part-Time Love"; "Who's Making Love") got the job with the Soul Stirrers.

EMULATING HIS NEW IDOL, Moore got his hair processed and tried to replicate Wilson's showmanship in the Overtown clubs. He got work with local singer and keyboard player Sam Early. When it came to singing rather than stagecraft, he tried to sound more like Willie John, whose most recent hit, three years or so after "Fever," was "Talk to Me." Others imitated John as well, Moore says, but "no one could touch him."

During this time, Moore maintains, he and Early wrote a song they called "Getting Paid." He came up with the lines: *"Money buys everything, it's true / What it don't buy, I can't use; I want money!"* He sang it slower than the song was done later, Moore says, in more of a Willie John flow. Early took it to Henry Stone, and Moore knew no more about it until he heard a local girl group, the Night Lights, singing it—faster—on a South Florida record company's 45. When Moore complained, Early said he would set up a meeting with Stone to settle the credits and royalties. That meeting never happened. Early ultimately admitted he'd gotten fifty dollars from Stone for the rights to the song, neglecting to tell Henry he had a cowriter. Moore knew nothing about copyrights, publishing, or writers' rights so he never challenged or pursued a claim for his lyrics. "Money" then became a hit for Barrett Strong on Motown, and the Beatles covered it in 1963 (the Rolling Stones also recorded it in 1964). The original and the cover versions credited Motown founder Berry Gordy and in-house colleague Janie Bradford as the songwriters, with Strong later claiming he deserved songwriting credit as well.

Decades later at Mary Wells' funeral, Moore says, he confronted Gordy, telling him, "BG, man, when you gonna take care of that? You know you owe me!" The way Moore tells it, the magnate told him, profanely, that he didn't owe him a thing.

In addition to working with Early, and occasionally with saxophone player Pee Wee Ellis (born in Bradenton, he would later play and arrange for James Brown), Moore was also fronting other groups who'd pick him up for club gigs, earning fifteen to twenty dollars for a weekend's work. But at this point he was a part-time musician and most-times hustler. For a while, he says, he pimped four young women in "the muck" north of Miami, as the Everglades region was called, selling their services to farmworkers for five dollars, as well as running dice games for that same "captive audience." When the police busted him for procuring, his fed-up mother and stepfather refused to pay for a lawyer, and he did eighteen months.

When he got out, Baby and Mr. Moore took Sam back into their home, where they were still raising Deborah. His mother fell gravely ill, and at last, Moore wrote in his memoir, "I was the son that she wished I had been," taking tender care of her and Deborah until Baby died of heart disease in 1960, at fifty years old. His grandmother died a year later.

Moore went back to singing and some of his hustles, including three-card monte, dice games, and bogus raffles. He also started working at the Liberty City club, the King O' Hearts—after, he says, with a sigh, "I had told another lie." The club, at 62nd Street and 20th Avenue, was run by John Lomelo, a big, imposing chain-smoker who would later serve as mayor of Sunrise, Florida, a tenure interrupted by his conviction and imprisonment for public corruption. The King O' Hearts was relatively new and well furbished, and at the time Liberty City was considered a better, safer neighborhood than Overtown. Lomelo had advertised for a comedian and MC to run Wednesday amateur nights, and Sam glibly told him and his father, Pops Lomelo, he'd had experience with both. "I told the one joke I knew, a knock-knock joke, over and over," Moore laughs, "and the people would just sit there looking at me." He was sure he was about to be fired when, one Wednesday night in late 1961 or early 1962, Dave Prater showed up to compete for amateur night's twenty-five-dollar top prize.

"I had heard about Dave," Moore says. "He was winning [other amateur-night contests] every place he went; somebody told me he sounded like Sam Cooke. So that night that I was sitting at the door, taking the names for the contestants that were going to do amateur hour. He tells me: 'Dave Prater.' I said, 'Oh, you going to do something by Sam Cooke?' And he says, 'No, tonight I'm gonna do Jackie Wilson, 'Dogging Around.' I'm surprised, but, hey, okay. He's cocky, confident he's gonna win again."

The way Moore remembers it, Prater was wearing a white shirt, white pants, and sneakers, because he'd come directly from his job at a bakery. In one, perhaps embellished, version of this story that Moore has told many times, he saw puffs of white flour coming off Prater as he approached the stage. Sam admits, though, that his own get-up was not exactly suave: He wore Capri pants he'd cut off himself, socks up to his knees and high-tops. "I must have looked like Rufus Thomas in drag."

Moore's friend Sam Early was on organ, leading the house band with a drummer and a sax. A local woman named Eloyce Foreman had already performed, and she brought the house down. Then, Moore says, when he called the newcomer to the stage, Prater confided that he didn't exactly know the words to "Dogging Around."

Nonetheless, Moore introduced him, telling the audience: 'Here's a young man going to sing some Jackie Wilson for you.' And usually I would step off the stage but that night, to this day I don't know why, I stayed up there. "So then he starts singing, '*You better stop, girl . . .*'"

Soon after, Prater lost the lyric and Moore stepped up to the lone mike, provided the next line, then moved back to the rear of the stage. That went on for a few verses and then, as Moore withdrew again, his foot got tangled in the microphone cord. "When that happened, I jumped forward and knelt down to grab the mike, and Dave did the same thing at the same time." When they came back up together, restoring the mike to its upright stand— both still belting out the song—the crowd, which had been indifferent, re-acted with loud approval. "They thought it was a set-up, part of the act," Moore says. Somehow they got through the rest of the song.

Prater didn't win, even with the extra help. Eloyce took top prize, and Prater got third (five dollars). A black Elvis impersonator won second (twelve dollars). Afterward Sam was occupying himself with a waitress in the basement when Pops Lomelo came looking for him, calling, "Moore! Moore!" He and John brought him to their office and told him, "That was great! Can you two put an act together for this weekend?"

Over the next few days the two hastily worked out some versions of Ray Charles, Sam Cooke, and The "5" Royales tunes at Sam's house, and they became a King O' Hearts fixture. "We got a local following," Moore says. "Sam and Dave got it packed in there Tuesday, Wednesday, Thursday and Friday nights." The Lomelos had come up with the name for the duo, Moore says, calling it Sam and Dave, rather than, say, Dave and Sam.

The two men, as Moore has always insisted, were very different: Moore, a couple of years older, called Prater "country," whereas he was more street-wise. Miami was then a city of more than a half-million people in 1960, some 225,000 of them African American. All of Irwin County, Georgia, which contained Prater's hometown of Ocilla, mustered a total population of 9,200.

Yet they were brothers in gospel. Prater grew up churched and came to Miami in his early twenties to sing leads with his brother, J. T. Prater (bass), in the successful gospel group the Sensational Hummingbirds and was looking to cross over to secular or pop music. Despite all their differences, the two men's voices just worked together, each augmenting and enhancing the other. Sam's was higher, a true tenor, and more polished, while Dave's was lower, sounding more like a baritone than a typical second tenor. "Dave would take it lower, much lower," Moore confirms. Neither man ventured much into falsetto range.

Prater couldn't rehearse much; he had day jobs, including baking, and a family to support. That, Moore says, led to their signature style. "We never harmonized, because Dave didn't have time to practice, and work those kinds of things out." Instead, they sang in unison or, even better, they alternated lines, mimicking the call-and-response patterns of black-church singing, which Liberty City and Overtown patrons recognized and loved. "We were preaching and shouting, and jumping all over the stage," Moore remembers. "The audience would go, 'Sing it, Sam!' or 'Do it, Dave!' 'Preach to me—tell the story!' Just like in the church." (In the early days Eloyce, the singer who won on that amateur night and also had gospel roots, would sometimes join them onstage.)

They had more energy than technique, but the duo's spontaneity, born of necessity, lent excitement to their live shows. At that point, the combined sweat and heat they produced was only earning them twenty to twenty-five dollars a night each, Moore thinks. But, equally important, "now I'm getting girls waiting on me" after performances.

Lomelo soon had them touring all over Florida—from Daytona to Jacksonville and St. Pete to Tallahassee, with more chitlin' circuit stops in between. Steve Alaimo, who was working for Henry Stone, convinced Lomelo, also the duo's manager, to let him record Sam and Dave.

With local musicians including Early and bandleader/sax man Dave "Dizzy" Jones, they cut two singles for Stone's Alston and Marlin labels, distributed—in southern Florida only—by Stone's company, Tone. Moore immediately recognized one song Alaimo worked up for them, which he was calling "No More Pain." "He took 'Jesus Be a Fence Around Me,' the gospel song the Soul Stirrers did with Sam [Cooke], and just changed the words," Moore says. (Alaimo concurs.) "Sugar," they sing, "let me tell you what I've done / I'll build a fence all around you to protect you from sorrow and pain."

The spare arrangement and instrumentation also evoked gospel: What sounds like just one snare drum socks out a basic beat with no variation or rhythmic fills, while a high-pitched, churchy organ swirls behind the vocal lines. Only the presence of horns, and perhaps the absence of tambourines, diverges from the gospel template. In what would become their classic style, Moore and Prater take alternate vocal lines, including on the fadeout, when they repeat and ad-lib on the phrase, *"no more pain."* Their voices actually show a bit more elasticity here and move into a higher range than was typical on the Stax hits to follow.

Soon thereafter Lomelo took the duo away from Stone and worked out a deal with Morris Levy and Roulette Records. Based in New York City, Roulette was one of the biggest independent companies in popular music, producing hits for Count Basie, Sarah Vaughn, Dinah Washington, Joe Williams, and Frankie Lymon. (Both Levy and his company were long thought to be mob-connected; he was later convicted of extortion but died in 1990 before serving any of his ten-year prison sentence.) Levy turned them over to top-flight producer Henry Glover; Alaimo also produced or coproduced some of the half-dozen Sam and Dave singles on that label, including another version of "No More Pain." None sold well, though, and Levy eventually released them from their contract.

Sam and Dave were still playing and doing well at the King O' Hearts. In the summer of 1964 Ahmet Ertegun, cofounder of Atlantic records with his brother Nesuhi; legendary A&R man Jerry Wexler, who reportedly coined the term "rhythm and blues" while writing for *Billboard* magazine; and producer Tom Dowd came to catch their act. Henry Stone was there as well; he did a lot of distribution for and with Atlantic and had "hipped me to the act," Wexler wrote in his memoir *Rhythm and the Blues*. The club was packed "wall to wall . . . in 100-degree tropical heat," Wexler recalled, and the local favorites soon "had me out on the floor boogying like a fool." He quickly signed Sam and Dave.

Moore, who had already lived part-time in New York, relished recording for Atlantic, the label of Ruth Brown, LaVern Baker, Big Joe Turner, the Drifters, the Coasters, and Ray Charles. (Aretha Franklin would sign with them in 1967.) This was the big-city big time, and he would be a part of it. Wexler thought otherwise, however, sending the duo to Stax co-owner Jim Stewart in Memphis, with whom Atlantic had an exclusive production and distribution deal. Stewart turned this new act over to the emerging songwriting and producing team of Isaac Hayes and David Porter.

Moore was disappointed. He had little sense of what Stax was turning out, or would turn into. He wanted to sing material like that Jackie Wilson was having so much success with. Still, he went. Moore was ready to realize the full value, artistic and financial, of his musical education in Overtown.

WHEN HE AND PRATER arrived in Memphis, Moore was not reassured to find out that one of his new producers, Porter, was still bagging groceries at the Big D grocery store across the street from Stax and the other, Hayes, worked in a meat-packing plant. But Porter and Hayes were just coming into their own as well. The first Sam and Dave single on Stax—"Goodnight Baby," a ballad with fairly insipid love lyrics, backed with "A Place Nobody Can Find"—came out in March, 1965. The arrangements included tambourines and tinkling vibes, which were featured on some Motown songs of the day. The mostly major chords and very familiar way the two voices fit together also had Sam and Dave sounding a bit like James and Bobby Purify, the other great soul duo from Florida, many of whose biggest hits tended toward sweeter sounds. The redeeming soulful elements are Prater's strong leads, and the more powerful, emotional singing they do when the songs go to minor-chord bridges.

Four months later the duo cut "I Take What I Want," a Porter-Hayes composition. The tempo is faster, the energy level higher, and as the title suggests, the lyrics are much more assertive and macho from the first verse, which begins with, "*I'm a bad go-getter, yes I am,*" and ends on: "*Cause I take what I want / and yeah, yeah, baby, I want you.*" "Although it didn't chart," writes Rob Bowman in his history of Stax, *Soulsville, U.S.A.*, "[that song] set the tone for the majority of Sam and Dave's Stax singles." Part of this new direction, he notes, was that "Sam assumed the role of lead dynamo, with Dave functioning as his foil. At Roulette, Dave was featured much more."

Porter later said of Moore: "He had some of the greatest pipes that I ever knew." (That take was echoed by *Rolling Stone* magazine some forty years later when they named Moore one of the "100 Greatest Singers of All Time.") Their next Stax effort, and their first chart hit, was "You Don't Know Like I Know," in 1966. In another example of soul's dependence on gospel—and Moore's transformation from gospel singer to soul man—this was an adaptation of the sacred song, "You Don't Know Like I Know What the Lord Has Done for Me."

Later that year the complex four-part coevolution of Moore, Prater, Porter, and Hayes reached its fulfillment with "Hold On, I'm A Comin'." On that tune an important force emerged that was integral to this hit and the ones that followed: the Stax horn players, including Wayne Jackson on trumpet and the late Andrew Love on sax. Later they would brand themselves the Memphis Horns, helping to create hits for everyone from Al Green to the Doobie Brothers. As on the best-known songs by Otis Redding, Wilson Pickett, and Eddie Floyd, the horns took over where other labels' arrangements would call for solos by guitars or other instruments.

In "Hold On" they are a powerful, sophisticated voice, taking the song's beginning, before the singers' voices come in, then surging and receding dynamically around and behind the vocal lines and supplying rhythmic counterpoint on the bridge. On the final fade-out, they form a combined third voice, along with Moore's and Prater's. Although horns were not customary in gospel, Moore maintains that the ones on his songs had a gospel antecedent: They took on the role of the church choir behind the lead preachers. According to Moore, these crucial horn parts and voicings were the work of Isaac Hayes.

"Hold On" was a #1 R&B hit, the duo's first, and reached #21 pop. "Said I Wasn't Gonna Tell Nobody" and "You Got Me Hummin'" followed and became chart hits as well. A rare slow song, "When Something Is Wrong with My Baby" and the mid-tempo "Soothe Me"—another gospel adaptation by Sam Cooke derived from "Save Me Jesus Save Me"—also did very well in 1967. That fall, Stax released single 45-231, "Soul Man." Musically, it seizes the listener from the first notes of Steve Cropper's guitar intro, followed immediately by accelerating, blasting horns. (This song also contains a very unconventional bridge that moves to chords not in the original key of G major.) Lyrically, Porter and Hayes' words were not quite as overtly, racially assertive as James Brown's "Say It Loud, I'm Black and I'm Proud," released the following year, or his "Soul Power." Yet the song clearly contained a message of black male empowerment, both in what it said and in the full on, prideful way the two singers delivered it: *"Got what I got, the hard way / And I'll make it better, each and every day / So honey, don't you fret / 'cause you ain't seen nothing yet / I'm a soul man."*

This declaration came out at a fraught, fiery time in race relations, in Florida and across the United States. Isaac Hayes said he got the idea for the song watching Detroit ablaze during the riots there, noticing that some boarded-up stores had "soul brother" or "black owned" written on them—a plea for solidarity and for those stores to be spared.

A few months earlier, the fatal shooting of unarmed nineteen-year-old black man Martin Chambers by a white policeman led to three days of burning and looting in Tampa's Central Avenue neighborhood. Muhammad Ali, who Moore became lifelong friends with in an Overtown barbershop, refused induction into the military and "the white man's war" in Vietnam in that same "Soul Man" year, 1967. The Reverend Martin Luther King, Jr. was denouncing that war as well as pressing for civil rights. In 1964 he protested a segregated restaurant in St. Augustine and was arrested, prompting his "Letter from the St. Augustine Jail."

After his assassination in April 1968, Sam and Dave, who had performed at some of Dr. King's rallies, sang at a memorial concert at New York's Madison Square Garden. (On April 4, 2014, forty-six years after King was assassinated on that date, Moore released a single of "They Killed a King.")

Clearly, references to coming up the hard way resonated with African Americans, as did the struggle to make it better. Importantly, though, the song's stance—and no doubt, its musical greatness—seemed to resonate with a broad swath of people whose way, generally speaking, was less hard: young, white Americans. In the days when mainstream AM radio stations still offered a variety of musical genres, white teenagers belted out the refrain, "*I'm a soul man!*" along with their car radios.

Sam and Dave's second #1 hit on the R&B charts, "Soul Man" reached #2 on the Hot 100 as well. ("To Sir with Love," sung by British songstress Lulu, from the 1967 movie of the same name, blocked "Soul Man" from reaching the #1 pop ranking.) "I Thank You," another soul classic and arguably their last great recorded single, followed in 1968. Again, it was delivered with great urgency, including when the duo trade off their signature, improvised exhortations on the fade-out.

In what must have been thrilling personally and still seems a startling cultural shift, Sam and Dave were not just recognized as nonpareil soul singers—they were pop stars. Along with Otis Redding and Aretha Franklin they became celebrated artists in the American mainstream. In 1967 they sang "Soul Man" and "Soothe Me" on an "American Bandstand" Top Ten Hits episode. The duo sang and danced on *The Ed Sullivan Show* in 1969; chatted with Dick Cavett on his new ABC prime-time talk show; and appeared on *The Mike Douglas Show* that same year. Their hits were collected on six albums, then a relatively new business for soul music, between 1966 and 1969 on Stax, Atlantic, and Roulette, which reissued their old material to cash in on their surging popularity.

With a band that grew to sixteen pieces, the duo toured the United States, Europe, and Japan as headliners, performing more than two hundred nights a year. In 1967 they were also part of a European tour by the Stax Revue, which included Redding, Carla Thomas, Arthur Conley, and Eddie Floyd, all backed up by Booker T. and the MGs and the Mar-Keys. Although Otis Redding was top-billed, Sam and Dave are said to have stolen the show on many a night, and afterward, their manager, Phil Walden, said, Redding refused to be on the same bill with the duo.

When they'd played the Apollo in New York before, they'd opened for Jackie Wilson or were billed below Solomon Burke, the Four Seasons, the Shirelles, and the Coasters. "*Everyone* was bigger than us," Moore laughs. But now they were the headliners. One of the supporting acts was the Jacksons, the family singing group from Indiana. Young Michael Jackson studied the older performers and absorbed their techniques. As Moore modeled himself on Wilson, Jackson built on what he'd seen James Brown, Jackie Wilson, and the Temptations do onstage—as well as the flashy styles and athletic dance moves of Sam and Dave. In the chapter on Jackson in her 1984 soul music book *Nowhere to Run,* Gerri Hirshey writes: "Even now he can describe a set of red suits worn by Sam and Dave: 'Vented sides . . . pegged pants . . . matching patent leather boots." In his later days as a solo artist, fans may remember, Jackson was partial to red sequined jackets.

THE DYNAMISM OF THE SAM AND DAVE live show, what so impressed young Michael Jackson, can still be witnessed today on YouTube. Most of the performance clips there show them in Europe, performing to overwhelmingly white audiences (some of whom may not speak English well), so there's little of the interplay the duo generated with their African American audiences back home. Nevertheless, Moore and Prater *bring it*, delivering equally passionate and more polished performances than they did earlier on the southern chitlin' circuit. The duo still delivers some "Holy Ghost preaching." "If you know what I'm talking about, I want you to do me a favor," Sam improvises at the end of one song, getting the Europeans to say, "Yeah!" At this point the two men's camaraderie is either genuine or well acted; either way, their collaboration is so successful, so musically profitable, that one wonders why the duo has virtually disappeared in soul and pop music. (Chapters 8 and 9, on James and Bobby Purify, respectively, also provoke that same question.) Two *can be* better than one. As Robert Gordon wrote of this duo in his book on Stax: "Both were high-energy performers, each at full tilt, exploding together with exponential force."

They're confident. It's good to be good at things, and they clearly know their level. Dave, wearing a double-breasted suit and bowtie in one YouTube reprise, is taller and thinner than Sam, though his voice is deeper. As he begins "When Something Is Wrong with My Baby" alone, his baritone is rich and resonant, sounding a bit like Joe Simon, perhaps. When they sing the concluding line together—"*Something is wrong with me*"—Prater's voice and

Shirts soaked through with sweat, Sam Moore, *left*, and Dave Prater pour it on, circa 1970. Photo by Michael Ochs Archives/Getty Images.

Moore's higher, suppler one lock into each other with amplified power and grace. If it's not harmony, as Moore insists, it's something equally stirring.

On "Hold On," filmed in 1967 in Norway, Sam takes the first verse at the front of the stage while Dave dances behind him. (This is before wireless mikes, so the singers must come to the equipment to be heard.) By the time that verse ends, sweat is dripping off Sam's broad face and high forehead. Usually the two wore matching suits, but here they're in light-colored slim-fitting beltless slacks and white shirts, sleeves still rolled all the way down. (The jackets may have already been thrown off, Jackie Wilson style.) Both men wear their hair in close-cropped naturals, and both have pencil moustaches.

Sam's a more demonstrative and a more limber dancer, while Dave stays more or less upright. At times their steps are synchronized as they switch places or turn back-to-back; mostly, though, they free-style independently. As the more-than-seven-minute song reaches its climax, the horns and rhythm section double-time the tempo and Sam jumps down off the stage and surges out into the audience. This and other video clips also show how renowned drummer Al Jackson, a mainstay of Stax, Booker T. and the MGs, and Memphis's Hi Records, propelled the musicians and the singers from a raised dais at the back of the stage.

They're not lip-synching and they're not autotuned; these Sam and Dave performances are live, superlative soul, and their talent—and the quality of their material—still pours out of even the tiniest screen or tinniest earbuds. One YouTube commenter, perhaps of an older generation, posted this plaintive reaction to a Sam and Dave clip: "One has to ask, whatever happened to true talent?"

> *"You didn't have to love me like you did*
> *But you did, but you did, and I thank you."*
>
> —*"I Thank You," by Porter and Hayes,*
> *performed by Sam and Dave*

YEARS AFTER MICHAEL JACKSON studied Sam and Dave at the Apollo, those two bumped into each other in Encino, California, where Moore was living with his wife, Joyce, and stepdaughter, Michelle. Jackson was in a limo, and he invited the older man inside to talk. This was in the early 1980s. The already troubled Michael, roughly twenty-five years Moore's junior, asked him, "Sam, how did you handle all that success?" Moore, who was sober at this point, told him the truth: "Very badly."

Success and excess performed their own call-and-response right along-side Moore and Prater. In 1966, Moore recounts in his book with Dave Marsh, "I'm at the pinnacle of my career. I'm living in New York City, and I'm popular." On one of those heady nights, after Sam and Dave played an Apollo show with Willie John, he and John went to Small's Paradise, the Harlem nightclub owned then by basketball star Wilt Chamberlain. In the bathroom there, Moore said, "Willie turned me out," using a pimp's term to convey that John gave him his first taste of heroin. Two years later, he was skin-popping and then, inevitably, mainlining, or injecting.

After 1968 Sam and Dave's best work as a duo was essentially done, their legacy established, though they continued to tour and record for an-other eight years or so. For much of that time they famously feuded—Sam and Dave broke up more than once and didn't speak to each other for years, except onstage, until they disbanded for the last time in 1981. Prater then went on the road with another man named Sam, and Moore sued to stop him from using the name Sam and Dave. Both men had been drinking and doing drugs during their partnership; the year before he died, in 1988, Prater was arrested for selling crack to an undercover officer. (Moore has said their rift was the result of Prater's violence toward his girlfriend, later his wife.)

Moore did dope for fifteen years; he had both the good fortune and the curse to be able to afford drugs for much of that time, but he eventually lost it all. In the early 1980s he had become involved with Joyce, the woman he'd known since 1968, when she came to the Knight Beat as a student at the University of Miami. She remembers a drug therapist telling her, "It's going to be almost impossible to save Sam." There was something in charge of him, she'd come to understand, "that [was] a demon." And she could not let the outer Sam, who she loved, blind her. The doctors gave him six months to live.

Initial treatment with legally dosed long-acting methadone (LAM) kept him comfortable and off street drugs. Working with Dr. Forrest Tenent and Don Smith, his drug counselor, Joyce then weaned him off methadone, without his knowledge, on a European tour. Then Sam took a course of nal-trexone, the opiate-blocker—which Joyce says she also secretly extended—relapsed once or twice, and finally got clean.

Joyce Moore also spearheaded a RICO lawsuit on behalf of Sam and more than a dozen other artists, charging that recording labels failed to report and pay earned royalties and make required pension and health-care contributions for years and years. They won redress for Moore as well as Motown's Mary Wells; the estate of Jackie Wilson; Curtis Mayfield; and Lester Chambers (of the Chambers Brothers), among others. Dave Prater's son was another of the plaintiffs.

Willie John died in prison at thirty. Sam Cooke was shot to death at thirty-three; Jackie Wilson made it to fifty. But Sam Moore survived. Toward the end of his drugging years, Belushi and Aykroyd's Blues Brothers TV act and first hit movie (1980) began bringing another young, white audience to soul music. Moore appeared in the second movie, "Blues Brothers 2000," appropriately enough, as a reverend opposite James Brown in a revival tent. "I always wanted to be a preacher," he laughs. His second career continued to flourish after Sam and Dave's induction into the Rock and Roll Hall of Fame in 1992. Throughout his sixties, seventies, and into his eighties, Moore has been in demand, in this country and abroad.

On this night, when Moore is first interviewed for this book, the Floridian-turned-Arizonian is about to perform in Tucson, headlining that state's sesquicentennial celebration. Waiting to go on in a makeshift dressing room near the outdoor stage that night, he is calm and patient with every well-wisher who wants to greet him or claim they somehow know each other or someone in common. Once he has learned or is reminded of a visitor's name, he uses it often to preface his remarks: "The thing is, John . . ."

His hair is both salted and peppered, cropped short. He wears a long-sleeve white waffle tee with a white vest over it, creased jeans, and tan lace-ups. Befitting the Southwestern setting, he has a ring with a big turquoise stone on his left hand, as well as a thin gold chain around his neck. Moore needs to conserve his energy, but there is clearly a good deal of it to conserve. Before performing on this chilly evening, he drinks a glass of warm water and whistles a few bars—"to warm up the vocal chords," he explains. "I heard Sinatra talk about this, and now I do it." Joyce rubs some cream on his lower back, and he walks a little stiffly to the stage on a pedestrian mall, as the band riffs on "Hold On, I'm A Comin'" and "Soul Man" as his introduction.

By his third song, Ray Charles' "I've Got News for You," he's warmed up and in good, full voice—but he's in control, not belting like the young Sam Moore. Unlike many vintage performers, Moore doesn't confine himself to a greatest hits show. Before "You Don't Know Like I Know" Moore sings "Let the Good Times Roll"; the Lee Dorsey tune "Get Out My Life"; and the song Ann Peebles made famous on Hi records, "I Can't Stand the Rain." Two female backup singers supply the responses to his calls, which seems to energize him. He's assembled some of his favorite players for this gig;

Moore pumps his fist as the horns end "Part-Time Love" with some high trumpet shakes.

Later, though, he explains, "I don't really follow or concentrate on the horns that much—I just use the trumpet for my pitch." Instead he says, he focuses on the drums and bass; if they're tight, he's all right. Drummer Omar Martinez, a Cuban-American from Miami who's also worked with Gloria Estefan and was a member of Paul Revere and the Raiders for more than twenty years, says: "Sam knows every little thing going on behind him. A lot of singers don't."

Moore is engaged, and funny, telling his Sam and Dave story, but the singer is most animated explaining the evolution of his craft. Conventional wisdom tells us that mastery requires ten thousand hours of practice. Moore's craft is built on some significant multiple of that number. "In my early years my voice was strong," he says, "Sometimes people compare me to Sam [Cooke] but mine is: *boom!* It's just booming. Sam was more of a crooner. Johnnie Taylor was a stronger singer than Sam, but he wasn't a powerhouse. Out of all of us the most powerful was Jackie. Oh, God, yeah."

As a young man he—and Dave—went full-out, attacking each song with the sheer strength of their voices and the athletic energy that became their trademark. Today the power vocalist possesses more finesse and command of his instrument. "Now I'm singing," Moore says. "Not over-singing. I don't do that anymore. Before, I didn't really know how to use my vocal capacity. I would come on really strong or hit a high note, because I know I'm going to get: *aaaahhhh!* [an audience response] But when you do that on every song, that's going to get kind of boring. At the end of the show where do you go, what do you have left? You got nothing."

He paces himself, both out of necessity and a fuller grasp of dynamics and stagecraft. "I'll take a little more time now, especially with slow songs. I can control the band and decide when I want to rest. In between lines I might say [singing very lightly], '*I love you, I love you.*' I'm resting." He didn't realize it at the time, but now Moore thinks that sometimes, when Jackie Wilson threw himself to the floor, he was not only inciting the crowd but also giving his voice a break. "You want to relax when you can, catch a little rest, gather yourself, get the song where you want it, then—sing."

The night before, during "Soul Man," a harmonica player approached the stage and asked to sit in. Moore let him, and he turned in a brutal solo. "Yeah, he was in the wrong key," Moore laughs the next day. "But guess what? It didn't take anything from me, and I could rest."

Moore explains another technique he took from Willie John. "When he hit a high note he was not struggling it was just . . . *easy*. But you know what made it easy, too? He didn't let the band overpower him. The band had to be down right here," he gestures, bringing his palm down below his waist. "I saw that, I learned that. I did it last night with 'Part Time Love.'"

What else differentiates the singer from the shouter? "First of all, *e-nun-ci-ate*," Moore says, stressing all those syllables. "Pronounce your words. You know whose enunciation is the best? Sinatra. Him, Nancy Wilson, Little Jimmy Scott, Arthur Prysock, Billy Eckstein. And Sam [Cooke]; his diction was beautiful."

"Another thing," he admonishes would-be singers: "Don't stay on the song too long. It's dumb to take one song and go 30 minutes—you're boring them. Sing it, tell the story and move on."

Even though he's considerably older Moore now sings the Sam and Dave hits in higher keys than he did originally. When Sam was working solo in the 1980s, Joyce relates, "he'd go out and sing these songs, and they just sounded a little dull without Dave for Sam to play off of." Isaac Hayes confirmed to her, she says, that they had originally cut the songs in "compromise keys" because of Dave's lower register and less expansive range. Without telling her husband, she got Sam's music director to raise those keys a half or even a whole step. Sam struggled at first and wasn't happy when he found out about the behind-the-back changes. "I got to tell you, though, it helped," he says. "Sure, you'll crack, and [my voice] cracked a lot initially. But the more you sing that way the more your vocal chords strengthen. I can take that now."

Moore also believes, as David Porter of Stax maintained, that singing at the top of one's range adds energy and urgency to the vocals. Barrett Strong sang "Money" that way, Moore says, and "Willie did that all the time."

Moore the mature performer is of course less of an athlete. "I'm not a dancer, and I'm not gonna do any splits." Instead he's thinking about "how to approach a song and make it my own, how to make the audience part of what you're doing, and get them to believe in what you're saying." In that 2014 Kennedy Center appearance, for example, his version of Al Green's "Take Me to the River" was clearly in the canon but not an imitation, resembling the honoree's original take but with just enough distinctive, assured differences. Moore paused at different points in the lyric, emphasizing different syllables, changed the words here and there, and ad-libbed a bit, making it his own.

In this second phase of fame, Moore says, he doesn't sit in on others' performances. "I don't go to other people's shows to be called up onstage. It ain't about me and I didn't get tickets to come and see me. They're probably singing in a different key [than he would prefer] anyway. So no, Sam don't jam."

He still studies, recording singers on TV and then scrutinizing their work. "I learn from those I consider the best," he says. Of all the celebrated singers he's worked with, he was most impressed by Amy Winehouse, who reminded him of Billie Holiday. (Winehouse died in 2011 after battling alcohol and drug problems). They sang "The Mighty Quinn" together on one of Jools Holland's New Year's TV specials in the United Kingdom. "Amy was a freak, by which I mean: She could sing the telephone book, and make it sound good."

Moore and Joyce, his wife of thirty-five years at this writing, are Floridians again. Since they moved back to the Miami area, the singer has been working to honor and document that city's rich musical history. (For more on this effort see the epilogue.)

Moore still has plans and ambitions as a singer as well. For one, he'd like to work with "someone I've known for years, since she was a little girl, and that's Gladys Knight. I would love that." His biggest unrealized goal is "a gospel album. I don't care about hits; it would just be a gift for myself, and to honor my mother and grandmother." He and Billy Preston discussed a gospel album, but the singer, songwriter, and keyboard player died in 2006.

Here the professional and the personal appear to be converging, in another improbable, serendipitous Moore story. In June 2016 the soul man learned—at eighty-one—that he has several half-sisters and brothers, more of Mr. Hicks' progeny, some of whom share his vocal gifts. Now Moore envisions the big, multivoice gospel choir he's always wanted to accompany him consisting of his newly discovered siblings and their singing children. The album is now in the planning stages. "I think we can bring something to the table with that," he says, smiling. "I really do."

8

James Purify

Pensacola

"Oh, I'm still singing," he says. "Most definitely. I'm in a gospel group; there are eight of us and we're called Joyful Noise. We get together three times a week. I sing lead and, not to toot my own horn, but they tell me I sound pretty good."

"So, you've still got the pipes?" he's asked, over the phone.

"Until it gets cold in here," comes the reply. "Then I get hoarse. But you can't control that."

The first singing he ever did was gospel, he continues. "My dad sang tenor with a group back in Pensacola, the Gospel Four. They rehearsed at my house and I would sit in the middle of the floor listening to them. I was always in love with spiritual music. So now it's no different—it's just that, well, I'm in here."

"Here" is Avenal State Prison in California, a low-to-medium security prison for men about an hour and a half north of Bakersfield. The man on the other end of the phone is soul singer James Purify.

In the 1960s and 1970s, soul music's golden age, Purify had ten hits significant enough to make the *Billboard* charts; the first and biggest was "I'm Your Puppet," which reached #5 R&B in 1966 and crossed over, climbing to #6 on the mainstream or pop chart, the Hot 100, as well. Not at all a typically soulful or funky tune, "Puppet" is light, sweet, and narrated by a hopeless, hapless lover. It's since been covered many times, including by Dionne Warwick, Irma Thomas, Motown's Marvin Gaye and Tammi Terrell, and Elton John with fellow Brit Paul Young. Used periodically in commercials, at this writing it's featured in a Nike ad starring NBA basketball player Blake Griffin.

A prominent pop critic suggested "I'm Your Puppet" might be the "coolest" soul classic of them all (more on that later); it's certainly quite popular on oldies radio. One such show, hosted by DJ Art Laboe, is available on the Internet radio channel tunein.com, and prisoners at Avenal are among his listeners. "Guys come over to my bunk telling me he is playing my song," Purify said, "and he's making a big thing about how 'I'm Your Puppet' is one of the most sought-after oldies. So now, I can't really go any place in the compound without getting recognition."

Purify, born in 1944, gained his fame as part of a duo: James and Bobby Purify, the closest rival to the other great Florida soul pairing, Sam and Dave. James and Bobby were billed as brothers, but Purify wasn't related to any of the three men who sang with him in that guise. Their producer just thought James Purify was the greatest soul name he'd ever heard, so, beginning at their first recording session in 1966, he told the other singer: "You're Bobby Purify."

James and Bobby toured Europe as well as the United States behind "I'm Your Puppet" and their other hits; stateside, they played prestigious African American venues like the Apollo in New York and the Howard Theater in Washington, D.C. Beyond his gifted singing, James was an entertainer and a handsome front man. Six feet tall, he wore a black moustache that slanted down, taking the opposite direction from his thick, upturned eyebrows. His hair was slick and processed over a high forehead.

When his ex-wife, Anner Purify, met him, she was sixteen, still in high school in Pensacola. He was twenty-three. "James just had a really soft look and voice and a beautiful smile, with dimples," she remembers, decades later. "He was very well built but slender, with a small waistline. James still doesn't have a butt." When interviewed for this book, she expected him to return to her and to Florida after serving his time in California: "When he gets out, he's coming back."

After fifteen or so successful years, Purify's career—his life, really—twisted in ways, and for reasons, that are hard to fathom. "He was the star," his former music producer said of their time working together, "and also the problem." A charming man with a beautiful voice, Purify committed crimes that even he says he doesn't understand and can't assimilate into the way he sees himself and the rest of his life.

Purify didn't want to be visited in prison, so we talked in a series of collect phone calls. California's public records are fairly opaque, but Purify

didn't hesitate to supply specifics. His sentence was "four years and eight months," he said. "But I hope to be paroled after two years, eight months. So if all goes well, I'm out next month." He gave the reason for his imprisonment just as readily: "Assault with a deadly weapon. In a domestic battery. I didn't plan it; it was just that heated moment . . ."

Papa Don Schroeder first heard James Purify sing at a Pensacola nightclub called Tom's Tavern, on Gonzalez Street, in 1965. The producer was coming off one of his first big hits, a bluesy cover of country singer Patsy Cline's "Sweet Dreams" by Mighty Sam McClain. McClain told him he had to check out the singer with his former group, the Dothan Sextet. They were based in Dothan, Alabama, close to the Florida Panhandle.

Purify, from Pensacola, had a fluid, higher tenor voice, lower than Smokey Robinson's but the same kind of smooth. He rarely strayed from the middle of his vocal range. Less piercing than Marvin Gaye, not as powerful as Solomon Burke, Purify's singing seemed to contain no strain, his timbre pleasing but still potent. His signature song at that time was Jackie Wilson's "Work Out." "Not tooting the horn," he said, "but I'm told I did a splendid job on that particular song. To be honest with you, I could do pretty much anything back then."

Purify grew up on Pensacola's black west side, living first in a neighborhood called the Tan Yards and attending Antioch Missionary Baptist church. The family moved to other west-side areas, but "you could say I lived at Belmont and DeVilliers," he laughs. "That was the entertainment area. We called it The Blocks or The Corner. That's where everybody would hang out, and I was down there all the time." Abe's 506 Club, originally at 506 West Belmont and later moved to #515, was one hotspot. In the 1960s, big-name acts, including Ray Charles and James Brown, played the main Ballroom and "local guys were in the smaller Stardust Room upstairs," Purify remembers. "Before the 506 time, another of the big clubs was the Savoy" on DeVilliers, he adds.

During the Purifys' heyday, Alabaman Peggy Scott-Adams was featured regularly at the 506. "Lover's Holiday," her duet with JoJo Benson, was a national hit in 1968. In the 1970s Abe's expanded to hold fourteen hundred customers; across the street was the Sugar Bowl, later renamed the Bunny Club, and the Sabre Club drew an after-hours crowd.

Back when Purify was coming up, a less upscale place called the High Hat—"that was more of a juke joint, a little hole in the wall," he says—sat outside this Little Harlem, in another black neighborhood called Shantytown. Trader John's was the classy white club downtown, on South Palafox. When the airmen from the nearby naval base got their wings and became part of the Blue Angels flying team, they'd have their celebrations there. "It was segregated," the singer says, "but not for entertainment; black bands played there."

The teenage Purify haunted them all, looking for a chance to sit in. He was listening to "Ted Taylor and blues singer Jimmy Reed, they were my favorites," Purify says. Taylor, who had a high tenor voice like Purify's, was ten years older; his big hit was "Be Ever Wonderful" in 1963. Purify also learned from Little Willie John, he says.

At seventeen he was hired for a time as the lead singer of a local group, Little David and the Mighty Rockers. They played Trader John's and Alabama venues as well. A few years later, the Dothan Sextet was one of the most popular groups to play Pensacola, and "I would always go to their dances," Purify says. "I'd go up and sing, along with other people; that was a regular part of their performances." So they knew his work, and when Mighty Sam left the group they asked Purify to take his place. "I was sweet 21," he says. "I turned 21 in May of that year [1965] and joined the group in September." Robert Lee Dickey—who'd be the first to take the name Bobby Purify—played guitar and sang with the Sextet.

When Papa Don Schroeder, another local, caught the Sextet and their new lead singer at Tom's Tavern (on the east side of town, not on the Blocks) he was just twenty-five, four years older than Purify. But he was already a published songwriter and Mighty Sam's producer, as well as a local DJ and promoter of shows at Abe's 506 (see chapter 10). He liked what he heard, and in the summer of 1966, Schroeder took Purify and Dickey to Fame Studios in Muscle Shoals, Alabama, where you could record on sixteen tracks. (Wilson Pickett, Aretha Franklin, and Joe Tex, among others, would also record hits there with the Muscle Shoals horns and the house rhythm section.)

Dan Penn and Spooner Oldham were prolific collaborators, studio regulars, and the in-house songwriting team. Oldham remembers that when the Pensacola contingent arrived at Fame, "Papa Don came dressed all nicely with the briefcase and had these two soul brothers with him that no one had ever met." Schroeder didn't have any songs in that briefcase, Oldham says, so they suggested he go upstairs and listen to some demo tapes the pair had recorded. "He came down after an hour waving this tape box saying 'I got one: the puppet!'"

As they usually did, the two songwriters had worked up "I'm Your Puppet" in the studio one evening, Penn on a little Stella (acoustic) guitar and Oldham on piano. The chords were simple: "A and G, then it goes to C," Penn says. They were mining country and pop veins, though some of their songs would later become soul landmarks, including "Sweet Inspiration," sung by the Sweet Inspirations, "Good Things Don't Come Easy," sung by Irma Thomas, and "Take Me (Just As I Am)," sung by Solomon Burke. "We weren't really about soul music back then," Penn says. "That hadn't even been named yet."

Schroeder didn't initially hear "Puppet" as a duet. He had Dickey singing lead, the producer says, and Purify doing background and harmony. (Purify doesn't remember it this way.) But as all the singers, studio musicians, and the producer stood on the brown carpeting in the middle of the high-ceilinged room and ran through the tune, "Dickey couldn't find the pocket," Schroeder says in a *Florida Soul* interview. "I was looking for a certain approach and he just couldn't do it. So then Purify showed him; he said,' 'Here's what he's talking about,' and just nailed it. So I changed the plan." When the duo put on their headphones and stood in front of the one shared mike to record, Purify was singing the lead. (Dickey was also notified of his name change at this session.)

Schroeder says "I'm Your Puppet" had already been recorded thirteen times as a country song (that's probably an exaggeration) and every one of them had tanked, including Dan Penn's version a year or two earlier. It's a slow, plaintive lament from a captive man who just doesn't want to be free: "*Pull the string and I'll wink at you / I'm your puppet / I'll do funny things if you want me to / I'm your puppet.*" The bridge makes his abject stance even more explicit: "*I'm yours to have and to hold / Darling, you've got full control, of your puppet.*"

The singers hated it. They sang soul with swagger and force, and this was more of a "Why Must I Be a Teenager in Love?" ditty than a grown man's declaration. (You'd never hear James Brown invite a lover to jerk him around like a marionette.) "We were strictly R&B," Purify said, "and their stuff was more pop and country."

But Papa Don wore them down—and, in the end, he had the power. "We just got so tired," Purify said, "and at one point 'I'm Your Puppet' became the focal point. But as far as it becoming a hit, we had no inkling whatsoever."

Penn felt the same way. The Purifys' version included some modifications of his tune—and he didn't approve. "It was 'I'm *The* Puppet' when we wrote it. But when James and Bobby started cutting it, every line said 'I'm *Your* Puppet.' I thought that was a mistake and that they played it too fast. I didn't like much about it. I was the engineer and I was thinking, 'There goes another one that ain't gonna happen.'"

Papa Don had a great ear and a visceral feel for soul, but he also had a strong pop sensibility. When he was still trying to be a singer he'd cut young love tunes, including his first release, "Melanie." He sensed that, in the same way Mighty Sam had infused "Sweet Dreams" with passion, blues, and gospel, laying soul vocals on top of "Puppet"'s poppy sweetness could yield a hybrid hit. "Don Schroeder was a very smart cat," Penn says, in retrospect. "He knew where the radio was."

Later Papa Don added horns and background vocals, featuring Doris Troy, whose bigger claim to fame is singing lead on "Just One Look." That night in the studio, though, he made a strange and risky move. The 1960s recording equipment allowed for one overdub, and Oldham, who'd played piano on the basic track (Barry Beckett was on the B-3 organ), spotted a glockenspiel in the studio. Schroeder told him to go for it. Oldham couldn't find the mallets used to play that high-pitched, tinkling instrument (like a xylophone with metal plates), so he used "a church key, you know, a beer can opener," he says, to strike the keys. Unaccountably, it worked. (Fifty years later a post on the musicians' site *Digging for Covers* declares: "The glockenspiel is the new guitar. Get on board.")

Not long after, Purify said, "we were riding down the highway coming from one of our engagements in Columbus, Georgia. We were listening to the radio and lo and behold, it pops up on the air and the DJ had a big rave about it. And after that, seemingly, every time, every station we turn to, there it was. It really was strange, to tell you the truth." Purify still can't understand it. "Until this very day, I do not see what was spectacular about 'I'm Your Puppet.'"

Ben Moore, the third and last Bobby Purify, who rerecorded the tune with James ten years later, disagrees. "To me 'I'm Your Puppet' was a classic tune to grab young people during that time," he said. "We're singing about being a puppet on a string and everyday kids—16, 17 years old— in love were grabbed by that." As proof of "Puppet"'s romantic resonance Moore says: "People tell me, 'My mom and dad say I was born off 'I'm Your Puppet.'"

It's slight, even in a pop music context, bordering on insipid. But as Chubby Checker said of his cover of "The Twist," the Purifys' singing took this sugar-and-soul mix to glory. The first "I'm Your Puppet"—the one with Dickey, released on Bell Records in 1966—sold more than a million copies, and the remake—with Moore, on Mercury ten years later—was a bigger hit than the first overseas.

Even the doubting coauthor Penn came around eventually: "When I got my first check I said, 'Hey, I like this.'" Musically he became a believer as well, and his appraisal may be the best at capturing "Puppet"'s appeal: "It's a real soft record that hits hard." Music critic and author Dave Marsh thinks the song's appeal lies partly in its relaxed, almost halting tempo, and the languorous ease of the duo's vocals. "If the best definition of cool is that which never has to expend any energy defining itself," he wrote, "then 'I'm Your Puppet' may be the coolest soul classic ever recorded."

WHEN "I'M YOUR PUPPET" hit it big, Schroeder had to rush an album out, which he did. *James and Bobby Purify* (recorded in Muscle Shoals, Alabama) delivered some strong singing on covers like "Knock on Wood" and Sam Cooke's "A Change is Gonna Come," along with the country-ish "You Left the Water Running (When You Left Me Behind)" and the teen-pop "Wish You Didn't Have to Go."

James Purify, *left*, with the first Bobby Purify, Robert Lee Dickey. Their fashions look quite "mod" in this 1960s promo shot, and they were very popular in the United Kingdom; this might have been taken at a London gig. Courtesy of the author.

The duo scored more hits straddling those same lines, combining and alternating R&B with radio-friendly pop, complete with strings Schroeder dubbed in. James and Bobby were in demand and well-paid, often touring as part of revues with other big-name acts, in the United States and abroad.

But Bobby Purify—that was still Robert Lee Dickey at this point—had a hard time flying, and for that and possibly other reasons he left the act. A second Bobby, real name James Grubbs, was hired and they released one single together, called "Section C." (This was a "social conscience" or message song; one snatch of lyrics described a public housing complex: "*I live in Section C, room 4B / eight of us in a room for three.*") Schroeder told soul blogger Red Kelly that this 1969 song marked "the only time I shared the lead on a James & Bobby Purify record. James was the Purify sound!" (Kelly's blogs, *The A Side*, devoted to hits, and *The B Side*, focusing on lesser-known soul cuts, are highly recommended.)

Grubbs died, drowned in a boating accident, and Purify performed solo for a while. Then in the early 1970s Papa Don took him to the 506 Club to hear Ben Moore, who was singing with the house band at that time, the Rounders. Purify sat in and the two did Sam and Dave's "When Something Is Wrong with My Baby" together. Purify told Schroeder: "This is the singer, if you can get him."

He got him: Less than a year after Grubbs passed, Ben Moore took over the harmony vocals and the guitar work as Bobby Purify. "Man, we got along just like scrambled eggs and bacon," Moore exclaims in a *Florida Soul* interview. (For Moore's story, see the next chapter.)

He and James Purify worked together for almost ten years. "James loved singing," said Moore, in his seventies, "and here's what I love about him: He *will* rehearse. See, practice makes perfect, and that was what he and I did. We rehearsed our harmonies so tight, that when we went into the studio, in two days 13 songs would be finished. Now it takes some people six months to finish an album."

The times he remembers most fondly, though, are backstage, before they performed, saying to each other: "Let's go get them baby. Let's go out there and tear 'em up."

As for Purify, he said Moore was the best singer he ever worked with. "His voice was much stronger than the other Bobbys', and he had the sound that I really prefer, the more gospel/soul sound." Then Purify laughed. "Now, onstage, Ben wasn't much of a showman, he really couldn't dance at all. I did all the dancing from that point on."

Moore concedes the point. "I wasn't no smooth mover, like James told you. I never could get my feet to do what my brain wanted them to do. He was the one to do the flaunting around on the stage. But when we got ready to really nail something down and sing, our voices blending so close, we had people in those places *crying*, man."

"There were a lot of duos out there during that time," Moore continued. "Mel and Tim, the Righteous Brothers, Sam and Dave. But James and I were burning the trails, I tell you. Sam and Dave had a fit with us. We played a lot of places they played, together, and when they heard James and Bobby were coming, I bet they said, 'Oh, boy, we got trouble.'"

Something like that. Sam Moore, formerly of Sam and Dave, says he wasn't cowed by James and Bobby by any means, but he did admire their singing. "With me and Dave Prater, it was more call and response," he said. "But those two sang true harmony."

THIS LAST JAMES AND BOBBY PURIFY DUO, the one with Ben Moore, disbanded in the early 1980s. Schroeder said at one point that Purify became unreliable, and Purify was upset by Papa Don's recording Ben Moore as a solo act. One former associate said the singer had a drug problem, but Purify flatly denied that, and Ben Moore also rejected that idea. "We would smoke a little marijuana back in the day," he says. "After the show, we'd sit down with a bunch of friends and light up a little joint and laugh and talk about how we tore the show up. But I never saw him with no strong habit or hard drugs."

Moore said Purify's temper may have gotten him in trouble at times. "He was a fighter. I'm a calm man," Moore continues, speaking in his Pensacola home. "I let things roll over me, but James couldn't do that, he wouldn't let nothing roll over."

Soon after the breakup Purify moved to California alone. He continued to perform solo when he could in the Bay Area, worked in a Sealy mattress plant, and managed an after-hours nightclub in Richmond, north of Oakland. Then in May 2009 he committed the assault with a deadly weapon on the woman he calls "my now divorced wife." (This was a California woman, not Anner Purify, his ex in Pensacola.)

In interviews Purify was thoughtful and polite, and he spoke with care and precision. He called when he said he would. The singer was modest—or he tried very hard to come off as modest—when talking about his talent or success, prefacing his remarks by saying, "Not to toot my own horn . . ." When he conceded that singing gospel in Avenal had kept his voice in good shape, he immediately followed with: "Let me backtrack. Everyone else thought so. I left that for them to say and not myself."

When asked about comparisons between the Purifys and Sam and Dave, he said quickly: "Oh, they were much better than we were. I actually idolized Sam and Dave. I'll put it to you like this: Any time you are doing someone else's material that means you must have an extreme liking for this artist's capability. And we did a lot of their music."

He's a religious man, he said in those collect phone calls. "It hasn't been completely consistent but I've never completely dropped out." Before he was imprisoned he was a deacon in training at an Oakland church, and sang in two church choirs. When he got out of Avenal, he hoped to resume that, and get some singing gigs, maybe through that Internet DJ who liked to play James and Bobby.

At one point he said something that indicated he had been in prison before. Asked, he said he didn't want to discuss it over the phone. He was released roughly two years early, in March 2012. Afterward, he said candidly that his other conviction was for "a sex offense," adding that it occurred in California around 1988 or 1989. Public records confirm the charges included "lewd or lascivious acts with a child under 14 years of age." At that time he was forty-five.

Could he . . . explain?

"That was an isolated incident," Purify began. "I'm sure somewhere in life something happened that you absolutely have no logical explanation for. Now that's one thing that I don't have any explanation for, because it was totally uncharacteristic. That's not the nature of me, and I never had any desire of anything like that.

"If I said that some teenage chick came on to me and I was unable to [resist], that would be passive, but I take full responsibility for what I did. Matter of fact it's something I'm totally ashamed of. You wouldn't have any idea just how ashamed. I've been beating myself up for years [but] comes a time when you've got to let it go. If I could undo it I wouldn't hesitate, but I can't. I just pray that whatever transpired doesn't have any lasting effect on her."

There's a medical term that is also a legal term, he said, for the two incidents that led to his convictions. "With my now divorced wife it was heat of the moment, passion," Purify said. "She was caught in a compromising situation, and I was just unable to contain myself. It's like you're momentarily insane. Temporary insanity, that's it. Passionate crimes . . . crimes of passion."

James Purify in Pensacola. Photo © Suzanne Williamson.

THE CONDITIONS OF HIS RELEASE were such that he had to stay in California for some time, Purify said. Approaching seventy years old, he returned to Oakland, where he was employed as a homecare worker in a facility for parolees and the mentally challenged. After a year or so, he returned to Florida, moving in with his ex-wife, Anner. She's been retired from teaching high school in Pensacola since 2003. They have a son, Jason, in his thirties, who graduated from Florida A&M and works for a charity in Atlanta.

Sitting in her—now their—neat brick one-story home with a pink door, Purify said he was eager to resume his singing career. He was still dapper, dressed for a photo shoot in red slacks, gleaming red shoes, and a bright yellow shirt with a wide collar that evoked the 1970s, the heyday of soul, and James and Bobby's. His hair, receded a bit, was cropped in a neat low natural. At one point he posed next to a framed gold "Puppet" record hung on a hallway wall.

Previously, Ben Moore says, James had asked his former singing partner to get back together. "He told me, 'Bro, I sure need you to come back,'" Moore remembers. Purify said he had producers interested in recording the duo again, but Moore told him he couldn't do it. "Man, we had such a friendship, such a brotherin' thing going, that I would love to. But I've got other obligations and a lot of people depending on me. I'll tell you what, though," Moore adds. "Ain't nothing happened to his voice. James can still sing."

He's back in church, at Antioch Missionary Baptist, the one he grew up in, singing in their male chorus. He's developed kidney problems that require three dialysis treatments each week. Purify doesn't listen to much of today's music, and what he does hear, he doesn't care for. "They call it rap; I call it crap," he said. "You do have some [neo-soul] guys trying to do songs done by Marvin Gaye and Johnnie Taylor, Tyrone Davis or Stevie Wonder. But how the hell are you going to try to record one of those guys' songs? Come on! Those singers were true originals. Nowadays everybody sounds alike."

The last time he was free and in Florida Purify showed up at the Pensacola church his former producer, Papa Don Schroeder, attends. The two hadn't seen each other for thirty years. If they had differences in the past, they seem to have reconciled. "He's walking with the Lord now, and I pray for him," says the producer, who owns a Christian radio station.

In 2015 Papa Don, almost seventy-five at this point, was making plans to take Purify to a Nashville studio to record again. (He wouldn't say what music he had in mind, but he didn't deny that a remake of "I'm Your Puppet" was part of the plan.) But Schroeder's severe back troubles flared up, and with Purify's ill health, "neither of us is really physically able to do a recording session," the singer said. "That requires a lot of energy and a lot of work. But I did tell him a few days ago that maybe we should have tried, anyway. I feel like we may have been able to pull it off. But that's could-a, would-a, should-a."

9

Bobby Purify

Pensacola

IF HE'D GOTTEN TREATMENT SOONER, the doctor told him, they might have saved his sight. This was around 1991, when Ben Moore had just turned fifty. "I was in a dark place," he remembers. "He said it was glaucoma, and that I had waited too long to act on it."

At this point his performances with James Purify were ten years in the past. But Moore, the third and last singer to go by Bobby Purify, was still better known by that stage name. After the duo broke up he worked solo for roughly ten years, recording both soul and gospel albums. "Then I started going blind, man," he says, "and it just took my heart away. I stayed off the road and didn't perform for almost three years. I wouldn't go further than my front porch. I was scared to get run over or that somebody's going to rob me."

At this writing Moore, in his mid-seventies, is not just singing again; he's surpassed his success as Bobby Purify, touring and performing all over the world. "I done won a Grammy, and I've sung for the first black President," he says proudly, sitting in the living room of his house in Pensacola. His way out of that dark place began with an unexpected phone call from another Florida soul singer, one of the greatest. It began this way:

"Bobby Purify? This is Ray Charles."

BENJAMIN DILLARD MOORE was the lead singer for the Echoes of Zion, a prominent gospel group in Atlanta, where Ben Junior grew up. His father taught him to play the guitar and at about fourteen, Ben started singing and playing with the group. "Later, we formed a group called The Moore Family," he says. "I was singing with my father, my mother and my two sisters. We sang all over Atlanta, and we sang for Martin Luther King, because my father had a big name.

"I started working in these little whiskey joints on my own and then one day a carnival came through and they needed somebody to play guitar, so I ran away with them. I was making $5 a day, and my father, who was a wire stringer for the phone company, made something like 50 cents a day. So I stayed with the carnival for about a year and sent money home to help the family."

When Moore returned to Atlanta he played local clubs on Albert Avenue—"I was underage but I always look older"—like the Peacock and the Fox. He and Spencer James recorded some songs for Atlantic as Ben & Spence in 1968, and then he joined the Rounders, an R&B group with a second, strange 1960s incarnation. "We were the Black Beatles," Moore remembers, laughing. "We would do our first set [singing R&B], then take a five-minute break and then the MC would say, 'Now, ladies and gentlemen, the Black Beatles!' And we'd run out in these long blond wigs and sing '*Oh, yeah, I'll tell you something*' and be shaking our long hair, and the people—black and white—went to howling and screaming."

Around 1974 the Rounders got a yearlong gig backing up Mighty Sam McClain at Abe's 506 Club in Pensacola. That's when Mighty Sam, who knew James Purify had just lost his partner—the second Bobby—suggested the singer and his producer, Papa Don Schroeder, give Ben Moore a listen.

"You know when you meet that person where it seems like you were meant to be together?" Moore asks. "That's how it was with James and me. That first night I asked him, 'Man, do you know 'When Something Is Wrong with My Baby?' And he came up and sang it with me, and man, it was beautiful. I stayed with the Rounders for a while after that and people would come up to me and ask, 'Is James gonna be with you tonight?'

"After that, boom, it just took off. When we'd get out there onstage, James would run from one end to the other; he had all the dance moves. But I'd just stand in one place because I was playing guitar as well as singing. And man, when we'd sing harmony together we had people *crying*."

Papa Don took them into the studio to record, and their cover of the Isley Brothers' "Do Your Thing" made the R&B chart in November 1974. That song was included on their 1975 Casablanca Records album, *You and Me Together Forever*. A 1977 Mercury album, *Purify Bros.*, included a redone

The Purifys' 1975 Casablanca album, which included their cover of the Isley Brothers' "Do Your Thing," an R&B chart hit in 1974. Courtesy of the author.

"I'm your Puppet." Schroeder says that though this version didn't chart in the United States, "it was bigger than the first one in England and Europe."

AFTER HE AND JAMES stopped working together Moore cut the soul/funk album *Slow Dancin'* and three gospel albums, including *Purified* in 1982. "He Believes in Me," from that album, was nominated for a Grammy in the Best Soul Gospel-Traditional category. (Al Green won.)

Then Moore began to go blind. He stopped going out, not straying farther than his kitchen. That meant he stopped performing and, without income, Moore lost his house. Friends took him in; "I even spent a few nights under the bridge down under Jordan Street," he remembers. "I could see a little bit out of my right eye then, like tunnel vision. That was scary, but the Lord brought me through it alright."

Nick Dotson, a drummer, also blind, bought Moore a guitar and tried to help him get local gigs so he could earn a living. Dotson says the singer had no clue about living without vision. "He was fumbly blind, as I call it. He'd get disoriented onstage; one time he fell and crashed into my drum kit." But Moore wouldn't get or accept any help.

Dotson sold and supported software for the blind, and one of his long-time clients was Ray Charles. "I told Ray about Ben and his predicament." So one day, out of the blue Charles called Moore from his Los Angeles home. "He told me not to be afraid," Moore says, "and not to give up my career. He said 'You don't need no eyes to have soul.' He really encouraged me."

Dotson guesses the love was considerably tougher. "I think Ray told him something like, '[N-word], get up off your ass.'"

Moore smiles upon hearing that and admits, "Yeah, it was something like that. He told me 'Don't sit your ass around, you've got a voice, use it!' And you know what? I think his words pulled me out of that deep thing that I was in, that fear, where I wouldn't even leave the house."

He began working with Independence for the Blind of West Florida, a local nonprofit. John O'Dylan, the director of vocational rehabilitation, helped him learn to do daily chores like cooking for himself. Moore wasn't the easiest client: "He didn't want to climb up the baby steps, he was used to hitting the big time," O'Dylan says. But he took to the cane. "The guy from the blind school got me out on the sidewalk," Moore says. "He held my wrist with the cane and said, 'Now, start walking.' I went about two blocks and I didn't step off the curb, didn't stumble. After I had that white stick, you couldn't stop me."

He's escaped that trap of fear. "Now, I fly all over the world by myself. I could get up right now, take my cane, and walk clear up to the avenue."

TODAY MOORE ENTERS THEATERS AND CONCERT HALLS wearing a black leather car coat with white lettering on the back. The words read:

BLIND BOYS OF ALABAMA
Five Time Grammy Award Winners
2009 Lifetime Achievement Award

On the front of his jacket, over the heart, more white letters say:

Ben Moore, Lead Singer

In 2005 he cut a Bobby Purify comeback album, *It's Better to Have It*, produced by Dan Penn. During those shut-in years Moore kept his voice in training by singing along with records, and he taught himself to play the guitar all over again—without looking at the fret board. Theirs was a long, grueling session, though, Penn says, because Moore didn't know the songs coming in and couldn't read the lyrics as he sung them: "It was hard to get all that in his memory," the producer says. Moore says he didn't mind at all. "When Dan Penn takes you to the studio you get ready to stay there until he says it's done. And he knows what he's doing."

The following year Moore heard that one member of the renowned gospel group the Blind Boys of Alabama was coming off the road due to health problems. Friends got him to New Orleans to audition.

"I went over to the House of Blues where they were trying out two or three blind guys," Moore says. "We sang 'There Must Be a Heaven Somewhere' and two or three others. Then Jimmy Carter—he's the boss man of the Blind Boys—said, 'Man, what other keys can you sing in?' I said, 'Call it,' and he went to calling out keys and I sang in every one, no problem. After all those years I've sung myself into a real tight, formed voice. I really listen to myself, and I don't go sharp and I don't go flat. They hired me that night."

"Ben had that soul sound," Carter remembers. He's standing just outside the Blind Boys' dressing room with fellow singer Ricky McKinnie before a gig in Charlotte, North Carolina. That night they're all wearing shiny green pinstripe suits, bright yellow shirts, and matching pocket squares. Carter finishes the outfit with a blue ball cap with the nickname "Jimster" on the front.

"We just had to indoctrinate him a little," Carter continues. What kind of indoctrination, he's asked? He and McKinnie act taken aback. "We're not telling you that," Carter replies instantly, either genuinely indignant or pretending to be. "That's Blind Boys' stuff."

When the concert begins Moore is on the far right of the audience facing the stage, seated in a row of four folding chairs. He's thinner than Bobby Purify was; his hair is gray, and the moustache, goatee, and soul patch a little whiter. Like the other Blind Boys he wears black wraparound sunglasses. Moore thumps the fist of his right hand, the one holding the microphone wand, on his thigh, keeping time and singing baritone and tenor harmonies.

He stands up to take a lead early in Curtis Mayfield's "People Get Ready," and sings out, "*All you need is faith to hear the diesels running.*" Then he improvises, jumping ahead of and then lagging just behind the beat. Moore goes silent and lets the background vocals take over briefly, and then

Ben Moore performing in Atlanta with the Blind Boys of Alabama, 2015. Photo by Chinita Tate-Burroughs.

powers back in over the others. When the lyric moves to *"I believe,"* he taps his chest with one hand and adds an improvised: *"Right here in my heart."*

His voice has a rich sonority, a deep southern soul timbre; there's some similarity to Sam Moore (no relation) of Sam and Dave. Like Sam's, Ben's voice carries more clarity than rasp; they're both singers now, not shouters, in command of their craft. And when all five Blind Boys' bodily instruments blend their power and grace, it's clear what this lead singer means when he says, "We are a mighty group."

There's a chill coming off the concrete floor, though, and as soon as Moore sits down he starts coughing; that continues the whole set. "Congestive heart failure," he explains later. After the last song, "Amazing Grace," Moore, Carter, McKinnie, and Paul Beasley file off the stage, each man walking with a hand on the forward man's shoulder and the fifth, sighted,

At home in Pensacola, Ben Moore holds the Grammy Award he won with the Blind Boys of Alabama. Photo © Suzanne Williamson.

member, Joey Williams, leading the gospel train. As they step down, Moore says, keeping his voice, low, "I just may be getting too old for this."

BACK HOME IN PENSACOLA, he's regathered his strength. His wife, Caroline, died a few years back, but Moore has since met and married Shirley Adams—also a gospel singer—who moved from Chicago to live with him here. On this day Moore says he will keep singing "until I drop onstage. For the rest of my life, man. Singing's all I know, and I love making people laugh and cry and jump up and shout. With the Blind Boys I do that for thousands, all over the world."

With the group his faith is affirmed—proclaimed—every night. Even at his most bereft, he insists, he knew despair but never doubted. Moore even sees divine reason for his blindness, saying: "God put me somewhere I couldn't get out of except by turning more completely to Him."

The late Benjamin Moore, Sr., would be proud for many reasons, including one based in a long-ago conversation. It started when his Daddy told him:

"You know, you make me mad at you."

"Why, what's going on, Dad?"

"I taught you how to play and sing. Then I go and pick up an album with your face on it, and it says Bobby Purify. That ain't your name—why are you doing that to me?"

The son explained it was simply the best opportunity to make a living. "Daddy understood it but he never did forget it. He never did."

The son says he's been "propositioned" quite a bit, meaning he's been asked to perform again as Bobby Purify, including by his former partner. But he's not going back, not even to reunite with James and reclaim "that brothering thing we had." He's with the Blind Boys now and has too many people depending on him, he explains. "Besides, I'm just not Bobby Purify anymore.

"I'm Ben Moore."

Papa Don Schroeder

Pensacola

HE'S TALL, SO GERALD SCHROEDER has the driver's seat of his black Buick LaCrosse pushed all the way back. In his early seventies, he's lean and fit-looking, wearing blue jeans, running shoes, and a light blue shirt the color of his eyes. His hair is short and neat, parted on the side, and sits high off his forehead. The cut is conservative, as is his overall affect. As he gives this road tour of Pensacola and Pensacola Beach, Schroeder looks very plausibly like a prosperous, Anglo-Saxon, born-again North Florida businessman and Christian broadcaster, all of which he is.

His car, clean and uncluttered, has the optional superior sound system. "Had to get that," Schroeder says with a quick smile. He slides in a CD and the 1974 hit "Everlasting Love," sung by Carl Carlton, fills the interior: *"Open up your eyes / Then you'll realize / Here I stand with my / Everlasting love."*

"My biggest record, ever," he says, and turns up the volume. Again. More. As he listens Schroeder pounds the steering wheel with the heel of his hand and then keeps time by thumping the top of the dashboard with a closed fist. A few minutes later, when the car's stopped at a light, James and Bobby Purify's up-tempo "Shake a Tail Feather" comes on and the seventy-something snaps his fingers, claps his hands, and bops forward and backward in his seat. To facilitate that or perhaps due to his abiding faith, he hasn't put a seatbelt on all day. "That's Doris Troy, who did 'Just One Look,' singing background," he grins. "I'd overdub her, Melba Moore and Ellie Greenwich onto my songs in New York."

A 1967 Schroeder recording session for singer Oscar Toney, Jr., backed by the Memphis Boys, at American Recording Studio. Papa Don is second from left; to his right is American co-owner and producer Chips Moman. Papa Don Schroeder/Phillip Rauls Archives.

"That was a tough session," he continues. "I must have been behind the recording console for at least 24 hours straight, to cut that one tune." (In another interview he says he and his colleagues took diet pills to stay awake.)

"I'm Your Puppet" follows, the original 1966 version and then the second one, released ten years later, with Ben Moore. "I think the second one's better," he notes, driving with his left hand and snapping the fingers on his right. "More strings."

After several more Purify tunes comes a track by Mighty Sam McClain, the Louisiana-born soul singer who had two notable singles in the 1960s.

The first is his heartfelt, mightily soulful cover of "Sweet Dreams," previously a country hit for Patsy Cline. Schroeder calls it "the best pop blues of
my whole life." McClain also covered Buster Brown's "Fannie Mae" (much
later a staple for Southside Johnny and the Asbury Jukes). When that second, raucous tune comes on, Schroeder grins and laughs; he's loving it.
"He [McClain] doesn't like me," Schroeder says evenly, moments later. ""I
couldn't ever break him into pop. But I tried, I really tried."

This born-again white man is also a soul man: a prolific producer, DJ,
and promoter who went by Papa Don Schroeder. He had a great ear for and
love of black music. More specifically and perhaps more importantly, he
had tremendous instincts for the black music that white people would buy.
"The Lord blessed me," he says. "I had a gift for hearing the hit. I could see
it before they sang it."

Papa Don is likely the most important record producer in Florida soul
after Miami's Henry Stone, operating from the opposite end of this long
state. As the "Papa Don's Greatest Hits" CD he's playing proves, a slew
of memorable, successful songs and important artists can be traced back
to this Pensacola source, the host of local radio's "Papa Ding-Dong Diddley Daddy Debatably Daring Dig'in Out Dash'n Dip Dig'in Don Schroeder
Show."

He drives past the place where his childhood home stood and his
mother raised him, at 18th Avenue and East La Rua Street. They lived in the
bottom left apartment and she rented out the other three. Young Gerald was
the yard boy and he painted the apartments in between tenants. "That's the
only way we could afford to live in this neighborhood," he says. "My mom
was very sharp, a hustler. She worked her butt off so I could go to college
and become a doctor."

Schroeder made it to college, a Baptist school in Arkansas. During his
first summer he was a waiter and a lifeguard who played guitar and sang
on the stand at a Michigan resort. He auditioned a teenage love song he'd
written called "Melanie" for one of the affluent clients, who got him to Vee
Jay Records in Chicago. In the doo-wop era Vee Jay had hits such as "Baby
It's You" by the Spaniels, and bluesmen Jimmy Reed and John Lee Hooker
recorded for that label. Schroeder recorded his tune there and fell in love
with black music in Chicago, too, especially the work of local acoustic bluesman Guitar Red.

He married and transferred to the University of Tennessee with his
wife, Gail. (He calls her Mama Gail; they're still married.) In Knoxville he

began working at radio station WATE and took the on-air name Papa Don at nineteen. "I wanted a handle that would make me sound older and blacker," he says. There was a DJ on WBOP, the R&B station back in Pensacola, who went by Papa Rock, "and I sort of stole his name." Soon he migrated to Nashville, worked in radio there, and produced demos for a music publishing company. He also apprenticed with John Richbourg, aka John R, the influential DJ on the powerful southern station WLAC, who also owned Rich Records. Schroeder was also writing songs and selling some of them, but "I was after Berry Gordy," he says. "I had eyes for becoming a hit-making independent producer."

He, his wife, and his baby girl named Melanie moved back to Pensacola and Mom's ground-floor apartment. Schroeder—or Papa Ding-Dong Diddley, etc.—began DJ-ing on WBSR. He claims he pulled a 78 share of the local radio audience, though there was still very little money in it. "But there's more than one way to skin a cat." He explains that as part of his compensation, he got a sixty-second spot, played once an hour, twenty-four hours a day. Papa Don used it to promote shows he was producing at local venues, including Abe's 506 Club on West Belmont. "That was the biggest club for black people in town," Schroeder says, "and they advertised on my show, 'cause all the black people listened to me." He copromoted local and touring acts there, including Wilson Pickett and James Brown.

He had a similar arrangement with Tom's Tavern, a less swank black club at Gonzalez and Railroad Streets. That's where he heard Mighty Sam McClain and was knocked out by his singing. Not too long afterward, in the summer of 1966, those two were driving to FAME Studios in Muscle Shoals, Alabama, in Schroeder's Jeep. He got himself and McClain "the going deal" for the session from Larry Utall, who ran New York–based Bell records: eight hundred dollars per single and an 8-percent royalty. After striking that verbal bargain, Schroeder says, he turned down more money from Jerry Wexler of Atlantic, and "Wexler never spoke to me again."

McClain's record is timeless, superlative soul. But its initial timing was unfortunate; when that single came out on Amy, a Bell subsidiary, in 1966 another version of "Sweet Dreams"—by a country singer named Tommy McClain, just to make things more confusing—was released at roughly the same time. "Sam was a great, great blues singer, maybe too much for the white market," Schroeder says.

Now the music playing in the Buick slows and Schroeder's dashboard drumming subsides as "For Your Precious Love" by Alabaman Oscar Toney,

Jr., pours out of the speakers. "That's the first time I used strings," he says over the music. "We recorded three violins later, and then I doubled them. And I wrote that intro, the part he speaks before he starts singing."

Strangely—and successfully, which was strange in itself—Papa Don would often arrive at a recording session with no or little material in hand, or even in mind. He'd listen to demos and choose tunes on the spot, with the artists and musicians already assembled. As piano man and songwriter Spooner Oldham confirms, that's how he fastened on "I'm Your Puppet" and "Wish You Didn't Have to Go," the Purifys' second hit. At other times Papa Don would turn to the singer(s) and ask what songs they thought they could cover well.

Schroeder brought Toney to a James and Bobby Purify album session at American Sound Studios in Memphis solely on Mighty Sam's recommendation; he'd never heard Toney sing. "Sam had a good ear," he shrugs. After grueling days and nights working on "Shake A Tail Feather" and the rest of the Purifys' second album, Schroeder turned to Toney, who'd been singing background and waiting his chance.

"What's the greatest old song you can do better?" Papa Don asked the singer. The producer was surprised at the answer, and replied incredulously: "You're gonna beat Jerry Butler?" But Toney insisted he wanted to cover "For Your Precious Love," Butler's 1958 classic—and proceeded to tear the song down. Unusually, Schroeder was satisfied in no time. "We cut it in 15 minutes," he says, shaking his head. "A smash." Toney's version of "For Your Precious Love" went to #4 R&B and stayed on the chart for thirteen weeks. "We're listening to the playback on these big Altec A-7 speakers, me and Chips Moman, who owned the studio, and Don Crews [another producer]," he remembers. "And we knew."

Schroeder gives a good deal of credit to the (all-white) house band at American, which became his go-to studio. "Reggie Young on guitar, Bobby Emmons on organ, Tommy Cogbill on bass, Gene Chrisman, the drummer—they did a fantastic job on that record." (A couple of years later, Elvis would launch a comeback by cutting "Suspicious Minds" and "In the Ghetto" there with those musicians, who became known as the Memphis Boys.)

"Let Love Come Between Us" by James and Bobby is next out of the booming dashboard. The melody and the lyrics are pure pop, bringing to mind heartsick teenagers and Top 40 songs of that era by young white artists. Yet Purify and Dickey's voices redeem all that sentiment—and even seem enhanced by it. Schroeder's true gift, and the appeal of his best songs, lay in the combination of the soulful singers he responded to so strongly with the saccharine material he was also drawn to (see "Melanie"). In songs like "Puppet," the soulful elements don't just redeem the more insipid ones; the hit-making catalyst may actually be the combination of these two opposing forces, a kind of musical fusion. Schroeder used the same positive dissonance on the soul versions of country tunes he recorded, as on Mighty Sam's "Sweet Dreams." Who else would even use the term "pop/blues," as he calls that record?

Once the twenty-seven-year-old producer got enthused about a pairing of artist and material, he overpowered everyone else, including the dubious. The Purifys famously hated "I'm Your Puppet" when they first heard the Penn version, and they were not exactly drawn to "Let Love," either, Purify says. But at this point, "Puppet" had become such a crossover success that they sang along willingly.

In the early 1970s Papa Don, a hustler in his momma's mold, got tired of hustling. He also says he got tired of dealing with James Purify (the two have since reconciled). Schroeder had previously owned a restaurant in Pensacola, Papa Don's Family Drive-In, with a piano and rehearsal space in the back by the kitchen. Now he opened a club, Papa Don's Skylark, on Navy Boulevard. He's proud, he says, that it drew a racially mixed audience. "The rest of the world was crazy, but we never had a problem." He was back on the radio as well, and in this small city (less than sixty thousand residents at the time), he was something of a celebrity, which he remains.

But Schroeder missed making records: "It's my life." So he agreed to produce the Purifys again, with Ben Moore replacing Dickey. Their album on Casablanca yielded one hit in 1974, their version of Isaac Hayes' "Do Your Thing," and the next year they collaborated on an album for Mercury that included the remake of "I'm Your Puppet."

In 1974 Schroeder came up with another surpassing cover, Carl Carlton's version of "Everlasting Love," recorded seven years earlier by Tennessee singer Robert Knight. Although Carlton was "not a great singer," Papa Don observes, his rendition, on Don Robey's Backbeat label (then part of ABC), was an R&B hit (#11) and did even better on the pop chart, reaching #6. "Everlasting" also has a mainstream or pop feel. It's got a simple, sing-along refrain, and upbeat energy, but certainly doesn't scream soul, and Carlton doesn't have an R&B voice. Lyrically, the ethos is undying devotion. By comparison, Carlton's next big song—without Papa Don—"She's a Bad Mama Jama (She's Built, She's Stacked)" from 1981, comes off as downright carnal.

The DJ who once went by Papa Ding-Dong Diddley Daddy Debatably Daring Dig'in Out Dash'n Dip Dig'in Don Schroeder, at his Pensacola radio station. Photo © Suzanne Williamson.

Schroeder quit the business again soon after that—not long after he "said yes to the Lord." Papa Don was in Nashville, mixing "Everlasting" with his friend and colleague Tommy Cogbill when he felt God speak to him. At first he attributed it to "bad pizza," and went back to work. A couple of days later, it happened again. After his awakening, Schroeder says in testimony he wrote for friends and family, he asked the Lord "to please help me never lose the way that I felt at the very moment I said yes to Him. He's been faithful."

On the way back to Schroeder's house, he again drives by his childhood home. There's a stand of pines nearby; in the 1950s Schroeder used to hide his cigarettes in a knothole in one of them. "Those were short trees then," he remarks. "Now they're tall."

During his second incomplete retirement, Schroeder went into Christian broadcasting and in 1980 bought a Pensacola AM talk station, 790 WPPN. In 1982 he produced Ben Moore's gospel album, *Purified*, with the Grammy-nominated single "He Believes in Me."

A couple of songs later the compilation he's been playing ends with two Schroeder-produced cuts by contemporary gospel singer Viney Williams. When "I'll Never Be the Same"—a slow number, with strings—comes on, Papa Don grins, then cocks an emphatic finger at the dashboard CD player. "That's the hit," he says.

Wayne Cochran

Miami

"FROM MIAMI BEACH, the sun and fun capital of the world, it's *The Jackie Gleason Show!*"

With that introduction from announcer Johnny Olson, the TV camera moves to "The Great One," as Gleason was known. The host of this hour-long CBS variety show is fifty, and not yet at his portliest. Gleason wears a reddish-brown jacket over a shiny black vest, black bowtie, and his trademark red-carnation boutonnière. In a sign of the times—this was broadcast in October 1966—he lights a cigarette and holds it smoldering in his left hand as he addresses the camera and the studio audience in the Miami Beach Auditorium (later renamed the Jackie Gleason Theater of the Performing Arts).

"Ladies and gentlemen," he begins, "occasionally I go to a nightclub." Laughter from the audience.

"One night I dropped into a place called The Barn, and what I saw there I have never seen before and I don't expect to ever see again."

More laughter.

"I'm going to introduce to you the wildest combination and the wildest guy I've ever seen in my life. Ladies and gentlemen, here he is, and I know you're going to be wild about him: Wayne Cochran!"

The camera cuts to a ten-piece band in black suits; the five horns, backed by both a trap drummer and a Latin percussionist, blast out up-tempo riffs. Still seen in a long shot, the singer comes on, a vision in a pastel yellow suit with narrow pegged pants, the broad collar of his white shirt extending out over the trim-fitting jacket. He picks up the big oblong mike by its handle and goes into some sliding dance moves on a narrow platform that juts out from the stage into the audience. He's a trim figure, fairly tall, topped by a massive head and an exploding pouf of bleached-blond hair. The camera comes in tighter and the true glory of that hairstyle is revealed. It takes the shape of a rooster's comb, jutting forward from his forehead like a bouffant Mohawk only wider, covering the entire top of his head.

"*I want everybody to let your hair down*," he roars, in a deep raspy baritone. Cochran then launches into a series of barely connected riffs—it's not a song, really—starting with his exhortation to "*Get down with it!*" as the band blasts away at a hyperfast tempo. "*I've got a brand new dance everyone can choose*," he continues. "*Come on baby, I want to see you move.*" The couples, seemingly all white, seated at little round nightclub tables get up on their feet and start to move.

As Wilson Pickett did in "Land of a Thousand Dances," his hit from that same year, Cochran quickly references the Jerk, the Swim, and the Watusi, with rhymes attached to each. *He's* moving, all right, his upper body bending side to side with the beat as his legs and feet move twice as fast below. His dancing has an unusual quality that evokes James Brown: From the knees down Cochran's lower legs and feet seem to scurry and jab independently, including splaying out to the sides, while his thighs remain more or less vertical.

"*Snap your fingers, stomp your feet; clap your hands with that beat*," he blasts. "*Come on!*"

Then Cochran and the band segue into "Satisfaction," the Rolling Stones' recent hit, then back to chanting, "*Get down with it!*" Cochran turns sideways to the audience and glides toward them just by torquing his feet in tandem, and then the song ends with a high blast of horns as the singer takes a bow.

It's a hyperkinetic, ultra-energized performance, as Gleason promised. Yet in the oeuvre of Wayne Cochran and the C.C. Riders, this TV spot is not all that "wild." In their nights as the house band at the Barn, on Miami's 79th Street Causeway, and in twenty-plus years on the road, his outfits were often more outrageous. There was the russet and black cape, for example, with an orange shirt underneath and black scarf around his throat. When Cochran spun and twirled, the cape billowed out to the sides, touching the two female backup singers on his flanks. For a time he favored a rose-pink suit over a white shirt with rose polka-dots—and a pink tint in his hair. "It was a subtle thing," he says in fond remembrance. "Unless you looked close you couldn't see it."

The dancing he sometimes did on one foot, with his back to the audience, was even more attention-grabbing than his "Gleason Show" steps. A
post on the *forgotten hits* blog by Chet Coppock testifies that "Wayne was
just the damndest night club soul man God ever put on earth. I recall one
night when he took the whole crowd out of The Happy Medium [a Chicago
nightclub] and led us on a snake dance up Rush Street." Another post on
that same site describes showmanship that would clearly not be suitable for
prime-time TV: "Saw him at the legendary Diamond Club in Dayton over
30 years ago. He was standing on a table singing with that gravelly voice.
He proceeded to fire a mostly drank bottle of Jack into the ceiling, breaking it into a hundred pieces." The post concludes: "If you couldn't dance to
Wayne Cochran, you were in a coma."

He is likely the most successful white artist in the Florida soul pan-
theon. (Other prominent blue-eyed Florida soul performers include Steve
Alaimo, whose work with and for Henry Stone is detailed in chapter 14;
Tampa's Rodney Justo, for years the lead singer with the Atlanta Rhythm
Section; and Linda Lyndell, whose story was told back in chapter 5.) Jeff
Lemlich, author and curator of the insightful Florida music blog *The Lime-
stone Lounge* declares in one post that "Wayne Cochran is the most authen-
tic-sounding white soul singer I've ever heard."

In his heyday, the 1960s and early 1970s, Cochran also played long,
regular gigs in Las Vegas. (There he crossed paths with Elvis Presley; Cochran claims the King took to wearing jumpsuits after seeing his.) Thanks
to those gigs as well as his touring, Cochran and Cochran style gained
national renown as he helped bring soul to the masses. Although he's at
no risk of being inducted into the Rock and Roll Hall of Fame, Cochran
made a lasting mark on popular culture. In the first Blues Brothers movie,
released in 1980, their manager urges the two black-clad, fedora-wearing
singers to update their act. "Times have changed," he tells them. "You have
the same act, the same suits. Why don't you guys get some jumpsuits like
Wayne Cochran and the C.C. Riders?"

In 2014 when David Letterman announced he would leave "The Late
Show," the *Daily Beast* quoted musical director Paul Shaffer on his initial
job interview with the host. Shaffer proposed that his house band play soul
and funk. "That sounds great," Letterman responded, adding, "I've always
considered myself the Wayne Cochran of comedy." True to that idea, Letterman had Cochran on his show in its first year.

Much of his appeal came from the spectacle of his outfits and antics,
and there was self-conscious humor to his act. But more than he was funny,

Miami-based circuit rider Wayne Cochran—aka the white James Brown—shows his bleached blond bouffant, probably in the mid-to-late 1960s. Courtesy of Glamour Studios.

Cochran was genuinely funky: He could dance and had a real, strong soul voice. Like James Brown, he carried and rehearsed tight, horn-driven bands. Those players, and the rhythm section and backup singers, dancing in choreographed steps, ratcheted up the hyperkinesis of Cochran shows even higher.

The James Brown comparisons are not coincidental. Cochran, who hailed originally from Thomaston, Georgia, was billed as "the white James Brown" (as well as the King of Blue-Eyed Soul). He maintains that he and Brown were friends from time they spent together in Macon and that the Godfather didn't mind the close homage.

Cochran didn't have much vocal range but didn't need it to put his songs across, belting them out, grunting like JB: "Uh! Good God!" He'd add some gospel exhortations as well, sounding like the preacher he'd become.

"ENERGY" IS HIS WATCHWORD, a Cochran mantra. When he was growing up in Thomaston, Georgia, and learning to play country music on the guitar, Cochran recalls, "The only music that was happening then—that was high energy at all—was Hank Snow. He had a song called 'I'm Movin' On,' and one called 'The Golden Rocket.' You had the beginnings of what would become known as rock and roll, with people like Ivory Joe Hunter, but there was no rockabilly yet, and no soul music. There was nothing but country and jazz, big band pop, and Frank Sinatra."

Born in 1939, Cochran was about eleven when Snow's hits appeared. Interviewed at seventy-three in a Miami Lakes hotel restaurant, he's animated in remembrance, breaking into song at various times to make a reference clearer. At one point he breaks into "Hadacol Boogie," a ditty praising a bottled health tonic recorded by Bill Nettles and His Dixie Blue Boys and later covered by Jerry Lee Lewis. "*If your radiator leaks and your motor stands still / Give 'er Hadacol and watch her boogie up the hill/ Do the Hadacol Boogie.*"

After Snow's the first music that really moved him was Elvis' early Sun singles. "I remember there was a little honkytonk club in Thomaston, had a juke box," Cochran says. "A friend said, 'You gotta come down here and listen to this song.' That was Elvis' 'Baby Let's Play House.' It was three songs for a quarter and I played it a dollar and ten cents' worth." In 1957, he felt the same way about "Whole Lotta Shakin'" by Jerry Lee Lewis: "a lot of high energy."

A couple or three years earlier he'd paid fifteen cents at the Ritz Theater to see the movie "The Glenn Miller Story." Cochran liked the swing of "In the Mood" and "String of Pearls"—"moving tunes," he called them. But the biopic also "showed them on a bus touring and getting stuck on the side of the road and all that, and I went 'My, that's so exciting.' So that was where I got my interest in being on the road."

Then, at nineteen or twenty years old, Cochran met Otis Redding. That soul titan, born two years after Cochran, was from Dawson, Georgia, and Cochran first heard him sing in Gray, fifty-some miles east of Thomaston. Redding was playing the all-black Club Fifteen with Johnny Jenkins and the Pinetoppers and the young white would-be singer was "amazed at what they sounded like." After the first two songs, he was a soul or R&B convert. "They had minor chords; I had never heard such a thing." He probably had and may have responded more to the singers' blue or flatted notes. In any case, he said, "It was so great I *had to* learn to sing that."

The two singers became friends and hung out at Cochran's house. "Otis was great at imitating Elvis," he says. "And my momma loved it 'cause she loved Elvis." Later the two shared some bills and sang together in some Memphis nightclubs. In his biography of Redding, Mark Ribowsky writes, "Wayne and Otis made for a wildly odd couple, but the trade-off of vocals between the two was so irresistibly fun that it always sold out the house."

Cochran, who was married with two children by age twenty-two, moved to Macon, where he got his next steeping in soul. James Brown was living there and was "king of the hill," Cochran says, after the success of Brown's (mostly instrumental) "Night Train." Then, in 1964, Brown came out with "Out of Sight" and Cochran thought: "Boy, oh boy." Little Richard (Penniman) was living and performing in Macon, too. "High energy" doesn't begin to describe these two great showmen's performances; together they shaped Cochran's stage command and, along with Redding, his singing style.

Back then, Cochran says, white music and black music were "interwoven," like his admiration for both James Brown and Jerry Lee Lewis. "We all knew each other. And here's another thing: We wasn't trying to create a new style of music. We were just playing what we liked, and adding what we liked. It turned out to be R&B. To me, R&B or soul was rock and roll with a little more intensity. Take it, make it really intense, growl and scream, you got R&B."

He wasn't yet a working professional, however, in any genre. Instead, he sold furniture, ran a dairy route, and worked construction. (He'd left school after the ninth grade.) But he'd had a realization: When his band, the Rocking Capris, played the VFW Club back in Thomaston, or the Lake Henry

Supper Club in Roberta on a Friday night, the quartet got paid sixty dollars total. "I'm thinking, my dad makes $25–$30 a week, working 40 hours at the cotton mill. In two nights a week I'll make as much money as he does."

In Macon he hired a four-piece outfit from Jacksonville, Florida, called Bobby Cash and the Nite Flyers, and went on the road with them for the first time. A club owner in Shreveport wanted a horn band, "'cause horns was big in Texas and Louisiana." Horns were also a crucial part of the James Brown sound, one that Cochran had been yearning for since JB's *Live at the Apollo* album came out in 1963.

After negotiating a pay raise from that club owner, Cochran added the horns from the Dixie Crystals and named the new nine-piece band the C.C. Riders, for Cochran's Circuit Riders. White bands like his weren't on the chitlin' circuit at the time, though later the Riders would become one of the very few. "Ours was more like the vaudeville circuit—white clubs," he says.

IN KEEPING WITH chitlin' circuit tradition, though, Cochran bought a new baby blue Cadillac and had his name inscribed on the side. "I was a big shot," he says. To carry the rest of the crew and equipment he added a fifty-dollar hearse. "You had to stop and put water in it about every 30, 40 miles."

A Riders set would include Redding's "Mr. Pitiful," "Night Train," and some Isley Brothers. Packed houses and return crowds in the South and Midwest led to a better pay scale that included some or all of the door, or cover charges. Cochran says he and the Riders could take in $1,000–$1,500 a night. After that breakthrough, did he go buy more Cadillacs? "Naw, I got a Lincoln."

In the mid-1960s Cochran and the Riders moved to Florida, and became the house band at the Barn, where Jackie Gleason caught his act. Cochran says the TV star and his crew had a section right in front of the stage reserved every Friday night and that June Taylor, the choreographer for Gleason show's dancers, took some ideas from the Riders' synchronized moves.

This one-story joint that held about four hundred patrons sat on the island between the mainland and Miami Beach called North Bay Village. Although it was billed as the House of Soul, the decor was faux farm rustic: rough, unfinished lumber; pitchforks on the walls; OshKosh overalls ads. For the next several years, the most successful of Cochran's career, "we were there eight or nine months a year. That was our base, our home."

He was carrying eight pieces at first, including four horns: baritone sax, tenor, alto, and trumpet. Later he added another trumpet and a trombone.

Cochran and the Riders held it down six nights a week, three shows a night. The Barn's four-drink minimum helped generate three to four hundred dollars a night for each musician, Cochran remembers.

Still in thrall to Brown's *Live at the Apollo*, Cochran staged his show like a continuous revue. "The band would play big-band jazz for 30 minutes before I came on. And they loved that because they didn't think they'd ever be able to play in a jazz band with horns, 'cause that was passé by then. But people dearly loved it. Then we had a group of girls called the Shirley Delights; they'd do two songs and then I'd come on do my show." He'd left the guitar-playing behind somewhere on the road. "By then I was strictly an entertainer." Cochran's opening number was either "You Don't Know Like I Know" or "Hold On, I'm A Comin'," both by Sam and Dave, or Redding's "Can't Turn You Loose."

During this time the Cochran hair that seemed to precede him onstage was in its glory, a character in its own right. That trademark style, dating back to his early circuit days, was another adaptation or cover of other artists' work. One night in Shreveport, Cochran went to see two young guys from Texas, billed as It and Them. "They were great, great musicians," he says, "and the two lead guys were albinos. They had foot switches for these red, green, and blue lights. And every time they changed the lights, their hair would change colors. And I'm thinking, 'Man, that is incredible!' So I started trying to find somebody who would bleach my hair that night." He used the colored lights as well, though he favored pink. The two albinos—brothers, it turns out—were Edgar and Johnny Winter.

Early on, his costuming was an homage to, or imitation of, James Brown. "I had me a floor-length cape, black satin with red velvet lining, like he had. And at the end of our show [a helper] would come out and put the cape on me, and I'd throw it off and they'd put it on again . . . So we did James Brown's *Live at the Apollo* show."

Cochran also got fashion sense from the flamboyant 1940s and 1950s wrestler Gorgeous George, a bleached blond who wore flamboyant sequined robes, and from actress Marilyn Monroe. Cochran remembers a newspaper story that showed her pulling up to an event with a police escort. "She got out of a beige Thunderbird and she had on a beige linen suit and her hair was dyed beige and she had a poodle and he was dyed beige. And I was thinking, 'Now that's the way to dress!'"

In 1965 and 1966, he put out singles on Mercury Records that became his signature tunes: a cover of "Harlem Shuffle," "Get Down With It," and "Back to Miami," which Cochran wrote for a *Gleason Show* appearance. The song began with just Cochran singing over pounding drum licks: "*Going back to Miami / Going back to my girl.*" (It was later covered by the Blues Brothers.) Chess, the Chicago blues label, released an album, *Wayne Cochran!*, in 1967. As was the case with singles he recorded on the Gala, Confederate, Aire, and King labels, it didn't do much business.

Cochran doesn't really understand why; it may be that the energy he and the Riders generated live simply didn't transfer to vinyl. For another reason, his act consisted mostly of covers, including versions of hits by Sam and Dave and Otis Redding; many fans already had or would buy the originals instead.

His most successful, and lucrative, recorded work is "Last Kiss," a lost-love anthem he wrote back in Thomaston. The familiar last lines are: "*Where, oh where, can my baby be? / The Lord took her away from me / She's gone to heaven, so I've got to be good / So I can see my baby when I leave this world.*"

Cochran cut it for Gala, a Georgia label, and later for King Records in Cincinnati, but neither version sold well. Cochran never performed it live: "That's a rockabilly song," he says. "People come to hear Otis Redding's 'Can't Turn You Loose' and then you turn around and sing 'Last Kiss'? Wouldn't work." Instead it was a big pop hit for J. Frank Wilson and the Cavaliers in 1964 and has been done by many others, including Pearl Jam. Cochran holds the songwriting rights and earns royalties.

While Cochran built a devoted following at the Barn, his reputation was spreading well beyond Miami. The *Soul Sheet*, a monthly newspaper, was sent out to fans across the country, and Cochran published and sold a southern cookbook, *Wayne Cochran's Soul Recipes.* He met the actress Ann-Margret and her husband in Miami, which led to the band's appearance in a 1970 B-movie starring her and former football star Joe Namath, entitled "C.C. and Company." Namath's character was named C.C. Ryder.

This in turn led them to Las Vegas, where the band alternated long gigs at the Flamingo and the International. A 1983 *Miami Herald* story said he commanded $14,000 a week for his "roaring, crazed blues act." In Vegas, appropriately enough, Cochran's sartorial style became even more garish. He had "Southern Plantation style" suits made by an L.A. tailor, with three-quarter-length coats, cut away in the front, worn over vests and lace shirts with Napoleonic collars. "They had a lot of beautiful embroidery and rhinestones on very exquisite material," he says. "There was nothing cheap about it." Cochran maintains that, after he shared a bill with Elvis Presley, he had similar suits made for the King, and that after he switched to jumpsuits, Elvis did, too.

"I NEVER HEARD RACE in the music," Cochran told a *Miami Herald* reporter. "It was just music that spoke to me. It moved me." There's no doubt his feeling for this music, and his talent, were genuine. Yet, as a white man cannily, consciously operating in and profiting from black music, the ways he lived race were necessarily more complicated. Despite his friendships and collaborations with Redding, Brown, and other African American musicians, Cochran remembers that when he left Louisiana and started working black clubs, "it was a strange sensation, 'cause I'm from Georgia." Unlike Miami blue-eyed soul singer Steve Alaimo, who says he was never challenged as a "white boy," Cochran recalls numerous race-based confrontations—though in his telling, he either bluffed or finessed his way through them all.

After their cover of "Harlem Shuffle" came out, the Riders got booked into some of the country's prominent black theaters, including the Royal in Baltimore. "We played three days and nights and walked off in dead silence," Cochran says. "And we were next to the closing act. [LaVern Baker was headlining.] The next show was at four o'clock in the afternoon and a lot of kids was there. It was packed and I'm doing a song I wrote called 'No Rest for the Wicked.' I cut the music down quiet, and I talked about how this song came about.

"I'm walking by the front of the stage, the spotlight's on me and a little of the audience, and there's this young black girl, she's about 10, 11 years old. She stands up and says, 'Go home, hillbilly!' And it just went silent.

"Now, I didn't have the nerve to do this or the creativity to think of it. But I just turned around and said, 'Honey, now, I got a story to tell. You listen if you want. But I gotta tell my story.'"

A middle-aged black woman in the balcony came to his rescue. "This lady said, 'Go on, honey, you tell your story, I'm listening.' And that broke the ice. We closed to a standing ovation."

At other times, when he sensed race would come into play, it didn't. In 1967 civil rights demonstrations were held in Milwaukee, and rioting broke out. Cochran and the Riders were playing a black club called the Scene. "I mean, this was a powder-keg time," he says. "And it's really weird: Guys would come in from picketing and lean their picket signs up against the back wall. Then they'd sit down and start drinking and watch the show."

Crucial to his success, Cochran brought close-to-authentic black music—or, to give him more credit, authentic black music transmitted via a white delivery system—to audiences who would never go see James Brown or perhaps even know who the Godfather of Soul was. He did it for the white patrons of the Barn, who would probably not go to Overtown clubs; for the vacationing masses in Vegas lounges; and for the millions who watched Gleason's show as well as those hosted by Dinah Shore, Merv Griffin, Johnny Carson, and David Letterman.

It's not too much of a stretch to assert that this white soul man is partly responsible for the genre's late-1960s crossover into mainstream success. In a way—his own, vastly entertaining way—he was inoculating the uninitiated, giving them a soul vaccination, as the title of a Tower of Power song puts it. And this shot would not make white listeners immune but, rather, susceptible.

He brought so much energy to his work and to the audiences, and Cochran seemed to genuinely be enjoying himself onstage. But by the early 1970s his wild stage behavior had become less entertaining and increasingly destructive. He smashed chandeliers, dishes, and stage lights. At this point Cochran was divorced from his first wife and broken up with his second, Monica.

Even he couldn't summon the energy for working six or seven nights a week anymore, for all the one-nighters with their constant setting up and tearing down. "It's a rough life," he says, "I wouldn't wish it on nobody." He took speed or cocaine to perform, "and then you'd have to take a downer to go to sleep afterwards. My downer was Southern Comfort."

He began looking for solace. He'd never felt much for traditional Christianity, so Cochran began reading up on Eastern religions, "pyramid power," and even positive thinking as espoused by Norman Vincent Peale. On the long bus rides he'd always find something in them that would excite him intellectually but not spiritually. "They would still leave me empty," he says. "It didn't touch my heart." He noticed, though, that many of those other sources invoked Holy Scripture to validate their own points of view. In one of his endless series of hotel rooms, he picked up a Gideon bible.

In 1979, after a gig in Toronto, he called it quits and came off the road. He returned to Monica, with whom he'd reconciled, heading south and dropping the band members off one by one. When he reached northern Florida he was driving, the only one left. "I'd been on the road since the mid-60s and I'd been in music almost 25 years," he says. "And what I had going for me was equity in my bus." He put a little combo together with players he found through a newspaper ad and his youngest daughter on vocals. Then Cochran started a Bible study group in his living room, which, in 1981, became the Voice for Jesus Church, the Wayne Cochran Ministries.

> *"You don't have to jump no pews,*
> *or run down no aisle,*
> *no chills run down your spine.*
> *But you'll know*
> *that you've been*
> *born again."*

PASTOR WAYNE IS conservatively dressed in tan slacks and a dark blazer, the only patch of bright color coming from his orange pocket square. He's smiling and confident as he sings his own mid-tempo composition in this Miami-area TV studio. The Cochran hair is now a grayish white, tamer and smaller, no longer bleached blond and with no rose tint. These days he wears a thin gray mustache that seems to come from and represent the past, an older generation's idea of manly grooming.

Cochran's voice has held up well. Reaching down for the last "born again," he taps into a low soulful timbre that's actually more melodious than his former belting. He's still got the gravel, a raspy blast, when he wants it. With a minimal backing group behind him, you can actually hear his singing better than you could back in his previous heyday.

This broadcast is an outreach effort for his Voice for Jesus Church, and Wayne Cochran Ministries. Since the early 1980s he's had various local cable shows, including one called "Miami Voice," a play on that era's hit TV show, "Miami Vice."

On Sundays, live services start at 10 a.m. in Theater 11 of the Cobb multiplex in Miami Lakes. Pastor José, who's assisting Pastor Wayne, explains that they are here temporarily; after they sell some land the ministry owns, he says, they'll build their own church.

Pastor Wayne looks dignified in a black suit. Older and sober, Cochran is still the star, clearly used to being a leader. He's his own man and a bit of a contrarian, even when it comes to his conversion to Christ. The lyrics of the song he sang in that TV appearance continue to deny that there were (or need be) any histrionics accompanying that life-changing event: *"My hands didn't shake, the earth didn't quake / no stars fell from the sky / But I know that I've been born again."*

At times he gets a little arch, not quite testy, at what he seems to think are ill-considered interview questions. "So, you wanted to play rock and roll at first?" he is asked during an interview. "Well, yeah," he says, "that's why I'm talking to you about it."

No one is as convincing as the convinced, and in most things, it seems, Cochran is sure. He has the confidence of the saved, and of someone who has relied on himself, worked for himself, and seen himself succeed in two careers, winning over two very different audiences.

Cochran's son Chris manages the ministry and this morning, two of the girls singing onstage are Wayne's granddaughter and great-granddaughter. On the screen at the back of the stage, projected words read: "Voice for Jesus: Tell My Children How Much I Love Them!" The musicians as well as the congregation are a mix of whites, blacks, and Latinos. Worshippers file in, perhaps forty of them, clutching well-worn Bibles with crinkled corners marking important passages.

After a half-hour of songs—high-energy ones with names like "Lord You Are Awesome" and "My God Is Mighty to Save"—he walks with a slight hitch to the center of the stage and stands behind a Plexiglas lectern. He wears a flesh-colored headset with a mike attached, glasses with gold-colored wire rims, and a crucifix on a chain around his neck. He joins the singing briefly, then starts this call and response:

> This is the day!" Cochran declares.
> "*This is the day!*" the faithful declare back at him.
> "The Lord has made!"
> "*The Lord has made!*
> "I will rejoice!"
> "*I will rejoice!*"

"Now, remember what 'rejoice' means," the former professional wild man intones. "It means to dance around in a circle. That's what David did. You don't have to do that but if you want to, just take off! I don't care. Hallelujah. Go ahead and praise Him!"

Next week, he announces, a former SEAL will give his testimony. "We're gonna have our own SEAL here, and he's still sniping—sniping the Devil!"

Today's sermon, he tells the assembled, has to do with wealth transfer. "Not Obama's socialist wealth transfer," he says, "but a supernatural wealth transfer. The world's finances are crumbling, the Babylon system is failing so God's system can take its place. The Kingdom of God will prevail but it can't rule unless He can rule over the finances. Whoever got the money got the honey," he cracks, to much laughter. The outcome—in this life, not in the next one, he stresses—has been foretold: "The wealth of the wicked will belong to the just."

His speech is vernacular, colloquial. "The Devil don't own this earth," he reminds them. "We do." Later he reminds them: "I've got a ninth-grade education."

As he did when that little girl interrupted him in Baltimore, Cochran tells the faithful he has a story to tell. This one's about his church in dire need. "Somebody stole over a hundred thousand dollars. From the church! And I didn't know it 'cause they were keeping the books! Looked like it was all over."

Instead, he relates, a benefactor bailed them out, donating $10,000 a week. And it turned out that benefactor "was wanted by the federal government for racketeering. He was facing 20 years in prison! They caught him. Put him in jail, and I took $10,000 he gave us and went and paid his bond. And he still lives here in South Florida."

Soon it will be time to take up the tithe and offering. First, though, Cochran concludes his sermon. "Listen to me," he says forcefully. "We're the children of the Most High God. We can believe Him and trust in Him. So when you see all the financial systems in the world falling apart, praise God. Praise God! Now say this:

"The wealth of the wicked"
"The wealth of the wicked"
"Is laid up for me!"
"Is laid up for me!
"I'm getting ready to receive it!"
"I'm getting ready to receive it!"
"I've planted my seed."
"I've planted my seed."
"My crop is coming."
"My crop is coming."
"I believe it"
"I believe it"
"In Jesus' name"
"In Jesus' name"
"Amen!"
"Amen!"

Willie Clarke
and Deep City Records

Miami

Prolific producer and songwriter Willie Clarke was one of two cofound-
ers of Deep City Records, with fellow FAMU alumnus Johnny Pearsall.
Proof is hard to come by, but Deep City, based in Miami's Liberty City
neighborhood, is reportedly the first black-owned record production
company in Florida. It was certainly one of the most notable and seminal music producers of its day. Working out of an office in the back
of a record shop the late Pearsall owned, he, Clarke, and songwriter/
producer Clarence Reid recorded some of Miami's hottest soul acts,
including Helene Smith, Paul Kelly, and Frank Williams and the Rocketeers, featuring guitarist Little Beaver. From 1964 to 1968 they scored
numerous regional hits and showcased the city's rich, deep talent
pool. In a 2014 documentary, *Deep City: The Birth of the Miami Sound*,
trumpeter and singer Paul Lewis says the label "gave the artists that
performed in the local nightclubs an opportunity to get our music out
there, kind of like what Motown did for artists in the Detroit area."

The name of their company and primary label was taken from that
of a Tallahassee nightclub. "It was underground," Clarke says in that
film. "I told Johnny, 'That's a nice name.' He said, 'Yeah, it reminds me
of Miami—the deepest city in the South.'" In 2006 Chicago-based Numero Group put out an outstanding compilation entitled *Eccentric Soul:
The Deep City Label* and issued a 2007 follow-up, *Eccentric Soul: The
Outskirts of Deep City*. The second album featured music released on

subsidiary and related labels that Clarke, Pearsall, and Reid had their hands in, including Lloyd (Pearsall's middle name), Sun Cut, Concho, and Solid Soul.

In the beginning, Clarke and Pearsall had their ears tuned to what Motown was doing: soul music aimed at the widest, most mainstream audience, and hitting it squarely. The music of their first and mainstay artist, Helene Smith, could be described, as it was in the title of her album, as sweet soul. (*Helene Smith Sings Sweet Soul* was the only album released on Deep City.) However, her sound and Deep City's extended beyond that tonal and commercial range from the start and continued to evolve. Numero's promotional materials describe Deep City's music as "proto-funk and echo-laden ballads."

Clarke and Pearsall brought some of the brassy aggression of FAMU's Marching 100 into their brand of Florida soul. On Smith's cover of the Otis Redding hit, "Pain in My Heart," for example, you can hear what sounds like a full marching-band drum section behind her. Fellow Rattler Arnold "Hoss" Albury, a trumpeter and organist, also orchestrated prominent parts for Deep City's horns; Clarke told the documentary filmmakers that Albury "would have five trumpets, three trombones, a whole band" on their recording sessions.

Early on Clarke, Pearsall, and Reid (who died in 2016) established Helene Smith, who was involved with and later married Pearsall, as the first queen of Miami soul. Then they discovered Betty Wright, launching and nurturing her career. Her first single for them, "Mr. Lucky," was released in 1967, when she was fourteen. In one of her earliest of many appearances on the *Soul Train* TV show, the very young-looking singer, her hair in an enormous Afro, tells the host and audience: "My producers are Willie Clarke and Clarence Reid."

With her, those two went on to become important figures in Henry Stone's hit-making T.K. empire. Clarke shared a 1975 Best R&B Song Grammy award with Wright and fellow T.K. producers Rick Finch and Harry Wayne Casey, the founders of the Sunshine Band, for Wright's performance of "Where Is the Love." (This is a different song from the Donny Hathaway/Roberta Flack duet of the same name.)

Most of the Deep City artists, including Freda Gray, the Moovers, and Johnny Killens and the Dynamites, have since slipped into obscurity, remembered faintly and by few, especially outside Miami. Yet much of the material the label produced, including the singing of its first star, Smith, is distinctive, and some of it is superlative. The heartfelt Clarke/

Reid composition "Am I a Good Man," sung by the strangely named duo Them Two (Larry Green and Larry Mobley), asks: *"Am I a good man? Am I a fool? / Am I weak? Or am I just playing it cool? / I have a woman, and I know she's no good / Still I keep my head up high, and try to do the things a good man should."*

The Numero Group materials declare this cut "Willie Clarke and Johnny Pearsall's enduring masterpiece," and *long play miami* blogger Alberto de la Portilla calls it "one of the most profound and soulful tracks to come out of Miami's soul scene of the 1960s." He also notes that it's been sampled by hip-hop's 50 Cent and The Game.

As Clarke likes to say, he's a storyteller. The songs he and Reid wrote—including Betty Wright's breakout hit about the "Clean Up Woman" who picks up men others foolishly neglect—were drawn from real-life situations and human dramas, including soap opera–like romance. Those two men also had a gift for songs narrated from female perspectives; Wright sang another woman-to-woman cautionary song about a sixteen-year-old "man-getter" called "The Babysitter." (Wright was all of nineteen when the single came out.) "Stay Away from My Johnny," by Freda Gray backed by the Rocketeers, was inspired by an overly ardent woman's pursuit of Pearsall. Paul Kelly's 1965 single "The Upset" was based on young Cassius Clay upsetting heavyweight champion Sonny Liston—in Miami Beach—in February 1964: *"My friends say my chances are dim / They say your love for him is much too strong; I'll lose before the fight begins / Watch me pull an upset, in the very first round, baby."*

Trim, mustachioed, and compact—his nickname was Pee Wee—Clarke was energetic, thoughtful, and opinionated in his *Florida Soul* interviews, as when he invoked the virtues of the segregated black communities he lived in as a young man. He's still producing; Clarke answers his phone with the one-word, all-business greeting: "Music." A raconteur in conversation as well as in songwriting, he narrates his Deep City story here in his own (edited) words.

I DON'T GIVE OUT MY AGE. I was born in Fort Gaines, Georgia, right outside of Albany. [Clarke was likely born in or around 1936.] Most of my relatives came from Macon.

My mama could really sing. She was so good she sang in more than one choir in the church here [in Miami], and a little while ago the church asked

Willie Clarke circa 1976, after the Deep City days, at the console in T.K.'s sixteen-track upstairs studio in Hialeah. Photo © Larry Warmoth.

me to produce an album, to raise money for them. I'll give you one, if you want.

This is what I do and what I'm used to doing. I only put out the best, from my judgment. If it's good I'll share the credit with everybody involved. If it's a failure, then I'll take all the blame. Therefore I have the last say-so. That's my philosophy as a producer. Producing this church album I picked the best of the lot regardless of whether it was choir number one, choir number two, three, or four. Some of these kids, the youth choir, they sounded like some frogs moaning in the forest after the rain. People are certainly not gonna put out $10 or $12 to hear this, and it could be embarrassing to the kids when they hear it. So none of them are on the record. And it turned out my mom was singing in three of the choirs I selected. I wasn't even looking at that; I just listened to the sound and the delivery.

I would ask "Hey, how's the album doing?" and nobody would answer me. Finally my momma broke down and she told me the whole story. They claimed favoritism, and that I disrespected the kids, so they never pushed the album to where it could sell. So I learned my lesson about church people. But I still go to church every Sunday.

Growing up where I did gave me my vision, my imagination. I loved it, because I could see the hill, the little river down below, and this winding path going down to the bottom of the hill. I'd trek down and bring back a loaf of bread for 33 cents. And I remember seeing this Indian lady, she was just . . . beautiful. She was like an angel. She would always be dressed in white with beautiful beads, and she would stand so still she was like a statue. That was my mystery growing up. And I remember seeing my grandfather in the fields, him shooting the shotgun and cussing out the foxes. Later they would tell me that Indian lady was my grandfather's wife.

Gospel music was a foundation from day one. I also grew up on country and western in the hills of Georgia, and songs like "On the Wings of a Snow White Dove." It was very vivid and descriptive; it painted a picture from Jump Street, from top to bottom. So I would imagine these scenes in my head. One song that I never will forget is called "Don't Fence Me In." Part of it goes: "*I want to ride to the ridge where the West commences, and gaze at the moon till I lose my senses.*" I remember that just gave me a feeling, and I could picture myself in that story: "*Let my mind be free, don't put a fence around me.*" Later I found out the moon can make you crazy; that's where the word lunacy comes from.

I was very young and I wasn't reading at the time, but every time I heard music on the radio it seemed to tell a story. And that story would have a beginning, a middle, and an end. We had no TV. All we had was radio music, and also the stories, like the Lone Ranger. That's another thing that got me—the narrative, that great story.

Soon I picked up on the idea of lyrics. These words had impact and they told a story directly to you. They had a grip on me. After I went to school I realized songs are stories, and you have to tell that story in just three minutes. You can make a movie and you don't have to give everything away for the first 30 minutes—you can just wait and build and build because you got an hour and a half. But with a song, if you don't sell it in the first 30 seconds—or the first 15 seconds, even—you might as well forget the next two and a half minutes. If somebody can't get into it, zip! They turn it off and go to the next one. So you have to hit them hard.

The first time I heard black music on the radio was when my mom and my stepfather brought us from Georgia to Miami in the early forties. I was about four years old. The first place she took us was a house on 8th Street, about half a block from the railroads. There was a chicken factory or plant next to the house. This was Overtown. The train came through there on schedule three or four times a day, you could hear it coming and it was like music to my ears, the clickity clack.

Our second place was on 7th Street between 3rd and 4th Avenues. It was a real village with a lot of alleys and little framed houses. They were made out of wood. But you know, the funny thing is, they withstood hurricanes because they were so close together. You could stretch out your arms and touch the next home. They weren't isolated.

Our house was the biggest property, with mango trees, avocado trees, a lot of fruit trees. It was owned by an undertaker who had a mansion directly across the street. We had the picket fence and my mom and her three sisters—full grown-up women—and my uncle, my oldest cousin, me, my two sisters, and my cousin Denny all lived in that big house.

She worked every day, and if I did anything wrong in the neighborhood my momma would know before she got home. She would be on the porch with the ironing cord [he makes a whipping sound]. That's where I learned how to plead for my life. That's also when I started listening to music on the black radio station, WMBM. In the morning from about 5 a.m. 'til about 12 you heard nothing but gospel music. Then from 12 'til about sundown that station had to sign off from black music. At night we got some country flavor and classical music. I really got into gospel: Sam Cooke, the Five Blind Boys, the Mighty Clouds of Joy. It was terrific. They were singing from the Bible, and all of this was filtering through my head as more storytelling.

At nights during elementary school we kids would put on a little program in front of somebody's house. Three of us would sing or one would sing a solo. We entertained each other. I would sit in the middle of a circle of my friends and tell stories. I was the leader of the 7th Street gang, just boys, but when I did storytelling girls could come. I would improvise. We all played the part of the hero and we would sing western songs and ride around on old mop sticks like horses. We would ride through the alleys until the tip of the mop stick was sharp.

On Halloween the junkanoo bands would march all night and we would march with them, the Halloween Parade, everybody joining in with their masks on. [For more on this influential Caribbean music, see chapter 20.] And every Christmas we would go around and sing carols in front of other people's houses.

Then I started writing letters to girls, probably third or second grade. I would always make them rhyme. I *really* learned the power of the pen from the very first time I wrote a girl a love letter and it sounded like poetry and she was very carried away. Douglas Elementary. It was on 12th Street so we walked to school, about six blocks. I followed this girl home and when I got home late afterward, the sun was going down and my mom was waiting on the front porch. But she was so happy to see me she didn't hit me. And I was on cloud nine: all those beautiful girls at school, with their pretty dresses and long hair. I was enthused.

In the fifth grade I started writing some poetry but it never dawned on me to sing it. At the time I was singing doo-wop songs. Me and my group, that 7th Street gang. We sang and then we would go to battle—if anybody bothered us we would put a whupping on them. But there was no such thing as stabbing or shooting; you could just get your arm broken. After a fair fight, you'd shake hands.

I went to a fantastic, all-black high school, Booker T. Washington, and our writing and creativity really started flowing then. Mr. Davis would let us stand up every Friday in front of the class and give an oral: five minutes long, with a subject, an introduction, a middle, a climax, and a conclusion. I would give orals from the songs and soap operas I would listen to on the radio, like one with the title "Don't Fence Me In" but with my own words and my own creativity.

Then one night a guy name Freddie Rutledge was supposed to play the drums for the talent show, but he told me he wasn't going to and I should do it. So I got on the stage, got my foot on the drum, and I'm sure all the other kids were praying, "Oh please Lord, let him do it." And I don't know how, but when my part came, I did it. That's why I believe in God. To this day I believe the Holy Spirit did that with me.

From then I had it in my mind that I could write songs because songs are set up around the beat. The marching band is not a marching band without the drums. We dictate how fast or slow they move, and how great they look. From then it started flowing like a river, and I started making up my own lyrics to the beat.

When I was still in high school, maybe tenth grade, we moved to Liberty City. That was more upscale than Overtown. The lawns were mowed, the neighborhood was clean, and there was a tennis court. Children had to go to school every day; if not the community centers that handled everything would know. It was public housing but there were rules. Back then you had a chance to move up because they were paying your rent and you had a chance to go to college.

It was rare that I saw a policeman back then, in Overtown or Liberty City. When you did policemen were seen as heroes, and they were friendly. The law was the law, but if you did something bad normally that just meant a whoop-ass by your parents. My mom and her friends would discuss what was happening in the neighborhood, like someone gave a report to my mom that I was stealing apples from the corner store. My mom and her friends would also talk about politics and they were observant. They did domestic work for the white folks, and the white folks would school them about everything they did.

Most of the people from that neighborhood in my time are very success-ful, turning out to be lawyers, doctors, teachers, politicians, working for the CIA—back then it was very hard for black people to not succeed and they didn't fill up the jails. Even though we were riding on the back of the bus, that was *our* back of the bus. When they moved us out [of Overtown, by run-ning Interstate 95 and I-35 through it in the early 1960s] they dispersed that cohesiveness between the black citizens, and that's when the police and the criminal justice system divided and conquered. Today the cops want [to ar-rest] young brothers so they can boost their checks; they harvest them right off the street.

But when I finished high school, even though we had these opportuni-ties, I didn't want to go to college. I thought 12 years of school was enough. Then I found out the only job that I could get was washing dishes. The manager at the restaurant at 54th Street and Biscayne Boulevard told me that with a high school diploma I could get a dishwashing job anywhere. After he told me that two or three times, I took his veiled message.

I told my guys at home I was going to college because I wanted to play in the band. To them it was the ultimate, shining achievement to play in the FAMU band. They said, "The drum is bigger than you, how are you going to play that?" At FAMU some of those drums weighed 40 pounds and I weighed about 115.

My first year there I tried to play the snare, and I got shot down. We had something called "shake the tree." All the participants had to line up on a stage in the park and the section leader would say "Willie!" and I would have to do the routine. Then he would blow the whistle and I would have to play it faster, and then faster. . . . They shot me down and I was out. The guys who were better got it. Then one day they asked if I wanted to play tenor drum. That was the first time I heard of it; the tenor drum is the one you play with the mallets. It's higher-pitched than the bass drum, and sits [in front of the drummer] like a snare. And the spot that was open was the section leader's spot.

Dr. [William P.] Foster was our leader, and band was hard work; it was on the level of the football team, and some guys said we worked even harder. Girls weren't allowed to be in the band because it was so rough. I really started liking it, how you spin those mallets—with the right hand, then the left hand, then you spin it twice. It made a flashy, showy thing and people couldn't wait for it.

My roommate was from Pompano, Boo Dentley, he played the snare and together we wrote about 30 new cadences. They gave me a new nickname: "Hot Tom." They were behind me 100 percent and I energized the section. We had 150 members overall, and maybe 22 tenor drums. I still hear them; it still turns me on to think about it. Those were glory days for me.

What they drilled into me with that band was not just precision and perfection but how it takes practice and togetherness. If you made a mistake everybody who you're working with will know, and they will work with you to correct that mistake. That's teamwork. When we started moving real fast, every once in a while somebody would fall down—the same thing that happens when you're doing a recording and the bass player misses a section. You keep going, then you go back and fix it. The only difference with a band is if you missed the direction you will physically get hurt. I've seen guys fall down and other guys walk all over them. Band taught me to be a leader. And unlike my 7th Street gang this time I was a leader in the eyes of the world.

Those teachers were something else. I learned how to study and how to interpret and how to really get into the meaning of words and how important they were. But I was an art major: art education. I remember this one book, *Creative and Mental Growth* by Viktor Lowenfeld. That's my bible. I was certified for special ed—that's what it was called then—all the way up to twelfth grade.

All this training and studying about people as mental and physical beings got me thinking: "Why do I like this song, why am I getting lost with this song?" And I figured out the hit songs are the ones I understand from beginning to end, the songs that make me want to sing along bob and weave and have a special feeling. And I realized I had a preference for writing them.

The Liberty City record shop owned by Johnny Pearsall. Deep City Records' office and practice studio were in the back; Miami singing star Betty Wright was discovered in the front. Courtesy of Helene Smith Pearsall.

The whole time at FAMU my partner Johnny Pearsall and I always had our head into producing records. He was going to be the money man and I was going to be the producer and the writer. He had a charisma that was out of this world. He was from Miami, too; his mother was a school principal. Johnny played the trumpet but he didn't make the band. He smoked too much to keep up. He was six feet one and slim; I don't think he wanted to do all that vigorous exercise.

Every summer Johnny and I would come home and we would attempt to do songs. After FAMU, I started teaching and he had Johnny's Records shop. I painted the name in dancing letters and did some graphics for him from my art class. It was on 60th Street and 22nd Avenue [in Liberty City], right on the corner. It's a barbecue place now. His daddy owned that whole building. Half was Johnny's record store and half was his dad's restaurant.

I had notebooks full of lyrics, because I'm a poet. But I didn't have connections with musicians. So I made up my mind on working with Clarence
Reid because he had the notoriety. While I was away at college he was in the
studio making a name. One day around this time people came to repossess
my car. Everything was mounting up against me. I was trying to live the
American dream. I had a plump wife, a little baby, and a house with the
backyard and the fence, and I'm out there trying to figure out what to do,
and my wife comes screaming that it's my turn to take care of the baby. I
was broke, we had nothing in the fridge, and I said, "It's a shame: I went
to college, I played in the band, I had talent, I was working, and I still can't
live."

So I told her, "See you later, I'm going to my mom's house." I went
over there to borrow $10, which was a lot of money back then. I decided I
couldn't depend on just teaching—I had to do something with my dream
to have a gold record. The first part of the dream was that I would be able to
hear one of my songs on the radio. Then the gold record. Then a Grammy
and a platinum record.

I got in my car that they were going to take [he doesn't explain how this
was possible] and said, "I gotta find Clarence." Miami is a big city and Clarence is a man who walks a lot, more than the Disciples. I'm driving around
in a Ford convertible, red with a white flip-top. Then I saw Clarence. He was
walking and I honked the horn and said, "Thank you God, I found him." I
introduced myself and told him, "I've got a bunch of lyrics here. We need to
get together and make these into some songs." He said, "Let me see them."
Then he passed over my good lyrics and went to the weird ones and he said
he liked those. I knew if I teamed up with him he could do chord changes;
he was a genius with chord changes. He also knew bass players and drummers and more musicians, so I knew it would work.

I didn't have a monstrous vocabulary but it was bigger than Clarence's,
so the best thing I learned from him is if he didn't understand the words,
then he didn't like the song, so I had to back up. Simplify. I would work
it out with the same meaning but different words, make it more for the
masses. It opened up my eyes that I wanted to reach everybody and I didn't
want my words to be too fancy and for people to get bored.

Helene Smith was in charge of the record shop, and when we started
Deep City, she was our first singer, the first artist we wanted to produce.
She had a voice of her own, very unique. Very small, petite, and a beautiful
voice. The records we put out on her in Miami went to like Fort Lauderdale
and Palm Beach—they were local hits.

She was a little bit shy, though. I used to take her to shows to perform, and one time I took her down to the Harlem Square [the Overtown night-club]. It was packed and they were getting down and saying, "Helene Smith is in the house," and she said, "I don't want to go on!" I said "What?" and she said, "Take me back to the record shop, I don't want to go on." I said, "Come on, come on, it will be all right." She came on and once she got into it, Helene kicked it, tore the house down.

We had more local hits with her and our other artists, too: Frank Williams and the Rocketeers, Freda Gray, the Moovers, and Them Two, who did "Am I A Good Man." Little Beaver was in the Rocketeers, their guitar player, and he started singing with them, too. I would come up with melodies and put them into chord changes, and do some of the writing. Clarence and I made one basic agreement: If you came up with the idea [for a song] it was worth 50 percent. You couldn't ask for 60 percent. Or if he ended up writing 90 percent and there were only three or four lines from me, we still split it 50/50. Songwriting is a team effort. Never believe writers do everything by themselves.

This is later, but on "Clean Up Woman," for instance, he came up with the idea, and he explained the chord changes. The lyrics weren't finished but the idea was there. It was actually supposed to be about a man, the Clean Up Man. But I insisted that Betty Wright was going to do it as Clean Up Woman. See, this woman was going to take up all the brokenhearted men that other women threw out to the curb. The Clean Up Woman takes all the love and polishes it and turns it into something good, something that you lost: a good man. [Jimmy Bo Horne sang the song from the male perspective on Stone's Alston label in 1972, the year after Betty Wright's hit.]

Then he left [the studio]. That was another habit we got into: It was up to me to produce and make the necessary changes, then he would come in and listen to it. The only person I was trying to satisfy was him. But after we did our rehearsals one-on-one, then Clarence had to leave or he and I would get into it. One time—it might have been Paul Kelly on "Chills and Fever"—we had this drummer, supposed to be one of the top drummers in Miami. But he's falling off a cliff. I said, "Clarence, that drummer, he's not playing man." He told me not to say nothing to him, and I told him I don't give a damn if he gets upset, I'm in here to produce a record. I need this to be right. Otherwise I might as well stay home and change diapers.

So when I spoke to the drummer he was like: "Oh, that's what you want? That's easy." And I looked around and said "Clarence, see," and

The late songwriter, producer, and performer Clarence Reid, shown here in 1975, was an integral part of both Deep City Records and T.K. Productions. Says former colleague Helene Smith Pearsall: "Clarence was a genius." Photo © Larry Warmoth.

he got mad with me, and he left. My horn man, Hoss [Albury], arranged and wrote the chords. Hoss had them playing like how I wanted them to; meanwhile Clarence is walking from the studio in Kendall to Lejeune Road to Liberty City—like 20 miles! [The eccentric Mr. Reid was an inveterate walker, known to chastise people who broke his concentration on those expeditions by offering him a lift, telling them: "You just cost me a hit record."]

Clarence was very strict and very moody, and very impatient. But I was used to that from being an art teacher, from being a special ed teacher. I could work with anybody.

[Clarke's phone rings. It's Clarence Reid.]

Hey, Clarence, I was just telling this guy you're the Devil's kinfolk.

Anyway, before we did anything with Henry Stone, still Deep City days, Johnny and I are paying $15 an hour for studio time with our teachers' checks. And we're post-dating those checks so they'll clear. We couldn't pay our people top dollar, that's why the records out of Deep City have a funky feel but they're not as dynamic as the ones that came out of T.K. I learned, though, not to substitute perfection for feel. If it feels good it's better than perfection.

So we found Betty Wright. Actually, Clarence found her first. He was telling us, "I met a girl, she's really young but she can sing, man, she can sing." She was winning all these talent contests. Then one day we're in the record shop, rehearsing a group in the back, and we hear this strong voice coming through the walls singing Billy Stewart's "Summertime." The record was down low but she had overpowered his lead voice. She just shut down our rehearsal.

Betty had come to collect her prize for winning a name-that-tune deal on the radio. I went out front and looked at her and said, "Are you the one singing that?" and she said yes. She had braids and long hair, and her cousin was with her. I didn't believe it was her. I asked Helene if it was her singing, but it wasn't. I told Betty to sing it again. I thought she would be shy but she did it again. Johnny liked her, and then Clarence told us it was the girl he was telling us about, so we went to recording her. On her first single [for Deep City, "Paralyzed" backed with "Good Lovin'"], one side was the #1 record in Miami, and the flipside was the #1 record in Tampa. We already had Paul Kelly, Little Beaver, Frank Williams and the Rocketeers, and Them Two, so we were rolling. But I had to convince Johnny that I could produce both female vocalists, Helene and Betty.

Johnny didn't really want to work with Betty. [Helene Smith disagrees with this assessment; see next chapter.] I only knew she was a great singer and she needed guidance, and she chose me to be her guide.

After a while there were so many Deep City productions on the radio, Henry Stone started calling. He wanted me, Johnny, Helene, Betty, and all the people who had pulled together to come and work for him at T.K. Johnny wasn't for it. I told him Stone wanted to put us in the studio and he would pay for it, and I wouldn't have to use my teacher's check. Henry had the means to get money and we were the wrong color to get a loan. They weren't giving them to chocolate people. But I think Johnny had seen too many things in Tallahassee, the lynching and all that, so he didn't trust any white person. I didn't see all that in Miami. I never really suffered because of the segregated environment; our parents and our relatives and our neighbors kept us sheltered from that bigotry.

Years earlier, before we were getting any action on the radio, Henry gave Johnny and me some input and a critique that stayed in my head to this day. He is the real father in my life when it comes to my music. He was the first adult male that actually gave me productive guidance.

He took us into his cubbyhole office in Hialeah, where he had a little bar and a desk. He gave us a drink and asked to hear what we got. We put a couple records on the turntable, including one of Helene's first records. It wasn't getting any action; we needed him to distribute to the record shops. He listened to maybe two songs, and then he put them aside silently and got the number-one record on the radio at that time, and put it on the turntable and said: "The first thing you need to do is be your own best critic and your hardest evaluator. Now, if you're going to have a party and invite all your friends, or people you're trying to impress, would you play your record or this record?"

Johnny and I looked at each other and realized we had a lot of work to do. After Henry finished with us, I went into the studio and made the song "Chills and Fever" with Paul Kelly. I kept hearing Henry Stone telling me that everything had to be right. This is the most competitive business in the whole world, you can become rich overnight or you can be poor your whole life. You have to be as good as the competitors or better, and you have to have a whole lot of drive.

When Henry put the word out that he wanted us, Clarence was already working with him. Clarence was more productive with me, but if he got pissed off at us, then he would go back to Henry, and if he got pissed off at Henry, he came back to us. So I came over from Deep City and brought Betty and worked with her and a female singer they had, Gwen McCrae. Both those girls had aggressiveness in their voices and that's their real personalities; they're what you call real women.

I began to work with the other people there—Timmy Thomas, Chocolate Perry, Benny Latimore—all of them were listening to me as their producer. The first thing I look for are mistakes, miscommunications. If I can't find any fault with a song, then I deem it ready to go. But if I can't praise it, then I give criticism with suggestions for betterment. If anyone had a problem with that, I'd say, "Hey, that label is gonna say, 'Produced by Willie Clarke.'" You have to take responsibility. After it comes out you can't say you tried to get the drummer or the bass player to do something else. Leadership qualities are what you need. That's how I feel about the president. That's the hardest job in the world, but you have to find a way to get all the people to work with you or else we need another president.

Choosing the right musicians is a big part of it. I knew which bass player I wanted, which drummer I wanted, which keyboard player. For certain songs I would want Timmy Thomas on keyboards; on others I would want Latimore, and on some I would sneak KC on there. Latimore was basically a gospel soulful type keyboard player, and Timmy Thomas had almost a happy, carnival sound with his organ—I would compare it to the ice-cream man coming. And KC was just a hard-rock-and-roll type.

Chocolate Perry was real funky, yet he was a disciplined bass player. You could be sure you would get even notes—precision. Now Ron Bogdon—he was a white guy from Boston—he was more of a straight-ahead groove. He could get a good groove and just lay with it and create a feel. There was also a Caribbean drummer, he played on "Clean Up Woman," his name was Breeze. He was one of the best drummers I came across. He played with a loping beat; it's different, kinda laid-back, part of the island sound, which is part of the Miami sound. The Miami sound is stirred up with the ingredients from the Bahamas, Jamaica, Alabama, Georgia, all mixed all together.

I was blessed to be able to be working with these talented people. Sometimes when I think about it I get chills. You're a lucky guy to get a keyboard master like Timmy Thomas; you're a lucky guy to have a funk master like Clarence Reid; you're a lucky guy to have a keyboard player like Latimore to play on your songs. I feel the same way about KC, this man was so funky. He was like the light that was so bright people would gravitate toward it like bugs, because he had charisma and that feel.

I remember he and Rick brought me the track for "Where Is the Love" and I wrote some lyrics to that and arranged the vocals and I had a lot of help from my girl Betty Wright. The gay people up North made it really big and it won a Grammy [for Best Rhythm & Blues Song in 1975].

When Rick and KC were working together, they called me over to listen to "Rock Your Baby." They got that title from the very last words Betty sang on "Babysitter." So I went upstairs and they had Timmy Thomas on organ, and they had the clip-clop [rhythm machine on his organ] going, and they started playing that instrumental track and KC said, "What am I gonna do with it? I can't sing it because it's not in my key." I think Betty had turned it down, Gwen McCrae had turned it down. I told him, get George McCrae. That was a real soul song, but they couldn't see it until he put the right voice on there. I knew KC had talent and after that was a huge hit, the doors really opened for him.

"Rockin' Chair" was one of best ones we had. Clarence was the first one to sing it, actually. It came out on the back of [the Dash single] "When My Daddy Rode the West." I wrote those lyrics, and he used some of his interpretation in there. [They shared writing credit on Reid's Dash single and on Gwen McCrae's smash version of "Rockin' Chair" on Cat.] I engineered the session but I wasn't there when Gwen came in to put her vocal on.

I was always around the studio; I was a studio-holic. They used to have to wake me up in the chair. In addition to producing and songwriting, I became the engineer. I would run that custom-made [mixing] board. Henry named his company T.K. after Terry Kane, the guy who designed and built that board, and it had a unique sound. All the big hits came from that board. I trained a bunch of other engineers because when I went on tour with Betty I didn't want to leave Henry flat. I taught Rick Finch, and then KC. I always felt like we were a family, so when people would say, "Willie, teach me the board," I said, "Okay, just come to the next session."

I got a lot of ideas for songs just from listening to conversations and watching movies. Take my song, "The Experts." I'm thinking: Who can I call an expert and really get people's attention? The expert lover. The song says: "*If I can learn to kiss like the experts / the only thing I would be an expert at is kissing you and loving you.*"

People used to say, "You've got your thing on a string," meaning you're the puppeteer, you're in control. So I made a J. P. Robinson song with that title and it goes: "*If you have a love that's true, that never do wrong to you / then you've got your thing on a string.*" Henry Stone said it's his favorite song. And J.P. Robinson is a great singer. [Robinson, from West Palm Beach,

Clarke, still actively producing in 2016, outside his Hialeah studio.
Photo © Suzanne Williamson.

later recorded for Atlantic.] He would really get into his songs to the point where I thought we needed a straightjacket. You know how people in the church get the feeling and the ghost hits them? That's how he was in the songs—near the very end you can hear him getting ready to let loose and start holy rolling.

This was an age where the nightclub was a very competitive place for you to perform and you had to leave the audience frantic, with their hands up, like in church. It was like an exorcism. That's how the performing artist had to be onstage, and on a lot of our soul records out of T.K., near the end they start building up into a crescendo or climax; we call it the vamp. So there's peaks and valleys—and you don't go out on no valley.

Speaking of church, besides that album I told you about—the one I got in trouble for, the one with my mother—I have another gospel project right now. There's a line in a J.P. Robinson song, *"I'm gonna keep on keeping on,"* and that's the inspiration. I produced this record back in the T.K. days; in that one he's gonna keep on keeping on for his woman, but now I'm transposing the lyrics to gospel lyrics. I sent the song to somebody I want to work with. And I'm working on some stuff for Helene to listen to. I still got a lot going on.

13

Helene Smith

Miami

When Helene Smith cut her first single in 1964—"The Pot Can't Talk About the Kettle," written by Clarence Reid and Willie Clarke, was the A-side—she was still in the tenth grade. She had been discovered by Deep City cofounder Johnny Pearsall, her future husband, and became that company's first singing star.

She had moved up a grade, Smith remembers, when "Willing and Able" became her second local hit. Roughly twenty songs followed (some 45s bore the name Helen Smith instead of Helene), mostly on the Deep City label and others on the Philadelphia label Phil-L.A. of Soul. "A Woman Will Do Wrong" made the national R&B chart, reaching #20, in 1967. Written by Reid and Deep City vocalist Paul Kelly, it was an "answer song" to Percy Sledge's "When a Man Loves a Woman," and was later covered by Irma Thomas, Dee Dee Sharpe, and Esther Phillips.

Clarke and Pearsall were initially focused on the Motown sound, hoping to emulate the Detroit label's success with girl groups such as the Marvelettes and female singers like Mary Wells. As the knowledge-able soul blogger who goes by Sir Shambling writes, Smith's vocals could sound less distinctive over that smoother, safer material, what he calls "the more poppy arrangements that her writers/producers asked her to sing in front of." But Smith's emotive vocal approach and the funky pulse of Miami soul were still felt in her music. Shambling concludes: "When given a decent ballad to interpret, she was able to let go with both power and passion."

"Willing and Able" opens with a strong horn flourish, including high-range trumpets, the work of Deep City arranger Arnold "Hoss" Albury. At a slow, loping tempo, Smith comes in, singing soprano: *"Darling, I'm willing to forget about our past / Darling, I'm able to make our love last."*

That's the sweetness. Smith then shows her strength and intensity when the song goes to the bridge, based in the sixth chord, and sings the rueful line: *"Merry Christmas to you and a Happy New Year / although you have someone newww."* Even when singing more powerfully Smith enunciates very clearly, with no trace of a southern accent; in that way she resembles her Motown counterparts. (This signature song, released as a single in 1964, may also remind listeners a bit of Barbara Lynn's 1962 hit, "You'll Lose a Good Thing.")

Her 1967 album *Helene Smith Sings Sweet Soul* was the only LP Deep City produced. (Four of that album's cuts are on the reissued Deep City compilation, Eccentric Soul, along with a cover of Otis Redding's "Pain in My Heart.") That vinyl LP is a coveted collector's item; a copy was recently on sale for 1,800 British pounds, or more than $2,800 USD.

Smith, born in Miami in 1947, is almost always mentioned in the same breath or sentence as Betty Wright, the next great Deep City discovery, also a prodigy. Wright may have sung background on some early songs for Smith, who is six years older. Both women recorded for Deep City for a time; then Clarke took Wright with him to Henry Stone's T.K. Productions, while Smith and Pearsall chose not to join them. Smith withdrew from music in the mid-1970s, around the birth of her daughter with Pearsall. Like her husband and Willie Clarke, she taught in Miami schools for decades, retiring from that in 2013.

Talking over her career in a *Florida Soul* interview, she is poised, grounded, and seemingly without regrets. Smith does take issue with some of the assertions about rivalry between her and Betty Wright in the 2014 documentary *Deep City: The Birth of the Miami Sound.* But her prevailing attitude is one of gratitude. "I knew other people in Miami who could sing just as well or better," she said over iced tea in a Panera Bread restaurant. "I just happened to be the blessed one, the happy one, to have the career that I did." (At this writing she and Clarke were discussing going into the studio together again.)

Their contemporaries say that while Wright was hell-bent on success from her very early years, Smith was shyer or less overt in her ambition. She admits to initial timidity about her singing and some stage fright (as well as fear of flying). But luckily, she says, while she attended Brownsville Junior High School in northwest Miami her music teacher recognized her talent and drew her out. Sometimes, Smith recollects, he did that quite forcefully.

HE THREW A BOOK AT ME! Mr. Roscoe Speed, our music teacher, had just told me: "Smith, I need somebody to sing this, and you can do it." I was a soprano and maybe a little louder than the other kids, so he'd heard me. But I was shy and a little nervous, so I said I didn't want to.

Boom! That book hit the floor right in front of me. That got my attention. So then I sang, and at the end of class he said, "Smith, stay after. I'll tell your Home Ec. teacher that you need to keep working with me." I loved him; everybody loved him.

Growing up around that time I remember Saturday mornings at home, and everyone doing their chores. I was the fourth of nine children. Mom and Dad would be singing, my mom playing the piano and my dad singing and playing the harmonica. He really excelled at that; he'd play at little juke joints and storefront places around town. My Dad's favorites were John Lee Hooker, B. B. King, and Bobby Bland. Everybody's dancing and singing, doing their chores, having a good time.

By middle school I was listening to the Marvelettes, Baby Washington, the Supremes, and Aretha Franklin. She's my favorite because she's well-rounded, so versatile. She plays the piano, too. One time Pavarotti got sick, couldn't go on, and she took his place. Can you believe that? [Smith remembers correctly; this happened at the 1998 Grammy Awards.]

Mary Wells—she's another one. Yes. I loved her. I used to wear her record out: [Sings] "You beat me to the punch."

I met Johnny Pearsall, at Brownsville Junior High. I was singing in the chorus, and after-school programs, and he told me he liked my singing, and that he was thinking of forming a group with me and some other girls from the chorus. John was tall and handsome and I don't know if the other girls really wanted to sing, or they wanted to go for that ring. But I wasn't thinking about that. I had my mind on singing. Besides I was only 13 and my dad was strict; he did not play that.

When Johnny was in school [at FAMU] his mom was buying property and building a building. She thought he was going to be a pharmacist, and that he'd have his pharmacy there. But he didn't want to be a pharmacist anymore and convinced his mom to open up a record store. I was in tenth

Helene Smith Pearsall surrounded by soul—vinyl by James Brown, Dionne War-wick, the Temptations, and the Jackson 5—in Johnny's Records. Courtesy of Helene Smith Pearsall.

grade then, and I came with some other girls and we did a lot of work, fixed it up and made it into Johnny's Records.

He already knew Willie Clarke from college and Clarke went out and found Clarence Reid. Johnny put a piano in the back of the shop, and sometimes people would come with guitars and drums and so on. We would rehearse and we had this big tape recorder, and we had to get it to sound good on that before we could take it to the recording studio. We couldn't do a million takes there; studio time cost money. That's why we rehearsed to the nth degree. Sometimes we would rehearse at Johnny's house, too. We had a great band working with us: Frank Williams and the Rocketeers, and Little Beaver was a monster for them on guitar.

We started recording when I was still in high school [at Northwestern], that's when I did "The Pot Can't Talk About the Kettle." And I recorded "Willing and Able" when I was in eleventh grade. Those first times, I was definitely nervous, but I wanted to do it. I'm nervous even to this day sometimes. I still have to calm myself down, tell myself, "You have to do this, and you can do it. Be your best."

I remember when I heard that first 45—I was happy, happy, happy. And the kids at school stopped calling me Helene and they'd say, "*Hey, Pot can't talk about the kettle!*" It was a big deal, but I was still just me, I still had my friends and all. After the next record, though, I was out of there.

Next Clarence and I went to Nashville and I recorded up there with [producer and publisher] Buddy Killen and I did a little touring in Florida and some more in Tennessee. That's when I really got afraid of singing, or of performing, really. You know why? Danger could come about. You're a young person, and people are doing whatever in those clubs. Well, I didn't drink and I've *never* done drugs. Never smoked either. You're in town and men think they can get with you, because you're a young girl. No. I didn't come for that reason. Let me sing and if you got money to give me, give me money for my work. That's it.

I continued to record, in Philadelphia for Phil-L.A. of Soul and on Deep City, with Clarence. You know what? Clarence is a genius. Now, he didn't get paid as a genius, but the music that man made . . . He couldn't read too much—he might say, "give me a C" or "give me a D," that's all. But when we got in the studio, that man had *music* ready. [The musicians] would look at him like "What are you doing?" But when they left they were amazed at him. He liked my voice but you had to work. He was all business, and that's what it takes.

I worked with all three of them together, really: Clarence, Willie, and Johnny. Clarence knew me well—I'm not a screamer. I have a voice but I wasn't that screaming kind. My voice could be more quiet. So usually he would want me to do those sweet songs. One time, though, he wanted me to sing one that was too sexy, something about "*hoochie coo.*" And I told him, "No, I can't do that."

Willie always wanted me to do more soulful songs, though, to sing like Otis Redding. He'd say, "Come on girl, you can do this!" And Johnny, he could sing a little bit and play the piano a little, but he knew music. He would be there and say, "Bring it down a little lower" or "Take it a little slower." And he wrote some of our material as well.

As Deep City was getting well established, I did quite a few singles and then we had enough music to make the album, *Helene Smith Sings Sweet Soul*. We probably had enough to make another album, but we never did. We also had other acts who were really good: the Rocketeers, the Prolifics—they sang backup for me on "I Am Controlled by Your Love"—and Betty Wright made her first record there [on Deep City's subsidiary Solid Soul label].

Arnold Albury wrote the sheet music, the actual charts for those who used them. He really helped create the Deep City Miami sound—that full, kick-butt sound, like the FAMU marching band with all the horns. For years, the FAMU band used to come here to Miami with their classic parade. They're marching down the street. Can't help but dance. Because they sound so good.

My daughter, even though she's so much younger, when she hears our Deep City sound, she says, "Mom, I love it. I love it." Before I used to play it too much and she'd say: "Play something else. You're wearing it out, mom." [Laughs]

We were like family, I will always love all those guys, and I loved recording, making new music, hopefully making something somebody would appreciate and identify with. "Willing and Able" is one of my favorites; to me, it's about a person—could be a man or a woman—telling their true feelings, saying what they feel is real. And I like music that tells a story. It talks about love and love is very important. That's what people buy—they buy love songs.

I must have sung in just about every nightclub in Miami: the Continental, the Double Decker, on Seventh Avenue and 79th Street. I sang for Butterball [the prominent local DJ who MC'd live shows], in the Overtown area, too: the Mary Elizabeth. The Knight Beat. The Island Club. I sang a little bit for mostly white kids over at the War Memorial [in Coral Gables]. I traveled around Florida with Sam and Dave—they used to call me Baby Sister.

I got to enjoy it better, to be less nervous and shy. I found out later a lot of people weren't shy because they were high, and I wasn't high. My dad even came to see me at the Double Decker one night and he asked me, "How are you able to get in front of all these people and do what you do? Are you drinking, are you high?" I said, "Daddy, you know I don't do that."

The singer at far left with her husband, Johnny Pearsall, and fellow Florida soul singer Linda Lyndell, *middle*, at a North Florida gig, mid-1960s. Courtesy of Helene Smith Pearsall.

He was impressed with me, because when he did what he did [performing on harmonica], he had a beer or two, and then he was good to go.

You know, a lot of places that I've sung in my life I didn't make money. It was just promotional, so people there would play my records. Once, Johnny, who was my manager, and I flew to Nashville. I was on this big revolving stage and there were about 21 men on that show and one or two ladies. We had a room together, separate beds, and you couldn't lock the room on my side. I said to myself, "If I had to come up here by myself, what

would happen?" Johnny was teaching school, so he couldn't come with me that many times.

Another time we went to Jacksonville, and then we went way out in the country to Palatka, to this place with a wooden floor, and so many people were in there. Afterward when we were driving back, it was so pitch black and we were a little bit lost. A policeman pulled us over, asked us where were we going, what we were doing out there and like that. I was afraid, because back then sometimes police were not too nice. But it worked out okay.

The only job I can recall right now that really gave me a little money is when I went to Washington, D.C., and played the Howard Theater. I was on that show with Solomon Burke and Brenda and the Tabulations. Oh, that was wonderful. We did the show throughout the week and they would show a movie after the show. Friday and Saturday we did five shows each.

Johnny and I got married on May 29, 1971, when I was 23. By the time we were married I believe Willie had already gone over to Henry Stone and T.K. Records, and Betty went with him. My husband had gotten into his education—his mom was a principal, and she told him: "You need to do this first and foremost. Do something that's going to be for real, that will last."

[The Deep City documentary quotes others saying that Pearsall didn't want to work with Wright.]

No, I don't think so. Though she was still so young, and with him being a teacher, he was concerned about getting sued. We would still see her and Willie but it wasn't like before. They also implied [in the documentary] that Johnny didn't want me to keep performing. No, he really did. My husband told me, you go ahead, I'm going to make some money for us. Johnny was getting his third advanced degree; he had two master's and he was getting a specialist's degree in administration. My husband wanted me to sing; I went to Palm Beach, I went to Tampa, Jacksonville, Tennessee, Philadelphia, Washington, D.C. I went places.

Helene Smith Pearsall in North Miami. Photo © Suzanne Williamson.

I don't remember when but at some point I did go over and record some for Henry Stone [one single was released on his Dash label]. I was working and going to school maybe three times a week. So I'd come home from work, make sure my house is in order. And then go to the studio to meet Clarence and record and sometimes I'm there till eleven o'clock at night. At one point I went back to finish up my recordings there and I was told they had been destroyed. By whom? I never knew and at this point, I don't even care. That's why I called Mr. Stone and I asked him if I could have my contract back. And he informed me, graciously, that yes, I could.

For a while I had a little group called the Diamonettes, with three other girls, but I stopped singing when I was pregnant, and I had my daughter Joi when I was 27. Back when I worked at the record shop, Johnny was always encouraging me to take some [college] classes. At the time, though, I just wanted to sing. But eventually I did that, and I taught preschool kids and worked in the libraries at different schools. When I finally started working in the classroom, I loved it. I taught everything: PE, Music, Art. And in those classes, you really have to teach.

When we were doing Science, sometimes I would teach them little songs about the water and the environment. We would sing it and they would love it. "Let's sing it again!" Oh, yes. I taught for a long time before I finally got my teaching certificate in 2006, and I retired in 2013. I love kids. I hated to leave when it was time.

I still sing in church sometimes, with the choir. And I'm rehearsing now, learning some material so we can do another album with Willie Clarke. I'm told, too, that my old album is going to be rereleased in Japan, and that if I wanted to go there and to Europe I could, because they still love that old music and they love my thing. So if that was offered to me, I would do it. This is a time in my life when I would have to just go for it, even though I'm afraid of flying.

When I started to let go of my music professionally, I was getting so into my family—wanting to have a child and then raising one—plus wanting to go to school. Besides, things just weren't happening like I wanted them to [in the music business]; there was just so much mess going on and people acting crazy. I just wanted to be a decent person, and have a good marriage. [Her husband, Pearsall, died in 2000.]

I loved my husband so much. He used to tell me, "I just love the way you talk."

I said, "Really? Why?"

And he said to me: "It sounds like you're singing."

Henry Stone

Miami

"THIS BOOK YOU'RE WRITING is about soul music in Florida, am I right?"

"Yes, absolutely."

"The thing is, I *am* the story of Florida Soul, so your book is really all about me."

"Well, you are certainly a very important figure . . ."

"So, I'm thinking, I should get a cut."

He's right. Not about being a coauthor, but about his prominence—his preeminence—in this story. Distributor, producer, and record-label owner Henry Stone had a hand in, and his hands on, much of the significant music in Florida's significant soul canon. The history of his hit-making is broad and long; he recorded both Ray Charles and KC and the Sunshine Band—two major acts, working thirty years apart, who bookend this music and its history in this book. In between, he recorded the original version of Hank Ballard's "The Twist" (as told in chapter 4). Through Stone's distribution deals with Atlantic, King, and other companies, he influenced national charts and radio airplay across the United States and, in so doing, helped write the story of soul overall. The success of his records in Europe and the United Kingdom make his impact international.

In the more than sixty-five years between his arrival in Miami in 1948 and his death there in 2014, Stone put out a prodigious amount of R&B, soul, funk, disco, and rap music, by Florida artists and many others. (In his spare time, Stone cut records on bluesmen Lightnin' Hopkins and Earl Hooker and gospel records for his Glory label.) Much of this music is immediately recognizable to soul fans, especially those who came of age during the 1970s or had a member of that demographic in their house, blaring the hits of the day. That's due to the artists Stone chose to work with, the quality of their work, and to its commercial success.

In addition to those already mentioned, his roster includes:

- Wilbert Harrison ("Kansas City")
- Sam & Dave (early work, including "No More Pain")
- James Brown ("Do the Mashed Potatoes"; "Rapp Payback")
- Betty Wright ("Clean Up Woman")
- Latimore ("Let's Straighten It Out")
- Steve Alaimo ("Every Day I Have to Cry")
- Timmy Thomas ("Why Can't We Live Together")
- Otis Williams and the Charms ("Hearts of Stone")
- George McCrae ("Rock Your Baby")
- Gwen McCrae ("Rockin' Chair")
- The Beginning of the End ("Funky Nassau")
- Peter Brown ("Do You Wanna Get Funky with Me")
- Anita Ward ("Ring My Bell")
- Bobby Caldwell ("What You Won't Do for Love")

The Charms' song listed above was a #1 R&B hit in the 1950s; he also wrote a hit for them entitled "Two Hearts, Two Kisses, Make One Love." But Stone's most dominant decade, the period in which his reach extended the farthest, was the 1970s. At that time, according to published accounts, his T.K. Productions was the biggest independent record company in the world. (The company was named after Terry Kane, the engineer who built Stone's studio.) That's when the George and Gwen McCrae songs listed above were #1 hits; so was Timmy Thomas' peace anthem, as well as Latimore's greatest hit, "Let's Straighten It Out," which stayed on that chart for twenty weeks. KC and the Sunshine Band had four #1 R&B hits and four #1 pop hits in that span, selling millions of records. Playing on and driving almost all these hits was a stellar, synchronous group of in-house musicians: studio regulars, assembled by Stone and his producers, who created a signature Miami sound.

Although it doesn't list any sources, a 1976 Associated Press story invoking that sound in its headline says the company grossed around $10 million in 1975 ($45 million in 2016 dollars), up from $5 million in 1973. That article also notes that both "trade Bibles," *Billboard* and *Cashbox* magazines, were devoting special issues to T.K.

Henry Stone gets the latest issue of *Billboard* magazine in 1976; more than likely some of T.K.'s hits were on the sales charts. Photo © Larry Warmoth.

Henry Stone music was released on a slew of labels he owned, including T.K., Chart, Rockin', Deluxe, Dade, Glades, Cat, Drive, Marlin, and Scott and Dash. One reason he had so many of them, Stone said in an interview two years before his death, was "there were times we had so many of our records on the charts at the same time, I didn't want anybody to realize it was all Henry Stone, stick their head up and wonder, 'Hey, what's going on here?'"

He hungered for hit songs, and that urge never abated. "I had my ear to the ground constantly; I worked with these young producers, looking for my next big song," Stone said. "He's a record junkie, is what he is," says Steve Alaimo, his longtime producing partner, adding that "he loves music much more than I do." The first time Stone was interviewed for *Florida Soul* he was ninety and about to release another Latimore album, a tribute to Ray Charles. "I've been working with him since the 70s," Stone said of Latimore. "I believe in him. I'm finishing the CD right now, and I know it's going to be huge."

What did Stone listen for, which musical elements or qualities whispered—or shouted—"hit" to him? "A lot of people start off with a lyric," Stone said, "but I always started off with the bass line, a good bottom-line funk, not so much what the song says. A good deal of these hits had that funky rhythm and bass." Stone had an eighteen-thousand-square-foot warehouse in Hialeah for his True Tone distributorship (usually just referred to as Tone) and, upstairs, a small eight-track recording studio. From his downstairs office, equipped with a piano and a bar, Stone could hear bass lines thumping through the ceiling. When a riff reached down and grabbed him, he said, he'd drop what he was doing and exclaim, "Wait— that's it!"

KC and the Sunshine Band's music featured prominent horn-section riffs, many of them written by arranger Mike Lewis (see chapter 20), and "Funky Nassau" featured memorable horn lines. Was that brass sound also important to him? The former brass man replied: "No, not at all."

Stone worked in the music business before it was corporatized, when a lone, entrepreneurial wolf could operate with impunity and dominate an entire state. "If you wanted to do anything in the music business in Florida, you had to come through Henry Stone," he declared, and to a remarkable extent that was true. That power made him not just a dominant figure but also a controversial one. As was often the case with soul label owners and producers (mostly white), some artists (mostly black) came to feel they'd been taken advantage of. For his part Stone insisted that he never took a songwriting credit if he hadn't contributed to that process, eschewing that standard grab by many of his contemporary R&B and soul producers.

As STONE SAT IN THE LIVING ROOM of the condo he shared with his wife, Inez, on Miami's Grove Isle, framed gold and platinum records hung on the wall behind him. Stone's white hair was tied back in a ponytail and he wore a long white goatee, along with a light green shirt and dark glasses. He went blind in the early 2000s, following failed surgery for glaucoma, "but I haven't lost my ears," he said.

He did note with some pride that during his heyday, "I was the king of payola." Now illegal, this was the practice of bribing DJs to play certain records on the air to get a competitive sales edge. "I think I can talk about that now," he said, as his wife tried to steer him away from this line of inquiry. "I mean, with the statute of limitations, and all."

HENRY EPSTEIN PICKED UP the trumpet at about twelve years old, at the Hebrew Orphanage Asylum in Pleasantville, New York. He was born in the Bronx in 1921, and when he was eight (he sometimes said five) his mother, who was raising him alone, placed him in the orphanage "due to the wonderful circumstances we had then in the Depression," as Stone put it. He kept playing during his high school years in New York City, studying with Charles Colin (whose company now publishes brass instruction and arrangements) and playing duets with Milton "Shorty" Rogers, later a renowned jazz trumpet player, when both attended LaGuardia High School on Manhattan's West Side. Stone fronted a band called Rocky Stone and His Little Pebbles that played Catskills gigs; that was presumably the origin of the professional name he would adopt later on.

As Epstein, he got drafted into the wartime army but luckily was sent to Camp Kilmer in New Jersey, where he played in a military big band—"Glenn Miller–type music"—and some smaller jazz combos. The army was still segregated, but for some good reason these bands were integrated.

"The great trumpeter Sy Oliver was in our band," Stone said. Oliver, ten years older, had arranged for Jimmy Lunceford and Tommy Dorsey. Before, Stone had been playing jazz and some pop, but now he got a feel for the blues—"not straight blues; mostly big-band stuff with a lot of blues intonations and jazz intonations. I guess that's where I picked up a lot of my soul," Stone said. "I got a good feel for black music."

After the war he assessed his options and decided, "I just wasn't good enough to compete and make a good living playing the trumpet. I'd been exposed to players like Shorty Rogers and others in that category, and I had also burned my lip out. The number-one function of the Camp Kilmer Band, besides playing dances, was to go down to the New York docks and play to the troops right when they embarked to go overseas. And at the hours they left it could be below zero." Playing in those conditions damaged his lip and thus his embouchure. "And we didn't have the option of saying, 'Oh, I'm not going to play today.' That was our job."

He went to California in 1946 or 1947 (this seems to be when he changed his surname) and worked for bandleader Ben Pollack, who had gone into the record business. As Stone would later allow other younger men to do, he learned the business by hanging around and doing odd jobs.

In a 2010 event at the Rock and Roll Hall of Fame in Cleveland, Stone described one of his first entrepreneurial hustles. While working for Pollack's Jewel Records, "I used to pick up the records for Modern, Excelsior, Cadet and Exclusive [other independent labels], take 'em down to the railroad station and sell them to the porters. They'd take 'em back to Chicago, St. Louis, and places like that where they couldn't get these records [before distribution became national]. It was quite a cute little gimmick and it worked."

He moved to Florida, unclaimed music industry territory, in 1948. On his way to get a Florida driver's license in Miami, he ran into a California acquaintance who needed help unloading ten thousand copies of his company's records. Stone, newly licensed, drove all over the state and sold them out of the trunk of his car, exclusively to jukebox operators. "There actually were no record stores back then," he said. He got paid in records, which, when he sold them, became cash.

Stone ended up spending a few months in Jacksonville at some early point, which is where he heard of the talented singer and piano player RC Robinson, later Ray Charles. In 1951 he recorded him in the back of his Seminole Record Distribution Company (a precursor to Tone) on Flagler Street in downtown Miami. Eddie Shaw, Stone's shipping clerk, was the sound engineer. "I had a little back room there," Stone said, "where I had a nice piano and an Ampex tape machine." Stone also recorded several blues songs by another of his shipping clerks, Willie C. Baker, on his Rockin' label.

In the 1950s he began distributing records for Syd Nathan's King Records, an important R&B label based in Cincinnati. "I was a record man, and Syd was a fabulous record man," said Stone, using an expression that would become the title of a 2015 documentary about him. "Later, I had my problems with Syd and we parted ways," Stone noted. (Their first falling out seems to have been over the proceeds of "Hearts of Stone.") Gradually he added "Atlantic, Motown, plus all the independents" to his distribution client list.

In 1955, Nathan called Stone from Cincinnati and asked him go to Macon, Georgia, immediately and find a group with a hot demo he'd heard about. The group was the Famous Flames, led by one James Brown. "I jumped into my old blue Buick and headed for Macon," Stone said. The demo causing all the excitement was called "Please, Please, Please." Stone hoped to pick it up for his Deluxe label, which King distributed. But Nathan hedged his bets and also dispatched someone from Birmingham to get the demo, and that emissary got there first. A day later, Stone met Brown, listened to the demo, and was floored by the singer's "raw emotion . . . I knew it was going to be an immediate smash hit. I told Brown that I was going to be very instrumental in promoting his soon-to-be-pressed demo." The song came out in 1956 on Federal, a King subsidiary. Stone worked it hard and it became the smash he predicted and eventually, he noted, "Brown's trademark song." (Stone said that Leonard Chess of Chicago's Chess label was after the same demo but got caught in a Chicago snowstorm and so was aced out by Nathan.)

Stone and Brown, two men of exceptional talent and commensurate egos, hit it off in Macon and formed a lifelong friendship. When he got back to Miami, Stone told the owner of the Palms of Hallandale, an important club on the black circuit, about Brown and the Flames and got them booked there just as "Please" took off. As Stone remembered, "Brown and his first-class backup band brought the roof down," to the extent that was possible at this open-air venue, a former drive-in theater. "Their explosive show stunned the audience," Stone said in the liner notes to a greatest-hits CD. He then negotiated additional, more lucrative, week-long gigs—instead of the usual one-night stands—there for the group. The money aside, these engagements were instrumental in raising Brown's profile and launching his career.

A few years later Brown was in Miami and told Stone he wanted to cut some instrumentals featuring his band, known as the JB's by that time. But Syd Nathan, with whom he was still under contract, wouldn't do it. Would Henry? Certainly. At this point Stone didn't have a suitable place to record as he'd been focusing on distribution, so he took the band to Criteria, a rival Miami studio run by a friend and fellow trumpeter Mack Emerman. (With Atlantic's ace producer and engineer Tom Dowd at the board, Aretha Franklin and Brook Benton would record there, along with reggae's Bob Marley and rock acts such as Derek & the Dominoes, Fleetwood Mac, and the Bee Gees, who cut their "Saturday Night Fever" soundtrack in Studio C.)

Stone's plan to help Brown—and infuriate Nathan, if he found out— was to record the band under a pseudonym. Nat Kendrick and the Swans, named after Brown's drummer, cashed in on and propelled the going dance craze with their "Do the Mashed Potatoes," Parts I and II, both released in 1960. "One of the repeated lines was for someone to shout 'mashed potatoes!'" Stone said, "and Brown volunteered. At the last minute I decided it was too risky using Brown's very recognizable voice and turned to him and said, 'You can't do that, I can't use your voice on this record because Nathan will be on our ass!'" Instead, Stone called on prominent local DJ Carlton

"King" Coleman and dubbed in his voice shouting that line. In the 1950s and early 1960s, Stone said, Coleman, originally from Tampa, was one of the most important DJs in Florida, along with Jack the Rapper Gibson in Orlando; Jockey Jack Gibson and Ed Cook in Miami; and Milton "Butterball" Smith, heard on WMBM, 1490 AM, in Miami.

The "Mashed" songs did very well, and despite his precautions, Stone says, "If you listen to the record very carefully, you can still hear Brown's voice in the background." Stone and Brown remained close. "He used to call me at least once a month whether he was in Europe or wherever," Stone said. When Brown was in Miami, "we used to drink our cognac together there at the bar I had in my office. Later on when I quit drinking he used to tell me 'Henry Stone, you mighta lost your drunk, but you never lost your funk.'"

In 1970 they launched a record label together, called Brownstone, which over many years released mostly singles by Brown's musicians and backup singers, including Bobby Byrd and Vicki Anderson. Announcing that joint venture on Larry King's CNN talk show, Brown, who was notoriously demanding and usually confined all his pronouncements to the subject of himself, was warm and effusive about Stone. "I love Henry," he said. "One of the finest people in the world. He did a lot for me, going back to 'Please, Please, Please.'"

BY THE 1960s, STONE SAID, "the music scene [in Florida] was me. I had such good control of my area, I broke all of these records, and then they spread. [Record companies] would send me acetates to test it out, and when I'd order 13,000 records, they knew they had a hit." He maintained that while Florida accounted for only 2 percent of record sales then, he sold 15 percent of the music he distributed. Although most companies had some promotion men of their own, the majors and the independents were still so dependent on him, Stone said, that they would give him, or have him keep the proceeds from, three hundred of every one thousand records he ordered. Later, when he became more prolific as a producer, music Stone produced would be distributed nationally through deals he made with Atlantic, Columbia, Warner Brothers, and others.

He moved all that product and met those expectations, Stone said, through "travel, pushing and connections. And I believed in the records, I knew they were hits." The ones he didn't believe in, "the stiffs," as he called them, "I wouldn't talk about."

Stone also had a way of reversing the distribution flow—and upping his take—through what he called "trans-shipping." His obituary in the *Miami New Times* explained that when Stone heard the funk and sensed a song released by one of his distribution clients could become a national hit, "he would order extra from the manufacturers, and send them to Philadelphia, New York, Washington, Detroit, and Chicago, where he had contacts to sell them for him. This angered some, but . . . there was nothing anyone could do about it. He was just too good at it."

To maximize return, Stone would push those songs with the important DJs of the day, as radio and record stores had supplanted the jukebox as the most important sales sources. That meant "taking good care of them," he said. At this point in the *Florida Soul* interview Stone's wife, Inez, asked: "Are you sure you want to talk about this? Can you talk about it and not get in trouble?" But he was undeterred.

"If I thought we were going to have a hit record, I saw to it that the manufacturers and myself weren't the only ones being compensated," he said. "I got a lot of free records, records which could be turned into cash. Or [he'd give DJs] 50 or 100 dollars. And I'd take care of booze."

Two years later he was blasé enough about any possible repercussions to publish an e-book with *Miami New Times* writer Jacob Katel called *The Stone Cold Truth on Payola in the Music Biz.* In it he said:

> You just gotta remember it's all done by people. And people like booze, drugs, hookers, expensive meals, and nights on the town. Especially DJs. And most of 'em will take bribes to play certain music. We never called it that though. [The term] "Payola" was invented by the media. Guys in the bidness, we just called it promotion.
>
> The name Alan Freed comes up a lot with the big "Payola Bust" around 1959. Freed was a DJ that admitted taking money to play records. Basically ruined his career. Everybody was takin' money to play records then, and they still are today. After that bust, DJs kept right on takin' money to play records, along with cocaine, hookers, and Mercedes.

During T.K. Productions' 1970s heyday, the less-exotic cash payments worked this way: Stone had a constant supply of free records from the labels he distributed. When it became clear that one or more of those singles was selling well or would do so, Stone would ship them by the thousands to "one-stops," the wholesale centers from which record stores bought their merchandise. The one-stops would pay Stone—or more often, an associate in Chicago, New York, or another big city—up front. That cash would be delivered to the right DJs, who would then play T.K.'s songs. With that airplay came demand, first in the major markets—he targeted the ten biggest cities to begin with—and then in the smaller ones.

Stone claimed he paid the late Frankie Crocker (the Chief Rocker) on New York's prominent black station WBLS "up to $10,000 at a time. Every eight weeks or so." After he bought a young, struggling Alan Freed seventy-five dollars' worth of groceries, Stone said, he never had to pay him again to get his records aired. The promoter also maintained that local DJ Bob Green, of Miami's WINZ, was cooperative without any cash payments: "He used to like steak and eggs three times a day, that's it." (None of these men survives to tell his side of the story. Crocker was convicted of payola-related crimes, though that conviction was later overturned; Freed pled guilty to two counts of commercial bribery. No published reports besides Stone's indicate that Green was on the take.)

The system worked for everybody, Stone concluded cheerfully. T.K. got the airplay it needed, the artists got the exposure their art deserved, and the DJs got paid for their contributions. As he related it, Stone's payola philosophy came down to this: "Make a buck, spend a buck, you know? If a record does well, I shouldn't be the only one to do well." He said that T.K. revenues eventually grew to $15–20 million a year, in which case there was certainly enough to spread around.

Top 40 radio was becoming the formulaic, play-list driven thing it is today, he explained—so DJs on pop stations were not bribable, or less so. "But R&B DJs could still play whatever they wanted," Stone said. "So I'd break all my records R&B, and then if they were strong enough, cross 'em over to pop. Even my white acts—KC and the Sunshine Band, Foxy, Bobby Caldwell—they all broke R&B first."

At the same time, he maintained that the hit songs he put his payola behind deserved their success. "They were hit records, man, and you can't buy a hit record. Really. If it's not a hit and the public don't want it, you can play the hell out of it, but it'll just pass. . . . But a hit record will stick, if you do all the right things to promote it, which is what we did in the 70s. They all stuck, man."

STEVE ALAIMO WAS A SINGER AND GUITAR PLAYER who combined teen-idol looks and star presence with a strong blue-eyed soul sensibility. Soon after he transferred to the University of Miami from Michigan in the late

The unprepossessing Hialeah building housing Henry Stone's Tone Distributors and the hit-making T.K. Productions. Photo © Larry Warmoth.

1950s, he and his band the Redcoats played weekend dances for Henry Stone, and Alaimo did some work at his Hialeah warehouse as well. "I picked up records and put them in piles and got orders out for the record stores," he says. "Henry paid me off not in money but in B. B. King albums. I had never heard of B. B. King. I grew up in Rochester, New York. There was Bobby Bland, too, Jimmy Reed, Jerry Butler. It was brilliant. Henry would give me those albums and say, 'These are $3.98. Here, you get ten albums, that's $39.' I didn't realize they were budget albums and they were really only worth 80 cents."

After roughly a decade performing and hosting Dick Clark's TV show *Where the Action Is*, Alaimo decided to become a producer and apprenticed himself to Stone. "Henry introduced me to everyone, including Ewart Abner from Vee Jay and Lew Chudd from Imperial," he says. "These were the real pioneers of the business, and Henry Stone was at the helm because he was their distributor. He taught me everything about the business, which was very difficult. It's really a ruthless business."

Alaimo, twenty years younger than Stone, eventually became a true producing partner and vice president of T.K. Productions. The name of T.K.'s Alston label came from the combination of Alaimo and Stone. At times Alaimo's work called for him to play good cop to Stone's bad. "Henry had a reputation that wasn't always rosy, to be honest," Alaimo says, explaining that Stone was known to get the best of the deals he was a party to. "Some people loved him and some people didn't like him. But Henry was smart enough to say, 'I don't need anybody to like me.'"

As Alaimo remembers it, John Lomelo, the manager of Sam and Dave in their early, Miami, days, "brought them to me to record some songs. They had been on a show with me. [Moore remembers this show and says it was a disaster, that the sock-hop audience only had eyes for Alaimo.] I said, 'I'd like to produce them,' and he goes, 'Yes, you can produce them but I don't want anything to do with Henry Stone.' I said, 'Don't worry about Henry Stone.'

"So I called Henry and said, 'These guys are great, but he doesn't want to do anything with you.' He says, 'Don't worry about it. I don't have to know—I don't know from nothing. If you think they're good, do it.' So we made the records and [at first] [Lomelo] didn't know Henry was involved. Of course, Henry was paying for the sessions." (When Lomelo found out, the Moores say, he hit the roof, wrested the duo and their masters away from Stone, and took the act to Roulette and Morris Levy.)

In later years, Alaimo said, "Henry gave interviews and said how he discovered Sam and Dave. One day he called me up and said, 'Steve, I told somebody I discovered Sam and Dave. Back me up.'" Alaimo did.

"Henry's contracts could certainly be one-sided," says a former business associate. "But if you signed it, he stuck to the terms of that contract." In at least one instance, says Alaimo, an artist produced by Stone thought they sold enormously more records than they actually had and concluded that Stone had been cheating them on royalties. "But it wasn't true."

Timmy Thomas, who worked for Stone as a promotions man in addition to recording for him, is even-handed in his assessment. "When I think about Henry Stone and all the years I've known him, I look at reality," he says, citing the release of his classic "Why Can't We Live Together." "This was in the disco era, remember," Thomas says, "but Henry [saw] that my song was something totally different: a world record, a message record. And if it were not for Henry Stone, nobody would have heard it." (See chapter 17 for the full story of Thomas' remarkably enduring song.) Thomas says the same dynamic applies to many of Stone's other artists, whether or not they acknowledge it: Stone got them and their music heard, and they had their success through him.

As a producer and owner, Stone said, his role was similar to that of a casting director in movies. "I would get the musicians together, cast the project, and pick the material. If the artist was not a songwriter, I would try to pick the material that would be good for them. I would get them into the studio, rehearse them, and do all the dirty work. Listening to the songs, going over the titles. . . . Those records never went out until I finished doing my job. All these records you see on the wall here? They had to go through Henry Stone as a record owner, as a producer."

In Alaimo's assessment, though, Stone was, at least some of the time, less hands-on and more of a big-picture facilitator. "Henry was a great idea man," Alaimo says. "He knew to hire the right guy and let him work." Besides Alaimo, another of the "right guys" Stone brought in to produce for him was Willie Clarke, co-founder, with Johnny Pearsall, of the Deep City label. As detailed in a preceding chapter, they, along with songwriter and producer Clarence Reid, were the first to record Betty Wright, and Clarke became a key engineer and producer for Stone at T.K. Recalling the help Stone gave him and Pearsall back in those Deep City days, Clarke calls Stone "the real father in my life when it comes to my music."

After the Deep City principals discovered singer Betty Wright, she recorded her first album (with Reid on piano) for Stone at fourteen. "Girls Can't Do What the Guys Do" was the most prominent song on that album, which came out on the Atlantic subsidiary Atco. When her biggest hit, "Clean Up Woman," came out on Alston in 1971 she was not yet eighteen. The song was cowritten and coproduced by Reid and Clarke: "*A clean up woman, is a woman who / gets all the love we girls leave behind.*"

At this point Wright had not yet developed or exploited her multioctave range, heard most vividly on songs such as "No Pain No Gain." "I don't think she even knew she had that range back then," says Alaimo. "But you can hear the talent just exploding out of her." The lyrics ruefully concluded: "*Jumping slick was my ruin / 'Cause I found out all I was doin' / Was makin' it easy for the Clean Up Woman / to get my baby's love, oh yeah.*"

"It was a simple little raggedy record," Alaimo says. "We made it on a two-track tape. Clarke and Reid wrote a great groove. We made groove records; when you heard them, you felt good. And Betty just got it right in the pocket."

Wright's gold record—at the time, that meant one million singles sold—launched her long and successful career. "When you pick the five greatest [female] R&B singers, Betty would be one of them," Alaimo continues (though he goes on to name only four). "Aretha's the best that ever did it. I think you have to put Christina Aguilera in there. You have got to put Mariah Carey in there and Betty Wright. I'm talking about her vocal ability, her songwriting, her stage presence, her showmanship." Other than that, he laughs, she is really nothing special.

"Clean Up Woman" is two minutes and forty-six seconds of classic soul. Like all classics, including prose, it seems wholly original and yet inevitable at the same time. Alaimo is asked what his contribution was to that particular session. "I got out of the way," he says. "When it works, it works."

IN THE LATE 1960S AND EARLY 1970S Miami-born Harry Wayne Casey was working at a record store there and would go by Stone's warehouse in Hialeah to pick up inventory. Casey began hanging out there after work, answering the phone—"no one else would ever answer it," he says—and even taking out the trash. In between that and chatting with the T.K. regulars, he'd fool around on the piano in Stone's back room and in the studio upstairs. (At one point, Stone said, Floridians and future Allman Brothers Duane and Gregg were broke and living up there while they worked with Steve Alaimo, but their music "didn't impress me that much.")

Casey originally hoped to meet songwriter/producer Clarence Reid there and possibly write songs with him, but Reid never seemed to show up. After Casey ingratiated himself, Stone gave him a key and let him and Rick Finch, a bass player who worked in the recording studio, experiment and write songs together after hours. "They were messing around with island music," Stone remembered. "Not pure island music; there was R&B involved, but they had the bass rhythms that I like. I had had a hit with 'Funky Nassau,' the first island music I did, and I was just hoping they would come up with some more hits like that." Beginning in 1973, they did, launching Stone's biggest act, the interracial KC and the Sunshine Band. (KC is a derivative of Casey; for more on him and the Band, see chapter 20.)

In just over two years, beginning in the spring of 1975 and ending in summer 1977, the Band had four #1 R&B hits, three of which, along with "I'm Your Boogie Man," went to #1 pop. Stone laughed remembering the anxious discussion in a staff meeting after the acetate, a preliminary version, of one of those songs played. The concern wasn't about the music but about the title: "(Shake, Shake, Shake) Shake Your Booty." In those pre–hip-hop days, some felt that was too risqué. "They said, 'You can't put that record out!'" Stone said. "I said, 'Come on, this is America!'" As it turned out, America was happy to hear it, and to shake it.

Casey/KC left T.K. in 1980; he felt the company was not making him enough of a priority. But, he says, that didn't change his regard for Stone, who he considers "like a father. Business is business. I had to move on. That had nothing to do with my feelings for Henry."

It's impossible to tell how much payola—"or promotion," as Stone called it—influenced T.K. Productions' success, and it's probably useless to speculate. What is clear from a thirty-year remove is that Stone and his cohorts produced captivating music, a classic soul repertoire rivaling anything other studios, including Stax and Motown, produced. As with the Funk Brothers at Motown, Booker T & the MGs at Stax, and the Memphis Horns (Stax and Hi Records), T.K.'s cadre of musicians, producers, and songwriters created a distinct, proprietary Miami sound. That sound, ubiquitous in the 1970s, was less pretty and polished than Motown's—funkier might be a good way to describe it. In one minor difference, T.K.'s soul music dispensed with the tambourine, that vestige of the black church, heard so often in Motown's. (For more on T.K.'s musical family, see chapter 15.)

Conversely T.K.'s soul was slicker than Stax's heartfelt, overtly emotional southern version. What made T.K. unique probably had more to do with irresistible songs—lyrically and, especially, rhythmically—than singers. Unlike Stax, home to Otis Redding, Sam and Dave, and other iconic, instantly recognizable singers, Stone and Alaimo really only had one spectacular vocalist: Betty Wright.

Due to Stone's ear and Miami's location, some T.K. work also showed Caribbean influences other labels didn't share. The Sunshine Band's sound was originally derived from Bahamian junkanoo music, and "Funky Nassau"—along with the group that performed it, the Beginning of the End—were Bahamian, imported by Stone. T-Connection, also from the Bahamas, had a hit with "Do What You Wanna Do" on Stone's Dash label, and "Calypso Breakdown" was a long (almost eight minutes) 1976 dance-jam led by percussionist Ralph MacDonald, whose family had roots in Trinidad and Tobago.

"We had a unique sound," says Alaimo. "Like Count Basie had a sound or Jimmy Dorsey had a sound, no matter who the musicians were or the arrangers. Ours was a mixture of rock and roll and R&B and Latin and Cuban music. Afro-Cuban is a big deal and we have them both here: We had Africans and we had Cubans."

What was the rock and roll component in T.K.'s Miami sound? "Bass lines," Alaimo says. "Take 'Get Down Tonight'—you can tell that's a white boy playing a bass line. There's a different beat. It's an off-beat." A white boy off-beat? "That's what I'm saying."

Since its demise "disco" has become something of a dirty word, including to soul purists. Stone didn't like to call his 1970s hits by that name, preferring "dance records." But he still claimed credit for breaking what he calls "the first real worldwide dance hit that began the disco era," referring to George McCrae singing "Rock Your Baby" in 1974. (Some say the Hues Corporation's "Rock the Boat," released earlier that year on RCA, should have that distinction.) Stone did have two songs, KC's "Boogie Shoes," and "Calypso Breakdown," on the soundtrack album from the 1977 movie and disco landmark "Saturday Night Fever." He also cut more than one hundred 12-inch or extended-play singles, a dance-club staple, so he was implicated in disco in that way as well.

In an important distinction from much disco music, the T.K. musicians, including drummers Robert Ferguson and Robert Johnson, aka Shotgun, actually played their instruments rather than relying on synthesizers and drum machines. In a 2013 post on his authoritative *long play miami* blog, Alberto de la Portilla wrote of "Rock Your Baby" that "the signature open hi-hat drum beat produced a chi-kee-chi-kee rhythm that would become a staple of dance music from Madonna to 90s house music." Occasionally Timmy Thomas would add drum patterns he programmed on his Hammond B-3 to the T.K. mix, but with the exception of his solo hit, "Why Can't We Live Together," they rarely if ever replaced actual drummers. For the sake of specificity, and to avoid any latent disco toxicity, the T.K. music of the mid-to-late 1970s should probably have its own category or label. Here, then, this important body of Florida work will be called "dance soul."

Like the MGs and Memphis Horns, the T.K. house band and producing family was integrated. One regular bass player, Ron Bogdon, was white, as Alaimo notes; Chocolate Perry, the other stalwart, was black. The cohort was "mixed" in another way as well: Though some, including Willie Clarke, were formally trained musicians, quite a few others, Perry among them, could not read musical notation. Trained B-3 organ player Timmy Thomas and keyboard/piano player Benny Latimore, who does not read, often played together and complemented each other. "Benny is bluesier, and he can do things I can't do," said Thomas.

"Chemistry" and "alchemy" are oft-used terms when describing the magic—there's another one—of collaborative music-making. Yet they seem quite appropriate here, along with another mysterious element often cited when histories of hits are written: serendipity. In 1974 George Mc-Crae drove down from West Palm Beach to T.K. to pick up his wife, Gwen, who was cutting some songs for Stone (and would have a major dance soul hit with "Rockin' Chair" the following year). As was common, she was still there at 2 a.m. when Casey and Finch came down from the studio to play a music track they were excited about for Stone. "I agreed with them that they had something," Stone said, "but that it needed lyrics [and] I was trying to figure out who should record it. The song was written too high for Casey."

In walked George, who had a fairly high voice and had sung some background there. "After about an hour," Stone said, "they came down from the studio with a finished take." In the liner notes to his "Heart of Stone" compilation the producer claims that "Rock Your Baby," featuring McCrae's falsetto runs, topped the British charts as well as both U.S. ones and eventually sold 6.5 million copies in fifty-four countries. (It was definitely #1 on the U.S. R&B and pop charts.) Stone also noted with glee at one point that the song was cut for something like $15–20, paid to Jerome Smith, the guitarist on the session and an original member of the Sunshine Band. Everyone else was on staff, salaried.

The talent amassed at T.K. was extraordinary. One of the quirkiest such talents was the late Clarence Reid, who charted singing his own composition "Dancing with Nobody But You" on Stone's Alston label in 1969 but whose primary and most valuable roles were as songwriter and producer. As discussed in previous chapters Reid worked with both Stone and Clarke when the latter was still at Deep City and then continued those collaborations at T.K. (He later created the bizarre and long-lived persona of Blowfly, an utterly obscene rapper.) Reid also brought Rick Finch, a founding partner in KC and the Sunshine Band, to Stone's attention. By some accounts he encouraged Casey to experiment with Bahamian junkanoo music, which was integral to that band's sound and appeal. Steve Alaimo goes so far as to say that Reid "was in many ways the guiding force for Henry and me."

Even with Stone's ear, and the combined instincts of Alaimo, Reid, and Clarke—plus all the talent in Miami and elsewhere willing to record for their labels—breakout songs remained elusive. "If you think about it, KC and Betty Wright were the only ones that we had repeat, really big hits on," Alaimo says. They developed an in-house testing method for material they thought had hit potential. "We'd bring the record to 10 people who worked there, like the secretaries," Alaimo says. "If everybody liked the record, it became a hit. If just one of those people said, 'Ah, it's not bad,' it wasn't. Nine-to-one wasn't good enough."

SOON AFTER CASEY AND HIS SUNSHINE BAND LEFT, in the early 1980s, T.K. Productions went bankrupt. Stone blames it on disco, or his association with it. A backlash—the rallying cries were "death to disco" and "disco sucks"—was already underway, most notoriously between games of a 1979 Chicago White Sox doubleheader, when a crate of records was blown up and the field damaged by near-rioting fans. The DJ character on the popular CBS sitcom "WKRP in Cincinnati began wearing a Disco Sucks T-shirt. On television, *60 Minutes* did an earnest, Dan Rather–led explanation of the disco phenomenon, which meant that it was near death or at least uncool after just three or four dominant years.

One of KC's last songs for Stone, the ballad "Please Don't Go," had been on the pop charts for twenty-six weeks and reached #1; Stone remembers that Bobby Caldwell's 1978 song "What You Won't Do for Love" had just been a huge success as well. But when his bankers heard all the dire pronouncements and disco animus, Stone said, they canceled the loans they had agreed to, and his business collapsed. He even lost $700,000 that his own publishing company, Sherlyn, owed him, which he had plowed back into T.K. At some point there was a warehouse fire, and valuable master recordings were destroyed.

Afterward Stone went into business with Morris Levy of Roulette Records for a while and had some success with a New York rap group called Newcleus ("I Wanna Be a B-Boy"). After forming another company of his own, Hot Productions, he produced Latin freestyle records, the rap duo Gucci Crew II, and some "Miami bass" 12-inches for the female duo L' Trimm. (In the late 1980s Stone's son Joe created and Henry recorded a rap parody group based on the controversial 2 Live Crew, which he called 2 Live Jews.)

In 1990 he sold all T.K.'s remaining assets to Rhino, the reissue specialist. Afterward he continued to put out records in Miami under the auspices of Henry Stone Music: new material by Latimore; vintage Joe Tex; and other compilations and reissues, such as "Best of Little Beaver." Despite his disco denials, he put out seven volumes of "Twelve Inch Disco Classics" as well.

The late Henry Stone at his Miami home in 2013. Photo © Suzanne Williamson.

After he lost his sight, Stone got training at the Miami Lighthouse and later made a gift of the Henry & Inez Stone Music and Sound Studio there, which opened in 2007. He put out his payola opus just a year and a half before his death and continued to produce—and hold forth about music and the music industry—until very near the end, in August 2014. "Now we're back to a singles business, with the [digital] downloads," he observed at one late juncture. "It's back where it was when I started." Stone did get to see the documentary on him, *Record Man*, which did not formally debut until after his death.

Stone's taking a percentage of the (mythical) *Florida Soul* book profits was initially discussed in a phone call. Later, it came up again in person, in his Grove Isle living room. "There's no ego talk here," he said forcefully. "Soul music in Florida was all me. The only thing all of these hits have in common is Henry Stone, with 25 gold records—more, I don't even know. The Miami sound, before Gloria and Emilio Estefan did their Latin Miami sound, was created right here in Hialeah and our records were #1 all over the world."

All that will be acknowledged, he was told. Without a doubt, his imprint and his sensibility are all over, and inseparable from, this rich musical heritage.

"I like the way you said that," he responded immediately. "My imprint, the heritage—keep that in the book."

15

The Miami Sound

Little Beaver, Chocolate Perry, and the T.K. Family

As the Funk Brothers were to Motown and Booker T & the MGs were to Stax, the house band at Henry Stone's Hialeah headquarters was vital to the studio's sound and to its success. In the 1970s, virtually all T.K. Productions' hits on Stone's various labels (and the music that did not sell as well, for that matter) featured the same group of studio regulars. The core group included: Latimore and Timmy Thomas on keyboards; Little Beaver (Willie Hale) on guitar; either Ron Bogdon or Chocolate Perry on bass; and Robert Ferguson or "Shotgun," aka Robert Johnson, on drums. Singers Betty Wright, Gwen McCrae, and George McCrae alternately sang leads and backed up the others vocally, as did Latimore. In the middle of that decade Sunshine Band principals KC and Rick Finch took their places there as well.

Late in the 1970s and into the 1980s Gloria and Emilio Estefan became known for their Latin dance/pop music, which was dubbed "the Miami Sound." (Their group went by the Miami Sound Machine.) But Timmy Thomas maintains, with good reason: "We were the original Miami sound."

Unlike the Funk Brothers, sidemen whose excellence in anonymity formed the basis for a 2002 documentary, *Standing in the Shadows of Motown*, many members of the T.K. ensemble were stars in their own rights, who had records released under their own names. (One exception was house horn and string arranger and tenor sax player Mike Lewis, who, like most arrangers, remained anonymous. For more on his contributions and the arranger's art, see chapter 20). "A lot of us had hits and we used to sing and play on each other's records," says Latimore. "I played keyboards on

KC, Gwen McCrae ("Rockin' Chair"), and her then-husband George McCrae ("Rock Your Baby") lay down vocals in the T.K. studio, circa 1975. Photo © Larry Warmoth.

practically all Betty Wright's early stuff, and for Gwen McRae, Little Beaver—all of them. Timmy did, too, as well as his own music."

"We didn't have a whole lot of rivalry among us," Latimore continues. "Everybody rooted for everybody else. I might be out there [at T.K.'s Hialeah HQ] and somebody says, 'Hey man, come and play on this,' or 'Help me sing a little background on that,' and I'd say, 'Okay, sure.'" Perry, who also produced at T.K., starting when he was just eighteen or nineteen, remembers their collaborations in much the same way. "We were a family," he says in a *Florida Soul* interview, "so you could tell somebody to sing this or play that without the ego trip."

To Perry the fact that the T.K. regulars were "name artists" actually led to fewer conflicts, not more. They grew up together and were secure enough in their talents and the progress of their careers to support one another. "Everyone's a star in the room," Perry remembers. "But I see people telling Betty Wright what to sing. Clarence Reid walks in and tells Latimore what to play. I thought—'Hold up, Benny Latimore, you're telling *him* what to play? You're telling *Little Beaver*, 'Don't do that, do this'? But hey, all right then, now I feel comfortable doing that myself."

Latimore, Beaver, and the other T.K. stalwarts all seemed to know how to "play what was needed, and *only* what was needed," says bass man Perry. "They'd come in and play parts on the songs I was producing that I would automatically love. That happened a lot, because all the musicians were the same time after time. We knew each other's rhythms, what we liked and didn't like—we kind of knew each other's souls."

This group almost never performed together outside of the studio, and when T.K. went under in 1981 they went their separate ways. Twenty years later, though, Betty Wright reached back and got the band back together. She'd become the vocal coach for young—as in sixteen—British soul singer Joss Stone and was coproducing an album for her.

"Betty called me," Thomas remembers, "and asked, 'Timmy, you game for this?' I immediately said yes."

Latimore also remembers getting his Wright call. "Betty told me there's this young white girl from England, she's very talented, and they want to do a thing like we did at T.K. years ago where we're all together, playing everything live, not programming, no sequencing." Wright, her sister Jeannette, and Gwen McCrae were going to sing backup on the CD. (It's not clear that McCrae ended up doing that.) "I didn't know who Joss Stone was at that time," he continues. "Nobody did. And you know, I don't play on anybody's records anymore." But then Wright told him: "I got Beaver, and Timmy."

"I said, 'You got Beaver? I haven't talked to Beaver in 20 years.' I'd seen Timmy maybe 10 years before that," Latimore remembers. "I didn't even ask Betty how much it was gonna pay, I just said: 'Count me in.'"

That record, *The Soul Sessions*, a collection of covers, is easily Stone's best work. Even Latimore was impressed by the young singer: "I told her she was a reincarnation of an old black man." On "Super Duper Love," Stone is heard urging the T.K. guitarist to solo, singing *"Play it for me, Little Beaver."* He complies, adding a few short runs that are both stinging and sweet—nothing spectacular, technique-wise, but that fit just right.

Latimore and Timmy Thomas are the subjects of their own *Florida Soul* chapters, as is Henry Stone. Betty Wright, unfortunately, declined through a representative to be interviewed for this book. Here, then, are short profiles of two other lynchpin T.K. artists: Little Beaver and George "Chocolate" Perry.

LITTLE BEAVER

His stepfather's box guitar just stood there, leaning up against the wall. The older man meant to learn how to play it, to strum with his gospel group in Forrest City, Arkansas, but he never seemed to get around to it. So young Willie Hale began plucking on it. He was already nicknamed Little Beaver, due to the configuration of his front teeth. A local man who went by Sarge showed the youngster some fingering and other basics. Then Beaver learned the three-chord blues progression and, the guitarist said, "For about a month, I thought I was a master."

Still playing in a bluesy style while developing his own R&B approach, Hale moved to Florida in 1963. There he became, in the words of authoritative Miami music blogger Alberto de la Portilla, "arguably the most important and accomplished R&B guitarist of Miami's soul scene of the 60s and early 70s." Little Beaver's work, de la Portilla writes, "can be heard on almost every Miami 60s/early 70s soul and funk record that was worth a dime." (Hale/Beaver could not be interviewed for the *Florida Soul* project.)

Little Beaver recorded singles and albums as a leader and notched five chart-making R&B hits from 1972 to 1976, all on Stone's Cat label. But his most important and enduring work was done as part of the T.K. studio band, from roughly 1970 to 1980. "Beaver's an outstanding guitar player," said Latimore, "and he had a real knack for coming up with great licks just like that," meaning quickly and spontaneously.

His best-known licks are those heard on the 1971 Betty Wright song, "Clean Up Woman." It begins with a chorded guitar riff in a 3–2 rhythm, evoking the five-beat clave pattern essential to salsa and other Afro-Cuban music. "The Latin flavor was something I picked up on in Miami," the Arkansan told the *Miami New Times*. "It has that African in it, so it was already in me. But when I hear it, it inspires me."

That opening riff is then joined by and intertwined with a lower, contrapuntal looping lick, operating like a bass line though it was produced on guitar. (Renowned finger-picking guitarist Leo Kottke used these opening chords and rhythmic vamp as the basis for a song on his 1986 album *A Shot Toward Noon*. He titled it "Little Beaver.") After two cycles of those lines, the Mike Lewis–arranged horns kick in, followed by the eighteen-year-old Wright's vocals. All told, it's perhaps the finest example of the T.K. ensemble at work together. The single just missed being a #1 R&B hit, reaching #2, and "Clean Up Woman" reached #6 on the pop chart. "Without a doubt," Henry Stone said, "it was Little Beaver, with his distinctive bass and two-string guitar riffs that helped tremendously in catapulting this single to gold status."

Was the in-house guitar wizard really that important? "No, Beaver wasn't 'important,'" contradicts T.K. producer Steve Alaimo. "He made the whole record."

Beaver, as everyone still refers to him, first came to Florida City, where he played at the Lucy Street Bar. He got his break at the Knight Beat club in the Sir John Hotel, playing and singing James Brown's "Please Please Please" to win a talent contest MC'd by DJ Butterball of local station WMBM. That led to his hiring by Frank Duboise and his Chicken Scratchers (with whom Latimore also worked). They held down the Tiki Club in Coconut Grove for some time; then, at nineteen, the guitarist joined trumpeter Frank Williams and the Rocketeers. De la Portilla calls the Rocketeers "the 'it' band of Miami's soul scene, heard day and night from Coconut Grove to Liberty City. . . . They backed up just about every artist that rolled through [the] Overtown club scene and recorded on their own as well." (The Rocketeers' drummer was Robert Ferguson, who would later be a T.K. regular.)

Joey Gilmore, the guitarist Beaver replaced in the Rocketeers, may have exaggerated when he told *Living Blues* magazine that in the 1960s and 1970s, South Florida was such a musical hotbed, "there was a club on every corner." Regardless of their exact numbers, however, many of those clubs held guitar rivals for the new arrival. One of the top dogs, Beaver remembered, was Stan the Man, who dominated Liberty City. Luckily, Stan and his brother, who played bass, were "really into hot cars, and racing cars," Beaver said. "So they wasn't full-fledged into the music. There was also Treetop. He was a big-time guy; reminded me of Chuck Berry. He was a solo artist, he always traveled alone."

Frank Williams encouraged him to sing, but Beaver's strength remained his idiosyncratic, crowd-pleasing guitar style. He didn't read music though he would learn to identify and play chords. Back in Arkansas, he'd played with a "clamp" or a capo, moving it on the fretboard to play in different keys with the same fingering. Without that device, he said, "you gotta finger it. That was hard. I didn't have them big buttermilk fingers like BB King. I couldn't reach the bass [the lowest-strung string, the top E]." He devised a way of reaching around the back of the neck with his thumb to dampen that E string—and at times, seemingly, the A string beneath it as well—instead of extending his fingers upward on the front of the fretboard. As many other memorable artists have done, he turned a disadvantage—or, the workaround for that disadvantage—into his own distinctive technique.

"There's only a few people that play with their thumb on the bass," he told de la Portilla, "and most of them came through me."

Beaver caught the ear of producer Willie Clarke, who brought him to T.K. "Beaver had a groovy overtone," Clarke says. "His guitar had more feeling in his notes and his chords had more of a voice." At T.K. Beaver recorded "Joey," a bluesy unfaithful-woman lament he wrote that reached #48 on the R&B chart.

Two years later Beaver heard a TV commercial, "one of those island commercials, like Jamaica [or] Tahiti, you know, with the girl in a little [bathing] suit with her hair hanging and it was like, *ting-tun-ting-tuun* . . . *ting-ku-ku-kun ting-tun* . . . over and over, and I said man, 'That's soothing.'" He had also been impressed by Marvin Gaye's "What's Goin' On," "which was different for R&B at the time with its rhythms and percussions," Beaver said. "So I started to put that together, and I came up with 'Party Down.'"

Beaver's playing, mostly in the guitar's higher range, sounds brittle and has some bite to it. Overall, though, it's a mellow midtempo groove record—so relaxed, it seems, that it can barely be bothered to change chords. "*Everybody have big fun, party down,*" he sings. "*Let the good times roll, you only got one time around / so make looooove together.*"

It sounds, as Beaver says it was, like it was written while the creators were, yes, partying. In fact the lyrics and music were born of and meant to evoke a marijuana haze and what he describes as a mellower, "carefree" era in 1970s Miami. "You could smoke all the weed you want and not worry about gettin' arrested, or gettin' stopped on the highway with the police searching you," he told the *New Times*. When he walked with his guitar to a regular gig at the Mr. James club on NW 2nd Avenue and 36th Street, he said, policemen who knew him would stop and give him a ride. "That's how cool it was back in the 60s and 70s," he maintained. "You didn't worry. Nobody was gettin' robbed and shot. There was no AKs [AK-47s]."

At times he doubles his guitar lines with his own vocals, singing the same notes in unison, as jazz guitarist and pop vocalist George Benson would later do on songs like "This Masquerade." "Party Down" lazed its way to #2 R&B in the fall of 1974 and lingered carefree on that chart for nineteen weeks.

As hit singles did in those days, that called for an album in a hurry, also called *Party Down*, which came out on Cat the same year. (Two of the seven cuts were versions of that song.) Latimore "played the keys and held it together for me," Beaver said. "Yeah, Lat was the man."

Little Beaver (Willie Hale). Courtesy of T.K. Productions.

Chocolate Perry played bass on all but one cut. On "I Can Dig It, Baby," that role was filled by twenty-year-old future jazzman and electric bass innovator Jaco Pastorius, best known for his work with Weather Report. According to Henry Stone, *New Times* writer Jacob Katel, and others, Pastorius so admired the self-taught Beaver that he used to hang out at the T.K. studio to see what the guitarist would come up with—and how he'd accomplish it. Author and Florida music expert Jeff Lemlich posts on his *Savage Lost* site that Pastorius played on Beaver's 1972 cut "Funkadelic Sound," the B-side of "Joey."

Today Beaver remains a cult figure among guitarists, and to soul fanatics. That mythic status is deserved and probably enhanced by his withdrawal from public musical life. After T.K. Records disintegrated at the beginning of the 1980s Beaver got a job, as Willie Hale, with Miami-Dade Transit, and worked there for thirty years, according to fellow musicians and published reports. He came out of retirement briefly in 2003 to join his former colleagues backing up Joss Stone on the *Soul Sessions* album. (The ensemble also reunited for Stone's next album, *Mind, Body & Soul*.) When that first album did well, the band, billed as the Miami All Stars, went to New York to appear on Conan O'Brian's TV show and play a gig at Manhattan's Joe's Pub. But, Latimore says, Beaver wouldn't accompany them. "He said, 'That part of my life is over,'" his colleague remembers. When Alfredo de la Portilla interviewed him at his home in Opa-Locka in 2014, Beaver got out a red Gibson at one point to demonstrate a technique. When he did, the writer noticed that the black guitar case had dust over the top, suggesting it hadn't been played in some time.

Around the time he emerged for *The Soul Sessions*, two Beaver songs were sampled by the L.A. hip-hop group People Under the Stairs; the cuts were entitled "Suite For Beaver, Parts 1 and 2." More than thirty years after it was initially released, Jay Z sampled his 1974 song "Get into the Party Life" on his 2007 *American Gangster* album. Beaver said he found out about it while checking entries on himself on Wikipedia. "I didn't have a clue who Jay Z was." (Jacob Katel of the *New Times* wrote that Beaver later got paid $60,000 for that sample.)

He may well have become a master, as he briefly, mistakenly, thought he was when he learned that I–IV–V progression back in Arkansas. Yet Beaver maintained that "it wasn't my goal to become some type of great guitar player." As he explained, he'd quit school in the tenth grade and music "was about all I could do. I didn't have no other trade, and I didn't go to school for music. I was fortunate to have creativity and talent to where people said, 'Oh, that's great!'" But to him, "I was just doing my thing."

CHOCOLATE PERRY

Latimore gave him the name. "I'm a kid," the bass player remembers, a half-century later. "I just turned 18 years old, and 21 is the legal age to be in clubs. So when Benny asked me to play behind him at the Castaways, I tried to dress the part." Perry wore an Afro wig, which for some reason he thought made him look older, and platform shoes to make himself taller. "I worked there with him for three years." (A photo of the underage Perry in his grown-up guise can be seen in chapter 18.)

One late night when the place wasn't too full, Latimore decided to introduce the band. He called guitarist Warren Thompson by his nickname, Roach. Freddy Scott, the drummer, was FDS. Then he got to George Perry and, at first, didn't have a clever name to call him by.

"I like chocolate candy, a lot," Perry laughs, in his home studio in Miami's Little Haiti neighborhood. "My teeth are gone now because of that. I always had a Mr. Goodbar, Hershey's kisses or Hershey's bar on me at all times. Latimore looked at me and says: 'I know what to call you . . . ladies and gentlemen this is Sweet Chocolate on bass.' It stuck. I asked him to drop the 'Sweet,' 'cause people were thinking the wrong thing, so he did. Everyone just called me Chocolate."

"I'll tell you, though, later on I worked with Robin Gibb of the Bee Gees for almost 30 years and he wouldn't call me Chocolate. He thought they were calling me Chocolate because I was black and that it was degrading and racist. Even after he knew what it was about, he refused to call me Chocolate his entire life."

Like many of his colleagues at T.K., Perry couldn't read music. But he could do bodywork on GM and Pontiac cars; program computers; platform dive; and fly planes (Perry took lessons in high school). Most importantly, he could play the electric bass like very few others. Henry Stone, an erstwhile jazz man and soul/funk specialist, described him as "one of the top two or three bass players in the world."

The most exceptional thing about Perry and his career, though, is likely that he played great bass in soul music—*and* did as well if not better in other, disparate genres. During and after his T.K. tenure he toured extensively with Stephen Stills, Crosby, Stills, and Nash, and Joe Walsh, recording with them as well as other hugely successful acts, including John Cougar (Mellencamp) and the Bee Gees. When the Gibb brothers were producing other artists in their Miami studio, they called Perry to play with Dolly Parton, Kenny Rogers, and Dionne Warwick, among others. Perry "got" Latin music as well, working with Jon Secada and Gloria Estefan. It seems, as he says, that "everyone wanted a piece of Chocolate."

Discogs.com, a reliable discography site, lists him playing on eighty-eight albums. A tall man of sixty with his hair in dreads at the time of this *Florida Soul* interview, Perry says he thinks that's about right, but that they missed a few. He also produced twenty-some albums, including those by T.K. artists Lynn Williams, Miami, Raw Soul Express, and the Blue Notes in the mid-1970s; reggae artist King Sporty; and jazz singer Bobby Caldwell. His most recent producing credits include a Gwen McCrae album in 2006 and three by old pal Latimore, for Henry Stone Music. "I'm playing bass, drums, guitar, and some piano, all on my keyboard and computer programs," Perry says. "I even did some horns on those, 'cause we didn't have [arranger] Mike Lewis anymore. I've got a unique way of doing them too. Everybody asks me: 'How you get them horns?' Well, I'm not gonna tell them."

Roach Thompson has known Perry since the beginning, when the guitarist and underage bassist both worked with Benny Latimore and the Kinfolk at the Castaways. "Chocolate is one of the baddest bass players I ever played with," he says. "He just has a natural feel; he just lays it in the pocket and you can't help but play great. Every time I've needed a bass player for my groups I've looked for another Chocolate—and I never found one."

Growing up in Hollywood, Florida, young George started out on six-string guitar. Lessons lasted about five days until he realized: "Wait a minute, you're not teaching me what I want to know. I want to know how to play in a soul band, how to play Aretha Franklin. I wanted to play songs, not notes. All that "da da da da, Every Good Boy Does Fine, who cares?" (Erstwhile music students may remember that the mnemonic device Every Good Boy Does Fine identifies the lines in the musical staff. Extra credit for knowing that the spaces in the staff spell out F-A-C-E from the bottom up).

So he practiced on his own, learning by ear. His mother sang around the house constantly; dad played saxophone; and an uncle had a soul band. "So music was all around me, big-time." His father showed him the basic boogie-woogie bass line, which made a deep imprint on the young guitarist. At thirteen or so, he formed a band with friends and a cousin: Mike

Chocolate Perry on bass at T.K., circa 1975. Photo © Larry Warmoth.

Washington and the Soulsters. In the mid-1960s it was still possible to rent out the local firehouse for dances and charge admission, and they played gigs at the local elementary school, Carver Ranches.

All the time, though, he had his eye on Poo Poo. That was the bass player in the group, real name Joe Monk. "I used to watch him playing bass with his thumb, and I always got interested—'How'd you do that?' It was very intriguing that you could play just four strings and, you were the center of the band, actually. Then Poo Poo got drafted to the army, and I switched from rhythm guitar player to bass."

Washington, who was older, somehow got them a recording gig. The studio was at Tone Distributors, which like most things in musical Miami, belonged to Henry Stone. When they were recording in the little corner room upstairs, Steve Alaimo, Stone's producer and VP, stopped in. After the session, Alaimo came up to Perry and told him, "You oughta come by here once in a while; sometimes we need a bass player."

After a year and a half passed, Perry drove by the studio one day, "just out of curiosity. I parked in front of the studio where all the musicians were hanging out. They used to come by whether they were [booked to work] that day or not. And it just so happened they needed a bass player to do a session for Clarence Reid. So I went in there, and Reid put this paper in front of me—the chord changes—and said 'I want you play this bass line like this.' Then he hummed that line, and it was easy for me. I added a little bit to it and he said, 'Yeah, that's it, do that!' So we did the song and then he told me to come back tomorrow; he had five more songs to record."

Taking his place in the house band at seventeen (fellow bass player Ron Bogdon was still doing sessions as well) he learned a lot from the older Miami regulars, he says, including "not to overplay. The groove is there if you just leave it alone. Don't try to fill every space. Leave some to be imagined. Sometimes playing nothing is better than playing something. It's been said to me another way, too: 'What you don't play really counts.'"

One of the T.K. all-stars who took his turn as a leader—with Perry behind him—was guitarist/vocalist Little Beaver. "I had Chocolate Perry just kickin' it so hard on the bass," he said of his 1974 *Party Down* album. "The bass player is just as important as the drummer when it comes to backin' the guitar and keyboard. The bass and drummer coordinate together, they gotta just be one sound."

They'd usually cut between four and five songs a day, Perry says. One day in 1974 or 1975, Clarence Reid called the team together to do a song he and Willie Clarke had written and Gwen McCrae was singing, called "Rockin' Chair." (Clarke is credited as the producer.) After he came up with an innovative bass line, Perry says, "Clarence gave me a piece [of the songwriting credit] of the song and we got a gold record for it; mine is hanging on the wall right here."

Perry also studied electric bass player Willie Weeks, who may have rivaled Perry in working in rock and pop as well as soul. (He played with the Doobie Brothers, George Harrison, and Billy Joel, as well as Aretha Franklin, Etta James, and Bobby Womack.) Weeks came to Perry's attention through his solo on the Donny Hathaway song, "Voices Inside (Everything is Everything)" on his 1972 *Live* album. "I had to learn the entire solo because it was so intriguing," Perry says, "the triplets and everything. He took bass playing to school: He started from first grade and he went to college [on that solo], graduating into the more difficult parts. Only real bass players knew, and I learned it all, lick for lick."

Years later Perry was playing with Joe Walsh, who shared a bill with Boz Scaggs. Scaggs' bassist was Willie Weeks. "I walked up to him to meet him, he said to me, 'Are you Chocolate Perry? I've been listening to you for years.' My God, I didn't know what to say. I'd practically learned to play bass from this guy! I guess at that point I realized the level of bass player I was at."

Perry quickly became indispensable at T.K. One day he saw "Henry Stone and Steve Alaimo having a little conversation over in the corner, then they came over to me, handed me some keys, and he said: 'We think you can do well here, here's the keys, go ahead and produce your own songs and your own groups, do what you want.'"

"I got an office, I got a weekly salary—my first anywhere—of 350 bucks a week, and I started producing my own acts. Matter of fact, they gave me the Blue Notes when Harold Melvin left. I'm a kid and I'm smiling—I'm doing what I always wanted to do, playing bass and making music for a living."

Like all families, including surrogate ones, T.K. folks had their conflicts. But Perry says the loyalty and empathy were real and extended beyond the producing of music. "People understood if you were down, or had personal things going on. I got married at 18, married an Irish girl, and I'd just bought my first Corvette. So I'm riding around in the Corvette with the top down and a white girl in the car. Society didn't like us being together, and that weighed on us a lot. I had just bought my first house, too, and we had those payments. I wasn't home a lot, either; I was constantly at the studio. So I had my days when I felt like I just couldn't work, that I wasn't going to do well."

On those days the T.K. family was understanding, he says. Chocolate the bass player came to appreciate that; Chocolate Perry the producer adopted that stance as well. "It wasn't like, 'Man you got to get this done now; I don't care what your problem is.' We didn't live under that. Henry Stone made it very comfortable for all of us."

T.K. was the dominant Miami soul studio at the time, and Criteria, on NE 149th Street, was where much of Miami's rock production took place. (There was overlap; Aretha Franklin and Wilson Pickett recorded some of their best-known work at Criteria.) Someone at Criteria, now the Hit Factory, asked Alaimo for a bass recommendation, and he gave them

Chocolate. After that night session, Perry remembers, "Stephen Stills approached me; I had no idea who he was. This was when he was going solo, doing his *Illegal Stills* thing, around '75. He asked me to go on the road for 250 bucks and I said, 'Man that's kinda cheap, I can't go on the road for $250 a week.'"

Turned out Stills meant $250 a night, playing four nights a week. "Plus, $100 a day to eat, and your hotels paid, your travel is paid. And there are people to tune your guitar and take your amp for you, and all you have to do is get dressed and get on a plane and get on a stage." He went with it.

Perry continued to work at T.K. while his rock and pop portfolio expanded, from Stills to Al Kooper to Crosby, Stills, and Nash ("I spent 16 years with those guys," Perry says) to Jay Ferguson, to playing on Bee Gees–produced albums. "That became my lifestyle: answer the phone, go to T.K.; answer the phone, go to Criteria; answer the phone, go to another studio. People were passing my number around so I was getting calls from people who I had no idea of: 'Uh, Dion, sure, I'll come play for you.'"

"That was the big thing about me," Perry says: "I loved rock and roll, I loved country, I loved soul, I loved every kind of music I could hear, because I could see how to play it. When I hear a song on the radio, I know the part. I can see it; actually, I see it on the bass. I can mentally feel the notes, where he's going, and exactly how he did it."

"So after I hear a song once, I pick up the bass, and play it right the first time. They used to call me One-Take Chocolate, because, for instance, when Clarence Reid would hum me a part, he never had to hum it again. The other cats had to over-dub their parts but I'm already finished. I would go sit inside the control room and see what they're doing behind the board. I think that's how I really learned [engineering and producing]; they already liked my part so I'm behind the board, asking how do you do this and do that."

Perry came off the road for good in 1992, when his agoraphobia, which he'd lived with for many years, made traveling to perform untenable. Looking back, he credits his eclectic ear—and career—to Top 40 radio. "When I was coming up the stations we got—WQAM, WFUN, and WMBM was the black station—played all kinds of music; they'd play Aretha Franklin and then turn around and do the Rolling Stones, the Who, James Brown, then Carly Simon. So if you were a musician back then you learned a lot of genres, and of course Latin music was on Miami radio, too."

"Later it became very easy to understand what Stephen Stills wanted," he says, "or what the Bee Gees wanted. It seemed like I understood automatically the bass part for each one of those genres, and I actually believe it was from listening to all those different types of music on the radio growing up."

Perry acknowledges that back in those radio days he was a bit of a "strange kid, because I lived in a black neighborhood but I played everybody's music—loud. I had one of the first boom box vans, you know, loud trucks coming down the street. I had my bass amp in there, with three 18s [18-inch speakers] and I used to play Jimi Hendrix at 11."

As in his soul efforts, not reading notation actually benefited him when he worked in other genres, Perry maintains. Those artists and producers didn't care "because I introduced my own ideas to their songs. They'd put a chord sheet in front of me and I would add my own bass lines. I took what Clarence Reid taught me: I didn't play notes, I played *parts*. Other musicians might see an A written, and they hit an A. Well, I play *a groove in A*."

Usually he would change musical hats, Perry says, to play in different styles. Sometimes, though, a rock act would ask him to put some Chocolate funk into what they were doing. "So I would dip a little soul into it—but only at their request. It can be a different syncopated timing, or it could be extra notes or the choice of notes, more like what a Willie Weeks or James Jamerson at Motown would do. Or I might try to add a different texture to a chord, like working around in D if they are in A."

On the Crosby, Stills, and Nash classic "Southern Cross," Perry's bass is simple, played in the bass's lowest registers. When they were recording "Buying Time," though, Stephen Stills told him: "I want some funk on this." The tempo and rhythm are reminiscent of "Love the One You're With," and there's a similar-sounding high-pitched organ wailing during the intro. Perry's work here is still subtle, forming a fat bottom but relatively spare. At times, though, including at the turns from some verses into the next ones, Perry adds quick repeated sixteenth notes. Overall, he alternates sustained notes with rapid riffs, often jumping up an octave or two to create those accents, then back down. "I put so much funk into that song."

At some point he became able to identify written notes; say, a C or an E-flat. "But all those little dots with the little dashes and the little flags and staph lines? Forget that." He admired the way the horn and string players Mike Lewis brought into the T.K. studio could "just scratch it out on the paper, change a line or a note. It was so easy for them. I still don't understand how you do that."

But he didn't envy them. He still prefers what he heard emanating from

Poo Poo's thumb and what resonates in his own ears. Perry's convinced that not learning music formally was crucial to his creativity. "When you are trained that 'This only goes this way,'" he says, "you're limited in your perspective. I would put things together that are not supposed to go together. I would do beats that people didn't understand until they learned them. Then they went, 'Oh, I didn't think of that, that's cool.' My not knowing all the notes opened my mind up to any possibility."

16

Frankie Gearing

St. Petersburg

THE TWELVE-YEAR-OLD put lipstick on, the way she'd seen her mother do. Then she picked up an eyebrow pencil, also borrowed, and traced above both eyes. After Frances Yvonne Gearing stepped into a pair of her aunt's high heels, she thought, "I look pretty grown up."

So Frankie, as she was called, left the house on 8th Avenue South on that mid-1950s evening and walked the short distance to St. Petersburg's premiere black entertainment venue, the Manhattan Casino. Top touring acts in jazz, blues, gospel, and soul had played there since the 1930s when Louis Armstrong took the stage. (The Casino never had gambling; that name was just thought to be classy, as was anything having to do with New York City. Across the bay in Tampa you'd find an Apollo, a Little Savoy, and a Cotton Club, all homages to Harlem.) Usually those touring names added St. Pete gigs midweek, in between weekend jobs in bigger cities, such as Miami, Jacksonville, or Atlanta, or elsewhere. On this particular Friday, the headliners were still emerging, based on their first hit, the searing "Please Please Please."

Gearing was dying to hear James Brown and the Famous Flames, to meet the lead singer, and to deliver a message she'd prepared. As she climbed the steep stairs to the second-floor ballroom and gathered the $1.50 or so admission, the young girl thought she looked of age and was on her way in.

Frankie was certainly wrong on one count, probably both. Sam Jones, one of the city's few black policemen, was working security that night—and he knew Gearing and her family. "I'm not gonna drink," she pleaded, "I just want to hear them sing. And I want them to hear me sing, too."

"Frankie, you know you can't be in here," he said, kindly enough, and walked her back downstairs.

The night wasn't lost; she went across 22nd Street South near the Sno-Peak ice cream place that also sold hamburgers and hot dogs and sat on one of their patio benches. From that angle, she says, Gearing could see silhouettes of the dancers and performers, and she could hear perfectly, as the Casino had no air conditioning and all the windows were wide open. She'd use the same strategy to catch Little Richard, Bill Doggett, Edwin Starr, Betty Everett, Maxine Brown, and other singers who played the Casino. Quite a few adults used to drive up, park their cars along 22nd Street, roll their windows down, drink the liquor they'd brought with them, and listen to the music—for free—in their private listening booths.

The ambitious, nervy singer wasn't done, though. As she says today, "I had my ways." The next night Brown's band had a gig at the Palms of Bradenton. Gearing found a ride and managed to speak with Brown. "I'm a singer, too," she told him, "and you're going to see me again, maybe on the same stage as you. You'll hear from me."

Just a few years later, he did. When Gearing was fourteen, she joined a couple of eighteen-year-old classmates at Gibbs High School in a girl group called the Co-eds. After they won the Wednesday night amateur talent contest at St. Pete's Royal Theater (also on 22nd Street South), a talent scout and producer who went by Jazzy Red took the trio to Miami. Gearing lived there with her father and recorded a few singles with the Co-Eds. Red also booked them into the Knight Beat, where they opened for Screaming Jay Hawkins, Dionne Warwick, Little Eva, Sam Cooke, Big Maybelle—and James Brown.

Gearing's best-known work came later, in the 1970s, as a member of another group of three female singers, Quiet Elegance, on what Florida DJ and author Kurt Curtis called "incredible, deep Southern soul gems." She had one certified hit with that group: "You Got My Mind Messed Up." Gearing also toured internationally with Al Green and O.V. Wright, and, as part of an ensemble, was managed by two of the Temptations. All told, she was the lead singer in four recording groups.

Résumé, credits, sales, and credentials aside—she can really sing. Still. At her first *Florida Soul* interview Gearing is asked what she thinks of as her best work. Instead of "Messed Up" she named "There He Is," which she recorded with another group, the Glories, on the Columbia subsidiary label Date, in 1959.

Asked for a rendition Gearing, seated at her kitchen table, stops smoking her extra-long, extra-thin cigarette, and closes her eyes for a moment. Seen in profile her cheekbones and nose suggest Native American heritage and, indeed, her paternal grandmother was a Miccosukee Indian. Then she opens her eyes and comes out with a couple of verses, beginning with: "*There he is, standing in the rain / just waiting for me to run and kiss him.*"

The British website *Soul Cellar* calls her "the big-voiced singer leading Quiet Elegance's best and deepest tracks," and indeed, her singing immediately fills the room, blotting out her granddaughter's talking and the TV in the next room. She doesn't just blast or blare, though; in her strong kitchen rendition there is both melody and a rich tremolo, as she continues: "*And I know he looks the same / and heaven knows how I miss him.*"

Getting even more committed to her singing, Gearing takes it up an octave and sings even more forcefully, adding repetition and melisma to extend some of the syllables: "*Theeere he is, standing in the ra-a-ain / just waiting, waiting for my love / and I just forgot the words . . .*"

Gearing stops and laughs. Nearly seventy, she has just delivered a stirring, heartfelt performance. "I recorded that with the Glories," she said, "but I also sang it live with Quiet Elegance because it was a hot number for us, a bring-the-house-down number. I always liked the lyric about him standing in the rain, and the music is so beautiful."

"I put my whole heart into it," she added. "That one meant a lot to me."

Why was that?

"At the time I thought I was in love, I guess."

THE BALLROOM IN THE TWO-STORY WHITE, flat-topped building wasn't big as dance halls go; the orchestras of Cab Calloway, Count Basie and Duke Ellington had to crowd onto the bandstand in one corner. There weren't any tables in the Manhattan Casino, either, recalled Buster Cooper, born in 1929, who played trombone there with his cousin George's sixteen-piece band, and others. "They had long benches around the sides, but the floor was clear for dancing," Cooper, who died in 2016, said in a *Florida Soul* interview. In Cooper's time there, the late 1940s, Casino shows cost less than a dollar, he thinks. Cooper made "maybe $2 a night. That's *maybe.*"

More than size, the Casino had stature—it was an integral center of African American life in St. Pete. Like Central Avenue in Tampa and Ashley

Louis Armstrong performing at the Manhattan Casino in 1957, before an audience that included white patrons. Locals say that was not unusual when big stars came to St. Pete. Bob Moreland/*Tampa Bay Times*.

Street in Jacksonville, 22nd Street South was the thriving main artery of the black business and entertainment district known as The Deuces, after the two two's in 22nd Street. In its heyday, the late 1950s and early 1960s, "The Deuces boasted more than 100 businesses," according to a series on the neighborhood by Jon Wilson of the *St. Petersburg Times* (now the *Tampa Bay Times*). Three-quarters of those businesses were black-owned. "That's when 22nd Street was *22nd Street*," Cooper says, with emphasis. "We had everything there that human beings need to live."

The Casino building, built by black entrepreneur Elder Jordan and opened in 1931 as the Jordan Dance Hall, was the center of the center. Starting in the 1930s the Casino's music was booked by George Grogan, a former New Yorker who had a connection to an important talent agency there, Universal Attractions. Grogan held that and other business interests down while teaching at Gibbs High. The popular acts who played the Casino kept St. Pete connected to the national black culture, and traveling black preachers and spiritualists who appeared there, including the famous Father Divine, maintained that connection as well.

Those visitors came and went, but the Casino was a constant, a social center for the community. Gibbs High held dances and graduation ceremonies there. There was a post office on the ground floor, among other businesses. The ballroom served as a training ground for local musicians who got a chance to prove themselves before a mostly forgiving home crowd. Established local acts like George Cooper's and piano man "Fess" Clark's outfit found steady work there as well. Above the stage, a sign spelled out the entrance policy for the card-carrying musicians of that city, who were many: "Union card members admitted free on local bands only—Big Bands NO!"

As young Frankie found, the Casino was for what some of today's black radio stations like to call "grown folks." At times it also hosted white folks: "Quite a few from around Tampa Bay would come to hear acts like Cab Calloway and Sam Cooke," Gearing says.

On any given Saturday night into the 1960s, Roseland, the Shangri La, the High Topper, the Black Cat, and the Champagne Lounge would also offer jazz and R&B in The Deuces. But the Casino was—to its partisans, at least—the classiest act. "The teachers, doctors, and lawyers we had, they'd dress up in their nice evening wear to go there," Gearing remembers. "Regular working people came too, to dance there and at the other clubs on 22nd Street." Besides the clubs, there were also a dozen or so bars and poolrooms up and down that same street.

"That was our community," Gearing says of St. Pete's south side, including The Deuces. "We had our own grocery stores, our own little shops and stuff. We knew where we were supposed to be [during segregation]. The only time we came to the other side of town was when our parents or grandparents were working over there," she says, referring to domestic or yard work.

As it did elsewhere, integration in housing and other legal remedies helped undo the cohesion of the black community. Perversely, reporter Wilson noted, expanded opportunity "shifted the center of gravity away from places like The Deuces toward white-majority shopping centers and entertainment venues." After close to forty vibrant years, the Casino stood shut and neglected for another forty, from 1968 onward. In 2011, the Casino was

Geech's barbecue restaurant on 22nd Street South, just a couple of blocks from the Manhattan Casino, was a fixture in The Deuces. Courtesy of the Pinellas County African American History Museum.

reopened by the city and private partners and attractively renovated, but was subsequently closed. When Cooper the trombonist was interviewed at eighty-nine years old, he felt he had outlived the bustling, hustling neighborhood that surrounded and supported the Casino. "There's nothing left," he said.

ONE ACT FRANKIE NEVER CAUGHT at the Casino, and sorely missed, was Etta James. "She was my idol," Gearing says. "When I was singing with the Co-Eds in high school, the Etta James songs we did were my songs. Pat [Patricia Newkirk] led on the songs by the Shirelles, the Chantels and the

Marvelettes; and Lynn [Lynette Herring] had a real pretty high falsetto and she sang Ted Taylor songs, like 'If I Thought You Needed Me.' All three of us were lead singers."

The song that won the Wednesday talent contest for the Co-Eds at the Royal Theater (also a movie house) was the Chantels' "Look Into My Eyes." That in turn got the group to Miami. Fairly quickly, though, the two older girls seemed to lose interest in the group, Gearing says, just as an all-male group, the Laddins, lost its lead singer. They were a New York act; like many others, they played Florida for much of the winter, including at the Peppermint Lounge and the Castaways in Miami Beach (where fellow Florida soul singer Latimore led the house band for a time). Gearing would have been just sixteen when she says her parents let her move to New York with the boys. One reason they did may have been because her mother was an entertainer, too.

Frankie's mother had her when she was just a teenager, and for years the daughter was raised by her grandmother in Daytona Beach. The grandmother had wanted to name her daughter after the actress Colleen Dewhurst, Gearing says, but she didn't know how to spell it and Frankie's mother's first name came out Corrielean, last name Hood. (Frankie's father, from whom she got the name Gearing, was an educator and insurance man, who died in his forties.) "As Mommy got grown most people couldn't pronounce her name right, so she would say, 'Call me Connie,'" Gearing says. "She sang and danced on the road with Bobby 'Blue' Bland and Mr. B. B. King, who just died, and she took a stage name, which was Tiny." (An adopted brother of Frankie's, deceased, who went by Johnny Starr, played guitar with Jackie Wilson and Little Richard.) After her mother passed, Corrielean came off the road, and she and Frankie moved to St. Pete in time for the girl to start fourth grade. The mother worked at the Kress department store downtown and at a restaurant, the Wedgewood Inn.

When her parents gave her permission to join the Laddins, the group— Earl Marcus, John Marcus, and Mickey Goody—was a strong live act, made more so with Gearing fronting them. In one notable instance, too strong. One of her first New York appearances with them was at Brooklyn's Brevoort Theater—opening for James Brown. She was scared to death, but their set went very well. Before the next show that same day, though, Brown's perennial colleague and confidant Bobby Byrd came to the Laddins' dressing room. "Mr. Brown says, that song you're doing, 'With Every Beat of My Heart,' just sing half of it," Byrd told them.

"I'm a teenager, trying to figure out how you sing a half a song," Gearing remembers. "And so we were told: 'Leave out the middle.' When we got to the bridge it would keep building and building and everybody in the theater would be screaming, and Mr. Brown didn't want that on *his* show."

The Laddins obeyed, and perhaps as a result, Gearing and the group got to work with him several more times. The Flames were "dynamite," she recalls, "the way they would dance and spin around. They were the Temptations of that earlier day. And we wouldn't have gotten those jobs if I hadn't been a nice little girl and sang that song short. We did what Mr. Brown said."

In 1966 the Laddins got a recording deal with ABC, where management changed their name to the Steinways. Three singles of theirs came out that year on the Oliver label, which ABC distributed. Soon thereafter, though, producer/manager Bob Yorey took her "from the guys back to the girls," installing her in the female trio the Glories, with Mildred Vaney and Betty Stokes. They signed with the new Columbia subsidiary, Date Records, which, as *Billboard* noted in April 1967, was thriving: "Further penetration into the pop R&B market is planned with the soon to be released 'I Stand Accused (Of Loving You)' by The Glories." Date had also just "inked," as Billboard liked to say, a deal with famed songwriters Leiber and Stoller to produce a new Coasters album.

The Glories put out sixteen songs in three years on Date, and Gearing can rattle off the titles of all eight A-sides of those 45s easily from memory. The first one, the song cited by Billboard, "I Stand Accused," briefly dented the R&B and the pop charts in 1967.

Columbia tried to fashion their girl group after Motown's Supremes, she says, and as a result "we kind of sounded white and our songs crossed over to the white radio stations. A lot of times we got booked at places where people thought they had booked a white act, and were surprised to see us."

On one southern swing, the Glories were staying at a hotel in New Orleans, and had a gig twenty or thirty miles outside of the city. "There was this big ballroom way out in the Louisiana woods," she says, "and we showed up, those cute little girls who could really sing—but they didn't know we were black. While we were doing one number some big white guy came and lifted Mildred straight up in the air—she was so tiny, the littlest of us—and we got worried. But he just said, 'You are so beautiful, little darling,' and poor Mildred just kept on singing and doing the routines up in the air while he was holding her up." They were kind to us, really, but we noticed there really weren't many females [of any color] at this place, so when we weren't singing we just stayed in our dressing room."

The road held other hazards for a very young woman on her own. The Glories opened for Little Richard at the Apollo in Harlem; Gearing had met him at the Manhattan Casino and told him, as she'd told James Brown, that she wanted to be a singer. This time Richard, not known as a model of probity or sobriety, took the time to school her. "He told me about the stage door Johnnies, telling me, 'Don't take any presents from these guys. They're pimps, and you don't want to be in debt to them.' And he warned me about all the drugs." When drugs aplenty were passed around at an after-party at the Theresa Hotel, Little Richard told the assembled musicians: "None for her."

Big Maybelle, real name Mabel Louise Smith, also mentored her. Maybelle, who reportedly had drug problems of her own and died in her late forties, "was like a Big Mama to me," Gearing says, meaning like a grandmother.

Roughly midway through their Date career, Gearing says, she and the girls told their management they wanted to sing and sound more soulful. Yorey and Date complied and sent the group to the American Sound Studio in Memphis. Aretha Franklin recorded her *Lady Soul* album there, including "Chain of Fools"; Bobby Womack was just starting to turn out a series of hits there; and Joe Tex would soon do the same. Dusty Springfield's classic 1970 album, *Dusty in Memphis*, also benefited from the crack studio band, the Memphis Boys—who, as it happens, were soulfully white.

The Glories' cover of Otis Redding's "Try a Little Tenderness" came out in 1969, as did "The Dark End of the Street," done earlier by James Carr, co-written by American founder/owner Chips Moman with in-house writer Dan Penn. These songs played to Gearing's soulful strengths—so much so that she would again be deemed a bit *too* strong, by another soul titan.

THE GLORIES SHARED SOME BILLS WITH THE TEMPTATIONS, including at least one at the Apollo. On one of those nights, it turned out, Aretha Franklin was in the house, along with her sister Carolyn and cousin Brenda Bryant, both of whom sang with her. After the show Dennis Edwards, the prodigious lead singer for the Temps who later had a successful solo career, relayed a good news/bad news message to Gearing from the Queen of Soul: "Tell her she's a singing little girl, but she needs to quit trying to sound like me."

She wasn't, Gearing insists, though of course she admired Franklin. "I just had that same soul, that same spirit. She was born in the Baptist church and I was too. It was that old church sound she heard, not me copying her."

Gearing and the Glories also made an impression on the Temps, and two of them, Otis Williams and Melvin Franklin, took over the trio's management. The group followed them back to Detroit, where Lois Reeves—a sister of Martha Reeves who sang with her backups, the Vandellas—replaced Dolores Brown as a Glory. In 1972 the group was relaunched—with Reeves, Mildred Vaney, and Gearing—and renamed Quiet Elegance.

What annoyed Aretha and impressed the Temps also caught the ear of Willie Mitchell, the famed lead producer at Hi Records who oversaw Al Green's million-selling secular work. Like Stax and American, Hi had its own renowned group of studio regulars, including the three brothers Charles, Leroy, and Teenie Hodges; drummer Howard Grimes; and Mitchell's brother James, who played saxophone and arranged horns. The Memphis Horns, who backed up Florida soul singers Sam Moore and Linda Lyndell, among many others, at Stax, contributed there as well. Hi was also based in Memphis and, like Stax, was situated in a former movie theater. This one was called the Royal, same as the St. Pete theater where Gearing and the Co-Eds won that Wednesday night talent contest.

"Willie liked the gospel feel in my voice," Gearing says, "and he thought of doing 'You Got My Mind Messed Up.'" Like "The Dark End of the Street," which Gearing covered with the Glories, this song had been done previously by James Carr. The strings and swelling organ in the opening are immediately recognizable from Green's hits and Mitchell's other productions. Gearing's lead is ruminative rather than declamatory, and the tone, as the title suggests, is rueful. *"For as long as I've been running around / I finally met a little boy who really got me down."*

"Messed Up" was the only Quiet Elegance song to chart, reaching #54 on the R&B chart in 1973. Gearing isn't satisfied with her performance, however. "I regret that I didn't take my time; I performed it better live," she says. "Still, everybody liked it." She'd do another take on her favorite, "There He Is," as well. Her heartfelt version was aimed at "old John Wesley," she reveals, a romantic interest during her New York days with the Glories. He wasn't a musician, "just a working fellow." If she redid that tune, Gearing says, she'd reverse the conventional gospel/secular conversion, turning this pop tune into something holy. "I'd change the words around so it's about

Jesus. Onstage I did it much slower and very soulful; it was very church-like, I would say."

With Mitchell and Dan Greer producing, Quiet Elegance cut eight singles (sixteen songs) for Hi between 1972 and 1977. "Mama Said" is one of the strongest and most typical of that label. The horns are punchy, the congas are mixed up high, and, over swelling organ fills, Gearing sounds a bit like her label-mate and good friend Ann Peebles (best known for "I Can't Stand the Rain"): *"Mama said you're selling your soul to the devil / Papa said I'm living a wayward life / Brother said my self-respect is in danger / Girl, don't you know this man got a wife?"*

During those Hi years Gearing's group toured with Green, opening for him and then backing the headliner. (They also recorded a song from his *Let's Stay Together* album: "Have You Been Making Out OK.") Quiet Elegance also backed up the English pop singer Engelbert Humperdinck, who Gearing calls "a class act, a kind-hearted person. And he knew how to work that stage and the audience."

Green left Hi in 1976, and Gearing thought Mitchell was demoralized and began to withdraw after that, including from Quiet Elegance. Hi was sold in 1977, when the last Elegance single was released, and Mitchell left in 1979.

GEARING WENT BACK TO ST. PETE and continued to perform and record a little on her own. One such album, *Just Frankie*, released in Japan, is much prized by contemporary soul fanatics. (At this writing a copy is for sale online for 100 Euros.) She also, like almost every other significant Florida soul artist, recorded a bit at Henry Stone's T.K. records in Hialeah, working with producer Clarence Reid in 1982.

Gearing, who's married, is raising her granddaughter, Christina, in north St. Pete. She occasionally sits in with acts she's friendly with, and Gearing still sings Etta James, including "At Last" and "Trust in Me." Both her former Quiet Elegance partners are still very active and earning, Gearing says. Mildred Vaney (who goes by Millie Scott) is singing backup with Aretha Franklin, and Lois Reeves rejoined her sister Martha in the Vandellas. "I'm the one who needs to get back to performing."

On a recent birthday her goddaughter took her out to dinner and then surprised her after when they stopped by the Ringside Café, "St. Petersburg's Home of the Blues" on 2nd Street North. "The lady who was performing called me up onstage and I wound up singing some blues for

Frankie Gearing outside the Casino. She tried to sneak in as an underage fan and later performed there as a successful singer. Photo © Suzanne Williamson.

them," Gearing says. "And my goddaughter's yelling, 'Wood Foot done it again, you stomped a hole in the floor!' That's what she calls me, 'cause when I sing I like to stamp my foot."

Wood Foot would like to do more singing and stomping, maybe with Ann Peebles, who's home taking care of grandchildren in Memphis, as Gearing is in Florida. "I'm trying to talk her into getting out there with me, behind her new CD," Gearing says. "She doesn't need the money, but I do."

Recently her former manager, Bob Yorey, called her and proposed sending her back out on the road, either in a trio or as a solo act. He told her vintage acts like the O'Jays, the Temps, and the Stylistics are making good money (usually with one or fewer original members) and that all the sampling of old soul material by contemporary artists was likely driving these revivals. "These hip-hop boys are bringing us back!" Gearing exclaims.

She's thinking about the Cuban market, too, and possibilities for performing there. "I understand that's going to open up, and there'll be more and more tourism," she says. "And I know the Cuban people are into some soul music." As Gearing points out, from where she sits in St. Petersburg, it's just a short plane ride away.

17

Timmy Thomas

Miami

"I GOT THE BASS LINE FIRST," he says, playing and repeating a series of eighth notes on the keyboard with his left hand. "That's just C and B-flat."

Timmy Thomas is seated at the dining room table in his home in northwest Miami, closer to Hollywood than to the beaches or downtown. He has the blinds, brown wooden slats, fully closed in the window behind him to block out the midday sun. The singer, songwriter, and keyboard man is dressed up for the photographs that have already been taken, wearing a navy blue blazer over a lighter blue sport shirt buttoned all the way to the top, and in his breast pocket there's a grayish blue pocket square. His close-cropped black hair forms an acutely angled widow's peak midforehead. The musician, teacher, and minister appears solidly middle-aged (he's seventy, actually) and middle-class. In the adjacent living room, where the pictures were taken, gold records and civic awards line the walls behind the leather couch.

"I use this little keyboard when I'm writing," he says, gesturing down at the small black plastic instrument at the head of the wooden dining room table. His real instrument, a full-size organ, lives at his church. "When I recorded this song," he continues, "I played the bass line with my foot, the foot pedal, on the Lowrey organ. I played the Lowrey before I went to the Hammond B-3." He pushes his glasses back up his nose, which makes him look even more professorial or teacher-like, and his explanations are pedagogic as well: patient and precise.

"Now," he continues, very much in lesson mode, "I thought: 'What kind of chord structure can I use with this bass line? I don't want to just use the same key, or stay in C.' So I went to A-flat major 7, and then a G minor 7 chord."

Thomas plays those two chords for the same number of bars, the sleeves of his blazer riding up both forearms. "See, I've still got the same bass line going," he adds, starting to rock slightly over the keyboard, "it's never changing."

"The major 7th gives that A-flat chord some of what we call color," Thomas instructs, meaning that in addition to the three notes in the basic A-flat chord or triad, he's added the seventh note in that major scale, G. The G-minor 7 chord he's paired it with contains a flatted third note—B-flat instead of the B—plus a flatted seventh note: F instead of F sharp.

He repeats those chords, then moves to B-flat, F, and C, that last chord echoing one of the two notes in his bass line. During that cycle or chord progression, his most famous song has begun to emerge. His next demonstration will make the identification complete. "In music you have a theme, a variation, a bridge, things like that," Thomas says, picking up a pen and pointing it at his listener. "So my thinking was: 'What can I do to go into the variation and then back to the theme?' And this is what came out."

From his right hand comes a burst of staccato Cs—the highest notes yet—over the far deeper Cs and B-flats from the bass line. All told he strikes those high Cs twenty percussive times. There's an off-beat or behind-the-beat cadence to those tweets, as he calls them; did he get that from Latin music, he's asked? "No, I didn't listen to much Latin back then, though I do now," Thomas responds. "I don't really know where I got that from. It just seemed right, and that became my trademark." He lifts his hands from the keyboard and rests them and his forearms alongside it, on the table. "So," he concludes, "that's how 'Why Can't We Live Together' was created."

His song, released on Henry Stone's Glades label, was a #1 R&B hit in 1972. Its unique sound—just Thomas and his organ with its built-in drum machine—and timely lyrical message made it a crossover hit as well; "Why Can't We Live Together" ("WCWLT") reached the #3 spot on the pop chart.

Thomas was also an integral member of Henry Stone and T.K. Productions' house band, adding his organ riffs to hits by Betty Wright, Gwen McCrae, and Latimore, among others. But "Why Can't We Live Together," his first recording, made when he was twenty-eight, is clearly, easily, his biggest achievement. It may also be the most distinctive and enduring song in the entire Florida soul canon.

A passionate plea for tolerance and peace, "WCWLT" is part of the soundtrack to the 1999 movie *Boys Don't Cry*, which dealt overtly with

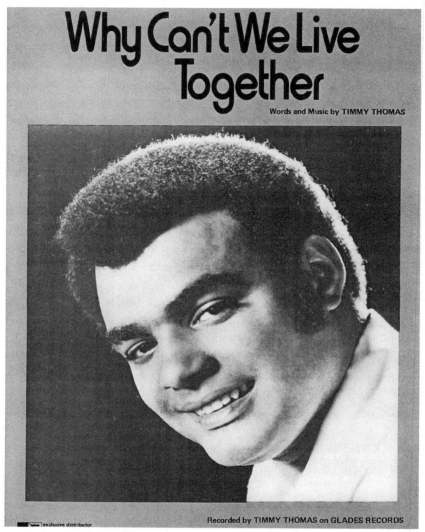

Sheet music for Timmy Thomas' enduring soul anthem. Courtesy of Timmy Thomas.

intolerance, in this case, centering on a transgender American youth. The song was also used prominently in the 2003 French movie *Monsieur Ibrahim*, which centers on the friendship between an older Muslim man and a young Jewish boy.

A global hit, it has since been covered by many prominent artists. (For some reason the title was never rendered with a question mark at the end.) The best-known version, after Thomas', is probably that of Nigerian-born singer Helen Folasade Adu, who goes by Sade, on her 1984 album *Diamond Life*. Soulful American singer Joan Osborne also covered the song, and Carlos Santana added searing guitar work to his versions, some done with British rocker and blues singer Steve Winwood. "WCWLT" already had an impressive half-life of more than forty years when the Canadian rapper/singer Drake extended it in 2015, using Thomas' instrumental track on his monster hit "Hotline Bling." That brought Thomas renewed attention, and he subsequently signed with a new Miami record label to record his first album in decades.

He's excited about the present, no doubt, but Thomas makes it clear that his song's greatest impact and most significant renderings actually came long ago. Over the years he played his song, which contains the line "*No matter what color, you are still my brother,*" several times in South Africa. The first time came during the years of apartheid, while Nelson Mandela was incarcerated, when Thomas' song had become an anthem of the black liberation movement. His last concert there was a celebration of Mandela's inauguration as that country's president. "Why Can't We Live Together" is a remarkably successful and enduring soul song, but it's also a legacy.

WHEN HE'S FINISHED EXPLAINING the song's musical underpinnings, Thomas sits back in his chair. "Actually," he says, "that's not how the song really started. It started in my bedroom in 1971. This was during the war in Vietnam. I turned on the TV news and Walter Cronkite took his glasses off and said, 'This many thousands of Viet Cong died today; and this many thousands of Americans.' [The daily "body counts," as they were known, were probably lower.] And I'd seen these poor Vietnamese kids walking around with half their skin off [from napalm].

"And I said, 'My God! These are humans. These are mothers' children! They're dying at 17, and 18 and 19; they don't even know what life is all about. Why are we hurting each other like this?' I walked back into the living room and I thought, 'This has to stop. Why can't we live together?'"

At the time Thomas was holding down a steady gig at a Miami Beach club that bore his name: Timmy's Lounge. He wasn't the owner; even now Thomas won't discuss it, but it seems to have been a mob-owned place, in the Lucerne Hotel, at 41st and Collins Avenue. He'd first established himself in Overtown, backing up big-name touring acts, including B. B. King and James Brown, at the Knight Beat. From there Thomas went on to draw good crowds working solo at the Satellite Lounge, around 62nd and 7th Avenue, and then at a beach spot called Sunny's. "People had seen trios but they had never heard one guy sound like three people, with my left hand on the rhythm, right hand playing leads on the organ, and left foot on bass. And of course I was singing at the same time. I was Timmy Thomas, the one-man band."

He'd come to Miami in 1969 or 1970 as a part-time musician; by day he was vice president for development at Florida Memorial College (now a university in Miami Gardens). When he was growing up, one of twelve children, in Evansville, Indiana, his father emphasized education and degrees. "He told me, 'You can play all the music in all the places you want to, but when you go to school, bring me back that piece of paper.' That meant that when I got through playing, I could fall back on teaching with those diplomas. 'Prepare yourself,' he said: 'You're not going to do this forever.'"

Between high school and college, though, Thomas got to attend a jazz clinic run by the Stan Kenton orchestra, and that spurred him to continue and deepen his playing. He got his B.A. from Lane College in Jackson, Tennessee, and studied administration at the University of Tennessee. He played keyboards for Phillip and the Faithfuls, who recorded for the Goldwax label in Memphis; worked as a session musician there; and had a regional hit of his own on that label in 1967 with "Have Some Boogaloo." (Goldwax also issued strong soul by James Carr—"The Dark End of the Street"—and O.V. Wright—"Pouring Water on a Drowning Man"—among others.)

Thomas played out a little on the chitlin' circuit—"mostly soul jazz, like what Jimmy Smith was playing on the organ, 32-bar blues"—including sideman gigs with Floridian saxophonist Cannonball Adderley and trumpeter Donald Byrd. But, as his father predicted, he didn't earn enough to support a family, and he'd married Lillie, still his wife, while they were in college. So he kept his day jobs, including when he headlined Timmy's Lounge at the beach.

"That was a big beautiful club," he remembers. "We had the Miss Black America pageant there once. I played a combination of jazz, pop, and R&B. I even had people ask me to do 'Fly Me To The Moon.' So one night right after I had written 'Why Can't We Live Together,' I tried it out at the club."

He begins to sing the first verse, the lyrics in A-A-B format, like the blues:

"Tell me why, tell me why, tell me why
Why can't we live together?

Tell me why, tell me why, tell me why
Why can't we live together?

Everybody wants to live together
Why can't we live together?"

When he finished his first live rendition, Thomas remembers, "They said, 'Sing that song again. Did you write it?'

'Yes.'

'Sing it again! We like it.'"

"It had the rhythm," he says, "but it also had what we called M and M: Music and Message. You get them on the floor first with the rhythm and then you ease in what you're really trying to say. Pretty soon, they're thinking about that message."

Response at the club was so strong that Thomas went to record the song at a small studio—"no bigger than this living room"—owned by Bobby Dukoff. "Where's everybody else?" Dukoff wanted to know when Thomas showed up. After Thomas convinced him that, yes, the entire band was in fact present, and no, he wasn't going to overdub himself but play all the parts at once, Dukoff put one mike by Thomas' foot and bass pedal and another by the left-hand side of the organ: "the part that sounds like a guitar." A third mike captured the sounds his right hand made on the keyboard "where I played the theme." Dukoff then positioned a boom mike for Thomas to sing into. The rhythmic drumming sounds, higher pitched like bongos, came from one of the preprogrammed buttons on the Lowrey; Thomas thinks it might have been labeled Samba.

With only three vocal verses, the song didn't take long to complete. Dukoff, who was also the engineer, stayed seated at the controls, waiting for the rest of it. Finally, he said, "Oh, you're finished?" The resulting eight-track recording on cassette cost the one-man band about $350.

Thomas knew some of the DJs at the black-oriented station WEDR, including James T., Sweetback, and Maestro Powell (who still holds forth at 99JAMZ on his *Gospel Sundays* show), as well as the station manager, Jerry Rushin. "I went over there; they were in a little old room on 36th Street. Years ago, you could do that, you could go into a radio studio as a local and ask them, 'Can you play my record?' They don't do that now.

"The DJs told the listeners, 'We've got Timmy Thomas, one of our friends, here and we're going to let you hear his record.' Then they punched it on, and all the phones started ringing. That was funny, too, because usually, nobody would play a record unless you had some money to give them."

Listeners wanted to know: Where could they buy that record? But, Thomas told the guys at WEDR, there weren't any records, just that cassette. "That station manager was smart," Thomas says. "He told the DJs, 'Stop, stop, don't play it any more, he's losing sales.' Because if there are none in the record shops when a person goes in there and asks for it, that person never goes back, so you've lost that sale."

Jamaican-born DJ, musician, and producer King Sporty (Noel Williams) was at the station that day, Thomas says, and offered to release the song on one of his labels, Konduko. He did but, Thomas recalls, "Konduko didn't have a lot of contacts or distribution outside of Miami." As the vinyl single of "WCWLT" continued to get local airplay, though, Henry Stone heard it, or heard about it, and made a deal with Sporty to sign Thomas and acquire the record. (Sporty, or Williams, cowrote the Bob Marley song "Buffalo Solider" and was married to Betty Wright. He passed away in 2015.)

"I hadn't heard of Henry Stone," Thomas says. "My work was mostly at universities; I didn't know who was who in the record business. But the biggest independent record company in the United States was T.K. Henry told me, 'There's a good record here that I'd like to promote and distribute.' That's when everything just started taking off. I couldn't believe it."

"No matter, no matter what color / You are still my brother
I said, no matter, no matter what color / You are still my brother

Everybody wants to live together
Why can't we live together?"

THOMAS' SOCIAL CONSCIENCE and his will to act on it were formed well before he wrote that M and M song, and before the Vietnam War that inspired it. "My wife and I walked with Dr. King," he says. "We were at Lane College [in Jackson, Tennessee]; I must have been 18 or so, in 1962. We both got training by his people. This was to be non-violent. He wanted people who could understand that we were trying to change things but we were trying to change them peacefully."

"We were the ones who integrated the Woolworths in Jackson. Young [white] guys were going by in their cars and saying the N-word but we were trained to ignore it. Lillie and I were just boyfriend and girlfriend then, and these four guys were standing in front of Woolworths and one of them did like this"—he makes a spitting sound—"he spit on her."

"This was the woman I was going to marry! You know I had red in my eyes. I dropped my placard, my sign, right on the ground. But I'll never forget, she told me: 'Don't do anything. You're not as big as the movement. Pick up your sign. Let's do what we were trained to do here.'

"And I did that. I picked my sign back up and kept walking. They called me everything but a child of God, but I kept on walking. We were very, very patient, and we integrated all the stores downtown."

As an even younger man, Thomas believes, he had a strong sense of fairness, inculcated in him by his father. "My daddy was very influential in my life," says Thomas, who remembers putting cardboard in his shoes and wearing them to the prom because the parents of the twelve Thomas children couldn't afford to buy him new ones. "We didn't have the world's greatest things, but we had clean clothes to go to school. We went to church every Sunday morning, we had a lot of love, and none of us were ever treated differently than the others. My daddy told me, 'Remember, there is always someone worse off than you, so just make the best of what you're doing.' So when I did my song, I had been taught those things through the relationship I had with my father and my mom."

After his parents' teaching, "Dr. King taught me about non-violence. When I wrote the lines, 'No matter what color, you're still my brother' and 'No more war; more peace in this world,' these were the things that he and the Kennedys stood for."

On paper the lyrics can seem a little simplistic. But when they're sung—by Thomas, Sade, Joan Osborne, Steve Winwood, and others—their simplicity becomes a virtue, a force that distills all the power and feeling Thomas meant to imbue his song with. As in classic blues songs and the hymn "Amazing Grace," the ideas—the ideals—it conveys and the words used to convey them are fundamental and familiar. Yet they invoke the most primal human needs and concerns, and listeners feel the urgency with which Thomas delivered his message—in person, on the radio, and on vinyl.

"IT WAS LUCK, AND THE OTHER THING WAS TIMING," Thomas says. By timing he means that listeners were ready for his message, after the assassination of Dr. King in 1968; the drawn-out Vietnam conflict; and, to some extent, awareness in the United States of the injustice of South African

Promotional photo of Timmy Thomas. "Why Can't We Live Together" was released on Henry Stone's Glades label in 1972. Courtesy of Timmy Thomas.

apartheid. The timing was good in another way as well: In the early 1970s, AM radio, still the dominant format, offered a broad variety of musical styles, black and white. Top 40 was both pervasive and inclusive; other contemporary pop hits surrounding Thomas' Hot 100 run included the smooth R&B classic "Me and Mrs. Jones," by Billy Paul; "I Am Woman," by Helen Reddy; "Baby Don't Get Hooked on Me," by country performer Mac Davis; "My Ding-A-Ling," by Chuck Berry (his only #1 pop hit); "I Can See Clearly Now," by reggae singer/songwriter Johnny Nash; and even "Ben," by Michael Jackson—an ode to a fictional rat. (Then as now diversity did not always equate to quality.) In that broad and varied context, it turned out, there was room for a soulful protest song with percussive organ "tweets."

Through luck, timing, and, yes, quality, "WCWLT" became a #1 R&B hit and the single stayed on that chart for eighteen weeks, even as it moved to #3 pop. When it took off, Henry Stone naturally, urgently, wanted a Timmy Thomas album to sell. The impresario assumed they would add all the usual instruments—guitar, horns, drums—on the LP, but T.K. producer Steve Alaimo intervened, Thomas remembers. "He said, 'No man, leave it just like it is. Don't touch anything.' So I did my whole first album as a one-man band." (Later Thomas albums would feature more players and instruments.)

That first album, also called *Why Can't We Live Together*, rushed out in late 1972, had ten of those solo tracks, including a longer version of "WC-WLT" with an extended organ introduction. "Rainbow Power" is another call for peace and brotherhood: "*Red, yellow, black and white / we need every color to make up the rainbow.*" "Take Care of Home" asks America to forget "trying to be Number 1 in the world" and do what the title suggests. "Opportunity" echoes the James Brown song of three years earlier, "I Don't Want Nobody to Give Me Nothing (Open up the Door I'll Get It Myself)." "Cold Cold People" is a little angrier—he calls those folks SOBs—but overall the album's ethos is assertive but positive, at times almost hippy-ish, as it might have been called at the time, as well as soulful.

While his organ lines on "WCWLT" are piercing and assertive, on many of the other songs his playing sounds more upbeat, energetic, even jaunty—more like the style he adopted while playing standards and pop hits at Timmy's Lounge and Sunny's. Willie Clarke, one of Thomas' T.K. producers, calls it "almost a happy, carnival sound." As on the title cut, Thomas' voice, on the high side, carries a lot of resonance and emotion throughout the album. There's a soulful strain in it, but his diction is clear and, as the only performer on the tracks, his singing and the lyrics are prominent and easily intelligible. Singing, he sounds a bit more southern than he does when speaking in person.

No more war, no more war, no more war
Just a little peace in this world

"No more war, no more war
All we want is some peace in this world

Everybody wants to live together
Why can't we live together?"

THE "WCWLT" SINGLE became an international hit, a "world record," as Thomas calls it. He eventually toured and performed in twenty to twenty-five countries, by his estimate, including many where English wasn't much spoken but his Music and Message still took hold. (When this writer attended a French university in the late 1970s, Thomas' song was heard in the halls of his dorm for foreign students, many of whom were from France's former colonies in Africa.) In 1974 the song's global appeal and impact drew him to Johannesburg.

"That was when Nelson Mandela was in jail," he says. "When I first got there, I was told, 'Mr. Thomas, you have a lot of people waiting for you at the airport.' And there were. You'll think I'm making this up, but because of the song, those people looked up to me like a savior. I couldn't believe it.

"Another thing I remember very well was coming to the Ritz Carlton Hotel. The mayor was there and it was a big deal. So I sing, and then at 9 p.m. the [black attendees] said, 'We have to go, because we have to be off the streets in Johannesburg.' The only reason I could stay downtown was because I was an American; otherwise I would have had to go out to Soweto, where the blacks lived. The situation there . . . sometimes it's difficult for me to talk about."

On that first visit, he played in a soccer stadium to more than one hundred thousand people, Thomas remembers. He went back in 1978, when Mandela was still imprisoned, and recorded his *Live in Africa* album (released in 1979), which opens and closes with "WCWLT" and includes "Rainbow Power" and a version of Ray Charles' hit, "Drown in My Own Tears." The album cover shows Thomas, in a white suit and with big, very 1970s sideburns, singing into a mike he holds in his left hand and reaching out with the right to touch several outstretched black hands. Still other black hands cling to both of his legs, in those white pants. That image vividly depicts how this Florida artist became a celebrity in that country and others on the African continent, and that his song was part of the growing chorus for revolution.

"On that second trip we performed and recorded in another stadium, closer to Johannesburg," Thomas says. "All these white policemen were standing around. I also made my first music video there, but I said I wasn't going to do it unless they brought in other races, the mulattos and the darker South Africans, which is what happened. I couldn't change any laws but I tried to change hearts."

In April 1994, Mandela was not only out of prison but also running for president. Thomas returned and remembers seeing "so many black people standing in line to vote for the first time. It seemed like you could use binoculars and still not see the end of the line. Then in May I got another call, saying, 'Hey man, your ticket is at the counter. They're asking for you to come and play to celebrate Mandela's inauguration.' Nelson Mandela was *President*—that was really something. Most people didn't see the change between those two eras, but because of my trips there I saw it.

"Of course I went. Can you just see me playing with tears rolling down my eyes?"

FIVE MORE TIMMY THOMAS ALBUMS followed that first one, and a dozen more of his singles made the R&B charts over the ensuing twelve years. After "Why Can't We Live Together," his next-biggest chart hit was "What Can I Tell Her" (another title lacking a question mark), which reached #19 in 1973. Most of this music was on Stone's labels; the last album and several singles were on Gold Mountain, a boutique label run by music executive Danny Goldberg and distributed by A&M.

Thomas did some promotional work for Stone, traveling around Florida a good deal. Often he'd perform for free at events promoted by local DJs, and in return they'd look favorably on his and Stone's product when it came to airplay. Thomas says it fell short of outright payola (which Stone freely admitted to). "It was you scratch my back and I'll scratch yours."

He continued to perform overseas; so much so, he says, that he'd wake up and ask himself, "What country is this?" But, he says, "that was still a very good time in my life. I have no regrets. I got a chance to be heard across the world, and whenever I'd go to another country, the first thing I would do was go to the educational system: the schools, the libraries. All the money that I was supposed to have gotten paid in South Africa I left there, for black kids to go to school."

On one such trip in 1992, he was in Rio de Janeiro, Brazil. They're just an hour ahead of U.S. EST, so timing his calls with his wife in Florida wasn't an issue, as it was elsewhere. But he could tell from Lillie's voice that something wasn't right.

"I said, 'What's wrong?'

"She said, 'I'm just watching the news, and a little middle-school boy here just shot another middle school boy. They asked him why and he said he just wanted to up his rep on the street.'"

She wasn't just upset; she had a message for the Music & Message man. "You're trying to save the world, traveling all over with your music," he remembers his wife telling him. "You need to come home, because these kids need to see somebody that's made it. You need to come home and teach music to these kids."

That was his last performance overseas, Thomas says. "I came straight home, went straight into Miami-Dade County public schools and I taught there for about 20 years."

THE SONG LIVES ON. Carlos Santana played it on his 2004 *Live at Montreux* album with vocals and keyboards by Steve Winwood. Both deliver fiery, moving performances; a video is on YouTube and highly recommended. (Winwood has also used "WCWLT" in his own live shows.) Less-known covers include a faster, disco-ish take by singer Mike Anthony in 1982; Maria Muldaur's 2008 recording; and one by Florida-based bluesman Lucky Peterson on his eponymous 1999 album.

The movies *Boys Don't Cry* and *Monsieur Ibrahim* helped bring the song back to prominence in 1999 and 2003, respectively, especially the former, after Hilary Swank won an Academy Award for her starring role. (Thomas' 1984 song, "Gotta Give a Little Love," was used in the Tom Hanks movie *Bachelor Party* that same year.)

Joan Osborne came to "WCWLT" relatively late; she was only ten years old in 1972 when it came out on Glades. She caught up with it when studying film at New York University and working the blues bars in New York's Chelsea and East Village. Thirty years after Thomas' song was first heard, she sung a powerful version on her 2002 collection of soul covers, *How Sweet It Is*. In a *Florida Soul* interview, she describes her response to and engagement with Thomas' song, in ways that perhaps only a fellow soulful singer and political artist can.

"You know," Osborne says, "the original recording was just a demo with him singing and playing the organ with that primitive drum machine. It's like a meditation in that way, more like someone communing with themselves, as opposed to a full band. That's a group experience and takes more arrangement. You can picture Timmy Thomas sitting there alone in a room, just connecting with the song, discovering things about it, and allowing that song to flow through him. He's communing with this lyric, and there's something very pure about it. That's what people connected to when the song became a big hit, I think, and that's what I connected to every time I heard it."

She liked the economy of it and that it was sincere but not strident. "The song doesn't overstay its welcome, and it's not hitting anybody over the head. It's just a very direct, simple statement and this emotional connection with the question: 'Why do things have to be this way?'"

Before recording her version Osborne intentionally didn't listen to other covers, such as Sade's. "I didn't want too many ideas cluttering things up, and if I heard something else that I liked, then I'd have to avoid it because they had already done it. So the less I listened to other people's versions, the better."

The goal she, producer John Leventhal, and producer/engineer Rick DePofi set for themselves in creating *How Sweet It Is* "was to reimagine these songs in a way that was respectful but also allowed people to hear them in new and different ways." For her "WCWLT" this meant using much more and different instrumentation than Thomas did. (Leventhal played a number of instruments, including guitar, and DePofi played percussion, keyboards, and horns.) "There's no point to doing the spare version of the Timmy Thomas song," she says, "because he'd already done that."

In Osborne's take, Leventhal's fuzz-tone guitar is almost as prominent as her voice, and his use of dynamics generates some of the same emotional force. She goes four minutes and fifty-nine seconds, a minute and ten seconds longer than the original, some of that attributable to a rhythmic, semi-scatted vocal fadeout.

Her "WCWLT" took on a different resonance, Osborne says, because of the 2002 timing. "When the record was released we were in this post–9/11 moment, almost a new world, and all the songs suddenly could be heard in that context. And I thought this song in particular really stood out, talking about, 'Why can't we live together?' I felt it really spoke very directly about the way a lot of people were feeling in that moment, this simple cry from the heart."

Thomas the educator, activist, and comeback performer, at his Miami home. Photo © Suzanne Williamson.

DRAKE'S REPURPOSING OF "WCWLT," singing over the original organ tracks on "Hotline Bling," "only" made it to #2 on the Hot 100. But it reached #1 on *six* other charts in 2015. Drake's lyrics deal with very different concerns than Thomas' original, as in: "*You used to call me on my cell phone / Late night when you need my love.*" Even if Thomas had wanted to, though, there was no escaping it.

"I got a call from one of my relatives in Indiana," Thomas says, "asking me, 'Have you heard Drake's new song?' I say no, then I get another phone call, telling me, 'Timmy they're playing your original track, not just covering your song. I just heard it two or three times on the Tom Joyner morning show.'"

Did he know who Drake was? "No, sir, I did not. I don't listen to the radio much anymore. My granddaughter had to tell me, 'Granddaddy, Drake is a super big artist.'" So on his next car trip he tuned in Miami's Power 96 and sure enough, on it came. "I had to pull over," Thomas says, "the same way I did when I first heard myself on the radio in 1972." Steve "Silk" Hurley was playing one of his old-school morning mixes, blending Drake's song with Thomas' original cut. "I loved it," Thomas says. "I'm so honored that with all the beats and rhythms that have come out between 1972 and 2015, Drake and his crew thought there was something special about my song."

The artist was also pleased that Drake didn't use profanity on top of his rhythms and chords, and very appreciative that the other performer licensed the use of his music "the right way. He gave me the credit, contacted my publishing company, so there's nobody running, as has happened so often in the past."

Based on his long-standing community work as well as this new notoriety, Thomas was a Grand Marshall of the 2015 Martin Luther King Day parade in Miami, along with his longtime musical associate Betty Wright. "I just want to say thank you to Drake," he says. "He's bringing Timmy Thomas back!"

He's back in the gym, anticipating more public appearances, and says he's lost between thirty and forty pounds. "I might have to get a weave in my [receding] hair," he jokes, "and try to look sexy again."

Retired from teaching since 2007, he's minister of music at his church. "I'm still trying to alleviate problems with young people like the bullying, the killings, the drive-bys," he says. "I just wish I knew the answers. These kids need jobs, I know that. Drake didn't deliver my message," Thomas acknowledges, "but what he did gives me an opportunity to talk to these kids and have them know me as the guy in 'Hotline Bling,' and that will help me get my message across."

At this writing he's preparing to go into the studio to record for the just-launched Allsun Records. (For more on this Miami start-up, see the epilogue.) He's got another message song in the works, "Wings of Change," which they plan to release before his as-yet-unnamed album. "There's still a lot of talent in Overtown," Thomas says of the hotbed where Sam and Dave was formed and countless other soul, funk, and hip-hop artists were nurtured. "We're going to record the singer, rappers and gospel choirs there and give these young people a voice."

Thomas is still called on occasion to deliver his message. In 2011, he was ready to sing, gratis, at the dedication of the Martin Luther King, Jr., Memorial in Washington, D.C., and honor the man and the cause he once served. But the timing changed and became unworkable, so that trip never materialized.

But with "so much unrest in the world, so many people hurting each other, including right here at home," Thomas knows it won't be long before someone else asks him to do what he's done all over the world. Seventy-one when he's interviewed again for *Florida Soul*, Thomas says, "I'll probably still be getting calls to perform 'Why Can't We Live Together' when I'm in a wheelchair. And I'll still do it, too. They'll say, 'Could you come? We need you to sing that song to our people one more time.'"

18

Latimore

Riverview/Miami

A GOLD EARRING IN THE SHAPE OF A G CLEF dangles from his ear. He's in his early seventies now, and his moustache and goatee are bright white, as is the big shock of hair that juts up from his head. There's much more of it in the center than on the sides, in something approaching, yet not arriving at, a Mohawk; it's more of a 'frohawk. He wears a gold bracelet and one of his front teeth shines gold as well.

Those glints aside, Benny Latimore, the soul singer and keyboard player who goes by his last name, is casually dressed in his denim work shirt and shorts, though a photographer's here to take his portrait. On another visit he wears a red Tampa Bay Bucs sweatshirt. He's very much at home—down-home, even—in Riverview, twenty minutes southwest of Tampa. (Previously he and his wife lived in Miami and Fort Pierce.) He keeps it his home, and not a place of business. "I don't gig around," he says, meaning, essentially: He doesn't play where he eats.

"I haven't done that for years," Latimore continues, sitting in the screened-in pool area behind their one-story house. "I worked a lot locally earlier on, in Miami, but when I started to have records that did well in other places I mostly stayed out. From here I can fly anywhere [using Tampa's airport] and I've got [Interstate route] 75, I can go up and down that, too."

It's not that touring artists tend to have higher status than local acts. Latimore's more concerned with grounding. "I keep my personal life separate from show business, and that's the way I've been able to stay in it so long. When I come home I want to be home. It's like taking off a pair of pants and throwing them over in the corner and then when I get ready to go out, I put them back on. I keep everything in perspective," he concludes. "Showbiz is part of me but not all of me. I don't let it consume me."

He's calm and convincing, and his fifty years as a working musician attest that his methods work—for Latimore. So many other artists describe their careers in traumatic terms, as hurtful addictions they were ultimately able or unable to kick, or failed life missions in which making a living constantly eluded them. Jacksonville singer Jackie Moore, who did well, still calls the music business "The Beast." Latimore's satisfied. After two dozen albums and fifteen singles on the R&B charts, he's still in demand at soul and blues festivals and plays out selectively; maybe two or three times a month.

His composition and signature song "Let's Straighten It Out" was a #1 R&B hit in 1974 and is still heard on R&B and "Quiet Storm" radio programs. Two TV appearances offer more evidence of his career longevity: He sang his "Somethin' 'Bout 'Cha" on *American Bandstand* in 1977, and in 2014, he sat in with the Roots on *The Tonight Show*, timed to the release of a Latimore greatest-hits album. His song "Move and Groove Together" had had an even longer half-life; released in 1968, it was heard forty-five years later in the hit Netflix series *Orange Is the New Black*.

"*Sit yourself down, girl, and talk to me,*" "Straighten It Out" begins. "*Tell me what's on your mind.*" A couple of verses later Latimore sings: "*Instead of you crying your eyes out, baby / you and me oughta be getting it on.*" Everyone sings about love, but in his singing and writing Latimore created and maintained a distinct persona, that of a love man who combines the romantic and the overtly sexual in just the right combination or alternations, and that's won him a loyal female following. (He appears bare-chested on many of his earlier album covers.)

He's a big man, always has been, weighing more than two hundred pounds at just over six feet tall. His head is big, too, and those two resonating chambers gave him a deep, forcefully resonant voice. His success has been more sustained and less dramatic commercially, but Latimore could be seen as a bluesier, grittier, and less hefty Barry White. Besides the deep voices, both wore beards and their most lucrative years came in the 1970s. But Latimore would never surround himself with a one-hundred-piece "Love Orchestra."

He's self-made in many ways, and self-determined in practically all ways. Latimore has approached his life and run his career from his own committed stance, and that's served him. He married a Cuban-American woman more than forty-five years ago, when that was very unusual, and accepted the consequences. Or, as he says about that and other race-based difficulties: "I rise above it."

The G-clef earring also signifies in an idiosyncratic way. This respected piano and keyboard man doesn't read music. He could have learned, certainly, but decided he didn't need to, that he would play his own way.

There was a piano in the Latimore home, out in the country near Charleston, Tennessee. His father worked the fields while his mother, Etna, looked after Benny and his three younger siblings. (The singer's full given name is Benny, not Benjamin, just as his father's was Eddie, not Edward.) Born in 1939, he was "a smart kid," skipping a grade and, no surprise, big for his age. Etna only had a fourth-grade education, and "when we were going to school my mother learned right along with us," he says. "She read every book that came in that house, and when she was no longer able to help me I helped her." The son remembers getting one B in high school—in algebra—and the rest As.

Everyone sang and his mother played the guitar. His two sisters took lessons; he didn't. "I played by ear and I learned over the years by trial and error." Benny sang in their Baptist church and listened to the nighttime R&B shows on Nashville's WLAC, but he didn't think about music as a profession until he went to Tennessee Agricultural and Industrial State College in Nashville (now Tennessee State). He was studying English and planning on becoming a teacher, but singing in a college group, the Neptunes, began to change his mind. Latimore also made extra money singing on country music demos for Nashville labels. "I had the right accent from growing up in Tennessee," he says. "We all [black and white] sound alike there."

A successful audition—as a vocalist, not a piano man—with Louis Brooks and His Hi-Toppers drove him to leave school. Brooks was a saxophone player whose biggest hit, with Earl Gaines singing, was "It's Love Baby (24 Hours A Day)" in 1958. When Latimore joined that year the Hi-Toppers played R&B with a doo-wop flavor, jazz, and pop. The woman who rented Latimore his room near campus had a piano, and he "drove that lady crazy, day in and day out," trying to hone his chops, working out the Hi-Toppers' songs by ear. He'd already begun to learn some chords from other players. "I'd ask them, 'What is this?' and they'd say: 'C major.' 'What about this?' 'C major seventh,' and so on." He fell in love with minor keys. "They can be dark but they're soulful." But his chords and his singing remained "my own things, I did them in my own style." Since he hadn't been trained, his fingering was different, and these "improper" techniques lent his playing unique colors.

Brooks tired of his piano player and asked Latimore if he would replace him. When the younger man said he wasn't able, the bandleader told him to come to his house every day, and he'd teach him. "He didn't teach me to read," Latimore says. "He'd play some chord changes, and then I would play them, and then go home and practice. Sometimes I didn't know what I was playing but I knew what I heard. I went through a hell of time trying to do it, but eventually I got Louis' repertoire down. Then one night we're playing and he says, 'Take a solo,' and I didn't know what to do."

Brooks told him, "Just sing with your fingers." That technique—playing what he would sing, hum, or whistle to that tune—along with much more practice, enabled him to solo. "I still tell young guys that today, including guys who have really studied music," he says. "Don't just do something that you heard somebody else do, and don't worry about 'What scale are we using?' It's supposed to be a solo, to be *your* thing."

After two years with Brooks he joined a friend from Nashville, singer Joe Henderson, who had a crossover hit with "Snap Your Fingers" in 1962. They'd promised each other that whoever made it first would give the other a job, and Henderson kept his word. "Sometimes I would open for him by myself, and I was his musical director," says Latimore. "And I can't even read music." That band toured from Maine to California and took Latimore to Florida for the first time.

Jackie Wilson was headlining this particular touring revue, and Hank Ballard's Royals (not to be confused with The "5" Royales) were on the bill along with Henderson. Like so many others in the post–World War II era, Latimore had Florida dreams. "Back in Tennessee, we knew a trucker who used to go there, and he'd stop at our house and show us pictures of the palm trees, fruit trees, oranges. You could pick oranges at the back of the yard! Florida was fascinating to me."

After those initial gigs, the Henderson band stayed in Miami for a couple weeks, playing the Knight Beat in Overtown. Latimore was about to win the amateur talent show competition with his version of Wilson's "To Be Loved," accompanying himself on organ, but someone pointed out he was a professional and he was disqualified. Still, Clyde Killens, the club's promoter, liked what he heard and invited Latimore to come back. As often happens to transplanted Floridians, winter weather—in this case the winter of 1961 or 1962—saw that he did.

"That was one of the worst winters ever," Latimore remembers, and the Henderson band got stranded in Gary, Indiana. "We were supposed to go to Minnesota, but they called us and said, 'Don't even think about it.'" Latimore made the call to Miami. It turned out the piano player in the house band, Frank Duboise and the Chicken Scratchers, had just taken sick, so Killens sent him a plane ticket. The job paid ninety dollars a week and came with an efficiency apartment in the hotel. Soon Latimore was switched to playing between the Scratchers' and the touring headliners' sets with a drummer who went by Bugs (for $110 a week). Their numbers included Jackie Wilson and Ben E. King songs, and "some Broadway tunes, like 'What Kind of Fool Am I' or 'The Greatest Love.' I'd mix it up."

Then he encountered his second great mentor, Joe Watson, who went by Black Magic. "This man was a world-class jazz piano player, a killer," Latimore says. "He worked in the [separate] lounge at the Sir John; he'd call me up to sing something, and we got to be really good friends. He showed me a lot of jazz chords and I told him, 'I think I want to learn to read music, and play like you do.' And he said, 'Don't worry about it. You got style. Work within yourself.'

"He told me reading music is—I'll say it the way he said it—'just doing what some other motherfucker did. Anybody can learn how to read, you gotta do what feels good to you. You internalize it first, and then let it come out.' I kept doing it my way and it's become like a trademark; people comment as much on my playing as they do on my singing."

Magic's playing was sophisticated but concise, a style Latimore naturally was drawn to. "You don't have to play a whole lot of notes to get it across," he says. "It's like some blues guitar players. They show you how fast they can play and it means nothing. Then you can take three or four little things and play it and it's meaningful. Magic told me, 'It's a conversation, and some people talk slower than others. Just concentrate on getting your message across, communicating.'"

Singer/songwriter and keyboard player Timmy Thomas, a trained, reading musician, worked frequently with Latimore at T.K. in the 1970s. He'd play off what Latimore was doing on the piano or electronic keyboards, layering in different chords and runs on his Hammond B-3 organ. "He's bluesier than I am," Thomas says, "and we blended very well." That Latimore doesn't read music doesn't stop Thomas, who's a trained musician, from admiring his work: "He can do things that I can't do."

Magic got him an afternoon gig at a Miami-area Sheraton, and the two began to work on Latimore's singing as well. He had good natural phrasing in his piano playing, Magic told him; that would help his singing, and in turn improved vocal phrasing would elevate his playing. "Listen to guys like Sinatra and Tony Bennett," Magic said. "Those guys don't over-sell the song with all kinds of vocal [tricks] and curlicues. Just tell the story." That's helped him over the years, Latimore says. "Having a good voice doesn't necessarily mean you can sing. Singing is using whatever voice you have to get what needs to be gotten out of that song. You're supposed to get lost in the song, and not get to where you are more important than what you're singing."

As much as he's found his own way, Latimore honors the debt he owes his teachers, especially Louis Brooks and Magic. "These men were old enough to be my father, and I'm from the old school where you honor older people. You don't want to get cocky as a young guy and think you know everything. You might be smart but you're not wise. Knowledge is passed on to you and wisdom comes from experience. Intelligence is like having a Ferrari and being wise is knowing how to drive."

AFTER INTEGRATION, the Knight Beat "started to dwindle down," Latimore remembers. Black people could now go to Miami's white clubs, including at the beach, so they did. Latimore migrated as well, holding down a steady gig in the Crystal Room of the Fontainebleau hotel. For a week or so, Frank Sinatra played the La Ronde room there while filming a movie locally, and he'd catch parts of Latimore's sets, preceded by bodyguards in black suits. "What does Frank think?" Latimore asked the hotel's entertainment director anxiously.

"Well, he hasn't complained," Latimore was told. "So I guess you're alright."

From there he moved to the touristy Castaways Hotel on Sunny Isles Beach, where he, guitarist Roach Thompson, and drummer Freddie Scott worked as the Kinfolk. (At different times this band was also billed as Freddie Scott and the Kinfolk; Freddie Scott and the Kinfolk featuring Latimore; and Latimore and the Kinfolk.) The Wreck Bar at the Castaways had a gimmick—"the music never stops"—so as one band finished their set, the next act would start taking their places and taking over their instruments in a seamless segue. The house dancers in bikinis were another memorable feature; they were known as the Treasure Chests. "But it was never anything vulgar," Latimore maintains. At times there were also Beach Boys, eye candy for the female clientele.

The Castaways' owner, Joe Hart, was a stickler for punctuality, which Latimore says has served him well throughout his career. He was intro-

Benny Latimore (*center*) and the Kinfolk, including drummer Freddy Scott, *lower left*, and underage bass player Chocolate Perry, *top right*. Courtesy of Latimore.

duced to another fact of musical life at the beaches: kickbacks. "I don't know about the other bands, but the black bands had to pay kickbacks to the entertainment directors to work on Miami Beach," he says. "On the books you'd be getting AA union scale, but you didn't actually get that. The guy who booked you there got his percentage, and the entertainment director got his percentage, too." Latimore got fed up and went to see Hart. "He said, 'What kickback?' I'm sure he knew about it, but he couldn't tell me he knew about it. So he gave me a raise, AA scale plus some more, and we stayed another six months."

On Sunday afternoons the Kinfolk played matinees at the Ocean Mist, right on the beach in Fort Lauderdale, and in 1970 or 1971 that became their next base. The three principal Kinfolk had worked together on and off since the mid-1960s, when they'd backed up some of Henry Stone's T.K. Productions artists on recording sessions and toured behind Steve Alaimo. They traveled with him to Tampa, where they played the Cuban Patio (which drew a predominantly white crowd) and the Oasis (mostly black). In Jacksonville they held down the Forum, where "the waiters and waitresses dressed in togas—short ones. That was a fabulous place where you'd dress up, and bring your wife."

To begin with, the band members were the only African Americans in the Forum, but the owner was open-minded, so Latimore and the other musicians went to the black neighborhood around Ashley Street and recruited. "Folks there would say, 'I can't go there, it's too expensive' or they thought they wouldn't be welcome. But we convinced them, and ended up integrating the place." A shy, nervous young singer who opened for them one time went by Aaron Neville.

At other white clubs in Florida, Latimore says, there was a place reserved for the black musicians to sit between their sets—usually in the kitchen or some back room. "I never did that and I wouldn't," he says, for both personal and commercial reasons. "I would go out and hang with the people, mingle, do the promotional thing. I was happy to do that," he says, and the owners came to see that it was good for business.

He did need a coping strategy, however, to deal with all that bonhomie. "The first thing people would want to do is buy me a drink. But I don't drink that much. So I'd work with the bartenders to fix me up something that looks like I'm drinking, but not with alcohol, and they're paying for a real drink. So they'd make plenty of money on the bar."

During this time when racial dynamics were changing, "we opened up a lot of doors in Florida," Latimore says. "The younger guys today just take a lot of things for granted; they don't have any idea about that. I wasn't trying to be a rabble-rouser, though, I just did my thing from a personal standpoint."

IN THE EARLY 1970S LATIMORE BECAME one of the go-to regulars in T.K.'s studio ensemble, backing up Betty Wright on all her early work, Gwen McCrae, Little Beaver, and others in Stone's stable. He took his turn as a leader as well and in 1972 Stone released a Latimore cover of the T-Bone Walker blues, "Stormy Monday." His version is much snappier and quicker than the usual treatment, including Bobby Bland's classic take, and begins with a jazzy/bluesy piano chorus. Latimore's not much for complication or adornment but was drawn to the song's subtly different chord progression.

"Monday" uses the traditional blues I–IV–V changes, beginning on the root chord, based on the keynote; say, G in the key of G. Then it moves to the chord based on the fourth note in that scale: in G, that's C. But before it moves to D, the V or dominant chord (the climactic one in the progression) the way a standard blues would, it moves to the II chord, the III, and then the flatted III (in this example, A, B, and B-flat). Latimore calls it "a little jazzy turnaround."

There's a solo by Latimore on the Melodica, a keyboard that's blown like a wind instrument; in "Monday," it sounds like a chromatic harmonica. T.K. session man Ron Bogdon played bass; Freddie Scott was on drums; Betty Wright, Gwen McCrae, George McCrae, and Latimore contributed backup vocals. At times Latimore's singing resembles that of the late Lou Rawls, who recorded "Stormy Monday" a decade earlier with jazzman Les McCann on piano. Latimore's version and Stone's promotion yielded "the first song I ever had that went outside of the city limits," he says.

"Monday" rose to #27 on the R&B chart, and he began getting out-of-town engagements. In 1973 his first album, entitled simply *Latimore*, came out on Stone's Glades label, and from then on the musician's last name alone became his stage name. The following year the two released his pivotal second album, *More, More, More Latimore*.

In a *Florida Soul* interview former T.K. vice president Steve Alaimo says that what he misses most about being a producer is "going in the studio and actually putting it together, getting something that just clicks." One night in 1974, Alaimo remembers, he and Latimore were holed up in the upstairs studio in Stone's Hialeah warehouse, working on a tune of Latimore's called "Let's Straighten It Out." This was a last-minute add-on, the artist says; they just needed one more song to fill out an album, and it was the only one in the collection he wrote.

"Just he and I were in there," Alaimo says, "and after about 11 hours, we hadn't gotten past the intro," the instrumental lead-in to Latimore's singing. "I was going insane. It's just the intro! He says, 'No, no, no, I've got to get it right.' And you know what? He was right. Believe it or not, it was fun."

Latimore concedes that he could be a perfectionist but doesn't remember the process the same way. "Steve must be thinking of another song we did together," he says with a laugh. "We did go at it at times, though, and I'd tell him: 'Don't mess with me.'"

His signature song was "inspired by some experiences, including some bad ones," Latimore says. "As much as I talk, I can still listen, and at that time there was almost a universal lack of communication and understanding between men and women. Mostly the men didn't understand the women."

The singer's persona is that of a man trying to get a woman to tell him what's bothering her, why she's tossing and turning in her sleep and, not least, why she doesn't want to have sex. As he urges and pleads with her, the song's title becomes its refrain. "I had this thing floating around in my head; in my life I used to tell people: 'Evidently something has gotten crooked. We need to straighten it out.' But my idea was you have to sit down and straighten out any kind of relationship you have," he says. "It doesn't have to be a man-woman relationship. It could be with your brother, uncle, boss, or your friend. With any two human beings there's gonna be a little bit of a clash and you have to straighten it out. I say that onstage a lot. No matter how old you are, how young you are, whether you're married, single, divorced, engaged, you gotta straighten something out sometimes."

The song's in one of his beloved minor keys: B minor. It begins with that long vibrato-laden intro on his Fender Rhodes electric piano, accompanied by Bogdon on bass and Scott on drums, using mostly cymbals. Latimore unhurriedly, thoughtfully interjects bluesy figures over a hypnotic repetition of just two chords, B minor and G minor. The vibe is introspective, moody, bordering on ominous. In the longer, LP version of the intro, Latimore also uses stop time; the music suddenly ceases twice before he comes in with these forceful lines: *"Sit yourself down, girl, and talk to me / Tell me what's on your mind / Don't keep on telling me everything's okay / 'Cause if it was then you wouldn't be crying."*

Latimore later dubbed in a second piano/keyboard part and his own background vocals. In a trope that recurs in the Florida soul story, the artist and producers had no idea "Let's Straighten It Out," the last song on the album's B-side, would attract any attention and had no plans to release it as a single. "Jolie," was the hit, the thinking went. "Straighten It Out" was filler.

The first time Latimore heard his tune on the radio, "I had just bought a new Thunderbird, the first car I had with nice-sounding speakers. I was living in Hialeah, on my way to Fort Lauderdale for my gig at the Ocean Mist, and it came on the air. It sounded great. Then a friend of mine called me from Atlanta, and said 'Man, that last cut on your album—people at house parties are playing that song and going crazy over it!'"

He called Henry Stone, who told him: "I know, I've had so many calls, we're getting ready to pull 'Jolie' and we're gonna put this out as a single." After that, Latimore recalls, "It just went crazy. To this day I don't really understand it. I mean, I don't look at it as an overwhelming musical triumph." He acknowledges that the song "has a mood to it, and it's withstood the test of time. It expresses how people feel."

A line that seemed to resonate with listeners was one Latimore and his producers had concerns about, when he sings: *"How in the hell do you expect me to understand, when I don't even know what's wrong?"* At the time saying or playing "hell" on the radio was not done and could have gotten the tune banned. "Got away with it," he says. "In fact, it became one of the lines people liked most." The song's #1 chart success also reinforced his commitment to recording more of his own songs, as opposed to covers.

Gender politics aside, it's masterfully sung, showcasing the power and soulful timbre of Latimore's voice. He attacks the lyric with intensity from the first line, and the abrupt transition from the more reflective instrumental intro into his vocals only emphasizes their fervor, which never lets up.

The story this song tells is set in the bedroom, and toward the end the sexual side of Latimore's musical persona emerges, merging with the sympathetic. The way he calibrates and delivers this admixture is no doubt important in the song's enduring appeal, and, in his overall body of work, one meaningful reason for his career longevity:

"If you're tired and don't want to be bothered, baby / Just say the word and I'll leave you alone / Instead of laying there crying your eyes out, baby / You and me oughta be getting it on

Let's straighten it out / Oh baby / Let's straighten it out . . ."

MANY MORE ALBUMS FOLLOWED, his own and others'. Then Latimore decided he'd only play on his own recordings, despite being a valued session man for much of his career. He made an exception about ten years ago, he's reminded, when he played on young British soul singer Joss Stone's early albums, *The Soul Sessions* in 2003 and *Mind Body & Soul.* "Yeah, I did that," he acknowledges with a laugh, explaining it was the chance to work with former colleagues Betty Wright (Stone's producer and vocal coach), Timmy Thomas, and Little Beaver. "I have a gold record on my wall due to that first one," he adds.

Unlike many R&B/soul singers, Latimore continued to thrive during the disco era, and his brand of romantic soul proved a sustained draw on the southern soul circuit. He did put out a single entitled "Discoed to Death," but in contrast to, say, Johnnie Taylor, who had his biggest commercial success with "Disco Lady" (a #1 R&B and #1 pop single in 1976), Latimore didn't have to adapt much to survive.

After Henry Stone's company went bankrupt in 1981, Latimore recorded for the southern blues label Malaco. He returned after Stone regrouped and formed Henry Stone Music, recording several more albums for him on their joint LatStone label, and that output continued until the impresario's death in 2014. As blues and soul cruises grew in popularity, Latimore added them to his festival gigs. He's always been a good draw in Europe; there's a ten-minute video of him doing a passionate "Let's Straighten It Out" in Vienna on YouTube. He performs all by himself on the Motif keyboard and wears a plain black T-shirt. He's smiling, clearly enjoying himself, and by song's end he has the initially restive, talkative audience enthralled.

His voice remains deep and strong, and he can still reach up into his falsetto range for emphasis. "I might put some of that in there, if I feel it," he says. "It's like the icing on the cake—but you have to bake the cake first." Like Sam Moore of Sam and Dave, Latimore says he "used to sing harder, but I learned not to sing as hard as I can. It's better to stay in your comfort range where you can use your voice better."

"That's why I admire stylists," he continues. "You may not have a great voice, like Luther Vandross, or Pavarotti or Barbra Streisand. But you still have a style that works for you. Like Willie Nelson. Or Jimi Hendrix—he had a style. Couldn't sing worth a shit, but his singing worked with his material."

Even in his seventies Latimore continues to work the Love Man persona as well—without seeming to embarrass himself. On the cover of the 2011 album *Ladies Choice*, he's shown reclining on a white fur throw rug, the first few buttons of his black silk shirt undone. A line in one of his compositions, "Bow Wow (I'm an Ol' Dog)," goes: "*I may be old but I ain't cold / I still know how to bury the bone.*"

That CD was done with Stone, T.K. bass player Chocolate Perry, and guitarist Roach Thompson, who played with Latimore in the Kinfolk. Thompson, whose given name is Warren, reveals how Latimore paid forward the mentoring he got from men like Louis Brooks and Black Magic. By his own account, when Thompson joined the Kinfolk, then known as Freddie Scott and the Kinfolk, he "sucked" as a guitarist. Luckily for him, he says, "most of the really good guitar players in Miami had their own bands," so he still got work as a sideman. The only reason he wasn't fired, he says, was that the other band members were afraid of losing the bass player, who had joined along with Thompson.

He was about twenty then and the band was working the Mr. James Club on NW 2nd Avenue and 36th Street, with singer Lee Eddy out front.

A promotional shot from Latimore's tenure with Malaco Records in the 1980s and into the 1990s. Courtesy of Latimore.

Like Latimore, Thompson doesn't read musical notation, so Latimore, as he was taught, schooled the guitar player in chords. "He didn't show me on guitar," says Thompson, who is five years younger. "He would hit a note on the organ, and I would find that note. Then he would say, 'This is the second note in this chord,' and I'd find that on my strings. After I had, say, C major, then he would say, 'This note makes it a ninth chord,' or 'this makes it a seventh,' playing it note for note on the keyboard. Through his help I learned minor chords, diminished chords, and I was like, 'Wow, man,' 'cause all I knew then was three-chord blues, the I–IV–V, and I was scuffling with that."

Latimore remembers that "Roach basically knew one solo. But like me, he had a good ear, and he became a dedicated woodshed man," meaning he practiced long and hard during their daytimes off. Similar to Latimore's unique fingering technique, Thompson invented and still uses an idiosyncratic tuning on his instrument. Eventually, Thompson says, "there came a point, man, when other guitar players ran from me."

In the mid-1970s Thompson joined the funk/soul band Notorious Miami, which at times just went by Miami. Willie Clarke was their producer; T.K. arranger Mike Lewis did the horns and strings; and the lead vocalist was Robert Moore from Jacksonville, who also led a notable soul band there called the Lemon Twisters. One of Miami's best-known songs was "Kill that Roach," which features a long screaming Thompson guitar solo. He went on to lead the Roach Thompson Blues Band for many years and continued to work with Latimore off and on. "We are pushing 50 years together now," he says.

Thompson's guitar is heard on "Move and Groove Together," the 1968 Latimore song used in *Orange Is the New Black*, and Latimore has recorded several tunes written by Thompson, including "A Woman's Love." In their later years Thompson, who was essentially retired and living near Fort Meyers, acted as his friend's driver and informal bodyguard (he's a martial arts practitioner), usually joining him onstage after they got to the gigs.

Like their friendship, Latimore the artist has had remarkable staying power. One reason, as David Whiteis points out in his book, *Southern Soul-Blues*, is that Latimore has successfully managed the transition from "live to synthesized recording techniques with a minimum of discomfort and little noticeable change in quality." The writer quotes Latimore saying: "Technology is a terrible master, but it's a good slave, if you know how to handle it. I use the new technology but we're all musicians; we don't just turn the machine on and let it play. . . . We play our stuff. We let technology do the heavy lifting. It's our slave."

That digital modernism comes up when Thompson is complimented on the memorable, bluesy guitar solos on that *Ladies Choice* album. "I don't solo on that record," he replies, "I just play rhythm." But he's the credited guitarist in the liner notes. "The solos are all Latimore," Thompson insists. "He's doing all that on his keyboard."

What turn out to be Latimore's "guitar" solos still sound a lot like Roach Thompson's style. "Well, he's taught me a lot," the guitarist says, "and I think he's learned some things from me, too."

Latimore at home in Riverview, Florida. Photo © Suzanne Williamson.

19

Jackie Moore

Jacksonville

JACKIE MOORE SAT ON THE PORCH of her mother's house on West 26th Street, pencil in hand and a brown paper grocery store bag on her lap. Her childhood home was "just the regular box house that most black folk lived in" on Jacksonville's West Side, she remembers. "It had the screened-in porch and the paved streets in the front." In 1970 this was still "the kind of neighborhood where everyone would get up and say 'Good morning' to you."

Moore was in her early twenties and much of her extended family lived within blocks. When she was growing up, her first cousin David Crawford lived just around the corner. Five or six years older than her, he would be an important musical partner, mentor, and conduit for her singing. At the time of this porch-sitting he had become a producer at Atlantic Records and Moore had just been signed to that prestigious national label.

Two years before, Crawford had come up with a short lyrical hook for Gainesville singer Linda Lyndell that turned into her biggest hit, "What a Man." To his cousin he had offered an even smaller remnant, just a repeated one-word term of endearment. "Dave had come up with the line, 'Precious, precious,'" Moore says, "and then I began to try to fill in the lyrics, and that bag was what I had to write on. Then when Dave and I next got together, we bounced that story off of each other, and there we were."

Their collaboration, a bittersweet piece of soul storytelling, begins, in part, like this: "*If you don't want me, honey, that's alright / If you ain't willin', baby, there sure won't be no fight / 'Cause I'm still satisfied in loving you / And I'll be waiting 'round when you get through.*"

Crawford put the musical accompaniment together, and they recorded a demo version in Jacksonville before laying down the finished Atlantic track in Miami's Criteria Studio. Cissy Houston and the Sweet Inspirations sang backup and a Louisianan named Mack Rebennack was an uncredited piano player; he was later known as Dr. John. Moore and Crawford thought his composition "Willpower" would be the hit from that Atlantic session. It's also told from the standpoint of a loving woman, done wrong, who vows to endure her man's wanderings with patience and determination. It's a driving up-tempo song, whereas "Precious" is, at least tempo-wise, more relaxed. The horns on "Willpower" pop louder, and that cut also ends with a real vocal climax, Moore's voice carrying over pounding horn and drum licks. For whatever reasons, though, Moore says with a laugh, "nobody bought one copy of 'Willpower.'"

She was out on a Crawford-arranged tour with the great (and too often overlooked) southern soul performer Joe Tex when some DJs turned their "Willpower" singles over and started wearing out "Precious, Precious" instead. The refrain was particularly sticky and sung along to: "*Oh, you're precious, honey / You're so precious / Precious baby, you're mine.*"

It was a huge hit, certified by the Recording Industry Association of America (RIAA) as a gold or million-selling record in March 1971. As that status suggests it crossed over from R&B success (#12) to pop, reaching #30 on the mainstream *Billboard* chart. "Precious" is one of fifteen Moore songs to crack the R&B best-seller list between 1970 and 1983. Her next best-remembered song is probably the 1979 dance-soul hit, "This Time Baby," which surpassed the O'Jays' original in sales and popularity.

"Precious" has become a classic, included on countless soul compilations and covered by many artists—including men, such as O.V. Wright; Otis Clay; and Toots Hibbert of Toots and the Maytals. Kanye West (with Ludacris) sampled "Precious" on his 2004 song "Breathe In, Breathe Out." It's the first song on a two-CD Moore set, "The Complete Atlantic Recordings," many of which were previously unreleased, issued in 2015 on the British label Real Gone Music.

Part of the song's appeal, its dramatic energy, may derive from the clash between the title endearment and the less-than-endearing behavior of the man it's addressed to: "*You've been in and out of my life / And, ooh, baby that hurts / You've been with every girl in this town / You've been dealin' in dirt.*"

Perhaps listeners knew from experience that love sometimes works in convoluted and contradictory ways and that those twists can make it even more intense. Just after that dirt-dealing—and the pain it causes—are exposed, the narrator comes back to confide: "*I look at love as a two-way street / You get the good with the bad / You take the bitter with the sweet.*" The lover in question is like two men wrapped up in one, and on balance, the singer and song circle back to conclude, "*You're precious, honey / You're so precious / Precious baby, you're mine.*"

That synthesis of opposites plays out musically as well. The song's relaxed tempo, the rolling, melodious horn lines (dubbed in later by the Memphis Horns) and the melodic sweetness of Moore's vocals, is juxtaposed with the tough, painful scenarios depicted. The three-and-a-half-minute single doesn't have any weak verses either; when the last well-crafted lines are sung, the story ends.

As sometimes also happens—see Florida soul singer James Purify, who was never a fan of his biggest hit, "I'm Your Puppet"—Moore wasn't particularly taken by "Precious." For a good long while, she thought: "'What is wrong with these people, that they love this song like that?' I just couldn't understand that vibe, because I was so into 'Willpower,' which didn't sell anything."

"Then I was performing in New Orleans one time," she continues, "and it hit me. I finally got that it was a great song and why both men and women love it. It comes down to what the lyrics say: 'You've been in and out, and that hurts; you've been with everybody in town, but I am still around.' And I somehow had just not gotten that before."

Moore also thinks the song benefited from its simplicity. "Simple songs sell," she says. "I tell people: 'When you write it, don't make it too complex.' Some songs are going here-here, and there-there. *No, no, no.* Just say what you're going to say. Because if people don't catch it in the first couple of bars you don't have nothing. I tell kids [aspiring musicians] today, whatever you're going to do you better hit it right away, because these record companies ain't fixing to give you but a minute to say what you're gonna say."

Brad Shapiro, a producer who worked with her at Atlantic and later signed her to his own label, Kayvette, doesn't consider Moore a funky, churchy deep soul singer like Aretha Franklin. He sees her as more of a "smooth, pop-sounding singer," though that may have a lot to do with the material he and other producers, as well as Moore herself, chose. On her stronger numbers and especially on gospel-tinged songs like "They Tell Me of an Uncloudy Day," Moore delivers a rich, feeling-drenched timbre that puts her right in the realm of other renowned soul sisters. In that more powerful approach her voice darkens into more of a contralto shade than her usual mezzo-soprano.

Shapiro mentions Etta James and that seems somewhat apt as, like Moore, James could sing sweetly ("At Last") as well as bluesy ("I'd Rather Go Blind"). Moore rarely if ever sounds that blue. Shapiro's word "smooth" might be apropos in that, even in the blaring dance soul number "This Time Baby," Moore's voice never becomes strident yet manages to cut through the accompaniment to be heard easily. Her enunciation is always clear and easily intelligible, with no trace of a southern accent; that may be traced to her early adoration of Motown's Mary Wells.

Moore's singing and Crawford's songwriting made many of their early 1970s collaborations memorable, still heard on soul radio and online more than forty years later. Mostly Moore sang love songs, but "If," on her 1973 Atlantic album, *Sweet Charlie Babe*, was a plea for peace and global justice: "*If it wasn't for this, and wasn't for that, it could be a better world.*" That song was later sampled by Jay Z in 2001 on his song "The Ruler's Back."

"Clean Up Your Own Yard" and "Joe," both included on the Atlantic reissue, were sampled by Christina Milian and Fat Joe, respectively. "This Time Baby," part of Moore's work done without her Jacksonville cousin, was used by the late Michael Jackson on "Love Never Felt So Good" in 2014.

Back in the summer of 1970, when "Precious" was surging up the charts, Crawford called Moore and told her she had to come off the Joe Tex tour and headline her own engagements behind that single. They were in Boston when she broached that with Tex (whose given name was Joe Arrington, Jr., and who hailed from Arkansas). He was agreeable to letting her leave his tour early but asked her to stay through their New York gigs, as he had a surprise for her. "When we pulled up to the Apollo Theater," Moore remembers, "Joe had my name up there under his name on the marquee. While I was boo-hooing, he told me, 'It's going to happen for you, and I just wanted you to see that now.' I later played the Apollo quite a few times, but that was an amazing moment."

It all started, she reflects, on a Jacksonville porch with that brown paper grocery bag. "I still have the bag," she reveals. "Oh, yeah. I had it mounted. That there is for my kids."

THE SIGN INSIDE THE WILLIAMS MEMORIAL CME (Christian Methodist Episcopal) Church tracks Sunday school attendance. The record, it says, is 102 attendees. On this Communion Sunday in early May, there were fifty-two students, yet by 11 a.m. perhaps a hundred and a half worshippers fill the pews arranged under the vaulted wooden ceiling. The range of ages extends from elderly ladies in striking Sunday hats to middle-aged couples, from teens to toddlers and babies with their young mothers.

The interior is clean, uncluttered, and looks freshly painted white, as does the exterior. A sign near the front entrance calls Jesus "The Unde-feated Heavyweight Champion," which may be a reference to the Manny Pacquiao/Floyd Mayweather fight the night before. Inside the congregants are enthused, ready to get prayed up. A three-piece live band kicks in and the choir lined up behind the pulpit, in black uniforms with red trim, sways as it sings into an array of microphones. Soon the cry rings out: "It's wor-ship time!"

"It's a lively church," says Jackie Moore Hopkins, seated in one of the pews toward the back on the left-hand side. Like many others, she fans her-self in these warm confines. Her husband, Calvin Hopkins, is the pastor of this church surrounded by others in what seems like a black religious dis-trict in northwest Fort Lauderdale. The New Hope Baptist Church, Church in the Lord Jesus Christ, Church of Christ, Mitchell Memorial Highway Church of Christ, St. Thomas True Tabernacle, and the Apostle Faith Church of Jesus (as well as a mosque) are all within a few short blocks. It's churchy around here.

Mrs. Hopkins wears a pink jacket over a pink and black skirt. Her lip-stick is bright red and her brown straight hair is parted in the middle. She keeps her gold-colored sunglasses on; they have "Vogue" emblazoned on one sidepiece. Reverend Hopkins, in a long black tunic with red but-tons, white clerical collar, wire-rimmed glasses and a salt-and-pepper beard, begins to preach. At sixty-five, he's about five years younger than she is. His oratory mixes colloquialisms, good humor, and some stern rebukes. "There's not a lot of things God hates," he declares, "but one thing we know He hates is a lying tongue." Along with others, his wife responds from her seat: "I know that's right."

For many soul singers, services such as these would be a spiritual and musical homecoming, a rerooting in the black church, where they first be-gan singing and their talent was first recognized, including by themselves. But despite her importance and allegiance here, church isn't those things for Jackie Moore. She didn't grow up singing there and has always resisted entreaties that she perform and record gospel. "That's just not me." She loves the Lord, she says, but her calling is to sing soul.

When she was growing up on Jacksonville's west side in the 1950s, ev-eryone went to church, including her family. "But I just never had a desire to sing in the choir," she says. "I already knew that was not where I was supposed to be." Instead, her musical epiphany came to her alone, and in a much different chamber.

Jackie was raised as an only child by an aunt and her husband; she only discovered in her teens that her young, unmarried birth mother had asked her sister to raise her. Jackie always sang around the house, and in her teens she was a huge fan of one Motown artist: Her yearbook described her as "the next Mary Wells." "One day I was in the bathroom," Moore says, "looking at myself in the mirror, and I started singing 'You Beat Me to the Punch.' And—I can remember like it was yesterday—I said, 'Oh I can *sing*.' I had a little vibrato to my voice and . . . I just knew. That was what I was meant to do."

She'd already been singing in school talent shows, and with a little group comprising her, her cousin David, and another cousin, Alvin Crawford. David was a piano prodigy who *did* get his start in gospel, and by the time Jackie was in high school Crawford was a disc jockey on Jacksonville's WOBS. His on-air moniker was the Demon, and, as she puts it, "he had inroads into the music business."

During high school Moore got some experience singing, mostly backup, in small Jacksonville lounges. Her being underage made it harder if not impossible to work in the better-known clubs on Ashley Street, but the lesser places weren't as strict. Besides Mary Wells, Moore was listening to Aretha Franklin, Gladys Knight, and the jazzier Nancy Wilson. When Wells' tune "Two Lovers" came out in 1963, Crawford wrote a takeoff he called "Three Lovers." Connections, confidence, and, the singer now thinks, naiveté, got them an appointment to offer the song and audition Moore at Motown.

"We drove all the way from Jacksonville to Detroit in some old car; I have no earthly idea how we made it," she recalls. "We practically got frostbitten. But we were determined, Dave and I both." Those two, plus cousin Alvin and one other male singer, did "Three Lovers" for William "Mickey" Stevenson, Motown's A&R man and a hugely important figure in the music business. When they finished he told Crawford (with Moore present): "She has a nice little voice. Let's give her a couple of more years to see if it's going to mature and then let's bring her back."

Back to Jacksonville. "But I was still convinced," Moore says. "I knew early on what my destiny was when it came to my music." She had also been singing in a three-person girl group, Jackie and the Jackettes, in high school, but stopped working with them, she says, because the other girls were not as committed. "I was serious. The call had already been made on my life. I remember the day I said, 'Nope, I'm going it alone.' I was very vigilant about this and I always have been."

When she graduated, Moore says, several colleges offered her music scholarships. But she didn't see any need for voice training or to be steeped in music theory. "I knew I could sing and it wasn't something learned, it was instinctive. Same thing with David: He did not read music; all you had to do was sing something, though, and he could play it."

Moore told her mother: "I know what I want to do. I want to record music. I really don't think it's fair for me to take your money and go to school when I know in my heart that's not what I want to do." She'd been spending summers with relatives in Philadelphia and she knew the music scene there was simmering. So she went, with her mother's blessing, to "see if I could wriggle my way in."

She stayed with her aunts for a while and then enrolled in a respiratory therapy course at the Albert Einstein Medical Center. "They paid me to go," she says. "I went to school in order to eat, because I was still dead-on trying to get somebody to hear me sing." Moore moved into a sort of dorm or rooming house at the center, with one shared bathroom, a shared hot plate, and one phone booth in the hall.

"Do you remember the old Wollensak recorder?" she asks. "Well, I made a reel-to-reel tape of some songs I had written—no music, just me singing. There was a club called Skylark, off of Broad Street, and every Friday all the local producers and singers would be there for talent scout night. I wasn't 21 yet, but every week I would go down there and see if I could get the bouncer to give my tape to—to whoever, I don't know—who might be there. Maybe Kenny Gamble or Bobby Martin." Gamble, Leon Huff, and Martin, a producer and arranger best known for his work with the O'Jays and Harold Melvin and the Blue Notes, were beginning to create the soul canon that became known as TSOP, the Sound of Philadelphia. (Early on Martin produced singles for two other Florida soul singers, Paul Kelly and Helene Smith.)

"I can hear that bouncer now," Moore says. "He would say, 'You the same little fat girl back here again, talking about 'Is Bobby Martin there?'" So . . . she was bigger back then? "Oh I was fat, I was huge. Just wait and see some of the pictures. But we'll get back to that."

One Friday the bouncer took the tape and came back to the door without it. "Okay," he said, "I gave it to Bobby Martin, I put it in his hands. Now will you go home?" Less than a week later, Moore says, "that one telephone we had in the hallway rang and it was Bobby Martin. He said, 'You can really sing, and I see you wrote these songs. I want to set up a meeting for you.'"

Martin paired her up with another affiliated producer, Jimmy Bishop. He produced her first singles in 1968 and 1969, including "Dear John" and "Loser Again," on the Shout and Wand labels. But Bishop was also working with Philadelphia-born singer Barbara Mason, who had a big hit in 1965 with "Yes, I'm Ready," and most of his attention was going to her, Moore says. Bishop's wife Louise had been appointed Moore's manager and, recognizing her charge was not going to flourish in the status quo, she arranged to sell her contract to Atlantic's Jerry Wexler. There, she would team up again with Crawford. "That's when I went back to Florida," Moore says, "and Dave and I began to work on 'Precious, Precious.'"

CRAWFORD WAS A TREMENDOUSLY GIFTED and accomplished figure, not just in Florida soul but in the history of soul music writ large. Besides Moore and Linda Lyndell, Crawford produced work by other Florida artists, including singer Gene Middleton (with whom Lyndell and sax man Charlie Blade worked) and the Tampa-based girl group the Lovelles, who became Faith, Hope, and Charity. He is also credited with writing "You Shot Me Through the Grease" for the Georgia Soul Twisters, led by Clarence Griffin of Eustis, Florida. In addition to his work as the Demon on Jacksonville's WOBS, he also DJ'd at Tampa's premier soul station, WTMP. (One of his colleagues at WOBS was Willie Martin, "Doctor Groove," with whom Crawford cowrote songs for Jackie Moore, Dee Dee Warwick, and Wilson Pickett.)

During his years working for Jerry Wexler at Atlantic and, later, on his own L.A. Records, as well as other companies, Crawford worked with Wilson Pickett, Sam and Dave (post-Stax), Esther Phillips, Baby Washington, and Archie Bell and the Drells. Beyond soul's usual boundaries, he also produced and wrote several songs on three pop-leaning B. B. King albums in the 1970s and 1980s, coproduced the J. Geils Band's first album, and worked with the hard-rock group Iron Butterfly.

Brad Shapiro was teamed with Crawford at Atlantic for several years and worked with him on much of Moore's work there after "Precious." Shapiro, who played bass on many of their sessions with Crawford on keyboards, was white, and Crawford was black. Wexler called them his "salt and pepper production team."

"Dave was a great piano player, fabulous," Shapiro says. "His playing was straight out of the church," Shapiro continues, "and he played that church groove, which was the heart of R&B. You don't hear that anymore in today's R&B—not at all."

His partner was deeply religious, Shapiro remembers. He even suggests that the Crawford tune "What a Man" was originally about Jesus and not a secular lover, as in Lyndell's rendition. Crawford clearly borrowed from and transposed some gospel songs and religious themes into pop, as Ray Charles had done so successfully at soul's beginnings. In another Crawford song Moore sang, the hard-driving "I Forgive You," that title is followed by: *"for you know not what you do."*

"They Tell Me of an Uncloudy Day," credited to Moore and Shapiro as well as Crawford, "came right out of the hymn book," she says. It's one of the most stirring, soulfully sung cuts she did for him and Atlantic, and it shows Crawford's gift for songs that were at once striking and original, yet immediately recognizable and easily appreciated, both by listeners steeped in soul and by pop audiences.

Many of his best songs are told from a female perspective and express unsurprising sentiments—on love, heartache, and those things in combination—in surprising ways. In one Crawford composition Moore sings this semi-ominous warning: *"Change me not / you may not like the change in me."*

Lyrically he used idiosyncratic word choices and phrasings, often followed by simpler, catchy choruses. In the late 1970s Crawford had several hits on Warner Brothers with Alabama-born singer Candi Staton, including "Victim" and "Young Hearts Run Free." Written and produced by him, they were dance-club favorites and the latter title became a ubiquitous #1 R&B hit in 1976, staying on that chart for twenty-one weeks, reaching #20 on the pop list as well.

In a 2010 interview with the *Oxford American* magazine, Staton recalled a conversation with Crawford in 1975. The singer was telling him about an abusive relationship she was in, and Staton noticed he was taking notes. She remembered him telling her, "I'm gonna write you a song [about this] that's gonna last forever." "Those were his exact words," Staton said. "And so he did."

That song, "Young Hearts," begins with the plaintive, distinctive question: *"What's the sense in sharing this one and only life / Ending up just another lost and lonely wife?"* The result, as Crawford wrote: *"You count up the years and they will be filled with tears."* Staton tells the young hearts listening to *"run free, and never be hung up, hung up like my man and me."*

After leaving Atlantic in the mid-1970s, Crawford became A&R director for ABC (at times known as ABC Dunhill) in Los Angeles, worked independently as a producer from Atlanta, including with Staton, and launched his own label, L.A. Records. That last venture did not do too well, it seems, and for a time Crawford returned to his former role as a DJ on a Miami gospel station. Moore has the sense that Crawford had a hard time making the transition in the late 1970s and early 1980s, as popular music changed "from the old rhythm and blues to more dance-oriented music. I'm sure he got caught up in that, and just wasn't able to turn it back around."

With his long face, Afro, and black beard, he resembled the young Gil Scott-Heron of the Last Poets and "The Bottle." Some who knew him describe Crawford as a frustrated performer. In an online interview Staton said Crawford "never got the kind of accolades he thought he deserved [as a singer]. He was a great producer and a wonderful writer but nobody was really drawn to his voice."

Florida soul singer Linda Lyndell believes Crawford, who wrote and produced her "What a Man," genuinely appreciated her as an artist. "I remember he called me from L.A when he was working with ABC-Dunhill and he said, 'You need to get out here, 'cause these people I'm producing can't sing.'" At the same time, she felt her natural singing ability rankled Crawford: "I think it ruffled his feathers somehow." Overall, though, Lyndell says, "I knew he loved me and I know I loved him."

Crawford's best-known work as a singer came on a song he wrote, "Millionaire," from the album *Here Am I*, which he put out on his own label in 1977. The lyrics, credited to Crawford, though there is an earlier, similar Billy Duke version on Capitol, are not his most memorable: "*If I had a quarter for every drop of water that fell from my eyes / from your goodbyes / I'd be a millionaire.*" On the 1975 Scorpio Records single version that's currently on YouTube, his vocals are unremarkable. On another version released long after his death, however, Crawford sounds much better, with backup vocalists accompanying him, evoking something like Marvin Gaye in the "Ain't that Peculiar" vein. Crawford also did an uncalled for but respectably sung disco version—lots of horns, congas, and strings—of Jim Croce's "Bad Bad Leroy Brown" on ABC in 1975. (Frank Sinatra made a similar mistake in judgment with that tune.)

Crawford died in 1988, when he was forty-eight or close to it. Little is known or discoverable about his death; he was reportedly murdered in Brooklyn, New York, and the killing appears to have gone unsolved. According to the *North Florida Music Hall of Fame* website, curated by Florida musician, teacher, and author Michael Ray Fitzgerald, "Crawford's songs—including a hit version of 'Whatta Man' by En Vogue and Salt-N-Pepa in 1993—would earn him [his heirs, presumably] roughly $500,000 during the decade following his death."

Moore says she had lost touch with Crawford after he left Atlantic and doesn't know much about his life after that. When Crawford died, she says, "I had not spoken to him for years and had no idea where he was."

"It's very, very sad, the ending of his life," she continues, "because he was so talented. A great producer, great writer. He and Candi did fantastic work together. The stuff he did with Wilson Pickett, the Mighty Clouds of Joy. . . . He made great music, and he loved what he did."

AFTER CRAWFORD, Moore was produced at Atlantic by LeBaron Taylor, an important figure in 1970s soul and one of the first African Americans to rise to high executive positions in the corporate music industry. (In addition to Atlantic, Taylor worked at Motown and Philadelphia International; he was also the station manager for important Philly soul station WDAS. When he died at sixty-five in 2000, he was senior vice president of corporate affairs for Sony Music and a vice president at Sony Software.)

In 1972 Taylor took her to Philadelphia to record, where he formed a production group called the Young Professionals with songwriter Phil Hurtt and singer/writer Bunny Sigler (formerly with Gamble and Huff). Those last two cowrote one of Moore's bigger hits, "Sweet Charlie Babe," which was also the name of her first and only Atlantic album, released in 1973. That single along with "Both Ends Against the Middle" had a light, bouncy pop feel, and both charted. Hurtt and Sigler wrote the "message song," "If," which didn't sell well. "Clean Up Your Own Yard" had the typical TSOP horns and strings, prominent in a long introductory sequence, and a less-global social message: *Before you judge someone else try taking a look at yourself—and shut your mouth / Clean up your own yard.*"

Moore's Atlantic contract expired in 1975, and the company didn't renew. Brad Shapiro had recently left Atlantic to go out on his own and was having success with Millie Jackson, so Moore signed with his Kayvette label, distributed by Florida kingpin Henry Stone. Almost immediately they scored one of her biggest songs, "Make Me Feel Like a Woman," written by Clarence Reid of Miami's Deep City label and T.K. Productions. This tune had a tougher, southern sound with less artful, more down-to-earth lyrics than much of her Atlantic work; it feels more like Ann Peebles' output on

Hi Records in Memphis. That single made it to #6 R&B—higher than "Precious"—but it did not reach that earlier song's "gold" sales benchmark.

Several other Moore-Shapiro collaborations charted before that collaboration, too, ended. "So I was looking for another deal," Moore remembers, "and I was looking to do something different." She discovered, however, that the music business was looking for something different, too—something different than Jackie Moore.

Despite her earlier successes, Moore couldn't even get appointments with the men running record companies' black music divisions—even those she knew. She and her entertainment lawyer couldn't understand it, but then one day her husband (she married Cal Hopkins in 1979) broke it down for her, telling his wife: "You need to lose some weight."

The business was changing, Moore says now, and she hadn't really understood that. "Before, there were lots of heavy women singers—Aretha, me, Denise LaSalle—and that was fine. But now it was becoming more about the visuals." Heavy wasn't sexy and salable anymore—even before MTV started broadcasting in 1981. She wasn't angry, Moore says, and didn't dwell on the unfairness of it; after all, "I was the same singer. It had nothing to do with my musical ability." With Calvin's help, diet, and exercise, Moore says, she dropped from 200-something to 136 pounds. "It was another obstacle," she says, "but I've always been willing to work hard and make sacrifices, because I had a goal; I was trying to get something *done*."

Finally she got LeBaron Taylor, who was by then head of "special markets" at CBS Records, on the phone and he suggested a meeting with one of his executives. Moore spent too much money on a new outfit for her meeting with Mickey Eisner, head of A&R at Columbia Records (part of CBS). She knew she looked good: "I was clean as the board of health." When Eisner, who knew her, came out to the waiting room, he had to look around a couple times, passing over her with his gaze, before recognizing the singer. He was expecting someone who took up more space. "Jackie!" he exclaimed, and a Columbia contract ensued.

Musically, Moore was ready for a new form as well. "I'd been working on the chitlin' circuit, or whatever you want to call it, for many years," she says. "I was still working with James Brown, including in some of the big theaters. But I wanted a complete new sound, more contemporary, with strings and horns—a classier style that was going to lift me out of just doing the circuit. And I had a new producer in mind: Bobby Eli, one of the studio musicians who was on *Sweet Charlie* at Atlantic."

Jackie Moore in 1979, the year of her biggest hit, "This Time Baby." Photo by Gems/Redferns/Getty Images.

Their first single was "Personally," written by Paul Kelly, who recorded as a singer and worked with Willie Clarke and Johnny Pearsall at Deep City. (Later it would be a pop hit for Karla Bonoff.) Next came the driving dance hit, "This Time Baby." Cal Hopkins "was the one who found the song," Moore says. "It was on the O'Jays' album with 'She Used to Be My Girl' on it [*So Full of Love*, 1978]. And when I was getting ready to go in the studio, he told me, 'Jackie, the O'Jays missed the hit.' When I heard it, I called Bobby and said, 'This is what I want to cut.'"

On this Philadelphia session she was backed by Atlantic Starr, best known for "Secret Lovers" and "Circles." "I remember telling the guys that day, when we were getting ready to cut it, 'Let me just tell you something:

If you put me in the groove, I'll sing it for you, and I *guarantee* you it's a hit.' When we finished it, we knew. I said, 'Okay guys, I'll see you on the charts.'"

"I was in New York when they added the strings and the horns," Moore continues, "and then they took the record to all the clubs before it was even mastered, and WBLS [probably the most important black radio station in New York at that time] jumped all over it."

When the single broke in June 1979, another important contingent embraced the song—and Jackie Moore. "I have had a very large and incredibly loyal audience in the gay community," Moore says. "Still do. If I wanted to work now, today, I could still be working for them. I've done some of the disco balls and such in earlier times. And it all started with that song; they really catapulted it."

After its strong start, Columbia put out an extended club mix, but today that 12-inch single sounds padded with unhelpful disco tropes, including much repetition and a series of introductory drum machine riffs. The original version, just under four minutes, is as strident and melodramatic as any of its disco contemporaries (Donna Summer comes to mind), but Moore manages to put some nuance and use dynamics in her singing, her voice carrying its usual tuneful resonance. It's rightfully a dance-soul classic.

The lyrics, by the team of LeRoy Bell and Casey James, whose best-known single is "Livin' It Up (Friday Night)," can be taken as sincere or ironic. The narrator concedes "*I've been selfish at times / Always trying to blow your mind*," and other improprieties, but the vocal hook insists: "*This time, this time, baby / We won't be in and out of love / in and out baby.*"

"This Time" became a #1 hit on the Hot Dance Club chart *Billboard* had added five years earlier in response to the disco phenomenon. Moore's song also went to #24 R&B and stayed on that sales ranking for fourteen weeks. A seven-minute version of the tune also appeared on her first Columbia album, *I'm on My Way*, in 1979. Yet Moore sees a cloud in what seems a silver lining. "'This Time Baby' should have been a number-one pop record, too, or at least top five," she says. It failed to make that chart at all. "You know how it is when you don't have your hookup right? Well, that's what happened here."

When the record came out, she maintains, the black music department at Columbia was having a hard time with disco in general and with their own company's dance music department in particular. "The dance people had immediately taken it to the clubs and the radio stations. By the time black music knew anything about it, it was already blasting, and they got upset. They thought, 'Here's Jackie Moore, [our] big-time soul girl—this should have gone through us!' So they did not push it like they should have. That was a big, political mess."

If there's cynicism in her explanation there is realism as well. When "This Time Baby" was released, Moore had been in the music business— the life she so wanted to be a part of—for a decade or more, and been on three labels. She was beginning to learn what the subsequent thirty-five years have made clearer: how ill-prepared so many artists were to handle the business aspects of their careers and how ill-served they often were by others.

Early in her career, "I was depending on David," she says. "He was the one who knew the business and I didn't. I wasn't getting no money like most of us, but the company was paying all my living expenses on tour—and I would say yes to anything if they let me cut records." She got cowriting credit on "Precious" and still gets royalties from that, but more often, Moore says, producers and other business types didn't give artists any publishing rights and royalties. "They just kept that for themselves." If artists didn't understand they were owed royalties—the families of deceased artists often were unaware of this as well—and didn't pursue them, "the record companies just kept that money," Moore says. "They're not going to be looking for nobody to pay." (Moore says one of the companies she recorded for decades ago claims she still owes them hundreds of thousands of dollars for recording expenses and the like.)

Even now when she is no longer active as a performer, "I'm still on my job," Moore says, meaning she—and her lawyers—closely monitor and pursue what they believe the industry owes her. When she was interviewed for *Florida Soul*, for example, Sound Exchange, the nonprofit that collects and distributes royalties from digital performances (via satellite, as with XM, and streaming music services like Pandora), was campaigning to get artists paid for work they did prior to 1972. According to Sound Exchange's website:

> Some of the biggest digital radio companies have decided to stop paying royalties to artists who recorded music before this time. That includes the hit makers of Motown, the legends of Jazz & Blues, and the people who gave birth to Rock n' Roll. . . . In one year alone, this practice caused artists and record labels to lose nearly $64 million in royalties. . . .

Based on their interpretation of copyright law, these companies believe that they can use pre-1972 recordings for free, forever.

Sound Exchange's efforts center only on performance royalties. Nonperformance royalties, for songwriting, publishing, and composition, are covered by other organizations. Fees for digital downloads, such as from iTunes, which are more lucrative for artists, are handled by those services.

For Moore the status quo means that "even though you hear 'Precious, Precious' all the time on satellite stations, I don't get paid for it." Even if payment was required and made by Pandora, for example, it would be as little as *one thousandth of a penny* per song, which would then be divided between the copyright holder (50 percent), the performer (45 percent), and the nonfeatured performers such as backup singers (5 percent).

"But we're working on that," Moore says, energetically. "And I've been very fortunate. I know I'm blessed because I still get checks. For so many of us, it's just a tragedy. There's been unspeakable joy and also unspeakable pain in music, because it's such a business—especially if you wear your heart on your shoulder."

A second Columbia album, *With Your Love*, followed in 1980, featuring covers of Wilson Pickett's "Don't Knock My Love" and Major Harris' "Love Won't Let Me Wait." Then that contract ended, and Moore had a short run with South Carolina–based Catawba Records, owned and run by former Columbia exec Richard Mack. The highlight there was a duet cover of "Precious, Precious" with Wilson Pickett. Her last recordings included a cover of the Kim Weston song tune "Helpless" on an indie label, which she remembers recording at the Miami home studio of KC, Harry Wayne Casey of the Sunshine Band. She worked with Crawford again briefly recording "Love Is the Answer" for Sunnyview. Finally, Moore cut "What Do You Say to a Lady," a duet with fellow Florida soul artist Timmy Thomas, released on Omega Records in 1991.

ABOUT FOUR YEARS INTO THEIR MARRIAGE, Calvin Hopkins, who had been a teacher and worked in real estate, got the call to join the ministry. They were living in Atlanta and moved to Florida soon thereafter. This massive life change coincided with the reemergence of "This Time Baby" as a club favorite. Based on that and Columbia's reissue of the 12-inch dance single in 1984, Moore was in renewed demand for live club performances across the country, including at many gay clubs. For her this precipitated a decade-long struggle between his sacred mission and her professional ambitions.

"I had some hardcore decisions to make," she says, "and it was very difficult because I tried to do both: be a minster's wife and maintain my career. I'd fly to New York, or to Hollywood sometimes, and do three clubs in one night. You do one at 10 o'clock, then you hop over to another one at 12, then do another at 4 o'clock in the morning. Then I'd fly home. So you can imagine what I looked like when I got back. Even if I made it for Sunday [services] at times my eyes would be all bloodshot . . .

"And to church folk, me flying around to all these clubs and then jumping up in here talking about 'Praise the Lord' on Sunday morning was hypocritical. I wasn't doing anything wrong, but the club environment—the drugs, the alcohol, the whole scenario—did not work with him trying to preach. But to his credit he never bothered me about it. He just let me work it out on my own."

The conflict was deep. "I didn't want to let go of that money—I'm just being truthful," Moore says. "But it wasn't only the money, it was also the fact that I had worked so hard and so long to do what I was doing, singing. All my life. It wasn't something somebody just handed me on a tray." She adds that she didn't have her two children until she was in her late thirties so her career would not get sidetracked: "I was dead into my music."

After ten years and much prayer, she determined that she could no longer merge her two identities as disco diva and "the First Lady of the church." Moore withdrew from performing; she remains active mostly in the monitoring of her fees and royalties, and doing publicity when called for, as when the two-CD Atlantic set was released. "I'm at a point now, as we move towards retirement, that I'm really happy," she concludes. Quickly she adds: "All I want is for people to give me some of my money. Then I'd be even happier."

Every once in a while, she will "crank it up in church," meaning she'll do some singing from other places than the pews. She has a heart condition now, though, and a defibrillator inside her. Even if she could physically, she continues to resist becoming a gospel singer. Someone in Fort Lauderdale recently suggested she cut an album and call it "From Precious, Precious to Precious Lord." "It's a cute idea," she says, "but it's going nowhere. Just because I'm not doing my [secular] music like I'd been doing, I'm not going to run over to the other side."

Over lunch in a waterfront Fort Lauderdale seafood restaurant, Moore explains that if she were ever to move into gospel, there could well be backlash. When some former R&B singers like her friend Candi Staton and Helen Baylor (who sang backup for Chaka Khan) did gospel albums, there was some acceptance, Moore says, but also pushback and resentment. It wasn't as heated as when Sam Cooke was ostracized for crossing over from gospel to pop in the late 1950s, "and maybe not of that magnitude. It's subtler," Moore says. "But it's there." Church folks can sometimes be a little hypocritical, too, she says. "After all, we've all had past lives."

Mostly, though, Moore won't move into gospel because "I'm not feeling it like that. And I never have. I always had a love for God, but my gift was to do something else." While staying resolutely on her side of the fence, Moore sees a strong commonality between soul and gospel. "We're both singing about love," she points out. "When I sing a gospel song or when I sing 'Precious, Precious,' you might see a difference, but to me there isn't any. I feel just as happy about either one and feel just as good doing it, because I know what I'm singing about is love, and that's universal."

"I'm not singing anything to harm anyone or anything," she continues. "And I've always been very particular about the kind of music I recorded." She means there's nothing too overtly sexual or obscene in her work. Jackie Moore sums it up this way: "I didn't sing anything my children can't hear."

KC and the Sunshine Band

Miami

HARRY WAYNE CASEY SAT ON THE MIAMI-BOUND PLANE, listening to music in his head. That wasn't surprising or unusual; the young man, twenty-one or twenty-two at the time, worked in the music business and, as far back as he can remember, was consumed by becoming a performer. "Never thought of anything else," he says today.

But the silent music he heard again and again on this trip was *new music*. For once he didn't hear the soul and R&B he grew up on: Ray Charles, Aretha Franklin, Motown, and Stax. That early education came through his very hip mother, a Miami housewife who loved to dance and was such a presence in Overtown clubs that acts like Sam and Dave would come over and chat with her. (Casey, born in 1951, says his father owned a furniture store and had no interest in music of any kind.)

On this early 1970s flight Casey was replaying the sounds of a recent wedding at Betty Wright's house. The ceremonies might have been for T.K. songwriter and producer Clarence Reid; the memorable part for this guest was the "Caribbean band with steel drums, horns and whistles." Wright, who was married to Jamaican-born musician King Sporty, hired a Bahamian junkanoo band for the occasion, and that music, Casey found, was "just infectious, it kind of takes your body over. It makes you wanna move."

It was right around that time that he'd flown to Washington, D.C., with T.K. recording artist Timmy Thomas. Casey had been hanging around Henry Stone's studio and warehouse in Hialeah, answering phones and running errands for free in pursuit of his musical career. On this trip he was assisting or maybe even "managing" Thomas. In D.C., the singer and keyboard player opened for Rare Earth, and during that concert Casey noticed "the entire crowd had whistles. I thought, 'Oh, my God, whistles are so popular, and that band I just heard was so infectious, this would be awesome, to get that sound on record.'" So on that plane ride home, with junkanoo in one brain lobe and whistles in the other, he wrote the tune, "Blow Your Whistle."

Casey may still have been enrolled at Miami Dade Community College, where he was nominally studying music; he's not sure. After playing keyboards and singing background on a few songs and doing a little songwriting with Reid, Casey had been given a key to T.K. and permission to experiment in the tiny eight-track recording studio upstairs. He and Rick Finch, another young hanger-on and aspiring producer from Opa-Locka, got some of the studio regulars together and cut a demo.

It's a two-and-a-half-minute party record that opens with some spoken greetings and exhortations—"*Hey, what's happening, man?*"—that echo the beginning of Marvin Gaye's "What's Going On?" Then a slew of percussion, including trap drums, cymbals, congas, and shakers, kicks in, along with vocals by Casey and three female backup singers. The lyrics are pretty much confined to "*Come on now, let me hear it, blow your whistle.*" More important are the syncopated instrumental breaks by what sounds like a large contingent of whistles. Although four horns are credited, they are muted, which is quite unlike the later work by this group. Casey and his band-to-be would continue to use overdubbing, which made their records sound as if many more were singing and playing.

Stone liked the groove, and he'd had a substantial junkanoo hit on his Alston label with "Funky Nassau" by the Beginning of the End, in 1971. He released Casey's tune in 1973 as T.K. Records single #1001, backed with "I'm Going to Do Something Good," written by Reid and Willie Hale, aka house guitarist Little Beaver. "Blow Your Whistle" hit the R&B chart and remained there for a good twelve weeks, peaking at #27. The writing was credited to H. W. Casey and the performers on that single went by K.C. and the Sunshine Junkanoo Band. The nickname or stage name K.C. was derived from the surname Casey, and the band that debuted with this single would become KC and the Sunshine Band, dropping the word "junkanoo." What derived from those other derivations is one of the most prolific hit-making machines in Florida soul history, eclipsed only by the artist at the opposite end of this musical timeline, one of Casey's earliest inspirations: Ray Charles.

KC leads the Sunshine Band at a free concert on Key Biscayne in August of 1975; three weeks later their song "Get Down Tonight" reached #1 on the *Billboard* Hot 100 chart. Photo © Larry Warmoth.

In the six years between September 1973 and September 1979 the Band had twenty hits on *Billboard*'s R&B chart, ten of which also made the Hot 100. Four of their songs—"Get Down Tonight," "That's the Way (I Like It)," "(Shake, Shake, Shake) Shake Your Booty," and "Keep It Comin' Love"— were #1 R&B hits and three of those, plus "I'm Your Boogie Man," were #1 pop hits. (Though RC Robinson had many more #1 R&B hits, eleven to four, KC and the gang actually had more #1 pop songs, four to three.) Casey had two more hits with other artists: "Yes, I'm Ready," a duet with Teri DeSario that became a gold single in 1980; and a collaboration with the 2 Live Crew, "2 Live Party," in 1998.

Fittingly, one of their songs, "Boogie Shoes," appears on the quintessential disco-era album, the movie soundtrack from *Saturday Night Fever*—one of the best-selling albums of all time, with a reported 15 million copies shipped. Moreover, as noted in the introduction to this book, KC and the Band continue to permeate our popular culture almost forty years after their last chart success. Casey, in his mid-sixties, is still performing with a fifteen-member iteration of the Band and at this writing appears not just permanent but resurgent; in 2015, he released two new albums after a twenty-year hiatus.

The Band's simplistic but utterly irresistible songs have their hooks, musical and otherwise, set deeply in the collective memories of multiple generations. They're seldom seen or thought of as a Florida band, though; few fans in the United States or abroad seem to give the band's locational title much thought. And virtually no listeners are aware of the group's original Bahamian influence. In some ways that's appropriate; dance-inciting, horn-driven, KC's signature tunes are a giddy, if somewhat guilty, pleasure shared well beyond the Sunshine State. Whether their work is most accurately called soul, dance soul, or disco, the argument can be made that this biracial, multicultural group of musicians—embraced by biracial, multicultural audiences for five decades now—is America's band.

Junkanoo music originated as a vital component of the annual Bahamian Junkanoo Festival, along with parades, costumes, and dancing. (Some, including *Black Miami* author Marvin Dunn, speculate that this celebration may have itself originated in Jamaica.) This festival began in the early 1800s as a celebration by slaves, who were given their three days off each year around Christmas. Because Junkanoo was raucous as well as joyous, and at other times a vehicle for political and racial protest, it was banned more than once in Nassau.

By the turn of the twentieth century, Dunn writes, "there was a growing Bahamian population permanently settled in various parts of Dade County. . . . When Miami was established in 1896 more than 40 percent of its black population was Bahamian." Those new Floridians, he notes, "brought their African-derived customs and traditions to South Florida."

No one knows how it got its name; among the numerous theories is one that claims a main character portrayed in the parades was named John Connu. Dunn tosses in the possibility that the name referred to "John Conny, a successful black merchant . . . on the Guinea Coast around 1720." Another theory holds that it's a devolution of the French words *gens inconnu*, referring to the masks marchers wore in the parade.

Not in dispute is that a musical genre, featuring the drums, whistles, and horns that so struck Harry Wayne Casey, grew out of this Mardi Gras–style celebration. In the Bahamas this music was first played—by huge groups and crowds—on goatskin and all manner of drums, cowbells, conch-shell horns, and other homemade instruments, as well as whistles. Gradually, European instruments, including the bugle, were added. One of the genre's best-known twentieth-century singers is Ronnie Butler, born in 1937; a younger singer, Kirkland Bodie, boycotted the 2015 Junkanoo in Nassau in protest over the "foreign" or non-Bahamian acts slated to perform. The junkanoo band best known in the United States is the Baha Men, who won a Grammy for their novelty hit—more of a chant than a song— "Who Let the Dogs Out." Although that song broke out in 2000, the group was actually long-standing, forming in 1979, when they were known as High Voltage.

KC and the T.K. musical family would add elements of 1960s soul and 1970s funk, including founding Sunshine Band partner Rick Finch on electric bass and the distinctive electric guitar playing of original member Jerome Smith. In a *Florida Soul* interview Henry Stone said of KC and the band's music: "There was some of the island rhythms that I like, and some of the bass. There was R&B involved, too. It was just a collaboration of sounds." In the booklet accompanying Stone's greatest hits CD he singles out Robert "Shotgun" Johnson on trap drums and Latin percussion player Fermin Goytisolo as vital to this ensemble sound. Overall, he concludes: "This band was hot, tight and funky."

IN 1973 STONE RELEASED another Sunshine Band single, "Sound Your Funky Horn," which, as the title suggests, did not stray far from "Blow Your Whistle." It did roughly the same as the first: "Made some noise [in the United States]," Casey says, "and started making some noise in Europe. Now there's talk about an album."

However, the next leap forward for the Band was propelled by a song that they didn't perform. Casey and Finch wrote and produced "Rock Your Baby," but T.K. singer George McCrae was the title artist. As discussed in the Henry Stone chapter, some consider this lilting melody, with what would become a familiar beat underneath, the first disco hit. Casey, or KC, as we will inevitably begin to call him here, says it was "number one all over the world." It was certainly #1 on both *Billboard* U.S. sales charts in 1974. According to the reliable site discogs.com, the song spent three weeks at the top of the U.K. singles chart in July of that year. The site goes on to describe "Rock Your Baby" as "one of the fewer than thirty all-time singles to have sold 10 million (or more) copies worldwide."

Although he acknowledges that McCrae's falsetto vocals helped make it a hit, KC says he thought of it as a Sunshine Band song. (They did a cover version of their own two years later.) Jerome Smith contributed memorable guitar work; his 2000 *New York Times* obituary cited his "suave sound" and the "signature riff" he supplied on "Rock Your Baby." Their next single, "Queen of Clubs," was a 1976 smash in the United Kingdom and Europe, though, KC says, "we couldn't give it away here" in the United States. A video on YouTube video showcasing that song in vintage performance opens with a close-up of Smith scratching out rhythm on guitar, and then the camera pulls back to show the seven-man outfit. Three are black and four white, it appears, including KC on keyboards and Finch on bass. In the back line sit a trap drummer and a conga player; all are, as the expression went, moving and grooving to the music they produce. With the horns blaring out a staccato riff behind him, a young, very 1970s-looking KC kicks off the vocals: "*In every nightclub across the nation / She's the life of the party, she's a real sensation.*"

His brown hair is long and shaggy, hanging down on both sides to touch the extra-long disco-era collar on his brightly patterned shirt. His bell-bottoms are tight to the knees and then flare. He's standing up behind his keyboard, smiling and energetic. Smith leans into KC's mike and joins him on the chorus: "*She's . . . the Queen of Clubs,*" and Casey lets out a high wordless shriek for emphasis. (George McCrae contributed uncredited vocals to the recorded version.)

At this point the band, if not fully evolved, is well on its way, and two mysterious—dubious, perhaps—factors in their success are already evident. For one, the lyrics are banal. "*If you throw a party and she ain't there,*" the song continues, "*people, let me tell you, that your party's nowhere.*" Generally speaking, their lyrics would get no more advanced in a literary sense—though the triptych "*Do a little dance / make a little love / get down tonight*" is such a quintessential distillation as to almost be poetic. Or maybe it is.

The band's second significant but somehow surmountable disadvantage: KC the soul singer is no Otis Redding; no Percy Sledge; and no Sam Cooke. He was and is nowhere near a great singer, and barely an average one—in a genre that exalts vocals. He's adequate. Then again, adequate means sufficient and, given KC and the Band's tremendous success, his vocals must be by definition good enough. Mike Lewis, who arranged the horns and strings and played tenor sax on almost all of the Sunshine hits, had this positive take: "I never thought KC was a great singer. But if he had been a better singer he might not have been believable. He was perfect for what he did." As KC's live shows reveal—to this day—he was and is a gifted

KC and the multiracial, multiethnic Sunshine Band taping an appearance on the *Mike Douglas Show* on Miami Beach, 1975. Photo © Larry Warmoth.

performer, a great energizer, and a shrewd recognizer and aggregator of talent.

Based on "Queen" and "Rock Your Baby," European distributors and Stone began clamoring for an album. Around the T.K. studio, KC the former gofer, booker, and acolyte noticed that his status in that family had changed. "Oh yeah," he says. "I've just given them a number-one record." His birth family evinced a tonal shift as well. "Up until that point my mom was telling me I should go get another job, do something else. She didn't want me to be in the music business 'cause she hung around all those people." She'd seen enough to know she didn't want that life for her son? "Correct." But at this point the senior Caseys came around. For KC, whose greatest success was still ahead, it already felt like "the culmination of the American dream."

The band's first album, *Do It Good*, with "Whistle," "Horn," and "Queen," did decently. The next one, however, *KC and the Sunshine Band*, released in 1975, blew the roof off. "That's the Way (I Like It)" and "Get Down Tonight" were #1 on both the pop and R&B charts that year. "(Shake Shake Shake) Shake Your Booty," from their third album, entitled *Part 3*, pulled off that same feat in 1976, and another cut, "Keep It Coming Love," just missed, hitting #1 R&B and #2 pop a year later.

KC says he did all the songwriting, while Finch "did a lot of the production work." But, he maintains, "I had a deal with Mr. Finch [in which] we split everything 50/50, no matter who did what." As his referring to the cofounder of the Sunshine Band as "Mr. Finch" might suggest, the two later had an acrimonious falling-out. Finch did refer to himself as the "kid engineer," but he certainly produced, played bass and occasionally the drums, and maintained he came up with some of their song titles as well.

The release of the *Saturday Night Fever* soundtrack album in 1977 pushed "Boogie Shoes," from the second album, onto both charts, three years after its initial release. Dance music, meant for clubs more than for radio airplay, was now dominant. The Bee Gees—three Gibb brothers from the United Kingdom—who had five songs on that *Fever* soundtrack, had the advantage of high and tight three-part harmony on top of their dance licks. But overall, insistent rhythm superseded pure singing; diva Donna Summer, for one, had composer Giorgio Moroder and producer Pete Belotte supplying dance rhythms and tropes that enhanced her strong but unmodulated voice. This shift may have made KC's vocal deficiencies moot. The music of these and similar artists took on a new name, which at this point was still a proud one: disco.

ESPECIALLY TOWARD THE BEGINNING, overdubbing and doubling of vocal and instrumental parts made the Sunshine Band sound bigger and fuller than it was. However, another element of behind-the-scenes music production was absolutely vital: the sweetening. That term refers to accompanying horns and strings, usually created and layered in separately from the vocals, rhythm section, bass, and percussion, which, in T.K.'s case, were recorded as an ensemble. T.K.'s sweetener in chief was Mike Lewis and his contributions to KC's success, especially the high-energy horn parts, were as vital as they are unrecognized. Among KC's contemporaries, the soul and funk bands of the day, the primacy of his horn parts was perhaps only surpassed by those in the music of the Average White Band, Tower of Power, and, in more of a jazz/rock vein, Blood, Sweat & Tears.

Those first two groups, analogous in some ways (both were interracial, like the Sunshine Band), certainly benefited from superior vocals by

Hamish Stuart (AWB) and Lenny Williams (Tower), among others. Yet the intricate funk rhythms Tower of Power used so masterfully were so complex, and shifting, as to make dancing to them difficult at times. Not so with KC's outfit. Their music, including the underlying rhythms and the catchy lyrics, was and remains easily accessible to the widest swath of mainstream listeners and dancers, drunk or sober. KC's songs aren't demanding, but for fun they're hard to beat: The titles and lyrics—"Get Down Tonight," "Boogie Shoes," "That's the Way (I Like It)"—say "party." The music does not disagree with that command in the least, and Mike Lewis' horns are a big part of that concordance.

Like T.K. impresario Stone, Lewis was a trumpeter who had trouble with his lip or embouchure; midway through his time at Florida State, Lewis switched to tenor sax (he already played piano). His sax idols were Charlie Parker, Phil Woods, Charlie Mariano, and John Coltrane. As Stone did, Lewis played in military bands, from 1960 to 1963. When Lewis got out he joined the Jimmy Dorsey band, which he calls "a ghost band." Dorsey died in 1958 and big bands had waned.

Since his wife had gotten "a real job" in Miami, the couple moved there and Lewis was soon gigging seven nights a week in the Deauville Hotel house band. Five years' work there allowed him to buy a house and drive a car, "just like regular people," as he puts it. In the early 1970s he made his first recordings with the pop/rock Florida group the Cornelius Brothers and Sister Rose ("It's Too Late to Turn Back Now," "Treat Her Like a Lady") at Miami's "other" studio—meaning the one not owned and run by Henry Stone—Criteria. Producer Brad Shapiro, who had played bass with Steve Alaimo's Redcoats, brought Lewis first to Alaimo and then to Stone and T.K. The first album he sweetened for them was Betty Wright's debut, *My First Time Around*. Lewis explains how that process worked:

> Sweetening means they go in first without me, with the rhythm section—sometimes the singers are on there, sometimes not—and they cut their track, and that's recorded to tape. They give me a copy of that and they say, "We'd like to have some horns or some strings (or horns *and* strings) added to this." So I bring home a copy of the cassette and play it back and forth a million times, and invent string and/or horn parts to go along with that.
>
> First of all, you think: "Do I want to have everybody play the same thing, or do I want two-part harmony, or four-part harmony?" That's just the arranger's decision. Think of an artist with a palate of colors.

With horns I've got four colors: two trumpets and two saxes, tenor and baritone. I can mix those colors any way I want.

Sometimes you'll have the horns playing in unison. [Lewis sings the introductory horn part from "Shake Your Booty"]: *da-da-da, da-da-da-da-da DAH!* But some figures sound better in harmony. [Sings the two-note background horn riff from later in the song, when the vocalists repeat "Shake, shake"]: *bap-bap, bap-bap* . . .

That's harmony, the two trumpets and saxes stacked up, playing different notes matching the chords.

It's a very spur of the moment kind of thing, too. If I wrote the same arrangement today I might do it completely opposite. I might make the part that was unison harmony and the one that was harmony, unison.

I found, though, that usually my first idea is my best. Arranging is almost like composing except what you're doing is taking an existing composition and embellishing it, enhancing it. Many times you're adding something completely different that then becomes a vital part of that record.

We'd go into the studio and play those arrangements live and mix them in. Usually there were 24 tracks to work with, though the tape was only an inch wide, sometimes two. Towards the end of the tape days, before it all went digital, it became a one-inch 32-track tape so you had 8 more tracks.

You may have a kick drum here on that track, you might have the high-hat here, the snare there, then you might have the bass, guitar 1, guitar 2, keyboard, that's eight tracks. Now you've still got 16 tracks, so we come in and we might put the violins here and here and the viola here and the cello here. Then we might double it, do them again, which makes it sound fuller. Then we put the horns here, more horns there. They'd use individual microphones, but they generally go into the same track. And then they've got the rest of the tracks for the vocals and background vocals.

They usually liked what I'd written, but nobody bats 1,000, so if they didn't like something I'd change it. "Okay," I'd tell the guys, "I told you to play this, but now I want you to try that."

The horns and strings would be done in separate sessions. Which was fine with me 'cause I made more money—I got paid per session.

Lewis also played tenor (and got paid for that) on the Sunshine Band sessions; the longest-running KC horn section also included Whit Sidener on baritone and Kenny Faulk and Vinnie Tanno on trumpets. When arranging, Lewis worked more with Rick Finch than he did with KC "I would sit there with Rick and we would play the track and sing parts back and forth. If Rick wanted a certain lick, he couldn't write it down [in musical notation] but thank God he could sing it. Then I could write it so my horn and string players could come in and read it. And I could write it down as fast as we'd sing it to each other, because it was really easy stuff."

"They were both smart guys," he says, "but they were—and I don't mean this in a derogatory way—musically illiterate. Doesn't mean they're not good musicians; they just can't sit down and look at a page full of notes and read those notes. I remember one time KC was playing me a new song he had just written and he's over there playing with three fingers and I said. 'What chord is that?' He said, 'I don't know.' He could play it but he couldn't verbalize it because he doesn't know harmony."

"I have to be honest with you," Lewis continues. "A lot of this music I didn't like. I did it for the money, the benefits, the pension from the musicians' union. The KC stuff was fun 'cause it was lively—only a couple were slow tunes. Many of the T.K. groups were great, some songs had great lyrics, and some of the performances were spectacular. It's just that they didn't lend themselves to any real creativity in the sweetening because the music was so simple. I was a jazz guy, and I've always had this elitist attitude that a song has to have really complicated chords to be good. But that means nothing to the record-buying public. You can't write augmented ninth chords over just a regular 1-3-5 triad [chord]. It sounds wrong. It was like after I'd read *War and Peace*, I'm now reading *Dick and Jane*. I had trouble at times thinking in such basic terms. Steve [Alaimo] would say, 'What are you trying to prove? You know we're not selling stuff to jazz people, keep it down.'"

Working on records by Bobby Caldwell, a jazz singer and T.K. artist, gave Lewis more chances to use the full range of his expertise. He actually had to sit at the piano to work these charts out; others, he could just do in his head. Caldwell, also a guitarist, actually *wanted* jazz complications in his music and put augmented ninth chords in his best-known composition, the 1978 crossover hit, "What You Won't Do for Love." With Caldwell's encouragement, Lewis used novel instrumentation for the bridge: clarinet, flugelhorn, tenor sax, French horn, trombone, and bass clarinet.

Before that, however, the song begins with a distinctive coda, a few bars long, that Lewis wrote. Along with some signature KC horn riffs, it is his most memorable work, the part the most listeners might recognize—even though no listeners outside the music industry would recognize the sweetener's role.

Lewis sits down at the piano in his home office/studio and knocks it out from memory, ending with two surprising, percussive 16th-notes that jump a whole step from E to F-sharp: ba bap! Those bars didn't exist in the song when he got it, Lewis says. And the horns played it in unison, he says, rather than in harmony.

Lewis' expertise gave him a huge advantage at T.K.: "I could ask for and get union scale." The musicians who couldn't read, he says, weren't secure enough in their abilities to demand the same. "One time they were passing out checks for what we had done the previous week and I remember my check was $1,200, and the bass player's check was $200. He said, 'Gee, how come your check is so much more than mine?' I said, 'Ask for it, tell them you want union scale.' He said, 'Oh no, they'll get somebody else.' But they couldn't get anybody else to do what I was doing."

Lewis loved playing in live ensembles, and he was very good at it. But a pre-T.K. encounter in the early 1970s with another sax player, when they were both working in Jackie Gleason's Miami studio band, led him to re-think his career. "I'm sitting there next to Paul Ricci [who also played clarinet and flute]," Lewis remembers, "and I was sort of in awe of him because I was in my 20s and he was maybe in his 50s. Then he said, 'Hey kid, are you working Saturday?' I said, 'Yeah, I think so.' He says, 'If you get another call, tell them to call me, I'm open.' And I remember saying to myself: 'Is this what I've got to look forward to? Thirty, forty years down the road hoping some kid will throw me a bone because I'm not working Saturday?' I said, 'Oh no, I do not want to go that route.' So I quit playing gigs about 35 years ago."

Over the years Lewis also worked at the Muscle Shoals studios, and for the blues label Malaco. Fittingly, perhaps, he arranged and sweetened several albums with the junkanoo band the Baha Men, though, he hastens to add, not on "Who Let the Dogs Out." "That's a chant, not a song," he says. "A perfect example of a horrible piece of music that became a big hit."

IN 1980 CASEY AND RICK FINCH, who'd had increasing conflicts, fell out permanently. Three years later, it seems, Finch sold (most likely) or relinquished his royalties to Casey. He later sued to recover them, claiming that he had been "manipulated" by Casey's lawyers "when I was not in a capacity to understand what was going on." He also claimed his representation had been inadequate. But two court rulings went against Finch, who moved to Ohio and produced other bands.

Around the time of his split with Finch, KC says, he began to feel "like T.K. was kind of ignoring me, and here I was, the guy who brought them all this success. So I thought it was time for me to leave." He produced the 1979 Casablanca album for Teri DeSario with their gold duet, "Yes, I'm Ready." Two KC and the Sunshine Band albums on Epic followed in 1981 and 1982 that didn't do as well as their earlier efforts, though the single "Give It Up" was a minor hit.

Some thirty-five years after their break, KC says he still thinks of Henry Stone "like a father. The company owed me money or whatever—I had to move on. That had nothing to do with my feelings for Henry." After Stone died in 2014 Rick Finch posted a similar statement that remains on the home page of his website: "The world of music has lost a trailblazer—a legend—but personally, I've lost the only father I've ever known." Of the Sunshine Band, Finch wrote, "We would have been nothing without him."

Together and separately, KC and Stone were both impacted by another early 1980s development. Disco, pop's reigning genre, became an epithet instead of an endearment. As Henry Stone relates in chapter 14, he was blindsided and severely damaged by disco's demise, which led to his company's bankruptcy. "I was trying to change somewhat anyway," KC says, "by putting out some ballads and stuff. Then they renamed me as 'disco.' But I've always believed that what I did was R&B."

He has strong support in that belief from a fellow Florida soul singer and bandleader who preceded him: Wayne Cochran, "the white James Brown." "One of the best groups to ever come out of South Florida is KC & the Sunshine Band," Cochran says in a *Florida Soul* interview. "They're great musicians and they wrote great songs. [Sings]: *'That's the way, uh-huh, uh-huh, I like it.'* Do you know what disco music is? It's the height of rhythm and blues. R&B progressed to disco. What can you call it, country? It's R&B. And from there it went to rap, which is crap."

When Cochran offered this contrarian take, in 2012, Donna Summer had just died. "She made great records," he said, but her reputation was sullied because snobbish fans, and especially musicians, looked down on disco. "And you know what? They're stupid. Musicians don't like anything popular. If you put out something nobody [listens to], they'll admire you."

In a newspaper interview that same year, KC also invoked the late disco queen. "Critics have almost succeeded in convincing me, and had her convinced, that disco was a bad word and a bad thing. And it's not."

At this writing Harry Wayne Casey has reconciled himself to wearing that label—"I'm gonna claim the disco moniker *and* R&B," he says. But he still feels that the great success of R&B or soul music in his day—in which he played a major role—has been slighted. "I just felt that it was a time [when] R&B music had finally broken through . . . nationally and worldwide. When they started giving it this new name, they took away the fact that R&B finally had its day. I felt like some of that glory [was] taken away from it."

In the early 1980s KC was in a serious car accident, followed by a year's recuperation, which included relearning how to walk. He has permanent nerve damage, he says, and underwent back surgery. KC later stopped making music and withdrew from the business again, for completely different reasons. He explained the second sabbatical this way in a 2013 interview on the website of the Grammy awards: "I kinda lost my mind. I was also on drugs." He credits talk-show host Arsenio Hall for urging him to get the Sunshine Band back together. "I came out of my stupor," he said, "went to rehab and I've been clean and sober ever since."

In 2015 KC released an album of his favorite 1960s hits by other artists. Songs covered include Smokey Robinson's "You've Really Got a Hold On Me," "Tell It Like It Is," and even Bob Dylan's "Blowin' in the Wind," backed on that tune by a gospel choir. With Medicare eligibility imminent at this writing, he is still touring, still leading crackerjack bands, and still performing with great energy, even as his songs, forty-some years old, continue to get airplay—not to mention wedding-band play. "I'm not 100 percent," he says. "I have numbness in my leg. But I can do my shows." All in all, he concludes, "it's been pretty amazing."

No one is more amazed than the sweetener, Mike Lewis. Thanks to his arranging and tenor playing on KC's hits, he still has regular checks coming in. Looking around the office in his Miami home, he quickly finds two, yet to be cashed or deposited. "Here's one I got last week for $1,200 for some KC stuff," he says. "We get those every few weeks; sometimes they're $10,000 or $15,000. Every time I get a check, one of us [horn players] will call the other and say, 'You know, Cole Porter couldn't write a tune, and George Gershwin couldn't write a tune. They're not making us any money. Harry Wayne Casey is my favorite composer!'" Lewis calls these deliveries "mailbox candy" and says: "We're making more money now than we did when we made the records 40 years ago."

Epilogue

The State of Florida Soul

"Ladies and gentlemen, it's star time!" declares Kenny "The Conductor" Eunice. The Soul Searchers, arrayed behind him in Gainesville's High Dive club on this night in 2016, have just finished their first number, James Brown's "Sex Machine." Now Eunice continues his introduction, bringing the featured singer on in the chitlin' circuit tradition—the way Brown's MC introduced him, and Lavell Kamma's MC brought him on when that Floridian was doing his version of the JB live show in the 1960s. "Please welcome the one, the only, Jake Mitchell! Give it up!"

The two hundred or so people in this downtown live-music venue do indeed give up their applause for this local act, opening for New Orleans' Rebirth Brass Band. Under the low ceiling, painted black, the noise is amplified and heat builds as a dapper African American man in a white three-piece suit and a shirt that either is purple or looks that color under the stage lights takes the stage. Mitchell is seventy-one, though his face appears younger, uncracked. Something about the arrangement of his features reinforces his earlier explanation that "my family, on my mother's side, is of Cuban heritage. We grew up in West Tampa and Ybor City." He's not a big man but not diminutive enough to earn him his stage name, Little Jake Mitchell. That was due to his age; Mitchell says he was a touring, recording professional at "12, going on 13."

The seven-piece Soul Searchers, including three horns, launch into the Johnnie Taylor hit, "Who's Making Love" and soon Mitchell's jacket is off. He clutches a white hand towel in his left hand, a microphone with a blue foam head in his right. His voice is still supple, modulating easily

Little Jake Mitchell at the mike at Sarah's Place in Gainesville, circa 1960, when he was still in high school, with two other singers in the Blenders vocal group. Courtesy of Charles Steadham & Johnny Moore, Sr.

as the songs move from the key of F to C, E, and A-flat. Not a gutbucket bluesy singer, Mitchell is more mellifluous than booming; he sounds a bit like smooth Chicago soul man Tyrone Davis. By the second or third tune, Mitchell is down off the stage, strolling and singing amid the patrons, who are mostly white and much younger. He's walking the floor, in the R&B/soul tradition.

Mitchell's set includes Jackie Wilson's "Lonely Teardrops" and Wilson Pickett's "I Found a Love" as well as some less familiar tunes of his own. He recorded "I Got to Know"—as Jock Mitchell—for the Detroit label Impact Records in 1967, and "Nomad Woman" appeared on his own label, Golden Hit Productions, the following year. He and the Searchers also reprise 1967's "Not a Chance in a Million," probably his best-known song and the title track of their 2016 CD. It's a mid-tempo jaunt that builds to a propulsive horn-driven climax and vocal vamp, with Mitchell singing: *"There's not a chance in a million of our love going wrong / not a chance in a million / 'cause I'll keep holdin' on . . . keep holdin' on."* The original version proved very popular with British northern soul fans; Mitchell and the Searchers recently played a series of gigs in Great Britain.

Mitchell traces his career all the way back to "when I was five years old. The Holsum Bread Company used to have talent shows once a month. They'd bring a wagon into the neighborhood and they had a stage and everything. Everybody would want to be in that talent show to win that bread. Yeah, you won loaves of bread!"

By the time Mitchell was twelve he was winning more contests with his version of B. B. King's 1953 hit, "Woke Up This Morning." When touring acts came to town, the youngster would sit in with or open for them. At one such gig, Mitchell recalls, "B. B. King let me sing, and called me his musical godson. Soon I was on the road with B. B. I had a private tutor who traveled with me." At that time there was a vogue for precocious singing talent, Mitchell remembers: "Frankie Lymon and Little Willie John were doing very well and that helped me."

Mitchell toured some with Roy Hamilton and cut some songs for Chess Records, the Chicago blues label, at twelve, which seem not to have been released. He then came back home and joined the long-running Tampa band the Skyliners, performing with them from about thirteen to fifteen years old. "I was a novelty," Mitchell sums up, "and I could really sing." At that time his main idols and influences were Gene Allison, best known for "You Can Make It If You Try" (1958), and Willie John.

From his earliest singing days to this writing, Mitchell (birth name Arnold) has been a consistent part of the Florida soul story. A keeping-on survivor, he's part of the connective tissue that binds this music and the people who created it. One such linkage is visible on the Gainesville stage: The Soul Brothers' bandleader, manager, promoter, and tenor sax man is one Charlie Blade. In the 1960s and 1970s, Blade (Charles Steadham) worked with Florida soul artists Linda Lyndell, Lavell Kamma, Gene Middleton, and Weston Prim.

During his Tampa years, young Mitchell took music lessons from "Professor" Michael Rodriguez, who also taught theory to tenor man Ernie Calhoun and wrote arrangements for Charlie Brantley and His Original Honeydippers, which at times featured Ray Charles. He also remembers opening for the Drifters in Miami and staying with them at Overtown's Sir John Hotel, which housed the Knight Beat club, where so many local and touring musicians made Florida soul history. That's where Sam Moore first caught Jackie Wilson live, which turned his life around. Mitchell's Drifters gig at the Knight Beat is also memorable, he says, as the time he got his first process, or hair straightening treatment, done by one of the older men in the group. "It burnt me! And when I came back home my mother said, 'Oh man, what y'all did to my child?'"

Before making his way to Detroit and Impact Records, Mitchell rode the rails as part of a distinctly Floridian tradition, the "Harlem in Havana" Review. An all-black traveling variety show owned by Leon Claxton of Tampa, "Harlem" featured musicians, acrobats, comedians, and, not least, scantily clad "brown showgirls" and performed at state fairs all over the country from the mid-1930s to the mid-1960s. Besides Mitchell this revue helped launch the careers of soul singers Rufus Thomas ("Walking the Dog") and Fontella Bass ("Rescue Me") as well as rocker Chuck Berry and comedian Redd Foxx.

As a 2015 *Tampa Tribune* article pointed out, "The show was called Harlem in Havana, but Tampa could stake as much a claim to it as the city in Cuba or the Manhattan neighborhood." This African American show traveled twenty-five thousand miles a year, but at almost all of those rail stops its performances were off-limits to blacks, except once an engagement, on "Negro Day." Mitchell also worked with the James E. Strates Shows, which traveled just as widely with carnivals and was based in Orlando. Tours of the Eastern seaboard with these two shows led to his recording a couple of sides in Philadelphia, as Arnold Mitchell, for New Town Records.

Jake Mitchell is also something of a Florida touchstone in the realm of race, another constant in the soul saga. In 1959—before Havana in Harlem and his Detroit sojourn—he formed a group, Little Jake and the Blenders, while living with his grandmother in Gainesville. They were more doo-wop than straight R&B and got regular work at University of Florida fraternity and sorority parties. As the fictional band Otis Day and the Knights portrays in the movie *Animal House*, black entertainers were often sought after, and found work, in Greek circles even when universities did not admit African American students. This held true at the University of Florida in Gainesville, which admitted its first black undergrads in the fall of 1962.

Two years earlier, in November 1960, Mitchell and his Blenders performed at the annual homecoming pep rally, the Gator Growl. "We integrated it," says Mitchell. "I was the first black artist to ever appear." The news stories that immediately followed this event don't mention race; they just say he performed. But Mitchell maintains that, when invited by Florida

Blue Key, the organizers, "I said I would only perform if my people would be able to come. They wanted me so bad that they accepted my proposal. They put 10,000 bleacher seats [for African Americans] in the end zone of the football stadium."

Forgivably, Mitchell says there were sixty thousand in attendance that day; the *Gainesville Daily Sun* had it at forty thousand. Today the Uncle Remus skit in the program would raise eyebrows, but, by all accounts, the event went smoothly. With Mitchell on first tenor, the Blenders sang three songs, backed by a group of white University of Florida students, the Pyramids. The Blenders were "a Lincoln High School group," promotional materials noted; Jake was sixteen.

In 2010, on the fiftieth anniversary of that event, the Gainesville City Council proclaimed Little Jake Mitchell Day. A video interview of him was shown at that year's Growl, and he, along with at least one of the original Blenders, rode in the homecoming parade. When asked by a reporter how he felt on receiving these honors, Mitchell said, "I got the chillbumps."

Back at the High Dive in 2016, Mitchell and the Soul Searchers close their opening set with "Turn On Your Love Light," a hit for Bobby Blue Bland. Through the thirteen songs Mitchell's energy doesn't flag; he's comfortable, clearly enjoying himself, and confident. Why not? He's been doing this for something like sixty years. Toward the end he asks the audience his trademark question, which is really more of an exhortation: "*You know what?!*"

The sweating dancers joyfully yell back: "*WHAT!!??*"

BETTY PADGETT ALSO ABIDES. The New Jersey–born singer who moved to Belle Glade, Florida, in the early 1960s was inspired by the Aretha Franklin, Gladys Knight, and James Brown songs she heard coming up from the restaurant jukebox beneath her aunt's apartment. After the family moved to Fort Lauderdale, she was old enough to frequent the Downbeat Club, the circuit stop on NW 15th Way. She began sitting in for a song or two with Joey Gilmore and the TCB Express; then Gilmore's lead female singer left and Padgett auditioned by singing a Betty Wright hit, "Pure Love." She was hired in 1971 and worked with his soul/blues/funk group for more than twenty years.

At twenty-one, she cut her first solo album, *Betty Padgett*, also known as *Sugar Daddy*, after the song that got the most notice. That piece of 1975 vintage vinyl was both rare and a collector's item, selling for as much as

Jake Mitchell with the Soul Searchers, including Florida soul stalwart Charles Steadham on tenor sax, *third from left, rear*. Photo by Randy Batista; Courtesy of Charles
Steadham / Blade Agency.

four hundred dollars, before it was reissued by the California label Luv N'
Haight in 2009.

Padgett continued to perform in South Florida, including with locals
Gwen and George McRae and KC's Sunshine Band, and recorded a sizable
handful of other albums. Like Mitchell, she is still active. Unusually, she
writes almost all of her own material, mostly having to do with domestic
drama. Her 2009 album *The Real Deal*, for example, features the song "Paying Bills and Poppin' Pills"; in another of her songs she tells a man he's got
to "*pay before you lay.*" "I'm a realist," she said in a 2011 interview. "I sing
songs about real life. Either [the drama in her songs] happened to me or I
know someone it happened to."

With her assertive lyrical stance and strong voice, her work comes off a bit tougher than that of smoother Florida soul singers like Gwen McRae. Although she can sound much sweeter on slower songs like "I Love You"—which also tend to be more upbeat—Padgett is often thought of as a "soul blues" or southern soul artist and compared to Georgia-born (and even bawdier) singer Millie Jackson. Padgett says she admires Jackson and agrees that her own vocals are different from "the typical Miami sound, which has a little more pop in it rather than the bluesy southern soul style."

She's managed to sustain her career into the hip-hop era, but like many other artists of her generation, Padgett is nostalgic for the times when classic soul ruled, in Florida and beyond. She notes sadly that the Downbeat Club she and others frequented for generations was demolished in 2012. When she was coming up, Padgett said, "everybody [who] was getting their name out there were real singers . . . and they were saying something. What you heard onstage were the real musicians playing. Nothing was fake. Now you wonder sometimes if the band on the stage is really playing. Are they really singing?"

In one of the songs on her album *The Real Deal*, Padgett exhorts listeners to "Let Your Mind Go Back" to the 1960s and 1970s. She paints a funky rosy picture of that time, referencing platform shoes, Afro hairdos and bell-bottom pants, and name-checking dances like the Jerk and the Fly. Women doing the Funky Chicken, she remembers, wore "miniskirts showing pretty legs." In her version of the day there was community: "*House parties was the thing / and everybody knew each other's name.*" She invokes a less violent time as well, claiming that folks "*didn't have to worry about date rape or checking guns at the gate.*"

Padgett is especially nostalgic for club and party life, describing dancers under a rotating disco ball: "*Everyone had a real good time / put on their platform shoes / and man they looked so fine.*"

When you really had it together, she sings, folks would say "*You're outta sight.*" Then she references another 1970s saying, asking her listeners: "*Can you dig it?*"

"*Let your mind go back,*" the chorus runs, "*let your mind go back. Let's go back in the day.*" Those back-in-the-day days are gone, and they are missed. Many of the artists who created Florida soul are gone, including circuit star Lavell Kamma; songwriter/producer Clarence Reid; and Miami mogul Henry Stone. More are fading: James Purify and Papa Don Schroeder recently canceled their planned recording reunion due to ill health; Ernie Calhoun can no longer physically handle his big tenor horn.

Beyond specific people and places, though, soul's lost its primacy. In Phyl Garland's introduction to *The Sound of Soul*, published in 1969, she declared that "soul music has become . . . a prime cultural force in both America and the world." As proof she cites that in the previous year soul acts occupied seven of the top twelve places in *Billboard's* year-end sales charts, "and Aretha Franklin . . . ranked as the year's number-one artist."

Most striking in a contemporary reading, Garland surveyed the aural and racial landscapes of her time and declared: "There is no conspicuous generation gap among blacks, so far as music is concerned." Today there's a huge, obvious chasm between middle- and Boomer-aged African American adherents of old-school soul and the newer, younger skool that grew up on and is devoted to rap or hip-hop. (The *Billboard* R&B sales chart is now called the Hot R&B/Hip-Hop chart.) Those who favor soul and listen to the Quiet Storm radio format—"grown folks' music" is one of this cadre's approving terms for it—often have little use for today's dominant form.

For the most part soul partisans know they have lost the war, and they are reluctant to accord the victor any respect. In their *Florida Soul* interviews singers Wayne Cochran and James Purify both delivered the same summary judgment on the rawer music that has much of young America, black and white, in its thrall, declaring: "Rap is crap." To Purify, "it's not even music. It's a disgrace to all the former artists. I was listening to a so-called song the other day and they were saying, '*I can hit it from the rear; you like me to hit it from the rear.*' I mean, come on." He doesn't even give younger soul revivalists much credit, calling them imitators. "There are a few guys trying to do songs by Marvin Gaye, Johnnie Taylor, or Stevie Wonder, but how are you going to pull that off? Those people were originals! Now everybody sounds alike."

Miami's Betty Wright seems to be the exception to soul's anti-rap rule, staying current and crossing over into other genres, including the unthinkable one. "I don't tell anybody how much I love rap music," she said in a 2012 interview. "But I got it bad, boy. Some of the subject matter is a little off-color. But some regular songs are off-color." She pointed out that soul artists, including her, Isaac Hayes, and Jerry Butler, who used spoken intros in their songs, "were the predecessors to what [rappers] do. Some of my biggest records have three minutes of singing and 10 minutes of talk."

Wright's hip-hop work goes back at least as far as her 2008 recording with rapper Lil Wayne, and he is heard on *Betty Wright: The Movie*, her Grammy nominated 2011 album with the Roots. In 2016 she was featured, along with Kendrick Lamar and Big Sean, on a single by Miami's DJ Khaled.

Wright has produced and acted as vocal coach for British soul singers Joss Stone and Angie Stone, and she's done similar work for Miami's reina of Latin music, Gloria Estefan, and Jennifer Lopez. She and Timmy Thomas were co-Grand Marshalls of Miami's most recent Martin Luther King Day parade. Much like Irma Thomas has done in New Orleans, Wright still reigns as her city's Soul Queen. (Showing even more range, she is also reportedly an ordained minister.)

SOUL IS NOT LOST. And there are signs that Florida soul in particular is newly, increasingly, found. Miami's Sam Moore is increasingly prominent, and revered, as a soul elder statesman. At this writing he has just performed in a White House tribute to fellow Florida soul legend Ray Charles; he sang "I Can't Stop Loving You," one of RC's beloved country tunes. And he is bringing that stature, and himself, back home. A recent *Miami Herald* story called him "one of the most famous African-American figures to hail from Miami," but added that "few young people, even in Moore's hometown, are familiar with his legacy."

That's changed rapidly since Moore and his wife, Joyce, moved back to the Miami area from Arizona, where they lived for many years. As part of the city of Miami Beach's one hundredth anniversary in 2015, March 26 was declared "Sam Moore Day," and in 2016 he performed with the Miami Symphony Orchestra. "I never thought I'd be able to come home to Miami and be celebrated, but it's happening," Moore said.

Moore's also come to realize that the musical heritage of Miami and Overtown—which he benefited from so much growing up, and then became a vital part of—has never been adequately documented. He's made it his mission, Moore says, to ensure that this history and influence are honored and fully understood. He and Joyce are working with Florida International University to create courses and workshops that will teach today's students about Miami's musical legacy.

Even as the ranks of this state's classic-soul-era musicians thin, recognition of their contributions—and, in the aggregate, their home state's—is growing. Some. Finally.

In downtown Tampa, the newly formed intersection of two equally new thoroughfares, Ray Charles Boulevard and Hank Ballard Street, pays homage to that city's soul heritage. Documentaries about Henry Stone (*Record Man*) and Deep City Records (*Deep City: The Birth of the Miami Sound*) were recently released; both are highly recommended. Anthony Bourdain interviewed both Helene Smith and Willie Clarke of Deep City Records in a 2015 segment of his CNN show, *Parts Unknown*.

As explained in chapter 17, Drake's use of Timmy Thomas' "Why Can't We Live Together" has brought the Miami musician and educator renewed attention and a bigger platform for his activism. Thomas recently signed with a newly launched Florida record company, Allsun Records, run by DJ, record dealer, and producer Jan Lisewski. Lisewski fell in love with this music in his native Britain when he first heard Otis Redding, and he became part of the northern soul movement before moving to Florida in 1992. As Soul Man Jan he cohosts a weekly radio show, "DooWop2Soul."

According to Lisewksi, Allsun is in negotiations to record Helene Smith, Little Beaver, and Latimore as well as Thomas. He also wants to sign young, up-and-coming soul singers and "record music that's still being written in the old style." Then he adds the obligatory: "Not rap and hip-hop and that junk." The label plans to make its music in a very old-school way. "I have five vinyl cutting machines," Lisewski says, "and we'll play on real instruments and record analog, on tape, and then to vinyl."

"The real soul music never went away," Lisewski maintains. "It's always been here; it's just been kind of underground in this other layer or dimension—kind of like 'the Matrix' in those movies."

Another simultaneous startup, Overtown Records, is run by Tom Bowker, who managed, produced, and played drums for the late Miami stalwart Clarence Reid in his Blowfly rapper persona. Overtown, its website declares, "is dedicated to the revitalization of the Miami Soul & Funk music. . . . We don't fake the funk!"

What hasn't expired doesn't need to be revived. Original soul artists—including the Florida contingent that includes Moore, Wright, Latimore, Mitchell, and Padgett—are still creating, still performing, here and overseas. For the past fifteen years or so, Daptone Records in Brooklyn, New York, has been putting out new soul with a vintage feel and a distinct in-house sound by Charles Bradley (born in Gainesville), the James Hunter Six and their breakout act, Sharon Jones and the Dap-Kings. (Jones passed away in 2016.)

Nationally and abroad, neo-soul artists are adding new elements and extending soul's musical half-life, already remarkable in its duration. Texan Erykah Badu is quirky, jazzy, and unpredictable, bending genres at times and then hitting an old-school pocket with the fed-up break-up tune "Tyrone." North Carolinian Anthony Hamilton manages to be both romantic and trenchant, and convincing in both modes. Young Brit Beverley Knight is promising; her compatriot, the late Brit Amy Winehouse—a uniquely, wildly talented singer and writer—made important contributions in her time.

To use Peter Guralnick's term, these latter-day soul artists are crafting their own messages from the heart. And as the late Sharon Jones was fond of saying: "What comes from the heart reaches the heart." In Fort Lauderdale, a young old soul is on a similar mission.

"I only meant to love you / Didn't you know it baby, didn't you know? / Why couldn't you be content / With the love I gave?"

SOUL COGNOSCENTI WILL IDENTIFY these words as the beginning of "Chokin' Kind," the #1 R&B hit in 1969 by the prodigious, underappreciated singer Joe Simon, later covered by British soul diva Joss Stone, among others. That lyric is also the first thing sung on *Soulful Classics*, a 2015 album by the young Floridian who goes by Urban Mystic. Heard anew, this neo-version of "Chokin'" evokes not just Simon's strong singing but the mood, feel, and vibe of classic soul.

The horn intro is familiar; the parts contributed by the female backup singers fit the genre; and the bouncy Latin percussion echoes the original. Mainly and most immediately, though, it's Mystic's voice that strikes that familiar chord. Vocally—improbably—the singer born Brandon Williams in 1984 has the timbre, depth, and richness of his predecessors, sounding like an older man and, as he is about five and a half feet tall and slender, a bigger one as well. Unlike Simon, Mystic ventures into the falsetto range and he improvises some new lyrics. He takes the song a tad slower than Simon did, managing to simultaneously convey passion and seem in control, taking his time. His version is not a carbon copy, like the one Chubby Checker made of Hank Ballard's "Twist"; it's a tribute but also an original statement.

Mystic can sound a good deal like Bobby Womack. (*Classics* includes two Womack covers, and the late singer's niece, Ja'Rae Womack, duets with Mystic on the album.) "I get that often," Mystic says in a *Florida Soul* interview. "I also get Sam Cooke; [the late] Joe Ligon—he's more gospel, from the Mighty Clouds of Joy—and K-Ci from Jodeci. It's cool, because these are guys I listened to coming up, but I'm not trying to sound like them. I was just blessed with this voice."

Contemporary soul man Urban Mystic in the recording studio, aka the Swag Labs, in Davie, Florida. Courtesy of SoBe Entertainment.

Mystic keeps his dark glasses on during the entire interview, which takes place in the blue-lit control room of SoBe Entertainment's studios in Davie, Florida. He's wearing a flat-brimmed black hat, black pants, and a black shirt and is festooned with gold chains, a chunky watch, and a sizable silver-colored ring. Superficially and stereotypically, he looks less like a soul man than a rapper or the new-school urban contemporary singer he presents himself as on his earlier albums, including *Ghetto Revelations* and *Ghetto Revelations II*. As it turns out he's comfortable with all those genres; his 2009 album *GRIII* is subtitled *Old School 2 Nu Skool.*

Mystic fits the traditional soul profile in at least one way: He grew up in the church. His father ministered at Mount Zion Missionary Church in Fort Lauderdale, and his mother was the organist. "I sang in the choir— I still sing in the choir." So it's not surprising to hear him acknowledge that "gospel started soul music, from back in the hymn days." He grew up listening to soul records played by his parents and three older brothers, including music by Florida artists Betty Wright and Latimore. "Soul music grabbed me from a toddler and sunk into me. I just took it and grew with it."

Echoing Sam Moore and others in his definition, Mystic says: "Soul music is about a feeling. There's some gospel you can listen to that touches you. It gives you the word that you need, but it doesn't give you that same feeling. Somebody might be going through something and hear a soul record and it touches them in a specific way," he continues, adding that the songs of Al Green, including "Love and Happiness," "got me through some times. Soul is definitely a healing aspect in life."

The music tracks for *Classics* were recorded in these studios, or Swag Labs. In choosing the musicians he told his musical director: "'If they're going to play for me they have to come from where I'm from.' I made sure everybody in the band grew up in the church and knows the old-school records I do. And it was like we already knew each other before we met."

The album took more than a year, Mystic says, of practically daily work. "We listened to the original records, and then we tried to get that same old-school sound, though we added bigger bass and bigger drums to make it sound a little more contemporary or up-to-date." He recorded the vocal tracks after the musicians got theirs down.

Besides Simon and Womack, Mystic covers Johnnie Taylor, Sam Cooke, the Temptations, and Otis Redding and reaches down into his lower registers to sound like Lou Rawls on "You'll Never Find." He's not entirely strict in his adherence to the classic canon, throwing in Rod Stewart's "Tonight's the Night" and even Prince's "Purple Rain."

Covering without copying was tricky, he acknowledges. "After I live with the records I try to put my funk on it, and make it mine. If I hear Bobby Womack went in a certain direction, I take that direction and flip it to make it more original, put more of a 2000-and-something frame on it." He's pleased that younger listeners are getting introduced to soul through him—though he often has to correct fans who think he wrote those classic tunes—and Mystic hopes to bridge the gap with older soul generations as well.

Like them this thirty-one-year-old is nostalgic for the creativity and originality of an earlier time—in his case, though, it's for old-school hip-hop. "Back when, people like Heavy D, Biggie and Tupac had messages in their records. But today," he continues, sounding a bit like rap-hater James Purify, "it's all about the beat; you can say anything so long as it's sounding good. The old-school peeps see that and they say, 'Okay you ain't really saying nothing, but you got a lot of money for it. And the man over here who took time to actually say something didn't get a lot of money for it.' So that weighs on people sometimes."

He realizes that many folks his parents' age think there's no good music being produced anymore, and they're especially down on hip-hop. "That even goes back to Heavy D, when he did 'Mr. Big Stuff,'" he laughs. In the video of that 1987 hit, Heavy D and the Boyz rapped over Jean Knight's 1971 Stax song while older black folks were shown covering their ears and saying things like, 'That's not music, that's noise.'" But in that short stage play, Mystic remembers, "when the song got to the hook, all the old-school folks got up and went to jamming and now you had everybody together."

Mystic admires soul contemporaries Anthony Hamilton and Fantasia (Barrino) and also hopes to work with the British pop/soul singer Adele: "I love her voice." His next album project, he says in 2016, will be entitled *Ghetto Gospel.* "I'm going to do a lot of writing and producing on it, and expand my sound." In terms of singing technique, he plans to use his falsetto range more—"the ladies like it." As for material, he says, "you're gonna get some hip-hop on there, and some R&B, but you'll still get the gospel feel and the soul feel. We're going to take some things people would consider not to be soul and mix them with soul, and that'll give us the ghetto gospel: the truth."

Two Florida soul greats meet again; new streets were named for them in Tampa's Encore! housing development. Courtesy of the author.

"Me, I'm for it all," he concludes. "Music is music. We, as artists, producers, singers, and rappers all have a great responsibility. Music is one of the most powerful forces on earth. So whatever we can do—if it's just a beat or it's a melody that can heal the people—we need to do it. And I'm definitely gonna keep playing my part, trying to keep soul music alive."

Can you dig it?

Acknowledgments

Firstly and mostly, I am extremely grateful to all the Florida soul practitioners who gave their time and shared their stories. Without their participation, patience, and generosity, this book would not exist. I learned a great deal from them, of course, but just as important these years of interactions have also been very rewarding and affirming for me personally. I hope my efforts live up to their contributions and expectations.

Some of the sources heard from here have since passed; special thanks and remembrance to Henry Stone, Lavell Kamma, June Watts, and Buster Cooper. (Thanks also to the Stone family, Inez and Joe.)

Among those talented and helpful folk, Charlie Blade (birth name Charles Steadham) of Gainesville was an essential guide to the musical history he's lived and continues to create and provided vital connections to other important artists and experts. Thank you muchly.

Joyce and Sam Moore were especially welcoming and generous; meeting and spending time with them is a highlight of this project.

One of the most gratifying parts of this mission has been the creation of the original photography seen here, contemporary portraits of Florida soul artists by Suzanne Williamson. She was also a valued photo editor on this project and in her other significant role—as my wife—was unfailingly supportive and inspiring. I aspire to be the same for her.

Musicians better versed in soul and gospel theory read and made suggestions on those portions of the manuscript: Big thanks to Tom Cohen, Scott Swan, Longineu Parsons, and Denny Leroux.

Friends and colleagues John Leland, David Friedman, John Atwood, and Dave Herndon provided encouragement throughout and early feedback on parts of this manuscript. I'm grateful and ever ready to return the favor. Hugo Lilienfeld's eagle eye for editorial improved the final product immensely. I also want to recognize the unwavering support of Eric Messinger and Tim Chung.

When I started this project folks who knew far more than I did about this music offered valuable counsel and expertise, starting with Michael Lydon, author of the rich and insightful biography *Ray Charles: Man and Music*. Florida author, record collector, and music expert Jeff Lemlich, who curates the Florida-centric *limestone lounge* blog, did likewise. Expert soul blogger Red Kelly (see *the A side* and *the B side*) was also generous and helpful. Preston Lauterbach, who wrote the definitive account of the chitlin' circuit, was very helpful on some key circuit points and sources. Alberto de la Portilla's *long play miami* site was a great source of information and enjoyment, and he was helpful to this author as well. Thanks also to South Florida's Angelo Angione and Tampa's Fred Hearns.

Singer/songwriter and expert soul source Ronny Elliott of Tampa was encouraging and helpful from the jump.

Appreciation and warm regards to Tampa DJ, producer, and expert Bob "Soul Man" Scheir for his help and suggestions.

Florida scholar Gary Mormino was encouraging from the start and made useful suggestions. I hope this book reads like one of his.

The University of Tampa, where I teach, offered important support of this project, including through a Professional Development Award, a sabbatical leave, and David Delo Research Professor Grants.

The University of Tampa's Creative Writing MFA program, which I'm proud to teach in, invited me to read a couple Florida soul stories in progress, putting them out into the world for the first times. Thanks especially to Director Erica Dawson, to my teaching colleagues, and to our students for their support and valuable feedback.

My student assistants at the University of Tampa did valuable work and made mine much easier: Thanks to Raychel Gadson, Kimberly Gordon, and Katherine Lavacca.

Respect and awe to research ninja Caryn Baird of the *Tampa Bay Times*, and thanks to the *Times* for publishing stories that came from or related to my *Florida Soul* research.

Jon Fink, editor of *Panhandler*, the literary magazine of the University of West Florida in Pensacola, saw fit to publish music stories of mine during my years of research, becoming an esteemed colleague and new friend.

The State Archives of Florida were a rich source of photography for this book and a pleasure to deal with, as was the Tampa-Hillsborough County Public Library System. Adonnica Toler and Yuwnus Asami of the

Ritz Theater and LaVilla Museum in Jacksonville graciously researched and supplied photos as well; thanks go out to them and to Sandra Rooks of the Pinellas County African American History Museum and the University of North Florida library. Many thanks also to ace photo editor Donna Cohen.

Thanks to Jeff Shepherd, who runs the jazz festival in Deland named for Noble "Thin Man" Watts, for his help with that chapter and to photographer/videographer Doug Braun.

Finally, I thank the University Press of Florida—especially senior acquisitions editor Sian Hunter and managing editor Marthe Walters—for believing in and publishing this book. If you are reading this, we must have pulled it off.

Notes

A Note about Sourcing

The information and accounts in this book are primarily drawn from my firsthand interviews with the creators of Florida soul music, as well as with living secondary sources. Whenever someone is quoted and the attribution is in the present tense—as in "she says," or "he adds"—and there is no attribution to another source, they said it to me, either in person or over the phone.

Information drawn from other published works, including interviews, is attributed in the text and sourced in the endnotes.

Statements on how songs and albums fared on *Billboard* magazine's R&B and pop sales charts are drawn from two authoritative reference books published by Record Research Inc. and compiled by Joel Whitburn:

Top R&B/Hip-Hop Singles 1942–2004, fifth edition (2004).
Top Pop Singles 1955–2002, compiled by Joel Whitburn, 10th edition (2003).

Introduction: The Soul State of Florida

That anticipatory song was a . . .: Joel Whitburn, *Top R&B/Hip-Hop Singles, 1942–2004*, Record Research Inc., 5th ed. (2004), page 510.
Press coverage declared that Charles . . .: Charles Mudede, "Seattle Pops: A Tribute to Ray Charles," The Stranger.com, June 2015. http://www.thestranger.com/events/21637849/seattle-pops-a-tribute-to-ray-charles.
Later in his career he . . .: Ibid., page 97.
In the otherwise excellent 2004 . . .: D. A. Pennebaker and Chris Hegedus (directors) and Roger Friedman (producer), *Only the Strong Survive*, (2002), documentary film.
In 1976 an Associated Press . . .: The Associated Press (no author byline), "'Miami Sound' Dominates Floors," April 4, 1976.
He already had the African . . .: Jacob Katel, " Little Beaver on 'Party Down," *Miami New Times*, September 22, 2014.
In her early (1969) and . . .: Phyl Garland, *The Sound of Soul: The Story of Black Music*, Pocket Books (originally published by Henry Regnery Company). (1969), page x.

In his book, Sweet Soul . . . : Peter Guralnick, *Sweet Soul Music: Rhythm and Blues and the Southern Dream of Freedom*, Harper & Row. (1986), page 2.

Author Guralnick puts it this . . . : Ibid., page 14.

In his book The New . . . : Richard J. Ripani, *The New Blue Music: Changes In Rhythm And Blues, 1950–1999*, University Press of Mississippi (2006), page 99.

(Ripani also says the biggest . . . : Ibid., page 97.

By the 1970s, when, as . . . : Ibid., page 121.

Natalie Cole's hit "I've Got . . . : Ibid., page 122.

As historian Gary R. Mormino notes . . . : Gary R. Mormino, *Land of Sunshine, State of Dreams*, University Press of Florida. (2005), page 19.

Between 1957 and 1959 . . . : John Broven, "King of the Road," in liner notes to *B. B. King: The Vintage Years* box set, Ace Records Ltd. (2002), page 37.

He made repeated stops at . . . : Ibid., page 38.

But as the late musician . . . : Preston Lauterbach, *The Chitlin' Circuit and the Road to Rock 'n' Roll*, Norton. (2011), page 12.

As an elderly man named . . . : Beau Halton, "The Great Black Way," *Florida Times Union*, July 26, 1998.

Between 1950 and 1970 in-migration . . . : No author byline, *Statistical Abstract of the United States 1973*, U.S. Bureau of the Census. (1973), page 29.

In an ironic twist—bitter . . . : Paul Guzzo, "Tampa-based Harlem in Havana Made Entertainment History," *Tampa Tribune*, February 8, 2015.

In his book The Real . . . : Hugh Gregory, *The Real Rhythm & Blues*, Blandford. (1998), page 145.

"Soul is a feeling," he . . . : D. A. Pennebaker and Chris Hegedus (directors) and Roger Friedman (producer), *Only the Strong Survive*, (2002), Documentary film.

CHAPTER 1. RAY CHARLES: GREENVILLE/JACKSONVILLE/ORLANDO/TAMPA

At that time this "undertaker" . . . : Ray Charles and David Ritz, *Brother Ray: Ray Charles' Own Story*, Da Capo Press. (1978), page 90.

While working some of his . . . : Ibid., page 68.

Of Orlando, Tampa, and other . . . : Ibid., page 42.

In his biography, Ray Charles . . . : Michael Lydon, *Ray Charles: Man and Music*, Riverhead Books. (1998), page 32.

The man himself could only . . . : Ray Charles and David Ritz, *Brother Ray: Ray Charles' Own Story*, Da Capo Press. (1978), page 8.

On the second page of . . . : Peter Guralnick, *Sweet Soul Music: Rhythm and Blues and the Southern Dream of Freedom*, Back Bay Books. (1999), page 2.

His great achievement, Guralnick writes . . . : Ibid., page 2.

The town produced cotton, cattle . . . : Michael Lydon, *Ray Charles: Man and Music*, Riverhead Books. (1998), page 4.

And of course this 1930s . . . : Ray Charles and David Ritz, *Brother Ray: Ray Charles' Own Story*, Da Capo Press. (1978), page 11.

There were two black enclaves . . . : Michael Lydon, *Ray Charles: Man and Music*, Riverhead Books. (1998), page 5.

We were back in the . . . : Ray Charles and David Ritz, *Brother Ray: Ray Charles' Own Story*, Da Capo Press. (1978), page 10.

"That's it, sonny! That's it!" . . . : Ibid., page 18.

As he wrote in Brother Ray . . . : Ibid., page 18.

In one later telling the . . . : Ray Charles, *My Early Years: 1930–1960*, Ray Charles Enterprises. (1995), page 3.

His mother took him to . . . : Ibid., page 3.

The school year had already . . . : Michael Lydon, *Ray Charles: Man and Music*, Riverhead Books. (1998), page 13.

When Robinson arrived, writes . . . : Ibid., page 13.

South Campus was for the . . . : Ibid., page 14.

"Imagine the nonsense of segregating . . . : Ray Charles and David Ritz, *Brother Ray: Ray Charles' Own Story*, Da Capo Press. (1978), page 22.

But to him it was always . . . : Ray Charles, *My Early Years: 1930–1960*, Ray Charles Enterprises. (1995), page 4.

He'd play "Honky-Tonk Train" . . . : Ray Charles and David Ritz, *Brother Ray: Ray Charles' Own Story*, Da Capo Press. (1978), page 38.

"The first time I wrote . . . : Ray Charles, *My Early Years: 1930–1960*, Ray Charles Enterprises. (1995), page 4.

As RC got older he . . . : Michael Lydon, *Ray Charles: Man and Music*, Riverhead Books. (1998), page 21.

The adult Charles was also . . . : Ray Charles Foundation website, Los Angeles: http://www.raycharles.com/RC/RC-WhoWasRayCharles.html.

Charles said he also had . . . : Ray Charles and David Ritz, *Brother Ray: Ray Charles' Own Story*, Da Capo Press. (1978), page 54.

Those first two were signs . . . : Ibid., page 41.

"If I was in a part . . . : Ibid., page 42.

He used this method his . . . : Michael Lydon, *Ray Charles: Man and Music*, Riverhead Books. (1998), page 19.

The fifteen-year-old trumpeter . . . : Ibid., page 53.

As he would later recount . . . : Ray Charles and David Ritz, *Brother Ray: Ray Charles' Own Story*, Da Capo Press. (1978), page 59.

"From these experiences as much . . . : Michael Lydon, *Ray Charles: Man and Music*, Riverhead Books. (1998), page 25.

"Silence and suffering also . . . : Ray Charles and David Ritz, *Brother Ray: Ray Charles' Own Story*, Da Capo Press. (1978), page 62.

An FSDB document obtained by . . . : Michael Lydon, *Ray Charles: Man and Music*, Riverhead Books. (1998), page 25.

In Charles' telling, however, leaving . . . : Ray Charles and David Ritz, *Brother Ray: Ray Charles' Own Story*, Da Capo Press. (1978), page 63.

The story, on owner James . . . : No author byline, "The James Craddock Enterprises," *Crisis*, January 1942, page 14.

Jacksonville went even further, calling . . . : Halton Beau, "The Great Black Way," *Florida Times-Union*, July 26, 1998.

"Ashley and Davis Streets was where . . . : Teddy Washington, *Life the Puzzle*, Self-published. (undated), page 14.

More importantly he was a . . . : Michael Lydon, *Ray Charles: Man and Music*, Riverhead Books. (1998), page 25.

Soon, RC wrote in Brother Ray . . . : Ray Charles and David Ritz, *Brother Ray: Ray Charles' Own Story*, Da Capo Press. (1978), page 69.

RC got occasional jobs with . . . : Ray Charles, *My Early Years: 1930–1960*, Ray Charles Enterprises. (1995), page 6.

Tiny York's smaller combo played . . . : John Carter, "Trumpeter Teddy Washington's Follies Awards recognized Jacksonville's unsung performers of the past," *Florida Times-Union*, October 22, 1999.

In Jacksonville, unlike in many . . . : Michael Lydon, *Ray Charles: Man and Music*, Riverhead Books. (1998), page 32.

Tiny York played New Year's . . . : Michelle Genz, "Antonio York Continues Family's Jazz Tradition," VeroNews.com, December 4, 2012.

"It became part of my education . . . : Ray Charles and David Ritz, *Brother Ray: Ray Charles' Own Story*, Da Capo Press. (1978), page 80.

Tiny York kept a second . . . : Michelle Genz, "Antonio York Continues Family's Jazz Tradition," VeroNews.com, December 4, 2012.

"We traveled down the highway . . . : Teddy Washington, *Life the Puzzle*, self-published. (undated), page 42.

A quarter century before Disney . . . : Department of Commerce, U.S., "1950 Census of Population," December 16, 1951, page 3.

As in Jacksonville, "musicians were . . . : Ray Charles and David Ritz. *Brother Ray: Ray Charles' Own Story*, Da Capo Press. (1978), page 76.

They showcased jazz as an . . . : Richard Severo, "Norman Granz, Who Took Jazz Out of Smoky Clubs and Put It in Concert Halls, Dies at 83," *New York Times*, November 27, 2001.

"Way down in Florida, those . . . : Ray Charles and David Ritz, *Brother Ray: Ray Charles' Own Story*, Da Capo Press. (1978), page 81.

Guitarist Charlie Christian . . . : Ibid., page 81.

"I sing a couple of . . . : Ibid., page 79.

Cole "changed my life," Charles . . . : Ibid., page 44.

Biographer Lydon, who got to . . . : Michael Lydon, *Ray Charles: Man and Music*, Riverhead Books. (1998), page 37.

"I didn't really think about . . . : Ray Charles and David Ritz, *Brother Ray: Ray Charles' Own Story*, Da Capo Press. (1978), page 72.

An alto player, the bandleader . . . : Ibid., page 85.

Harris also played piano and . . . : Kurt Curtis, *Florida's Famous & Forgotten*, Florida Media, Inc., Books. (2005), page 320.

It remained hard to categorize . . . : Ray Charles and David Ritz, *Brother Ray: Ray Charles' Own Story*, Da Capo Press. (1978), pages 86, 87.

McKee sang a little along with . . . : Michael Lydon, *Ray Charles: Man and Music*,
   Riverhead Books. (1998), pages 46, 47.
He met and impressed her . . . : Ray Charles and David Ritz, *Brother Ray: Ray
   Charles' Own Story*, Da Capo Press. (1978), pages 90.
RC's song was originally written . . . : Kurt Curtis, *Florida's Famous & Forgotten*.
   Florida Media, Inc. Books, (2005), page 170.
"Ever since I was a . . . : Ibid., page 88.
"We played all the country hits . . . : Ray Charles and David Ritz, *Brother Ray: Ray
   Charles' Own Story*, Da Capo Press. (1978), page 87.
If true, it's amazing that . . . : Ibid., page 88.
Confounding expectations, Charles' version of . . . : Joel Whitburn, *Top Pop Singles,
   1955–2002*. Record Research Inc., 10th ed. (2003), page 121.
Modern Sounds *topped the album* . . . : No author byline, Billboard.com (undated):
   http://www.billboard.com/articles/news/958003/ray-charles-on-the-charts.
Those same producers and executives . . . : RayCharles.com: http://www.raycharles.
   com/RC/RC-DiscographyAlbums.html.
It included "Your Cheating Heart . . . : Joel Whitburn, *Top R&B/Hip-Hop Singles,
   1942–2004*, Record Research Inc., 5th ed. (2004), page 113.
He may have paid as . . . : Michael Lydon, *Ray Charles: Man and Music*, Riverhead
   Books. (1998), page 47.
Whatever else he thought and felt . . . : Ray Charles and David Ritz, *Brother Ray: Ray
   Charles' Own Story*, Da Capo Press. (1978), page 89.
"It suddenly dawned on me . . . Ibid., page 92.
The older Ray Charles recounted . . . : Ibid., page 93.
He undercuts the serendipity of . . . : Ibid., page 94.
In the Lydon biography, however . . . : Michael Lydon, *Ray Charles: Man and Music*,
   Riverhead Books. (1998), pages 49, 50.
The reason he could hold . . . : Ray Charles and David Ritz, *Brother Ray: Ray Charles'
   Own Story*, Da Capo Press. (1978), page 97.
"Confession Blues," his composition, became . . . : Joel Whitburn, *Top R&B/Hip-Hop
   Singles, 1942–2004*, Record Research Inc., 5th ed. (2004), page 112.
One of the singles from . . . : Ibid., page 112.
Then Atlantic Records founder Ahmet . . . : Jerry Wexler and David Ritz, *Rhythm and
   the Blues: A Life in American Music*, Alfred A. Knopf. (1993), page 105.
Charles based it on a . . . : Peter Guralnick, online post on peterguralnick.com:
   http://www.peterguralnick.com/post/44057575074/rb-the-transition-years.
British critic and author Hugh . . . : Hugh Gregory, *The Real Rhythm and Blues*,
   Blandford Books. (1998), page 146.
Whatever the exact admixture of . . . : Joel Whitburn, *Top R&B/Hip-Hop Singles,
   1942–2004*, Record Research Inc., 5th ed. (2004), page 112.
(A later version charted again . . . : Ibid., page 112.
Guralnick, admittedly a soul partisan . . . : Peter Guralnick, *Sweet Soul Music:
   Rhythm and Blues and the Southern Dream of Freedom*, Back Bay Books. (1999),
   page 63.

Jerry Wexler, his producer at . . . : atlanticrecords.com: http://www.atlanticrecords.
   com/posts/ray-charles-makings-soul-legend-18226.
"The minute I started being . . . : Ray Charles and David Ritz, *Brother Ray: Ray
   Charles' Own Story*, Da Capo Press. (1978), page 148.
His imitating others, especially Nat . . . : Ibid., page 149.
Charles was "the first self-produced . . . : Jerry Wexler and David Ritz, *Rhythm and the
   Blues: A Life in American Music*, Alfred A. Knopf. (1993), page 108.
Unusual as it was for . . . : Ibid., page 103.
His goal and guiding vision . . . : Ray Charles and David Ritz, *Brother Ray: Ray
   Charles' Own Story*, Da Capo Press. (1978), page 148.

CHAPTER 2. ERNIE CALHOUN: TAMPA

Percy Mayfield, who's been called . . . : Joel Whitburn, *Top R&B/Hip-Hop Singles,
   1942–2004*, Record Research Inc., 5th ed. (2004), page 385.
He settled in for a while . . . : Cuban Information Archives, "Miami Night Life
   Guide 1956": http://cuban-exile.com/doc_176-200/doc0196.html.
(In Hawkins' obituary New York . . . : John Wilson, "Coleman Hawkins, Tenor
   Saxophonist, Is Dead," *New York Times*, May 20, 1969.

CHAPTER 3. NOBLE "THIN MAN" WATTS: DELAND

That bandleader and baritone sax . . . : Joel Whitburn, *Top R&B/Hip-Hop Singles,
   1942–2004*, Record Research Inc., 5th ed. (2004), page 627.
"Noble was a star with . . . : Eric Snider, "'Thin Man' Watts has a Full Lifetime of
   Playing the Blues," *St. Petersburg Times*, May 29, 1987.
"Noble 'Thin Man' Watts is . . . : Richard Williams, "Fat Grooves from the Thin
   Man," *Times*, November 14, 1987.
Wagging "a long, bony finger . . . : Eric Snider, "'Thin Man' Watts has a Full Lifetime
   of Playing the Blues," *St. Petersburg Times*, May 29, 1987.
"They used to say I was . . . : Ibid.
Watts made his first recordings . . . : Richard Defendorf, "Sanford's Midnight Creep-
   ers Found a Solid-Gold Sax in 'Thin Man' Watts," *Orlando Sentinel*, November
   10, 1985.
The magazine called it a . . . : No author byline, "Review Spotlight," *Billboard*,
   August 19, 1957.
"Noble 'Thin Man' Watts, a . . . : Arnold Shaw, *Honkers and Shouters: The Golden
   Years of Rhythm & Blues*, Macmillan. (1978), page 471.
In December 1957 Watts' . . . : Joel Whitburn, *Top Pop Singles 1955–2002*, Record
   Research Inc., 10th ed. (2003), page 756.
As Nat Adderley once said . . . : Eric Snider, "'Thin Man' Watts has a Full Lifetime of
   Playing the Blues," *St. Petersburg Times*, May 29, 1987.
Watts wrote and recorded two . . . : Kurt Curtis, *Florida's Famous & Forgotten*, Florida
   Media, Inc. (2005), page 880.
(King Snake, based in a . . . : Jim Abbott, "Old Sanford Blues Studio Gone—But
   Music It Birthed Lives On," *Orlando Sentinel*, June 1, 2008.

Greenlee, who died of pancreatic . . . : Jim Abbott, "Musician And Blues Record Producer Bob Greenlee Dies At 59," *Orlando Sentinel*, February 13, 2004.

In 1987 King Snake put . . . : Kurt Curtis, *Florida's Famous & Forgotten*, Florida Media, Inc. (2005) page 877.

(Though People *did call his* . . . : No specific author byline; reviews credited to Ralph Novak, Andrew Abrahams, Lisa Shea, Michael Small, "Picks and Pans," *People* magazine, August 27, 1990.

CHAPTER 4. THE TWIST CAME FROM TAMPA: TAMPA/MIAMI

Ballard's original version, on Cincinnati-based . . . : Joel Whitburn, *Top R&B/Hip-Hop Singles, 1942–2004*, Record Research Inc., 5th ed. (2004), page 44.

That simple, catchy two-and-a-half-minute . . . : Jim Dawson, *The Twist: The Story of the Song and Dance That Changed the World*, Faber and Faber. (1995), page 43.

Checker's Ballard cover also made . . . : Joel Whitburn, *Top R&B/Hip-Hop Singles, 1942–2004*, Record Research Inc., 5th ed. (2004), page 114.

A year and change later . . . : Joel Whitburn. *Billboard Hot 100 Charts: The Sixties*, Record Research Inc. (1990), page 124.

Ballard's "Twist" was rereleased in . . . : Joel Whitburn. *Top Pop Singles 1955–2002*, Record Research Inc., 10th ed. (2003), page 44.

In the early 1960s, seemingly everyone . . . : Jim Dawson, *The Twist: The Story of the Song and Dance That Changed the World*, Faber and Faber Inc. (1995), page 34.

The East Room of the . . . : Guido van Rijn, *Kennedy's Blues: African-American Blues and Gospel Songs on JFK*, University Press of Mississippi. (2007), page 48.

The St. Petersburg Times *confirmed* . . . : No author byline, "Everybody's Twisting It—No Sense Missing It," *St. Petersburg Times*, December 3, 1961.

In 2008 Billboard *ratified that* . . . : No author byline, "'The Twist' top song of Billboard Hot 100 era," Associated Press, September 11, 2008.

Ballard wrote the song, . . . : Joe Sasfy, *1960: Still Rockin'*, Time-Life Music, 1989.

In the 1993 documentary Twist . . . : Ron Mann, producer and director. Triton Pictures/New Line Home Video, 1993.

In his introduction to Ballard's . . . : P. W. Fenton, "A History of the Blues in the Tampa Bay Area," produced for the Suncoast Blues Society, aired on and © by WMNF-FM Tampa (2002).

According to Green this lyrical . . . : Jim Dawson, *The Twist: The Story of the Song and Dance that Changed the World*, Faber & Faber. (1995), page 10.

As author Dawson points out . . . : Ibid., page 2.

Duke Ellington recorded "Harlem Twist . . . : Ibid., page 4.

"The sexual implications of the . . . : Ibid., page 4.

The Miami song was narrated . . . : Ibid., page 12.

It became the group's biggest . . . : Joel Whitburn, *Top R&B/Hip-Hop Singles, 1942–2004*, Record Research Inc., 5th ed. (2004), page 44.

Then, DJs and listeners recognized . . . : Ibid., page 44.

Dave Appell, who produced Checker's . . . : Chuck Darrow, "How Chubby Checker and the Twist leaped into Legend," *Philadelphia Daily News*, July 9, 2010.

When Checker's "Twist" made the . . . : Joel Whitburn, *Billboard Hot 100 Charts: The Sixties*, Record Research Inc. (1990), page 34.

"Let's Twist Again" was Checker's . . . : Joel Whitburn, *Top Pop Singles 1955–2002*, Record Research Inc., 10th ed. (2003), page 124.

In October of that year. . . . : Jim Dawson, *The Twist: The Story of the Song and Dance that Changed the World*, Faber & Faber. (1995), page 63.

This effort made #4 on . . . : Joel Whitburn, *Top R&B/Hip-Hop Singles, 1942–2004*, Record Research Inc., 5th ed. (2004), page 114.

In February 1962 that . . . : Jim Dawson, *The Twist: The Story of the Song and Dance that Changed the World*, Faber & Faber. (1995), page 65.

A seven-page text-and-photo . . . : No author byline, "A Pulsating, Gyrating, Hip-Swinging Mania Sweeps the U.S. and Europe: and Now Everybody is Doing It," *LIFE* magazine, November 24, 1961, pages 74–80.

The St. Petersburg Times sent . . . : Gloria Biggs, title of article illegible, *St. Petersburg Times*, January 23, 1962.

"I think I'll take my . . . : Bill Dunn, "Everybody's Trying the Twist at Lounge," *St. Petersburg Times*, December 17, 1961.

Over the following New Year's . . . : Frances Protiva, title of article illegible, *St. Petersburg Times*, January 14, 1962.

Arthur Murray, the nation's dance . . . : Jim Dawson, *The Twist: The Story of the Song and Dance that Changed the World*, Faber & Faber. (1995), pages 56–58.

One Tampa Bay area psychologist . . . : Frances Protiva, title of newspaper article illegible, *St. Petersburg Times*, January 14, 1962.

The Society of New Jersey . . . : Jim Dawson, *The Twist: The Story of the Song and Dance that Changed the World*, Faber & Faber. (1995), page 60.

Dwight Eisenhower, who had just . . . : Ibid., pages 130–131.

In the Soviet Union . . . : Ibid., page 125.

"We discourage all weird or . . . : No author byline, "Tampa Bans the Twist," Associated Press, January 4, 1962.

"We won't ever ban fad . . . : No author byline, "Councilman Dances the Twist, But . . ." Associated Press, January 5, 1962.

Irwin Stambler cited the Midnighters' . . . : Irwin Stambler, *Encyclopedia of Pop, Rock & Soul*, St. Martin's. (1989), page 29.

CHAPTER 5. LINDA LYNDELL: GAINESVILLE

The company released the single . . . : Rob Bowman, "What a Woman: The Saga of a Soul Queen," *The Oxford American*. (August 2001), page 61.

Lyndell told Rob Bowman, author . . . : Ibid., page 62.

Meaning, the author says: "He . . . : Ibid., page 59.

"What A Man" (released on . . . : Joel Whitburn, *Top R&B/Hip-Hop Singles, 1942–2004*, Record Research Inc., 5th ed. (2004), page 368.

It didn't help that the . . . : Jerry Wexler and David Ritz, *Rhythm and the Blues: A Life in American Music*, Alfred A. Knopf. (1993), page 235.

Al Bell later said the . . . : Rob Bowman, "What a Woman: The Saga of a Soul Queen," *The Oxford American*. (August 2001), page 59.

CHAPTER 6. LAVELL KAMMA AND THE 100 HOUR COUNTS: JACKSONVILLE/ PAHOKEE

"Musically, he had no background . . . : Scott Swan, "'Music Is My Vessel': An Exploration of African American Musical Culture Through the Life Story of Lavell Kamma," a Florida State University Master's thesis. (2003), page 53.

They traveled, according to Kamma . . . : Ibid., page 102.

In his thesis Scott Swan . . . : Ibid., page 57.

To inculcate that close connection . . . : Lauren Flannery, "Chitlin' Circuit great Lavell Kamma dead at 73," *Gainesville Sun*, April 3, 2015.

CHAPTER 7. SAM MOORE, SOUL SURVIVOR: OVERTOWN

When Sunday came, after a . . . : Sam Moore and Dave Marsh, *The Sam and Dave Story*, Avon Books. (1998), page 24.

(Most Overtown houses in the . . . : Marvin Dunn, *Black Miami in the Twentieth Century*, University Press of Florida. (1997), page 164.

Music critic and author Dave . . . : Ibid., Introduction, page x.

"Soul Man," #1 on that . . . : Joel Whitburn, *Top R&B/Hip-Hop Singles, 1942–2004*, Record Research Inc., 5th ed. (2004), page 510.

and won a 1967 Grammy . . . : No author byline, "1967: 10th Annual Grammy Awards." Grammy.com, (undated): http://www.grammy.com/nominees/sear ch?artist=Sam+and+Dave&field_nominee_work_value=Soul+Man&year=196 7&genre=All

"Dave was much more serious . . . : Sam Moore and Dave Marsh, *The Sam and Dave Story*, Avon Books. (1998), page 47.

Overtown, formerly known as Darkey . . . : Marvin Dunn, *Black Miami in the Twentieth Century*, University Press of Florida. (1997), page 151.

In Moore's day it was . . . : Jordan Levin, "The Sweet Sound of Overtown," *Miami Herald*. February 1, 2009.

As Miami Herald *reporter Jordan* . . . : Ibid.

Then, as also happened in . . . : Marvin Dunn, *Black Miami in the Twentieth Century*, University Press of Florida. (1997), page 156.

After the Knight Beat show . . . : Sam Moore and Dave Marsh, *The Sam and Dave Story*, Avon Books. (1998), page 24.

For a while, he says . . . : Ibid., page 29.

His mother fell gravely ill . . . : Ibid., page 31.

The club, at 62nd Street . . . : Alan Cherry and Christy McKerney, "Mayor Lomelo Did It His Way," *Sun Sentinel*, June 30, 2000.

"I must have looked like . . . : Sam Moore and Dave Marsh, *The Sam and Dave Story*, Avon Books. (1998), page 40.

Miami was then a city . . . : U.S. Bureau of the Census, U.S Censuses of Population and Housing: 1960. Census Tracts. Final Report PHC(1)-90. U.S. Government Printing Office, Washington, D.C., 1962.

All of Irwin County, Georgia . . . : No author byline, "Irwin County," Georgia Info. Digital Library of Georgia, (2015): http://georgiainfo.galileo.usg.edu/topics/ counties/irwin.

(Both Levy and his company . . . : No author byline, "Morris Levy Is Dead; Power in Recording and Club Owner, 62," *New York Times*, May 23, 1990.

Henry Stone was there as . . . : Jerry Wexler and David Ritz, *Rhythm and the Blues: A Life in American Music*, Alfred A. Knopf. (1993), page 177.

"Although it didn't chart," writes . . . : Rob Bowman, *Soulsville, U.S.A.: The Story of Stax Records*, Schirmer Books. (1997), page 69.

Part of this new direction . . . : Ibid. Page 66.

Porter later said of Moore . . . : Ibid. Page 88.

"Hold On" was a #1 . . . : Joel Whitburn, *Top R&B/Hip-Hop Singles, 1942–2004*, Record Research Inc., 5th ed. (2004), page 510.

Sam and Dave's second #1 . . . : Ibid. Page 510.

The duo sang and danced on . . . : "The Ed Sullivan Show," TV.com: http://www.tv.com/shows/the-ed-sullivan-show/ may-25-1969-sam-and-dave-mary-hopkin-theodore-bikel-louis-nye-107143/.

. . . chatted with Dick Cavett on . . . : "The Dick Cavett Show," IMDB.com: http://www.imdb.com/title/tt1934863/.

. . . and appeared on The Mike . . . : "The Mike Douglas Show," TV.com: http://www.tv.com/shows/the-mike-douglas-show/october-18-1968-1294779/.

In the chapter on Jackson . . . : Gerri Hirshey, *Nowhere to Run: The Story of Soul Music*, Times Books. (1984), page 224.

As Robert Gordon wrote . . . : Robert Gordon, *Respect Yourself: Stax Records and the Soul Explosion*, Bloomsbury USA. (2013), page 98.

CHAPTER 8. JAMES PURIFY: PENSACOLA

In the 1960s and 1970s . . . : Joel Whitburn, *Top R&B/Hip-Hop Singles, 1942–2004*, Record Research Inc., 5th ed. (2004), page 476.

In the 1970s Abe's expanded . . . : Jessica Forbes, "Belmont-DeVilliers' Rich Musical History," *Independent News*, November 26, 2015.

The first "I'm Your Puppet . . . : Joseph Murrells, *The Book of Golden Discs*, Barrie & Jenkins. (1978), page 210.

"If the best definition of . . . : Dave Marsh, *The Heart of Rock & Soul: The 1001 Greatest Singles Ever Made*, New American Library. (1989), page 219.

Schroeder told soul blogger Red . . . : Red Kelly, "James & Bobby Purify—Section C (Bell 774)," The A Side. (March 1, 2011): http://redkelly2.blogspot.com/2011/03/james-bobby-purify-section-c-bell-774.html.

Public records confirm the charges . . . : Florida Department of Law Enforcement "Sexual Offender / Predator Flyer." (undated): http://offender.fdle.state.fl.us/offender/flyer.do?personNbr=79620.

CHAPTER 9. BOBBY PURIFY: PENSACOLA

Papa Don took them into . . . : Joel Whitburn, *Top R&B/Hip-Hop Singles, 1942–2004*, Record Research Inc., 5th ed. (2004), page 477.

After he and James stopped . . . : Kurt Curtis, *Florida's Famous & Forgotten*, Florida Media, Inc. Books. (2005), page 649.

Chapter 10. Papa Don Schroeder: Pensacola

(In another interview he says . . . : Bill Dahl, "Papa Don Schroeder reminisces about producing James & Bobby Purify, Mighty Sam and Oscar Toney, Jr. for Amy/Bell/Mala Records," Sundazed.com, (undated): http://www.sundazed.com/scene/exclusives/papa_don_exclusive.html.

Toney's version of "For Your . . . : Joel Whitburn, *Top R&B/Hip-Hop Singles, 1942–2004*, Record Research Inc., 5th ed. (2004), page 584.

He was back on the . . . : No author byline, "Number of Inhabitants," U.S. Census Report, 1960, Table 8, page 11–16.

Although Carlton was "not a . . . : Joel Whitburn, *Top R&B/Hip-Hop Singles, 1942–2004*, Record Research Inc. (2004), page 104.

After his awakening, Schroeder says . . . : Gerald Schroeder, "Papa Don's Revised Testimony," self-published document, (1998).

Chapter 11. Wayne Cochran: Miami

Jeff Lemlich, author and curator . . . : Jeff Lemlich, *Limestone Lounge* blog post, May 29, 2002: http://limestonelounge.yuku.com/topic/371/Wayne-Cochran?page=#.VvMIbRi8mwo.

"That sounds great," Letterman responded . . . : Lloyd Grove, "Paul Shaffer's Life With Letterman," *Daily Beast*, (August 29, 2014): http://www.thedailybeast.com/articles/2014/08/29/paul-shaffer-s-life-with-letterman.html.

In his biography of Redding . . . : Mark Ribowsky, *Dreams to Remember: Otis Redding, Stax Records, and the Transformation of Southern Soul*, Liveright. (2015), page 67.

A 1983 Miami Herald story . . . : Fred Grimm, "Sin City And The CC Rider Give Their Blue-Eyed Soul To God," *Miami Herald*, June 30, 1983.

"I never heard race in . . . : Joe Cardona, "How Miami Got Its Groove with Wayne Cochran and the C.C. Riders," *Miami Herald*, October 21, 2011.

Chapter 12. Willie Clarke and Deep City Records: Miami

Proof is hard to come . . . : Dorothy Jenkins Fields, "New Film Celebrates 'Birth of the Miami Sound,'" *Miami Herald*, September 10, 2014.

In a 2014 documentary, Deep . . . : Marlon Johnson, Chad Tingle, and Dennis Scholl, *Deep City: The Birth Of The Miami Sound*, WLRN (Public TV documentary). (2014).

"It was underground," Clarke says . . . : Ibid.

He also notes that it's . . . : Alberto de la Portilla, "Soul Flashback—July 1967: Am I a Good Man," *long play miami* blog, (July 28, 2013): https://longplaymiami.wordpress.com/2013/07/28/soul-flashback-july-1967-am-i-a-good-man/.

[Jimmy Bo Horne sang the song . . . : No author byline, discogs site entry (undated): https://www.discogs.com/artist/37413-Jimmy-Bo-Horne?filter_anv=0&subtype=Singles-EPs&type=Releases.

The gay people up North . . . : No author byline, grammy.com, (undated): http://www.grammy.com/blogs/the-grammys-trailblazing-women-part-two.

Chapter 13. Helene Smith: Miami

"A Woman Will Do Wrong . . . : Joel Whitburn, *Top R&B/Hip-Hop Singles, 1942–2004,* Record Research Inc., 5th ed. (2004), page 535.

Written by Reid and Deep . . . : Kurt Curtis, *Florida's Famous & Forgotten,* Florida Media Inc. (2005), page 746.

As the knowledgeable soul blogger . . . : Sir Shambling, "Artist Index: Helene Smith," *Sir Shambling's Deep Soul Heaven* blog, (undated): http://sirshambling.com/artists_2012/S/helene_smith/.

[Smith remembers correctly . . . : Tim Smith, "Opera Speaks to Vox Pop at Grammys," *Sun Sentinel* (March 8, 1998): http://articles.sun-sentinel.com/1998-03-08/entertainment/9803050169_1_aria-nessun-dorma-aretha-franklin.

Chapter 14. Henry Stone: Miami

Although it doesn't list any . . . : Associated Press (no author byline). "'Miami Sound' Dominates Floors," April 4, 1976.

The Charms' song listed above . . . : Joel Whitburn, *Top R&B/Hip-Hop Singles, 1942–2004,* Record Research Inc., 5th ed. (2004), page 114.

At that time, according to . . . : Jacob Katel, "RIP Henry Stone, King of Independent Records, Dead at 93," *Miami New Times,* August 8, 2014.

That's when the George and . . . : Joel Whitburn, *Top R&B/Hip-Hop Singles, 1942–2004,* Record Research Inc., 5th ed. (2004), page 389.

. . . so was Timmy Thomas' peace . . . : Ibid., page 577.

. . . which stayed on that chart . . . : Ibid., page 341.

KC and the Sunshine Band . . . : Ibid., page 315.

While working for Pollack's . . . : Interview by Dr. Lauren Onkey, "From Songwriters to Soundmen: The People Behind the Hits," symposium at the Rock and Roll Hall of Fame and Museum (May 19, 2010).

(Stone said that Leonard Chess . . . : Kurt Curtis and Henry Stone, "Heart of Stone: The Henry Stone Story," CD booklet, Henry Stone Music. (2002).

"Their explosive show stunned the . . . : Ibid.

The money aside, these engagements . . . : RJ Smith, *The One: The Life and Music of James Brown,* Gotham Books. (2012), page 85.

(With Atlantic's ace producer and . . . : Michael Limnios, "Criteria Recording Studios, Miami, FL—An Interview with studio manager Trevor Fletcher," Blues.gr: http://blues.gr/profiles/blogs/criteria-recording-studios-miami-fl-an-interview-with-studio

The "Mashed" songs did very well . . . : Kurt Curtis and Henry Stone, "Heart of Stone: The Henry Stone Story," CD booklet, Henry Stone Music. (2002).

Later on when I quit . . . : Jacob Katel and Henry Stone, *The Stone Cold Truth on Payola in the Music Biz,* Henry Stone Music (e-book). (2013).

He maintained that while Florida . . . : Interview by Dr. Lauren Onkey, "From Songwriters to Soundmen: The People Behind the Hits," symposium at the Rock and Roll Hall of Fame and Museum (May 19, 2010).

His obituary in the Miami New Times . . . : Jacob Katel, "RIP Henry Stone, King of Independent Records, Dead at 93," *Miami New Times*, August 8, 2014.

You just gotta remember . . . : Jacob Katel and Henry Stone, *The Stone Cold Truth on Payola in the Music Biz*, Henry Stone Music (e-book). (2013).

The promoter also maintained that . . . : Ibid.

"They were hit records, man . . . : Ibid.

Wright's gold record—at the . . . : Joel Whitburn, *Top R&B/Hip-Hop Singles, 1942–2004*, Record Research Inc., 5th ed. (2004), page 638.

In just over two years . . . : Ibid., page 315.

. . . along with "I'm Your Boogie . . . : Joel Whitburn, *Top Pop Singles, 1955–2002*, Record Research Inc., 10th ed. (2003), page 375.

In a 2013 post on . . . : Alberto de la Portilla, "The Making of 'Rock Your Baby,'" *long play miami*, (2013): https://longplaymiami.wordpress.com/?s=The+Making+o f+%27Rock+Your+Baby%2C%27%27%27.

In the liner notes to . . . : Kurt Curtis and Henry Stone, "Heart of Stone: The Henry Stone Story," CD booklet, Henry Stone Music. (2002).

(It was definitely #1 on . . . : Joel Whitburn, *Top R&B/Hip-Hop Singles, 1942–2004*, Record Research Inc., 5th ed. (2004), page 389.

One of KC's last songs . . . : Joel Whitburn, *Top R&B/Hip-Hop Singles, 1942–2004*, Record Research Inc., 5th ed. (2004), page 375.

Chapter 15. The Miami Sound: Little Beaver, Chocolate Perry, and the T.K. Family

Then Beaver learned the three-chord . . . : Alberto de la Portilla, "Little Beaver, Part 1," *long play miami*. (January 11, 2014): https://longplaymiami.wordpress. com/2014/01/11/little-beaver-part-1/.

Little Beaver's work, de la Portilla writes . . . : Ibid.

"The Latin flavor was something . . . : Jacob Katel, "Little Beaver on 'Party Down,'" *Miami New Times*, September 22, 2014.

The single just missed being . . . : Joel Whitburn, *Top R&B/Hip-Hop Singles, 1942–2004*, Record Research Inc., 5th ed. (2004), page 638.

"Without a doubt," Henry Stone . . . : Henry Stone and Kurt Curtis, "Heart of Stone: The Henry Stone Story," CD booklet, Henry Stone Music. (2002).

De la Portilla calls the Rocketeers the . . . : Alberto de la Portilla, "Little Beaver, Part 2," *long play miami*. (January 11, 2014): https://longplaymiami.wordpress. com/2014/01/25/little-beaver-part-2/.

Joey Gilmore, the guitarist Beaver . . . : Scott M. Bock, "Taking Control of His Own Destiny," *Living Blues* (June 2009).

One of the top dogs . . . : Jacob Katel, "Little Beaver on 'Party Down,'" *Miami New Times*, September 22, 2014.

Without that device, he said . . . : Alberto de la Portilla, "Little Beaver, Part 1," *long play miami*. (January 11, 2014): https://longplaymiami.wordpress. com/2014/01/11/little-beaver-part-1/.

"There's only a few people . . . : Ibid.

At T.K. Beaver recorded "Joey . . . : Joel Whitburn, *Top R&B/Hip-Hop Singles, 1942–2004,* Record Research Inc., 5th ed. (2004), page 355.

Two years later Beaver heard . . . : Alberto de la Portilla, "Little Beaver, Part 2," *long play miami.* (January 11, 2014): https://longplaymiami.wordpress. com/2014/01/25/little-beaver-part-2/.

He had also been impressed . . . : Ibid.

In fact the lyrics and . . . : Jacob Katel, "Little Beaver on 'Party Down,'" *Miami New Times* (September 22, 2014).

"Party Down" lazed its way . . . : Joel Whitburn, *Top R&B/Hip-Hop Singles, 1942–2004,* Record Research Inc., 5th ed. (2004), page 355.

Latimore "played the keys and . . . : Jacob Katel, "Little Beaver on 'Party Down,'" *Miami New Times* (September 22, 2014).

Author and Florida music expert . . . : Jeff Lemlich, "Jaco Pastorius' Funkadelic Sound: A 1971 Session," *Savage Lost* blog, (September 2015): http://savagelost. com/jaco-pastorius-funkadelic-sound-a-1971-session.

When Alfredo de la Portilla interviewed him . . . : Alberto de la Portilla, "Little Beaver, Part 1," *long play miami.* (January 11, 2014): https://longplaymiami.wordpress. com/2014/01/11/little-beaver-part-1/.

Beaver said he found out . . . : Alberto de la Portilla, "Little Beaver, Part 2," *long play miami.* (January 11, 2014): https://longplaymiami.wordpress. com/2014/01/25/little-beaver-part-2/.

(Jacob Katel of the New . . . : Jacob Katel, "Little Beaver on 'Party Down,'" *Miami New Times,* September 22, 2014.

Yet Beaver maintained that "it . . . : Ibid.

Discogs.com, a reliable discography site . . . : No author byline, "Chocolate Perry," Discogs.com (undated): https://www.discogs.com/artist/546512- George-Chocolate-Perry?subtype=Instruments-Performance&filter_ anv=0&type=Credits&page=1.

He also produced twenty-some . . . : Ibid.

"The bass player is just . . . : Jacob Katel, "Little Beaver on 'Party Down,'" *Miami New Times,* September 22, 2014.

Chapter 16. Frankie Gearing: St. Petersburg

Red also booked them into . . . : Kurt Curtis, *Florida's Famous & Forgotten,* Florida Media Inc. (2005), page 291.

Gearing's best-known work came . . . : Ibid., page 291.

She had one certified hit . . . : Joel Whitburn, *Top R&B/Hip-Hop Singles, 1942–2004,* Record Research Inc., 5th ed. (2004), page 479.

The British website Soul Cellar . . . : Tom de Jong, "The Stray Soul of Frankie Gearing." (Undated). http://www.soulcellar.co.uk/frankieg/FrankieGearing.html.

In its heyday, the late . . . : Jon Wilson, "The Deuces—What Was, Is No More," *St. Petersburg Times,* July 28, 2002.

There was a post office . . . : Ibid.

Perversely, reporter Wilson noted, expanded . . . : Ibid.

They signed with the new . . . : No author byline, "Date's Success Spurs Expansion of Artist, Property Purchases," *Billboard*, April 1, 1967.

The first one, the song . . . : Joel Whitburn, *Top R&B/Hip-Hop Singles, 1942–2004*, Record Research Inc., 5th ed. (2004), page 231.

The Glories put out 16 . . . : Kurt Curtis, *Florida's Famous & Forgotten*, Florida Media Inc. (2005), pages 292, 293.

"Messed Up" was the only . . . : Joel Whitburn, *Top R&B/Hip-Hop Singles, 1942–2004*, Record Research Inc., 5th ed. (2004), page 471.

CHAPTER 17. TIMMY THOMAS: MIAMI

His song, released on Henry . . . : Joel Whitburn, *Top R&B/Hip-Hop Singles, 1942–2004*. Menomonee Falls, Wis.: Record Research Inc. 2004, page 577.

Its unique sound—just Thomas . . . : Ibid., page 577.

After "Why Can't We Live . . . : Ibid., page 577.

Top 40 was both pervasive . . . : No author byline, "The Hot 100–1972 Archive," billboard.com (undated): http://www.billboard.com/archive/charts/1972/ hot-100.

Five more Timmy Thomas albums . . . : No author byline, *discogs* site (undated): https://www.discogs.com/artist/32166-Timmy-Thomas.

Drake's re-purposing of "WCWLT," singing . . . : No author byline, "Drake: Chart History," billboard.com (undated): http://www.billboard.com/artist/301284/ drake/chart.

But it reached #1 on . . . : Miles Raymer, "The Mysterious Power of 'Hotline Bling,'" GQ.com (October 10, 2015): http://www.gq.com/story/ mysterious-power-of-hotline-bling.

CHAPTER 18. LATIMORE: RIVERVIEW/MIAMI

His composition and signature song . . . : Joel Whitburn, *Top R&B/Hip-Hop Singles, 1942–2004*, Record Research Inc., 5th ed. (2004), page 341.

"Monday" rose to #27 . . . : Ibid., page 341.

He did put out a single . . . : Ibid., pages 568, 569.

One reason, as David Whiteis points out . . . : David Whiteis, *Southern Soul-Blues*, University of Illinois Press. (2013), page 46.

CHAPTER 19. JACKIE MOORE: JACKSONVILLE

It was a huge hit . . . : Recording Industry Association of America's Gold and Platinum Database: http://www.riaa.com/gold-platinum/?tab_active=default-awar d&ar=JACKIE+MOORE&ti=PRECIOUS%2C+PRECIOUS.

As that status suggests it . . . : Joel Whitburn, *Top R&B/Hip-Hop Singles, 1942–2004*, Record Research Inc., 5th ed. (2004), page 412.

"Precious" is one of fifteen . . . : Ibid., page 412.

Wexler called them his "salt . . . : Jerry Wexler and David Ritz, *Rhythm and the Blues: A Life in American Music*, Alfred A. Knopf. (1993), page 236.

Written and produced by him . . . : Joel Whitburn, *Top R&B/Hip-Hop Singles, 1942–2004*, Record Research Inc., 5th ed. (2004), page 549.

She remembered him telling her . . . : Wes Enzinna, "Musician of the Month: Candi Staton," *Oxford American*, December 2, 2010.

According to the North Florida . . . : Michael Fitzgerald, *North Florida Music Hall of Fame* site: http://larrycohenproductions.com/N_Fla_Music.htm.

That single along with "Both Ends . . . : Joel Whitburn, *Top R&B/Hip-Hop Singles, 1942–2004*, Record Research Inc., 5th ed. (2004), page 412.

That single made it to . . . : Ibid., page 412.

"This Time" became a #1 hit . . . : Joel Whitburn, *Billboard's Hot Dance/Disco 1974–2003*, Record Research Inc. (2004), page 178.

Moore's song also went to . . . : Ibid., page 412.

According to Sound Exchange's website . . . : No author byline, "SoundExchange Launches 'Project72' Campaign in Support of The RESPECT Act," SoundExchange.com, May 29, 2014: http://www.soundexchange.com/pr/soundexchange-launches-project72-campaign-in-support-of-the-respect-act/.

Even if payment was required . . . : Steve Knopper, "The New Economics of the Music Industry," *Rolling Stone*, October 25, 2011: http://www.rollingstone.com/music/news/the-new-economics-of-the-music-industry-20111025.

Based on that and Columbia's . . . : Kurt Curtis, *Florida's Famous & Forgotten*, Florida Media Inc. (2005), page 541.

CHAPTER 20. KC AND THE SUNSHINE BAND: MIAMI

"Blow Your Whistle" hit the R&B . . . : Joel Whitburn, *Top R&B/Hip-Hop Singles, 1942–2004*, Record Research Inc., 5th ed. (2004), page 315.

In the six years between . . . : Ibid., pages 315, 316.

(Though RC Robinson had many . . . : Ibid., pages 112, 113 (Ray Charles' hits) and 315, 316 (KC and the Sunshine Band's).

Casey had two more hits . . . : Ibid., page 316.

(Some, including Black Miami *author* . . . : Marvin Dunn, *Black Miami in the Twentieth Century*, University Press of Florida. (1997), page 16.

Because Junkanoo was raucous as . . . : Janet L. DeCosmo, "Junkanoo: The African Cultural Connection In Nassau, Bahamas," *Western Journal Of Black Studies* 27.4. (2003).

By the turn of the . . . : Marvin Dunn, *Black Miami in the Twentieth Century*, University Press of Florida. (1997), page 16.

Dunn tosses in the possibility . . . : Ibid., page 17.

Another theory holds that it's . . . : Janet L. DeCosmo, "Junkanoo: The African Cultural Connection in Nassau, Bahamas," *Western Journal Of Black Studies* 27.4. (2003).

Gradually, European instruments, including the . . . : Harold Chipman, *The Concise Garland Encyclopedia of World Music*, Routledge. (2004), page 258.

In the booklet accompanying Stone's . . . : Henry Stone and Kurt Curtis, "Heart of Stone: The Henry Stone Story," Henry Stone Music (CD booklet). (2002).

According to the reliable site discogs.com . . . : No author byline, "Rock Your Baby" entry on *discogs* site (Undated): http://www.discogs.com/George-McCrae-Rock-Your-Baby/master/138521.

Jerome Smith contributed memorable . . . : No author byline, "Jerome Smith, 47, of K. C. and the Sunshine Band, the Hit Disco Group," *New York Times*, August 10, 2000.

"That's the Way (I Like . . . : Joel Whitburn, *Top R&B/Hip-Hop Singles, 1942–2004*, Record Research Inc., 5th ed. (2004), page 315.

Finch did refer to himself . . . : Carl Wiser, Untitled interview with Rick Finch, songfacts.com, (November 11, 2009): http://www.songfacts.com/blog/interviews/rick_finch/.

He later sued to recover . . . : Ibid.

He produced the 1979 Casablanca . . . : RIAA Gold and Platinum Database: http://www.riaa.com/gold-platinum/?tab_active=default-award&se=yes+im+ready-search_section.

After Stone died in 2014 . . . : Richard Finch, "R.I.P Henry Stone." (Undated post): http://www.richardrfinch.com/welcome.

"Critics have almost succeeded in . . . : Tom Conway, "KC Proud of the 'Sunshine' His Music Made," *South Bend Tribune*, September 20, 2012.

I just felt that it . . . : Ibid.

He explained the second sabbatical . . . : J. Poet, "Harry Wayne Casey: The Boogie Man Returns," on Grammy Awards website (March 28, 2013): http://www.grammy.com/news/harry-wayne-casey-the-boogie-man-returns.

EPILOGUE: THE STATE OF FLORIDA SOUL

An all-black traveling variety show . . . : Paul Guzzo, "Tampa-based Harlem in Havana Made Entertainment History," *Tampa Tribune*, February 8, 2015.

Besides Mitchell this revue helped . . . : Ibid.

As a 2015 Tampa Tribune . . . : Ibid.

Forgivably, Mitchell says there were sixty thousand . . . : No author byline, *Gainesville Daily Sun*, November 13, 1960.

In 2010, on the fiftieth . . . : Bill Dean, "Mitchell Honored at Gator Growl," Gainesville.com, October 14, 2010.

"I'm a realist" . . . : Malik Abdul-Rahmaan, "Betty Padgett's Resurrection," *The Revivalist*, September 1, 2011.

When she was coming up . . . : Ibid.

In Phyl Garland's introduction to . . . : Phyl Garland, *The Sound of Soul: The Story of Black Music*, Pocket Books (originally published by Henry Regnery Company). page ix, (1969).

As proof she cites that . . . : Ibid., page 5.

"I don't tell anybody how much . . . : Jesse Serwer, "Miami Soul Queen Betty Wright Talks the Roots, Lil Wayne, and 'Old Songs,'" *Miami New Times*, May 2, 2012.

A recent Miami Herald story . . . : Jordan Levin, "R&B singer Sam Moore is Miami's 'Soul Man,'" *Miami Herald*, February 10, 2016.

Soul cognoscenti will identify these . . . : Joel Whitburn, *Top R&B/Hip-Hop Singles, 1942–2004*. Record Research Inc. (2004), page 527.

Bibliography

Bowman, Rob. *Soulsville, U.S.A.: The Story of Stax Records.* New York, N.Y.: Schirmer, 1997.

Charles, Ray, and David Ritz. *Brother Ray: Ray Charles' Own Story.* New York, N.Y.: Dial, 1978.

Curtis, Kurt. *Florida's Famous & Forgotten* (Volumes I and II). Altamonte Springs, Fl.: Florida Media, 2005.

Dawson, Jim. *The Twist: The Story of the Song and Dance that Changed the World.* Winchester, Mass.: Faber and Faber, 1995.

Dunn, Marvin. *Black Miami in the Twentieth Century.* Gainesville: University Press of Florida, 1997.

Garland, Phyl. *The Sound of Soul.* Chicago, Ill.: Henry Regnery, 1969.

Gordon, Robert. *Respect Yourself: Stax Records and the Soul Explosion.* New York, N.Y.: Bloomsbury, 2013.

Gregory, Hugh. *The Real Rhythm and Blues.* London: Blandford, 1998.

Guralnick, Peter. *Sweet Soul Music: Rhythm and Blues and the Southern Dream of Freedom.* New York, N.Y.: Back Bay, 1999.

Hirshey, Gerri. *Nowhere to Run: The Story of Soul Music.* New York, N.Y.: Times, 1984.

Lauterbach, Preston. *The Chitlin' Circuit and the Road to Rock 'n' Roll.* New York, N.Y.: W. W. Norton, 2011.

Lydon, Michael. *Ray Charles: Man and Music.* New York, N.Y.: Riverhead, 1998.

Marsh, Dave, and Sam Moore. *Sam and Dave: An Oral History.* New York, N.Y.: Avon, 1998.

Ribowsky, Mark. *Dreams to Remember: Otis Redding, Stax Records, and the Transformation of Southern Soul.* New York, N.Y.: W. W. Norton, 2015.

Ripani, Richard. *The New Blue Music: Changes in Rhythm & Blues, 1950–1999.* Jackson: University Press of Mississippi, 2006.

Ritz, David, and Jerry Wexler. *Rhythm and the Blues: A Life in American Music.* New York, N.Y.: Alfred A. Knopf, 1993.

Shaw, Arnold. *Honkers and Shouters: The Golden Years of Rhythm and Blues.* New York, N.Y.: Macmillan, 1978.

Smith, RJ. *The One: The Life and Music of James Brown.* New York, N.Y.: Gotham, 2012.

Stone, Henry, and Jacob Katel. *The Stone Cold Truth on Payola in The Music Biz.* Miami, Fl. (e-book): Henry Stone Music, 2013.

Washington, Teddy. *Life: The Puzzle.* Self-published: Undated.

Whitburn, Joel. *Top R&B/Hip-Hop Singles, 1942–2004.* Menomonee Falls, Wis.: Record Research, 2004.

Whitburn, Joel. *Top R&B/Hip-Hop Singles, 1955–2002.* Menomonee Falls, Wis.: Record Research, 2003.

Whiteis, David. *Southern Soul-Blues.* Champaign: University Press of Illinois, 2013.

Index

Page numbers in *italics* refer to photographs.

ABC, 311
Abe's 506 Club, 152, 163, 173
Abner, Ewart, 84–85, 231
a capella, 98
Ace Records, 105, 110
"A Change is Gonna Come," 155
Adams, Shirley, 169
Adderley, Julian "Cannonball," 18, 29, 59, 71, 130, 274
Adderley, Nat, 18, 59, 71, 73–74
Adele, 347
Adu, Helen Folasade, 273. *See also* Sade
Afro Soul revue, 114, 120
Aguilera, Christina, 234
"Ain't That Peculiar," 311
Alaimo, Steve, 8, 129, 136–37, 180, 187, 222, 223, 230–32, 235, 237, 245, 251, 279, 295
Albert Einstein Medical College, 308
Albertina Walker and the Caravans, 105, 131
Albury, Arnold "Hoss," 18, 193, 205, 212, 216
Ali, Muhammad, 139
Alligator Records, 74
Allison, Gene, 336
Allman, Duane, 74, 234
Allman, Gregg, 74, 234
Allman Brothers, 77, 92, 234
"All of Me," 69
Allsun Records, 285, 343
Alston, 4, 203, 233, 237, 321
"The Alvin Twist," 88
"Amazing Grace," 167, 277
American Bandstand, 77, 87, 91, 140, 288
Americano, 62

American Sound Studios, 14, 174, 265, 266
"America the Beautiful," 31
"Am I a Good Man," 194
Ammons, Gene, 73
Anderson, Joe, 38
Anderson, Vicki, 228
"Annie Had a Baby," 76
"Annie's Aunt Fanny," 80
Anthony, Mike, 282
Antioch Missionary Baptist Church, 152, 161
Apollo, 58–59, 150, 265
Appell, Dave, 86
April Follies, 34
"April Love," 73
"A Rainy Night in Georgia," 126
Archie Bell and the Drells, 309
Armstrong, Louis, *260*
A Side, The, 157
Atco, 233
"A-Tisket, A-Tasket," 94
Atlanta Rhythm Section, 180
Atlantic Records, 8, 105, 108, 137, 173, 209, 309, 312
"At Last," 267, 305
"At the Hop," 73
Autry, Gene, 80
Avenal State Prison, 149–50, 158
Average White Band, 327–28
"A Woman's Love," 300
"A Woman Will Do Wrong," 211, *218*
Axton, Estelle, 105
Aykroyd, Dan, 125, 145

Baby. *See* Robinson, Louise
"Baby, Baby, Baby," 11
"Baby Let Me Hold Your Hand," 49
"Baby Let's Play House," 182

"The Babysitter," 194, 208
"Back to Miami," 185–86
"Bad Bad Leroy Brown," 311
Badu, Erykah, 343
Baha Men, 324
Baker, Lavern, 137, 187
  "Jim Dandy," 76
Baker, Willie C., 226
Ballard, Florence, 80
Ballard, Hank. *See also* Hank Ballard and the
  Midnighters
  childhood of, 80
  children of, 80
  death of, 80, 92
  description of, 17, 128
  "Is Your Love for Real?," 84
  photograph of, 79
  physical appearance of, 76, 81
  Henry Stone and, 84–85
  "Teardrops on Your Letter?," 85–86
  "The Twist," 10, 77–78, 81–86, 91, 93,
    129, 344
Banks, Richard E., 56
Barksdale, David, 92
Barn, the, 178–79, 184, 186
Basie, Count, 64, 137, 235, 259
Bass, Fontella
  "Rescue Me," 18, 337
Bateman, 68
Baton Records, 72–73
Baylor, Helen, 319
Beasley, Paul, 167
Beatles, The, 77, 133
Beckett, Barry, 154
Bee Gees, 227, 249, 250, 254, 327
"Be Ever Wonderful," 152
"Begging," 118
Beginning of the End, The, 222, 235, 321
Bell, Al, 105, 108
Bell, LeRoy, 315
Belotte, Pete, 327
Belushi, John, 125, 145
"Ben," 279
Bennett, Tony, 292
Bennett, Wayne, 118
Ben's Cotton Club, 87
Benson, George, 246
Benson, JoJo, 152
Ben & Spence, 163

Benton, Brook, 69, 227
  "A Rainy Night in Georgia," 126
Berry, Chu, 64
Berry, Chuck, 18, 72, 77, 115–16, 118, 279
Berry, Robert, 12, 100, 102, 112, 117–20, 122
"Best of Little Beaver," 238
"Betty Is My Love," 117
Betty Padgett, 338
Betty Wright: The Movie, 341
Big bands, 9, 28
Biggs, Gloria, 88
Big Maybelle, 74, 87, 258, 265
Big Sean, 341
Billboard, 137, 222, 264, 303, 315, 341
Bill Nettles and His Dixie Blue Boys, 182
Billy Ward & His Dominoes, 132
Birdland, 129
Bishop, Jimmy, 309
Black Cat, 261
Blacklash, 14, 109, 121
Black Magic, 291, 298. *See also* Watson,
  Joe
Black Miami, 323
"Black Night," 42
Blade, Charlie (Charles Steadham), 98, 100,
  102–3, 108–10, 114, 118–19, 121, 336
Blanchard, Harold, 75
Bland, Bobby "Blue," 98, 118, 119, 213, 231,
  263, 294, 338
Blenders, The, 338
Blind Boys of Alabama, 165–66, *167–68,*
  169
Blood, Sweat & Tears, 327
Blowfly, 121, 237, 343
"Blowin' in the Wind," 333
"Blow Your Whistle," 321
Blue Notes, 250
Blues Brothers, 125, 145, 186
Blues with a Groove, 81
Bobby Cash and the Nite Flyers, 184
Bobby Williams & His Mar-Kings, 122, 140
Bodie, Kirkland, 324
Bogdon, Ron, 8, 207, 236, 241, 295
Bonds, Gary U.S., 88
Bon Jovi, 125
Bonoff, Karla, 314
"Boogie Shoes," 236, 322, 327, 328
Booker T. & The MGs, 110, 143, 235, 236,
  241

Booker T. Washington High School, 130, 198
B-3 organs, 64, 154, 291
Boston Chop House, 33
"Both Ends Against the Middle," 312
Bound Sound, 4
Bourdain, Anthony, 342
Bowker, Tom, 343
Bowman, Rob, 105, 109, 138
"Bow Wow (I'm an Ol' Dog)," 298
Boys Don't Cry, 271–72, 282
Bradenton, 133
Bradford, Janie, 133
Bradley, Charles, 343
Bradshaw, Tiny, 72
Brantley, Charlie, 43, 45, 69, 71
"Breathe In, Breathe Out," 303
Brenda and the Tabulations, 218
Brevoort Theater, 263
"Bring Your Love Back to Me," 105
Brooks, Louis, 292, 298
Brother Ray, 22, 27, 30, 34, 40, 42, 52
Brown, Buster
  "Fannie Mae," 73, 171
Brown, Charles, 24, 53, 56
  "Black Night," 42
  "Driftin' Blues," 41
Brown, Dolores, 266
Brown, James, 4, 12, 80, 98, 104, 139, 152, 173, 222
  Famous Flames, 18, 80, 226, 257
  Lavell Kamma and, 115
  "Night Train," 183
  "Out of Sight," 183
  "Please, Please, Please," 86, 226, 227, 228, 245
  "Say It Loud, I'm Black and I'm Proud," 139
  "Sex Machine," 334
  Henry Stone and, 226, 227, 228
Brown, Maxine, 258
Brown, Peter, 222
Brown, Ruth, 9, 40, 71, 137
Brownstone, 228
Bryant, Brenda, 265
B Side, The, 157
"Buffalo Soldier," 276
Bunny Club, 152
Burke, Solomon, 9, 110, 141, 151, 218

"Take Me (Just As I Am)," 153
Butler, Jerry, 174, 231, 341
Butler, Ronnie, 324
"Buying Time," 255
Byas, Don, 64
Byrd, Bobby, 228
Byrd, Donald, 274

Cadet, 226
Cadillac Hotel, 62
Caldwell, Bobby, 222, 238, 330
Calhoun, Alexander, 56
Calhoun, Ernie, 9, 13, 18, 55–67, 336
  Ray Charles and, 21–23, 30, 44, 52
  childhood of, 56–57
  Ernie Cal and the Soul Brothers, 65
  in Korea, 60, 67
  in Manzy Harris Orchestra, 60, 61, 62
  Percy Mayfield and, 55–56, 59–60
  military service of, 60, 66–67
  musical education of, 58–59
  photographs of, 57, 66
  physical appearance of, 64
  as sideman, 63
  as tenor, 64–65
  Noble Watts and, 68–69
Calloway, Cab, 32, 58, 71, 81, 259
"Calypso Breakdown," 235–36
Camel Walk, 106
Cameo Parkway, 77, 86–87
Camp Kilmer Band, 225
"Can't Turn You Loose," 185, 186
Carey, Mariah, 234
Carl Fischer Saxophone Method, 55
Carlton, Carl, 170, 175
Carmichael, Hoagy
  "Georgia," 75
Carnegie Hall, 39
Carr, James, 265, 274
Carter, Benny, 39
Carter, Jimmy, 166, 167
Casey, Harry Wayne, 2, 13, 193, 234, 320, 323, 325. *See also* KC and the Sunshine Band
Cashbox, 222
Castaways Hotel, 292
Castleberry, Robert, 100
Catawba Records, 317
Cat label, 222, 244, 246

"Caveman Rock," 130

Cavett, Dick, 140

C.C. Riders, 14

Central Avenue district, 15–16, 45, 58, 69, 93, 93, 139

Central Hotel, 58

CETA. *See* Comprehensive Employment and Training Act

"Chain of Fools," 100, 265

Chamberlain, Wilt, 144

Chambers, Lester, 145

Chambers, Martin, 139

Champagne Lounge, 261

Chantels, The, 262

Charles, Ray, 21–54, 125, 152

  academic life of, 29

  "Baby Let Me Hold Your Hand," 49

  big band influence on, 28

  birth of, 25

  blindness of, 30–31, 35, 38, 165

  boyhood home of, 26

  Charles Brown and, 41–42

  Ernie Calhoun and, 21–23, 30, 44, 52

  "Come Back Baby," 49

  "Confession Blues," 38, 49

  death of, 23

  description of, 13

  "Drown in My Own Tears," 280

  early history of, 22–23, 26–37

  gait of, 21–22, 44

  "Georgia on My Mind," 23, 46

  gospel singing by, 24

  "Hit the Road Jack," 46, 55

  "I Can't Stop Loving You," 46, 342

  "I Found My Baby There," 41–42, 45, 47

  "I Got A Woman," 24, 49, 51

  "I'm Wonderin' and Wonderin'," 41

  influence of, 6

  "It Should've Been Me," 49

  "I've Got News for You," 145

  "Mess Around," 49

  Nat King Cole imitations by, 42, 52

  in Orlando, 37–39

  personal losses that affected, 31–32

  photograph of, 3f

  in Seattle, 48

  Seattle Symphony tribute to, 2

  singing by, 53

  Henry Stone and, 40–41, 84, 226

  "St. Pete Florida Blues," 41–43, 45, 47, 53

  in Tampa, 43–45, 47

  "This Little Girl of Mine," 51

  "Walkin' and Talkin' To Myself," 41, 53

  "Why Did You Go?," 41

  "You Are My Sunshine," 46

  "Your Cheating Heart," 46

Charlie Brantley and His Original Honey-dippers, 43–44, 69, 72, 336

Chart, 222

Checker, Chubby, 10, 78

  "Let's Twist Again," 87

  "The Twist," 77, 86–90, 89, 92, 155, 344

Chess, Leonard, 227

Chess Records, 84, 186, 227, 336

Childs of Friendship, 43

"Chills and Fever," 203, 206

Chipmunks, 88

Chitlin' Circuit and the Road to Rock 'n' Roll, The, 16

"Chokin' Kind," 344

Chords, 10–12

Chrisman, Gene, 174

Christian, Christian, 39

Chudd, Lew, 231

"Circles," 314

Civil rights movement, 9, 14, 139, 187

Clapton, Eric, 126

Clara White Mission, 35

Clark, Dick, 77, 86, 88, 231

Clark, "Fess," 261

Clarke, Willie, 6, 8, 14, 18, 192–210, 236, 246, 279, 300, 343

  at Florida Agricultural and Mechanical University, 199–01

  gospel influences on, 196

  photographs of, 195

  poetry by, 198, 202

  producing by, 195, 207

  Helene Smith and, 214

  Henry Stone and, 233

  upbringing of, 194–95

"The Class," 86

Claxton, Leon, 337

Clay, Cassius, 194

Clay, Otis, 303

Clayton, Artis, 82

"Clean Up Woman," 5, 19, 128, 194, 203, 207, 222, 233, 234, 244

"Clean Up Your Own Yard," 305, 312
Cline, Patsy, 151, 171
Clinton, George
    "Flash Light," 12
Club Bali, 98
Club El Morocco, 99, 111–12
Coasters, The, 137, 141
Cobb, Arnett, 63–64
Cochran, Wayne, 14, 178–91, *181*, 332, 341
    "Back to Miami," 185–86
    childhood of, 182
    costuming by, 185–87
    "Get Down With It," 185
    "Harlem Shuffle," 185, 187
    "Last Kiss," 186
    Las Vegas shows by, 186–88
    as pastor, 189–91
    religious conversion of, 188–89
    Wayne Cochran and the C.C. Riders,
        179–80, 184, 185, 187
Co-eds, 258, 262, 263, 266
Cogbill, Tommy, 174, 176
"Cold Cold People," 279
Cole, Natalie
    "I've Got Love on My Mind," 12
Cole, Nat King, 33, 128
    Ray Charles and, 42, 52
    "Laura," 42
Coleman, Carlton "King," 227–28
Colin, Charles, 225
Coltrane, John, 64, 328
Columbia Records, 313
"Come Back Baby," 49
Como, Perry
    "April Love," 73
"Complete Atlantic Recordings, The," 303
Comprehensive Employment and Training
    Act, 65
"Confession Blues," 38, 49
Conley, Arthur, 140
Conley, Edwyn, 85
Connery, Sean, 88
Continental, 216
Cook, Ed, 228
Cooke, Sam, 40, 117, 197, 346
    "Cupid," 76
    death of, 145
    musical collaborations by, 125–26
    "Twistin' the Night Away," 77, 88

"Wonderful World," 76
Cooper, Buster, 259
Cooper, George, 261, 262
Coppock, Chet, 180
Cornelius Brothers and Sister Rose, 328
Cougar, John, 250
Counts, The, 99, 111–22. *See also* 100 Hour
    Counts
Coward, Noel, 87
Craddock, James, 32
Crawford, Alvin, 307
Crawford, Dave, 8, 105–6, 108, 303, 305,
    309, 310
    death of, 311
    "Millionaire," 311
    physical appearance of, 311
    "Victim," 310
    "What a Man," 14, 97, *107*, 108–10, 302,
        310–11
    "Young Hearts Run Free," 310–11
Crawford, Hank, 53
Creative and Mental Growth, 200
"The Creep," 72
Crews, Don, 174
Crisis, 32
Criteria Studio, 227, 253, 303
Croce, Jim, 311
Crocker, Frankie, 230
Cropper, Steve, 9, 106, 139
Crosby, Stills, and Nash, 249, 254, 255
Cuban Center, 62
Cuban Club, 22, 44
Cuban Patio, 62
"Cupid," 76
Curtis, King, 9, 11, 68, 71
Curtis, Kurt, 45, 258

Dade, 222
"Dancing with Nobody But You," 237
Danny and the Juniors
    "At the Hop," 73
Daptone Records, 343
"The Dark End of the Street," 265, 266, 274
Darty, David, 118
Dash label, 235
Date Records, 259, 264
Davis, Billy, 80–81, 83, 92
Davis, Eddie "Lockjaw," 64
Davis, Sammy, Jr., 100, 117–18

Davis, Tyrone, 161, 335
Davis Sisters, 131
Dawson, Jim, 82
"Daytona Blues," 74
D&B Records, 105
"Dear John," 309
Deauville Hotel, 328
Dee, Joey, 87
Deep City: The Birth of the Miami Sound, 192, 212, 342
Deep City Records, 6, 8, 14, 192–212, 233, 312, 314, 342, 343
Deland, 68, 74–75
de la Portilla, Alberto, 194, 236, 244, 246, 248
Deluxe, 222
Dentley, Boo, 200
DePofi, Rick, 283
Derek & the Dominoes, 227
Desario, Terry, 322, 332
Deuces, The, 15, 260, 261, *262*
Diamond Life, 273
Diamonettes, The, 220
Dickey, Robert Lee, 152, 153, 156. *See also* Purify, Bobby (Robert Lee Dickey)
Diddley, Bo, 77
DiNicola, Joseph, 87
Disco, 9, 74, 232, 236, 238, 315, 332, 333
"Discoed to Death," 297
"Disco Lady," 297
Dixie Hummingbirds, 10
DJ Khaled, 341
"Dock of the Bay," 110
Doggett, Bill, 258
"Honky Tonk," 64, 74
"Dogging Around," 134–35
Do It Good, 326
Domino, Fats, 72, 86
"Don't Fence Me In," 196, 198
"Don't Knock My Love," 317
Doobie Brothers, 252
Doo-wop, 9, 11, 80, 86, 117, 127, 337
Dorsey, Jimmy, 235, 328
Dorsey, Lee, 145
Dorsey, Tommy, 28, 225
Dothan Sextet, 151–53
"Do the Mashed Potatoes," 222, 227
Dotson, Nick, 164–65
Double Decker, 216

Dowd, Tom, 137, 227
"Do What You Wanna Do," 235
Downbeat, 112, 338, 340
Down Beat Records, 41, 49
Downing, Al, 65
"Do Your Thing," 163, 175
"Do You Wanna Get Funky with Me," 222
Drake, 284–85, 343
"Hotline Bling," 2, 284–85
Drifters, The, 137, 337
"Driftin' Blues," 41
Drive, 222
"Drown in My Own Tears," 280
Duke, Billy, 311
Dukoff, Bobby, 275
Dunn, Bill, 88
Dunn, Marvin, 123, 129, 323
Dusty in Memphis, 265
Duty, Ralph, 64
Dylan, Bob, 333
Dynamites, The, 100, 114, 119

Early, Sam, 133–34, 136
Earth Wind & Fire, 12
Eccentric Soul: The Deep City Label, 192
Eccentric Soul: The Outskirts of Deep City, 192
Echoes of Zion, 162
Eckstine, Billy, 65, 128
Eddy, Lee, 298
Eden Roc, 62
Edrington, David, 83
Ed Sullivan Show, 87, 140
Edwards, Dennis, 265
Egmont Hotel, 34
Eisenhower, Dwight, 91
Eisner, Mickey, 313
Eli, Bobby, 313
Ellington, Duke, 32, 64, 83, 259
Elliott, Ronny, 76, 81, 89, 91
Ellis, Pee Wee, 133
Emerman, Mack, 227
Emmons, Bobby, 174
Encore!, 94
Encyclopedia of Pop, Rock & Soul, 92
Enjoy Records, 68
Entertainment districts, 15–16
En Vogue, 97, 109, 312
Epic, 332
Epstein, Henry, 225. *See also* Stone, Henry

Ernie Cal and the Soul Brothers, 65
Ertegun, Ahmet, 49, 137
Ertegun, Nesuhi, 137
Esquire Show Bar, 63
Estefan, Emilio, 239
Estefan, Gloria, 146, 239, 250, 342
Eunice, Kenny "The Conductor," 334
Evans, Ernest, 86. *See also* Checker, Chubby
Evans, Herschel, 64
Everett, Betty, 258
"Everlasting Love," 170, 175, 176
"Every Beat of My Heart," 80
"Everybody's Twisting," 88
"Every Day I Have to Cry," 222
Excelsior, 226
Exclusive, 226
"The Experts," 208

Faith, Hope, and Charity, 309
FAME recording studio, 4, 14, 153, 173
Famous Flames, 18, 80, 226, 257
FAMU. *See* Florida Agricultural and Mechanical University
"Fannie Mae," 73, 171
Fantasia, 347
Faulk, Kenny, 330
Federal Records, 80
Fenton, P. W., 82
Ferguson, Jay, 254
Ferguson, Maynard, 72
Ferguson, Robert, 241, 245
"Fever," 76, 111
Fiesta Club, 128, 132
Finch, Casey, 5, 237
Finch, Rick, 5, *13*, 193, 208, 321, 324, 327, 331
"Finger Poppin' Time," 77
Fitzgerald, Ella
    "A-Tisket, A-Tasket," 94
Fitzgerald, Michael Ray, 312
Five Blind Boys, 197
"5" Royales, The, 127, 290
535 Club, 128
"F.L.A.," 74
"Flap Jack," 72
"Flash Light," 12
Fleetwood Mac, 227
Flemmings, Marvin, 93–94
Flora-Bama soul, 6
Florida

cities in, 15–16
population growth in, 16–17
segregated communities in, 15
Florida Agricultural and Mechanical University, 6, 11, 17, 17–18, 68, 71–72, 130, 199, 201, 216
Florida Funk: 1968–1975, 121
Florida Memorial College, 274
Florida Playboys, 2, 46
Florida School for the Deaf and Blind, 27
"Florida Shake," 74
Florida soul
    geographic influences, 6
    styles in, 6
Florida Soul, 8, 82, 90, 112, 125, 129, 157, 242, 259, 286, 332
Floyd, Eddie, 115, 138, 140
"Flying Home," 63
"Fly Me To The Moon," 274
Fontainebleau, 62, 292
Foreman, Eloyce, 134, 136
Fort Lauderdale, 111–12, 129–30, 293, 306, 338, 344, 346
Forum, The, 294
"For Your Precious Love," 173–74
Foster, William P., 200
Four Seasons, The, 141
Foxx, Redd, 337
Francis, Panama, 40
Frank Duboise and his Chicken Scratchers, 245, 291
Frankie Lymon and the Teenagers, 69
Franklin, Aretha, 9, 125, 137, 140, 153, 213, 227, 253, 265, 267, 304, 307, 338
    "Baby, Baby, Baby," 11
    "Chain of Fools," 100, 265
    Lady Soul, 265
    "Respect," 11
Franklin, C. L., 125
Franklin, Melvin, 266
Frank Williams and the Rocketeers, 192, 203, 215, 245
Freddie Scott and the Kinfolk, 292, *293*, 298
Freed, Alan, 229–30
Fulson, Lowell, 49
"Funkadelic Sound," 248
Funk Brothers, 235, 241
Funky Broadway, 106
"Funky Nassau," 6, 222, 224, 235, 321

Gaines, Earl, 115, 289
Gainesville, 95–110, 337
Gainesville Daily Sun, 338
Gala, 186
Gales, The, 130
Gamble, Kenny, 4, 308
Garland, Phyl, 8, 341
Garnett Mims and the Enchanters, 115
Garret, Milt, 50
Gaye, Marvin, 149, 151, 161, 341
    "Ain't That Peculiar," 311
    "Mercy Mercy Me," 11
    "What's Goin' On," 246, 321
Gearing, Frances Yvonne. *See* Gearing, Frankie
Gearing, Frankie, 13, 257–69, *268*
"Georgia," 75
"Georgia on My Mind," 23, 46
Georgia Soul Twisters, 105, 309
"Get Down Tonight," 1, 236, 322, 327, 328
"Get Down With It," 185
"Get into the Party Life," 248
"Get It," 76, 80
"Get Out My Life," 145
"Getting Paid," 133
Ghetto Gospel, 347
Ghetto Revelations, 346
Ghetto Revelations II, 346
Gibb, Robin, 249
Gibson, Jack, 228
Gillespie, Dizzy, 40
Gilmore, Joey, 245
"Girls Can't Do What the Guys Do," 233
"Give It Up," 71, 332
Glades, 4, 222, 271, 295
Gleason, Jackie, 178, 184, 331
Glenn, Lloyd, 49
Glockenspiel, 154–55
Glories, The, 259, 264, 265, 266
Glover, Henry, 86–87, 137
Goldberg, Danny, 281
Golden Hit Productions, 335
"The Golden Rocket," 182
Gold Mountain, 281
Goldwax label, 274
"Good Lovin'," 205
Goodman, Benny, 28
"Goodnight Baby," 138

"Good Things Don't Come Easy," 153
Goodwill Revue, 115
Goody, Mickey, 263
Gordon, Dexter, 63–64, 73
Gordon, Robert, 141
Gordon Henderson and the Blues Rockers, 98
Gordy, Berry, 11, 133, 173
Gospel, 8, 52, 127, 130–31, 135–36, 196, 210, 318–19
Gospel Four, 149
"Gotta Give a Little Love," 282
"The Grand Canyon Suite," 75
Grant, Joseph, 16
Granz, Norman, 39
Gray, Freda, 193, 194, 203
"The Greatest Love," 291
Green, Al, 12, 110, 126, 138, 258, 266
    "Love and Happiness," 346
    "Take Me to the River," 147
Green, Bob, 230
Green, Cal, 82, 84–85
Green, Larry, 194
Greenberg, Joyce, 129
Greenlee, Bob, 74
Greenville Training, 27
Greenwich, Ellie, 170
Greer, Dan, 267
Gregory, Hugh, 18
Griffin, Clarence, 105, 309
Griffin Brothers, 72
Griffith, Nelson, 43, 121
GRIII: Old School 2 Nu Skool, 346
Grimes, Howard, 266
Grits and Soul, 105
Grofé, 75
Grogan, George, 260–61
Grubbs, James, 157
Gucci Crew II, 238
Guralnick, Peter, 9, 24, 51, 344

"Hadacol Boogie," 182
Hale, Willie, 6, 241, 244–49, 321. *See also* Little Beaver
Hall, Arsenio, 333
"Hallelujah, I Just Love Her So," 24, 52
Hamilton, Anthony, 343, 347
Hamilton, Roy, 336

Hammond B-3 organs, 64, 154, 236, 291
Hampton, Lionel, 63–64, 72
  "Flying Home," 63
Hank Ballard and the Midnighters, 76
  "Annie Had a Baby," 76
  "Annie's Aunt Fanny," 80
  early history of, 80
  "Finger Poppin' Time," 77
  "Get It," 76, 80
  "Henry's Got Flat Feet (Can't Dance No
    More)," 76
  "Let's Go, Let's Go, Let's Go," 77
  "Sexy Ways," 76
  "The Twist," 77–78, 81–85, 92–93
  "Work With Me Annie," 76
Hank Ballard Live at the Palais, 92
Hank Ballard Street, 342, 348
"Hard Times (The Slop)," 64, 72–74
"Hard to Handle," 110
"Harlem in Havana," 18, 337
"Harlem Shuffle," 185, 187
Harlem Square, 128–29, 132, 203
"Harlem Twist," 83
Harold Melvin and the Blue Notes, 308
Harris, Manzy, 22
Harris, Wynonie, 40
Harrison, George, 252
Harrison, Wilbert, 222
  "Kansas City," 73
Hart, Joe, 292–93
Harvey, Bill, 58
Hathaway, Donny, 252
"Have Some Boogaloo," 274
"Have You Been Making Out OK," 267
Hawkins, Coleman, 36, 64
Hawkins, Erskine, 32
Hawkins, Screaming Jay, 258
Hayes, Isaac, 6, 108, 110, 123, 137–39, 147,
  175, 341
Hearns, Fred, 89–90, 94
"Hearts of Stone," 222, 226
Heavy D, 347
"He Believes in Me," 164, 176
Helene Smith Sings Sweet Soul, 212, 216
"Helpless," 317
Henderson, Enoch "Sticky," 114, 118, 120
Henderson, Joe, 290–91
Hendrix, Jimi, 77, 255, 298

Henry & Inez Stone Music and Sound
  Studio, 239
"Henry's Got Flat Feet (Can't Dance No
  More)," 76
Henry Stone Music, 298
Here Am I, 311
"Here Am I," 105
Herring, Lynette, 263
Hialeah, 9, 224, 231, 242, 295, 320
Hibbert, Toots, 303
Hicks, John Richard, 124, 148
High Hat, 152
High Topper, 261
Hightower, Cy, 100
Hi Records, 5, 143, 266, 267
Hirshey, Gerri, 141
History of the Blues in the Tampa Bay Area,
  A, 82
Hit Factory, 253
"Hit the Road, Jack," 46, 55
Hodges, Charles, 266
Hodges, Leroy, 266
Hodges, Teenie, 266
"Hold On, I'm A Comin'," 1, 11, 124, 131,
  138–39, 143, 145, 185
Holiday, Billie, 148
Holland, Jools, 148
Holsum Bread Company, 336
"The Honeydripper," 43
"Honkers," 71
Honkers and Shouters, 71–72
"Honky Tonk," 64, 74
Hooker, Earl, 221
Hooker, John Lee, 119, 213
Hopkins, Calvin, 306, 313, 314, 317
Hopkins, Jackie Moore, 306
Hopkins, Lightnin', 221
Horne, Jimmy Bo, 203
"Hotline Bling," 2, 284–85
Hot Productions, 238
"Hot Tamales," 72
"Hound Dog," 87
Houston, Cissy, 68, 303
Houston, Joe, 71
Howard Theater, 150, 218
How Sweet It Is, 282–83
"Hucklebuck," 69, 74
Hues Corporation, 236

Huff, Leon, 4, 308
"Hully Gully," 111
Humperdinck, Engelbert, 267
Hunter, Ivory Joe, 182
Hurley, Steve "Silk," 285
Hurtt, Phil, 312

"I Am Controlled by Your Love," 216
"I Am Woman," 279
"I Can Dig It, Baby," 248
"I Can See Clearly Now," 279
"I Can't Stand the Rain," 145, 267
"I Can't Stop Loving You," 46, 342
Ichiban, 74
"I Don't Know," 107
"I Don't Want Nobody to Give Me Nothing
    (Open up the Door I'll Get It Myself),"
    279
"I'd Rather Go Blind," 305
"If," 305, 312
"If I Thought You Needed Me," 263
"I Forgive You," 310
"I Found a Love," 335
"I Found My Baby There," 41–42, 45, 47
"I Got a Woman," 24, 49, 51
I–IV–V chord structure, 10, 248, 295, 299
"I Know Where It's At," 121
"I'll Never Be the Same," 176
"I Love You," 340
"I'm Movin' On," 182
I'm on My Way, 315
Impact Records, 335, 337
"I'm Your Boogie Man," 234, 322
"I'm Your Puppet," 6, 11, 149–50, 151, 153,
    154, 155, 164, 170, 174, 175, 304
Independence for the Blind, 165
Instrumentalists, 9
"In the Ghetto," 174
"In the Mood," 182–83
Island Club, 128, 216
Isley Brothers
    "Do Your Thing," 163
    "Twist and Shout," 77
"I Stand Accused (Of Loving You)," 264
"Is Your Love for Real?," 84
"I Take What I Want," 138
"I Thank You," 124–25, 140, 143
It's Better to Have It, 165

"It Should've Been Me," 49
"It's Love Baby (24 Hours A Day)," 289
"It's Now or Never," 77
"I've Got Love on My Mind," 12
"I've Got News for You," 145
I–VI–II–V chord structure, 11
I–VI–IV–V chord structure, 11

Jackie Gleason Show, The, 178, 180, 185
Jackie Gleason Theater of the Performing
    Arts, 178
Jackson, Al, 106, 143
Jackson, Bull Moose, 40
Jackson, Michael, 141, 143, 279
Jackson, Millie, 312, 340
Jackson, Wayne, 138
Jackson, Willis "Gator Tail," 71
Jacksons, 141
Jacquet, Illinois, 22, 63–64
"Jailhouse Rock," 73
James, Casey, 315
James, Etta, 115, 252, 262, 267, 305
    "At Last," 305
    "I'd Rather Go Blind," 305
    "Roll With Me, Henry," 76
James, Spencer, 163
James and Bobby Purify, 155
James E. Strates Shows, 337
James Hunter Six, 343
James Knight and the Butlers, 121
"JATP" records, 39
Jayville, 4
Jay Z, 248
"Jazz at the Philharmonic" records, 39, 48
Jazzman Records, 121
JB's, 227
Jewel Records, 226
J. Frank Wilson and the Cavaliers, 186
J. Geils Band, 309
"Jim Dandy," 76
"Jingle Bell Boogie," 31
Jodeci, 344
"Joe," 305
Joel, Billy, 252
"Joey," 248
Joey Dee and the Starlighters
    "Peppermint Twist," 77
Joey Gilmore and the TCB Express, 338

John, Elton, 149
John, Little Willie, 17, 76, 116, 128, 133, 145–46, 152, 336
    "Fever," 111
Johnny Killens and the Dynamites, 193
Johnny's Records, 201, 201
Johnson, Alice, 29
Johnson, Henry, 29
Johnson, James Weldon, 32
Johnson, Marv
    "You Got What It Takes," 76
Johnson, Plas, 71
Jolly, Clarence, 44
Jones, Bill, 120
Jones, Dave "Dizzy," 136
Jones, Quincy, 31
Jones, Sam, 257
Jones, Sharon, 344
"Jookin'," 64, 73
Jordan, Elder, 260
Jordan, Louis, 9, 22, 24, 34, 58, 71
Jordan Dance Hall, 260
Joylocks, 117
Joyner, Tom, 284
Jump-blues, 9
Junkanoo, 321, 323–24
Junkanoo Festival, 323
Just Frankie, 267
Justo, Rodney, 180
"Just One Look," 154, 170

Kamma, Lavell, 6, 14, 16, 111–22, 340
    "Begging," 118
    Robert Berry and, 112, 117–20, 122
    James Brown and, 115
    childhood of, 117
    death of, 112, 122
    "I Know Where It's At," 121
    leadership of, 120
    Linda Lyndell and, 99–100, 102
    obituary for, 122
    100 Hour Counts, 99, 111–22
    photograph of, 113
    promotional posters for, 113, 114
    "Soft Soul," 121
    "Try to Keep Yourself Uptight," 118
Kane, Terry, 208, 222
"Kansas City," 73, 222

Kari, Sax, 16
Katel, Jacob, 229, 248
Kayvette Label, 304, 312
KC and the Sunshine Band, 5–6, 222, 230, 320–33
    "Boogie Shoes," 236, 322, 327, 328
    disco and, 332, 333
    Do It Good, 326
    Rick Finch and, 331–32
    "Get Down Tonight," 1, 236, 322, 327, 328
    "Give It Up," 332
    "I'm Your Boogie Man," 234, 322
    Junkanoo, 321, 323–24
    KC and the Sunshine Band, 326–27
    "Keep It Comin' Love," 322, 327
    Mike Lewis and, 325, 328–29, 330, 333
    Part 3, 327
    photographs of, 322, 326
    "Please Don't Go," 238
    "Queen of Clubs," 325
    "(Shake, Shake, Shake) Shake Your Booty," 235, 322, 327
    "Sound Your Funky Horn," 324
    Henry Stone and, 234–35, 324, 332
    sweetening, 327, 333
    "That's the Way (I Like It)," 1, 322, 327, 328
    "Yes I'm Ready," 322, 332
KC and the Sunshine Band, 326–27
"Keep It Comin' Love," 322, 327
Kelly, Paul, 192, 206, 211, 308, 314
Kelly, Red, 157
Kendricks, John. See Ballard, Hank
Kennedy, Jacqueline, 78
Khan, Chaka, 319
Kickbacks, 293
Killen, Buddy, 215
Killens, Clyde, 132
"Kill that Roach," 300
Kinfolk, 292, 293, 298
King, B. B., 16, 58, 117, 213, 231, 263, 273, 309, 336
King, Ben E., 115, 291
    "Stand By Me," 11
King, Martin Luther, Jr., 108, 139–40, 276, 277, 286
"The King of the Boogie Sax," 74
King O' Hearts, 124, 134, 137

King Records, 80, 85, 186, 226
King Snake Records, 74
King Sporty, 276
Knight, Beverley, 344
Knight, Gladys, 148, 307, 338
Knight, Jean, 347
Knight Beat, 128–29, 132, 134, 144, 216, 258, 273, 290, 292
"Knock On Wood," 115, 155
Konduko, 276
Kooper, Al, 254
Kottke, Leo, 244
Ku Klux Klan, 103, 108

Laboe, Art, 150
Laddins, The, 263, 264
Ladies Choice, 298, 300
Lady Soul, 265
Lake Henry Supper Club, 183–84
Lake Okeechobee, 120
Lamar, Kendrick, 341
"Land of a Thousand Dances," 179
L.A. Records, 311
LaSalle, Denise, 313
"Last Kiss," 186
Latimore, 295
Latimore, Benny, 207, 222, 223, 236, 241, 242, 243, 250, 263, 271, 287–301, 343
    Black Magic and, 291–92
    childhood of, 289
    "Jolie," 296
    "Let's Straighten It Out," 222, 288, 295–96, 297, 298
    in Louis Brooks and His Hi-Toppers, 289
    Love Man persona of, 298
    "Move and Groove Together," 288
    photographs of, *293, 299, 301*
    physical appearance of, 287–88
    "Somethin' 'bout 'Cha," 222, 288
    Timmy Thomas and, 291, 297
LatStone label, 298
Lauderdale, Jack, 41, 44, 49
"Laura," 42
Lauterbach, Preston, 16
Lavell Kamma Band, 117, 122
LaVilla, 15–16, 32, 117
"Lawdy Miss Clawdy," 63, 111
Lawrence, Joe Lee, 28

Lee, Laura, 115
Lemlich, Jeff, 180, 248
Lemon Twisters, 300
Leon, 4
Lester, Lazy, 74
"Let Love Come Between Us," 174
"Let's Go, Let's Go, Let's Go," 77
Let's Stay Together, 267
"Let's Straighten It Out," 222, 288, 295–96, 297, 298
"Let's Twist Again," 87
"Letter from the St. Augustine Jail," 139
Letterman, David, 180
"Let the Good Times Roll," 145
"Let Your Mind Go Back," 340
Leventhal, John, 283
Levin, Jordan, 128–29
Levy, Morris, 129, 137, 238
Lewis, Jerry Lee, 72, 182
    "Whole Lotta Shakin' Goin' On," 87, 182
Lewis, Meade Lux, 26
Lewis, Mike, 224, 241, 244, 250, 255, 300, 325, 328–29, 330, 333
Lewis, Paul, 192
Liberty City, 136, 192, 199, 245
LIFE, 88
"Lift Every Voice and Sing," 32
Ligon, Joe, 344
Lil Wayne, 341
Limestone Lounge, The, 180
"Lipstick Traces (on a Cigarette)," 12
Lisewski, Jan, 17, 343
Little Beaver, 6, 8–9, 121, 192, 215, 241, 243–48, 247, 294, 297, 343. *See also* Hale, Willie
Little David and the Mighty Rockers, 152
Little Eva, 258
Little Harlems, 15
Little Jake and the Blenders, 337
Little Richard, 4, 98, 183, 258, 263, 265
Little Savoy, 81
Live, 252
Live at Montreux, 282
Live at the Apollo, 184, 185
Live in Africa, 280
"Livin' It Up (Friday Night)," 315
Lomelo, John, 134, 232
Lomelo, Pops, 134–35, 137
"Lonely Avenue," 31, 52

"Lonely Teardrops," 132, 335
"Look Into My Eyes," 263
Lopez, Jennifer, 342
Lord Calvert Hotel, 128
"Lord You Are Awesome," 190
Lorraine Motel, 108
"Loser Again," 309
Louis Brooks and His Hi-Toppers, 289–90
Love, Andrew, 107, 138
"Love and Happiness," 346
"Love Is the Answer," 317
Lovelles, The, 309
"Lover's Holiday," 152
"Love Won't Let Me Wait," 317
Lowenfeld, Viktor, 200
Lucerne Hotel, 273
Lucy Street Bar, 245
Lunceford, Jimmy, 58, 225
Luv N' Haight, 339
Lydon, Michael, 22, 27, 31, 42
Lymon, Frankie, 100, 117–18, 130, 137, 336
Lyndell, Linda, 95–110, 114, 180, 266, 336
    childhood of, 97
    "Here Am I," 105
    "I Don't Know," 107
    Lavella Kamma and, 99–100, 102
    musical education of, 95, 98
    in 100 Hour Counts, 99–102, 120–21
    on promotional posters, 100, 101
    photographs of, 96, 101, 104, 217
    physical appearance of, 100
    racial issues, 102–3, 108, 120
    singing power of, 98–100
    stage persona of, 99
    threats against, 108
    "What a Man," 14, 97, 107, 108–10, 302, 310–11
Lynn, Barbara, 212

MacArthur, John, 130
MacDonald, Ralph, 235
Mack, Richard, 317
Macon, Georgia, 4
Mahal, Taj, 74
Majestics, 130
"Make Me Feel Like a Woman," 312
Malaco Records, 298, 299, 331
"Mama Said," 267
Mandela, Nelson, 2, 280, 281

Manhattan Casino, 58, 257, 259, 260, 261, 262, 265, 268
Manzy Harris Orchestra, 21, 45, 60, 61, 62, 69
Marcus, Earl, 263
Marcus, John, 263
Mariano, Charlie, 328
Mark IVs, 98, 109
Marley, Bob, 227, 276
Marlin, 222
Marlin Records, 4, 130
Marsh, Dave, 90, 125, 127, 155
Martha Reeves and the Vandellas, 100
Martin, Bobby, 308, 309
Martinez, Omar, 146
Marvelettes, The, 211, 213, 263
Mary Elizabeth Hotel, 40, 128, 132, 216
May Alley, 56
Mayfield, Curtis, 145, 166
Mayfield, Percy
    Ernie Calhoun and, 55–56, 59–60
    "Hit the Road, Jack," 55
    "Please Send Me Someone to Love," 55
McCann, Les, 295
McClain, Mighty Sam, 151, 163, 170, 173
McClain, Tommy, 173
McKee, Gosady "Gossie," 43, 45, 48, 50
McKinnie, Ricky, 166, 167
McKnight, Sarah, 118
McKuen, Rod, 88
McNeely, Big Jay, 71
McRae, George, 222, 236, 237, 241, 242, 295, 324, 339
    "Rock Your Baby," 208, 222, 236, 324, 326
McRae, Gwen, 207, 208, 222, 237, 241, 242, 252, 271, 294, 295, 339, 340
McSon trio, 48
"Me and Mrs. Jones," 279
"Melanie," 154, 172
Mellonaires, The, 130
Melodica, 295
Memphis, 4
Memphis Boys, 174, 265
Memphis Horns, 138, 235, 236, 266, 304
"Mercy Mercy Me," 11
"Mess Around," 49
"Messed Up," 258, 266
"Messin' Around," 83

Messinger, Elena, 1
Methadone, 144
Miami, 5–6, 8, 15, 63–64, 128, 135, 192–210
Miami Herald, 187, 342
Miami New Times, 229, 244
Miami sound
   Little Beaver, 6, 8–9, 121, 192, 215, 241,
     243–48, 244–49, 247, 294, 297, 343.
     See also Hale, Willie
   Chocolate Perry, 8, 13, 207, 236, 241, 242,
     248–56, 293, 298
   T.K. Productions' contributions to, 235
Miami Sound Machine, 241
Middleton, George S., 56, 309, 336
Middleton Senior High School, 56, 57
Midnight Creepers, 74
Mighty Clouds of Joy, 197, 312, 344
Mighty Dogcatchers, 121–22
Mighty Good and Strong, 43
"The Mighty Quinn," 148
Mike Douglas Show, The, 140
Mike Washington and the Soulsters, 250–51
Milburn, Amos, 9
Millinder, Lucky, 24, 39, 58
   "Shorty's Got to Go," 39
   "That's All," 39
   "Who Threw the Whiskey in the Well?,"
     39
"Millionaire," 311
Mind, Body & Soul, 248, 297
Mitchell, Arnold, 337
Mitchell, James, 266
Mitchell, Jock, 335
Mitchell, Little Jake, 18, 334–38, 335, 339
Mitchell, Louise, 45, 48
Mitchell, Willie, 266, 267
Mobley, Larry, 194
Modern, 226
*Modern Sounds in Country and Western
   Music*, 46
Moman, Chips, 171, 174, 265
"Money," 147
Monk, Joe, 251
Monroe, Bill, 98
Monroe, Marilyn, 87, 185
Monsieur Ibrahim, 271, 282
Montereys, 43, 121
Montgomery, Wes, 118–19

Moore, Ben, 18, 155, 157, 162–69, 167. *See
   also* Purify, Bobby (Ben Moore)
   in Blind Boys of Alabama, 165–66,
     167–68, 169
   blindness of, 162, 164–65
   childhood of, 162, 163
   photographs of, 167–68
   vocal quality of, 167
Moore, Charles "Charlie," 124, 131
Moore, Jackie, 8, 105, 288, 302–19
   "Both Ends Against the Middle," 312
   childhood of, 307
   church involvement by, 317–19
   "Clean Up Your Own Yard," 305, 312
   in college, 308
   Dave Crawford and, 305, 309, 310–12
   "If," 305, 312
   "Joe," 305
   "Love Is the Answer," 317
   "Make Me Feel Like a Woman," 312
   "Personally," 314
   photograph of, 314
   physical appearance of, 306
   "Precious, Precious," 303, 304, 305, 309,
     313, 317
   royalties disputes, 316–17
   "Sweet Charlie Babe," 312
   "They Tell Me of an Uncloudy Day," 304
   "This Time Baby," 13, 303, 305, 314, 315,
     317
   "What Do You Say to a Lady," 317
   Williams Memorial Christian Methodist
     Church, 305–6
   With Your Love, 317
Moore, Joyce, 129, 143–44, 342
Moore, Melba, 170
Moore, Robert, 300
Moore, Sam, 8, 16, 84, 123–48, 158, 266,
   342, 346
   at Booker T. Washington High School,
     130
   childhood of, 123–24
   children by, 130
   drug use by, 144
   father of, 124
   "Getting Paid," 133
   gospel influences on, 127, 130–31
   Only the Strong Survive, 4, 20

photographs of, 7, *142*
physical appearance of, 145
in Sam and Dave, 134–36. *See also* Sam and Dave
singing advice from, 146–47
in Soul Stirrers, 128, 131–32
"They Killed a King," 140
Moovers, The, 193, 203
More, More, More Latimore, 295
Morehouse College, 62
Mormino, Gary R., 15
Moroder, Giorgio, 327
Morris, Joe, 49
Morton, Jelly Roll
"Turtle Twist," 83
"Winin' Boy Blues," 83
Motown, 4, 11, 14, 133, 211, 235, 241, 307, 312
Mount Zion Missionary Church, 346
"Move and Groove Together," 288, 300
"Mr. Big Stuff," 347
Mr. James, 128, 298
"Mr. Knockout," 100, *113*, 114
"Mr. Lucky," 193
"Mr. Oliver Twist," 88
"Mr. Pitiful," 184
Muldaur, Maria, 282
Murray, Arthur, 90
Muscle Shoals, 4, 6, 14, 108, 153, 155, 173, 331
"My Ding-A-Ling," 279
My Early Years, 28
Myers, Bill, 92
My First Time Around, 328
"My Foolish Heart," 65, 66–67
"My God Is Mighty to Save," 190

Nash, Johnny, 279
Nathan, Syd, 85–86, 91, 226, 227
Nat Kendrick and the Swans, 227
Neal, Kenny, 74
Nelson, Willie, 298
Neville, Aaron, 294
New Blue Rhythm, The, 10
Newcleus, 238
Newman, David "Fathead," 24, 53, 64
New Orleans, 4, 12
Newsweek, 88
"Nightie Night," 130

Nightingales, The, 130
Night Lights, 133
"Night Train," 183
Nixon, Richard, 88
Noble & Nat, 74
"Nomad Woman," 335
"No More Pain," 136–37, 222
"No Pain, No Gain," 233
"Not a Chance in a Million," 335, 336
Notorious Miami, 300
Nowhere to Run, 141
Numero Group, 192, 193, 194

Oasis, 294
Ocean Mist, 293
"Octaves" technique, 119
O'Dylan, John, 165
O'Jays, 269, 314
Oldham, Spooner, 6, 153, 154, 174
Oliver, Sy, 225
Oliver label, 264
Olson, Johnny, 178
Olympics
"Hully Gully," 111
100 Hour Counts, 99, 111–22
Only the Strong Survive, 4, 20
"On the Wings of a Snow White Dove," 196
Opa-Locka, 321
"Opportunity," 279
Orange Is the New Black, 288, 300
Osborne, Joan, 2, 273, 277, 282, 283
Otis, Johnny, 80
"Every Beat of My Heart," 80
Otis Williams and the Charms, 222, 266
"Out of Sight," 183
Overtown, 15–16, 123–48, 197, 199, 285, 320, 343
Overtown Records, 343
Oxford American, 106, 310

Padgett, Betty, 338–40
Painia, Frank, 105
"Pain in My Heart," 11, 193, 212
Palms of Bradenton, 258
Palms of Hallandale, 16, 227
Palms of Jacksonville, 117
Papa Don's Family Drive-In, 175
Papa Don's Skylark, 175

Paradise Club, 114
"Paralyzed," 205
Parker, Charlie, 36, 39, 328
Parliament, 12
Parsons, Longineu, 11
Part 3, 327
Parton, Dolly, 250
"Part-Time Love," 115, 127, 133, 146
Party Down, 246, 252
"Party Down," 246
"Pass the Buck," 71
Pastorius, Jaco, 248
Paul, Billy, 279
Paul Revere and the Raiders, 146
Paul Williams and His Hucklebuck Boys,
    69, 72
Pavarotti, 298
"Paying Bills and Poppin' Pills," 339
Payola, 224, 229, 230, 235, 239
Pearl Harbor Club, 102
Pearsall, Helene Smith, *214, 219. See also*
    Smith, Helene
Pearsall, Johnny, 14, 18, 192, 193, *201*, 211,
    213, *217*, 233
Peebles, Ann, 269
    "I Can't Stand the Rain," 145, 267
Penn, Dan, 6, 153, 154, 155, 165, 166, 265
Pennebaker, D. A., 20
"People Get Ready," 166
People Under the Stairs, 248
Peppermint Lounge, 87–88, 263
"Peppermint Twist," 77, 87
Perry, Chocolate, 8, 13, 207, 236, 241, 242,
    248–56, *293*, 298
"Personality," 63
"Personally," 314
Peterson, Lucky, 74, 282
Philadelphia International, 312
Phil-L.A., 215
Phillip and the Faithfuls, 274
Phillips, Esther, 211, 309
Pickett, Wilson, 105, 115, 138, 153, 173, 179,
    253, 309, 317, 335
Pimping, 133–34
Pinkett, Charley, 130
Pinkett, Estelle, 130
Pitman, Wiley, 26
"Please, Please, Please," 86, 226, 227, 228,
    245

"Please Don't Go," 238
"Please Send Me Someone to Love," 55
Pollack, Ben, 225, 226
Porter, David, 6, 123, 137–38, 147
"Possum Belly Overalls," 69
"The Pot Can't Talk About the Kettle," 211,
    215
"Pouring Water on a Drowning Man," 274
Powell, Maestro, 275
Prater, Dave, 134–35
    death of, 125, 144
    photographs of, *7, 142*
    Sam and Dave, 124, 134–35. *See also* Sam
        and Dave
Prater, J. T., 135
"Precious, Precious," 303, 304, 305, 309,
    313, 317
Presley, Elvis
    "Baby Let's Play House," 182
    "Hound Dog," 87
    "In the Ghetto," 174
    "It's Now or Never," 77
    "Jailhouse Rock," 73
    "Suspicious Minds," 174
Preston, Billy, 126, 148
Price, A. C., 38
Price, John, 117
Price, Lloyd, 63
    "Lawdy Miss Clawdy," 63, 111
    "Personality," 63
    "Stagger Lee," 63
Prim, Weston, 14, 98, 109, 121, 336
Prima, Louis, 88
Prince, 347
Process, 103–4, 133
"Pure Love," 338
Purified, 164, 176
Purify, Anner, 150, 160
Purify, Bobby (Ben Moore), 18–19, 138,
    162–69
    childhood of, 162, 163
    "I'm Your Puppet," 6, 11, 164
    "Let Love Come Between Us," 174
    photograph of, *164*
    James Purify and, 150, 157–58, 163, *164*
Purify, Bobby (James Grubbs), 157
Purify, Bobby (Robert Lee Dickey), 157
Purify, James, 19, 138, 149–61, 340, 341
    childhood of, 150, 152

crimes by, 158–59
imprisonment of, 149–51, 158
"I'm Your Puppet," 6, 11, 149–50, 151, 153, 154, 155, 175, 304
"Let Love Come Between Us," 174
Papa Don Schroeder and, 152–54, 157, 158, 161
parole of, 160
photographs of, *156, 160*
Bobby Purify (Ben Moore) and, 150, 157–58, 163, 164
physical appearance of, 150, 160–61
Purify Bros., 163
"Purple Rain," 347
Pyramid Hotel, 59, 81

"Queen of Clubs," 325
Quiet Elegance, 258–59, 266, 267

Rabinowitz, Sol, 72
"Race records," 9
Racial issues, 102–3, 108, 120, 139
Radio stations, 4
"Rainbow Power," 279–80
Randolph, Robert, 126
"Rapp Payback," 222
Rare Earth, 321
Rawls, Lou, 295, 346
Raw Soul Express, 250
Ray Charles. *See* Charles, Ray
Ray Charles: Man and Music, 22
Ray Charles Boulevard, 342, *348*
Ray Charles Orchestra, 24, 31
Ray Charles Trio, 49, 50
R&B. *See* Rhythm and blues
Real Deal, The, 339, 340
Real Gone Music, 303
Real Rhythm and Blues, The, 18
Rebennack, Mack, 303
Rebirth Brass Brand, 334
Recording Industry Association of America, 303
Record Man, 239, 342
Redding, Otis, 98, 105, 125, 138, 140, 183, 215, 325, 346
"Can't Turn You Loose," 185, 186
"Dock of the Bay," 110
"Hard to Handle," 110
"Mr. Pitiful," 184

"Pain in My Heart," 11, 193, 212
"These Arms of Mine," 11, 110
"Try a Little Tenderness," 265
Reddy, Helen, 279
Reed, Jimmy, 152, 231
"Reet Petite," 132
Reeves, Lois, 266
Reeves, Martha, 266, 267
Reid, Clarence, 121, 192, 193, 202, 203, *204,* 205, 206, 211, 214, 215, 233, 234, 237, 242, 252, 255, 312, 320, 340, 343
"Rescue Me," 18, 337
"Respect," 11
"Return of the Thin Man," 71, 74
Rhino, 238
Rhythm and blues
AAB lyrical structure of, 10
chord structures in, 10–11
description of, 8–9
musical forms derived from, 9
origination of term, 137
soul versus, 8
Rhythm and the Blues, 137
RIAA. *See* Recording Industry Association of America
Ribowsky, Mark, 183
Ricci, Paul, 331
Richbourg, John, 173
Rich Records, 173
Ridgley, Tommy, 104
"Ring My Bell," 222
Ringside Café, 267
Ripani, Richard J., 10, 12
Ritz Carlton Hotel, 280
Roach Thompson Blues Band, 300
Robey, Don, 118, 175
Robinson, Aretha, 23, 31
Robinson, Bailey, 25
Robinson, J. P., 208, 210
Robinson, Louise, 123–24, 134
Robinson, Mary Jane, 25, 34
Robinson, Ray Charles. *See* Charles, Ray
Robinson, Smokey, 333
Rock and roll, 9, 236
Rocketeers, The, 194
Rockin', 222
"Rockin' Chair," 208, 222, 237, *242,* 252
Rocking Capris, 183
Rocking Chair, 48–49

Rockin' MB Lounge, 62–63
Rockland Palace, 128
"Rock the Boat," 236
"Rock Your Baby," 208, 222, 236, 324, 326
Rocky Stone and His Little Pebbles, 225
Rodriguez, Michael, 44, 58, 336
Rogers, Kenny, 250
Rogers, Milton "Shorty," 225
Rogers Hotel, 59, 81
Rolling Stone, 138
Rolling Stones, The, 133, 179
"Roll With Me, Henry," 76
Roots, The, 288, 341
Roseland, 261
Roulette Records, 129, 137, 238
Rounders, The, 157, 163
Rowland, Linda, 95, 110. *See also* Lyndell, Linda
Royals, 80, 83, 290
Royal Sons, 127
Royal Theater, 263
"The Ruler's Back," 305
Rushin, Jerry, 275
Rutledge, Freddie, 198

Sabre Club, 152
Sade, 2, 273, 277, 283
"Said I Wasn't Gonna Tell Nobody," 139
Salinger, Pierre, 78
Salt-N-Pepa, 97, 109, 312
Sam and Dave. *See also* Moore, Sam; Prater, Dave
   description of, 1, 5–6, 98, 115, 124–27, 135, 222
   disbanding of, 144
   formation of, 127, 133–36
   "Goodnight Baby," 138
   gospel influences on, 135–36
   "Hold On, I'm A Comin'," 1, 11, 124, 131, 138–39, 143, 145
   "I Take What I Want," 138
   "I Thank You," 124–25, 140, 143
   live shows by, 141
   "No More Pain," 136–37, 222
   performing styles of, 141, 143
   photograph of, *126, 142*
   as pop artists, 140
   Rock and Roll Hall of Fame induction of, 145

"Said I Wasn't Gonna Tell Nobody," 139
   singing style of, 136–37
   "Soothe Me," 139–40
   "Soul Man," 123–24, 139–40, 145–46
   touring by, 140
   "When Something Is Wrong with My Baby," 139, 141, 157
   "You Don't Know Like I Know," 124, 138, 145
   "You Got Me Hummin'," 139
Sam and Dave: An Oral History, 127
Sanderson, Watts, 22, 62
Santana, Carlos, 2, 273, 282
Sasfy, Joe, 81
"Satisfaction," 179
Saturday Night Fever, 322, 327
"Saturday Night Fever," 227, 236
"Save Me Jesus Save Me," 139
Savoy, 58
"Say It Loud, I'm Black and I'm Proud," 139
Scaggs, Boz, 253
Scheir, Bob, 81
Schroeder, Gail, 172
Schroeder, Papa Don, 6, 14, 170–77, 340
   childhood of, 172
   "I'm Your Puppet," 6, 11, 149–50, 151, 153, 154, 155, 164, 170, 174, 175
   "Melanie," 154, 172
   photographs of, *171, 176*
   James Purify and, 151, 153, 154, 157, 158, 161
   physical appearance of, 170
Scorpio Records, 311
Scott, Clifford, 64
Scott, Freddy, 249, 292, 295
Scott, Joe, 119
Scott-Adams, Peggy, 152
Scott and Dash, 222
Scott-Heron, Gil, 311
Seaboard Line, 60
Seattle Symphony, 2
Secada, Jon, 250
"Secret Lovers," 314
"Section C," 157
Segregation, 9, 15, 56, 94, 97–98, 128–29, 206
Seminole Record Distribution Company, 226
Sensational Hummingbirds, 135

Sensational Nightingales, 82–83
"Sex Machine," 334
"Sexy Ways," 76
"Shake, Rattle, and Roll," 71
"(Shake, Shake, Shake) Shake Your Booty,"
    235, 322, 327
"Shake a Tail Feather," 170, 174
Shambling, Sir, 211
Shangri La, 261
Shapiro, Brad, 8, 304–5, 309, 310, 312, 313,
    328
Sharon Jones and the Dap-Kings, 343
Sharpe, Dee Dee, 211
Shaw, Arnold, 71–72
Shaw, Eddie, 226
Shellman, Frank, 43–44
"She's a Bad Mama Jama (She's Built, She's
    Stacked)," 175
"She Used to Be My Girl," 314
Shiloh Baptist Church, 26
Shirelles, The, 141, 262
"Shorty's Got to Go," 39
Shot Toward Noon, A, 244
Shout label, 309
"Showtime at the Apollo," 69
Sigler, Bunny, 312
Simmons, Frederica, 43
Simmons, Lydia, 43
Simon, Joe, 141, 344
Sinatra, Frank, 88, 114, 182, 292
Singing techniques, 8
Singleton, Charlie "Hoss," 33–34
Sir John Hotel, 78, 128–29, 132, 290, 336
Skyhaven, 45
Sledge, Percy, 211, 325
"The Slide," 72
Slim, Guitar
    "The Things I Used to Do," 49
Slim, Root Boy, 74
Slow Dancin', 164
Small, James P., 32
Smith, Buster, 64
Smith, Don, 144
Smith, Helene, 6, 192, 193, 202, 203, 206,
    211–20, 308, 343
    childhood of, 212–13
    at Deep City Records, 211–12, 216
    Helene Smith Sings Sweet Soul, 212, 216
    "I Am Controlled by Your Love," 216

musical influences on, 213
Johnny Pearsall and, 213–16, 217, 218
photographs of, 214, 217, 219
"The Pot Can't Talk About the Kettle,"
    211, 215
in teaching, 220
"A Woman Will Do Wrong," 211, 218
"Willing and Able," 211, 212, 215, 216
Betty Wright and, 212
Smith, Jerome, 237, 325
Smith, Jimmy, 274
Smith, Lawyer, 29
Smith, Mabel Louise. See Maybelle, Big
Smith, Milton "Butterball," 228
"Snap Your Fingers," 290
Snow, Hank, 182
SoBe Entertainment, 346
Society of New Jersey Chiropractors, 91
"Soft Soul," 121
So Full of Love, 314
"Somethin' 'bout 'Cha," 288
Sony Music, 312
"Soothe Me," 139–40
Soul
    definition of, 8
    history of, 14
    instrumentalists in, 9
    rhythm and blues versus, 8
    verse structure in, 11
Soul Cellar, 259
Soulful Classics, 344
Soul Has No Color, 105
Soulman, 81
"Soul Man," 123, 124, 139–40, 145–46
Soul Searchers, The, 334, 336, 338, 339
Soul Sessions, The, 243, 247, 297
Soul Sheet, 186
Soul Stirrers, 128, 131–32
Soulsville, U.S.A.: The Story of Stax Records,
    109, 138
Soul Train, 193
Sound Exchange, 316–17
Sound of Soul: The Story of Black Music, The,
    8, 341
"Sound Your Funky Horn," 324
South Africa, 2
"Southern Cross," 255
Southern soul, 10–11
Southern Soul-Blues, 300

Southern Tones
  "It Must be Jesus," 49
"South Shore Drive," 71
Southside Johnny and the Asbury Jukes, 171
South Street Casino, 38
"Spanish Eyes," 33
Speed, Roscoe, 213
Spellman, Benny
  "Lipstick Traces (on a Cigarette)," 12
Sporty, King, 250, 320
Springfield, Dusty, 265
Springsteen, Bruce, 125
Spruill, Jimmy, 73
"Stagger Lee," 63
Stambler, Irwin, 92
"Stand By Me," 11
Standing in the Shadows of Motown, 241
Stan Kenton orchestra, 274
Stan the Man, 245
Staples, Mavis, 110, 126
Stardust Lounge, 108
Star Lighters, 82
Starr, Atlantic, 314
Starr, Edwin, 258
Starr, Johnny, 263
Station Five, 25
Staton, Candi, 310, 312, 319
St. Augustine, 29–30, 32
Stax Records, 5–6, 14, 95, 98, 108–10, 125,
  137, 235, 266
Stax Revue, 140
"Stay Away from My Johnny," 194
Steadham, Charles, 98, 339. See also Blade,
  Charlie (Charles Steadham)
Steinways, The, 264
Stevenson, William "Mickey," 307
Stewart, Billy, 205
Stewart, Jim, 105, 137
Stewart, Rod, 347
Still Rockin', 81
Stills, Stephen, 249, 254
Sting, 125
Stitt, Sonny, 64
Stokes, Betty, 264
Stone, Angie, 342
Stone, Henry, 9, 13, 17, 19, 35, 40, 42, 45, 53,
  84, 129–30, 133, 136, 171, 193, 203, 205,
  206, 207, 208, 212, 220, 340

Steve Alaimo and, 230–32, 235, 251
  artists who have worked with, 222
  James Brown and, 226, 227, 228
  Ray Charles and, 40–41, 84, 226
  childhood of, 225
  Willie Clarke and, 233
  death of, 221, 223
  documentaries about, 342
  Hialeah headquarters of, 9, 224, 231, 242,
    295
  KC and the Sunshine Band and, 234–35,
    320, 324, 332
  labels owned by, 223
  musical elements, 224
  payola by, 224, 229, 235, 239
  photographs of, 223, 239
  physical appearance of, 224
  as producer, 233
  record distribution by, 228–30
  Timmy Thomas and, 232–33
  T.K. Productions, 6, 8, 11, 13, 193, 206,
    208, 212, 222, 229, 230, 235, 237, 241,
    249, 253, 267, 271, 276, 294, 321
Stone, Inez, 224, 229
Stone, Joss, 243, 247, 297, 342, 344
Stone Cold Truth on Payola in the Music Biz,
  The, 229
"Stormy Monday," 294–95
"St. Pete Blues," 41–42, 45
"St. Pete Florida Blues," 2, 41–43, 45, 47, 53
St. Petersburg Times, 72, 78, 88, 92, 260
St. Pete's Royal Theater, 258
"Strangers in the Night," 33
Streisand, Barbra, 298
"String of Pearls," 183
Strong, Barrett, 133, 147
Stuart, Hamish, 328
Stylistics, The, 269
Sugar Bowl, 152
Sugar Daddy, 338
Sugar Ray's, 68–69, 73
"Suite for Beaver, Parts 1 and 2," 248
Summer, Donna, 327, 332
"Summertime," 205
Sunny Isles Beach, 292
Sunshine Club, 38, 40
Sunshine Junkanoo Band, 2
"Super Duper Love," 243

Supremes, The, 100, 213, 264
Sure Shot label, 118
"Suspicious Minds," 174
Swan, Scott, 10, 117, 121–22
Sweetback, James T., 275
Sweet Charlie Babe, 305, 313
"Sweet Charlie Babe," 312
"Sweet Dreams," 151, 171, 173
Sweetening, 327, 333
Sweet Inspirations, 153, 303
"Sweet Inspirations," 153
Sweet Soul Music: Rhythm and Blues and the Southern Dream of Freedom, 9, 24
Swing bands, 9

"Take Care of Home," 279
"Take Me (Just As I Am)," 153
"Take Me to the River," 126, 147
Tampa, 57–58, 84, 337, 342
Tampa Bay Jazz Association, 65
Tampa Bay Times, 260
Tampa Red, 26
Tampa Tribune, 337
Tangerine, 29, 55
Tap Room, 32
Tate, Buddy, 64
Taylor, Johnnie, 115, 128, 133, 146, 161, 297, 334, 341, 346
Taylor, June, 184
Taylor, LeBaron, 312, 313
Taylor, Sam "The Man," 71
Taylor, Ted, 115, 152, 263
T-Connection, 235
"Teardrops on Your Letter?," 85–86
"Tell It Like It Is," 333
Temptations, The, 265, 266, 269, 346
Tenent, Forrest, 144
Tennessee Agricultural and Industrial State College, 289
Terrell, Tammi, 149
Tex, Joe, 153, 238, 265, 303, 305
TGener, 4
Tharpe, Rosetta, 40
"That's All," 39
"That's the Way (I Like It)," 1, 322, 327, 328
Them Two, 194, 203
"There He Is," 258, 266
"There Must Be a Heaven Somewhere," 166

Theresa Hotel, 265
"These Arms of Mine," 11, 110
"They Killed a King," 140
"They Tell Me of an Uncloudy Day," 304, 310
"The Things I Used to Do," 49
Thin Man Watts Jazz Fest, 75
"This Masquerade," 246
"This Time Baby," 13, 305, 314, 315
Thomas, Carla, 98, 105, 115, 140
Thomas, Irma, 149, 211
  "Good Things Don't Come Easy," 153
Thomas, Rufus, 74, 115, 134
  "Walking the Dog," 18, 337
Thomas, Timmy, 6, 10–11, 207, 243, 270–86, 342
  childhood of, 274, 277
  "Cold Cold People," 279
  "Gotta Give a Little Love," 282
  Latimore and, 291, 297
  "Opportunity," 279
  Joan Osborne and, 282–83
  photographs of, *272, 278, 284*
  "Rainbow Power," 279–80
  Henry Stone and, 232–33
  "Take Care of Home," 279
  in teaching, 282
  "What Can I Tell Her," 281
  "Why Can't We Live Together," 2, 14, 222, 232, 236, 271, 273, 274–75, 279, 280, 281, 283, 286, 343
Thompson, Fred, 34
Thompson, Lena Mae, 34
Thompson, Lucky, 64
Thompson, Sonny, 85
Thompson, Warren "Roach," 249–50, 292, 298, 299, 300
Thornton, Big Mama, 9, 87
Three Blazers, 41
"Three Lovers," 307
Tighten Up, 106
Tiki Club, 245
Time, 88
T.K. Productions, 6, 8, 11, 13, 193, 206, 208, 212, 222, 229, 230, 235, 237, 241, 245, 247, 249, 253, 267, 271, 276, 294, 312, 321, 327
"To Be Loved," 132, 290

WINZ, 230
"Wish You Didn't Have to Go," 155, 174
Witherspoon, Jimmy, 49
"With Every Beat of My Heart," 263
With Your Love, 317
WJAX, 4
WLAC, 173
WMBM, 4, 197, 228
WMNF, 81–82
"Woke Up This Morning," 336
Womack, Bobby, 252, 265, 344, 347
Womack, Ja'Rae, 344
Wonder, Stevie, 161, 341
"Wonderful World," 76
Wood Foot, 269
Woodruff, Bill, 83
Woods, Phil, 328
Woods, Sonny, 80
Woolworths, 276–77
"Work Out," 151
"Work With Me Annie," 76
WRBD, 129
Wreck Bar, 292
Wright, Betty, 5, 19, 78, 92, 193, 205, 219,
 243, 271, 295, 297, 341
 "Clean Up Woman," 5, 19, 128, 194, 203,
 207, 222, 233, 234, 244
 "Girls Can't Do What the Guys Do," 233
 "Good Lovin'," 205
 "Mr. Lucky," 193
 My First Time Around, 328
 "No Pain, No Gain," 233
 "Paralyzed," 205
 "Pure Love," 338

Helene Smith and, 212
Wright, O. V., 258, 274, 303
Wright Spiritual Singers, 128
WTMP, 4, 93, 309

Ybor City, 18, 62
"Yes I'm Ready," 322, 332
Yorey, Bob, 264, 265, 269
York, Tiny, 13, 34, 36–37
You and Me Together Forever, 163
"You Are My Sunshine," 46
"You Beat Me to the Punch," 307
"You Can Make It If You Try," 336
"You Don't Know Like I Know," 124, 138,
 145, 185
"You Got Me Hummin'," 139
"You Got My Mind Messed Up," 258, 266
"You Got What It Takes," 76
"You Left the Water Running (When You
 Left Me Behind)," 155
"You'll Lose a Good Thing," 212
"You'll Never Find," 346
Young, Harold, 30
Young, Lester, 39, 64
Young, Paul, 149
Young, Reggie, 174
"Young Hearts Run Free," 310–11
Young Professionals, 312
"Your Cheating Heart," 46
"You Shot Me Through the Grease," 105,
 309
"You've Really Got a Hold On Me," 333

Zucchero, 126

John Capouya teaches journalism and nonfiction narrative at The University of Tampa. He mentors students in UT's low-residency Creative Writing MFA program, as well as working with private writing clients. During his journalism career he was an editor at *Newsweek* and *SmartMoney* magazines, *New York Newsday*, and the *New York Times*. *Florida Soul* is his third book; his previous one, the biography *Gorgeous George*, is being adapted into a feature film.